Routledge Revivals

Social Welfare in Developed Market Countries

First published in 1989, this book analyses social welfare in countries with highly developed economies, at that time. For each country it considers the ideological framework underlying the social welfare system and describes the historical development of both the system and the political and socio-economic context. Each chapter looks at the structure and administration of the systems in place and how these are financed. This is followed by a consideration of the nature of different parts of the welfare system, a survey of social security, personal social services and the treatment of the following key target groups: the aged; those with disabilities and handicaps; children and youth; disadvantaged families; the unemployed; and the sick and injured. Each chapter concludes with an assessment of the effectiveness of the system considered.

Social Welfare in Developed Market Countries

Edited by
John Dixon and Robert P. Scheurell

First published in 1989
by Routledge

This edition first published in 2016 by Routledge
2 Park Square, Milton Park, Abingdon, Oxon, OX14 4RN
and by Routledge
711 Third Avenue, New York, NY 10017

Routledge is an imprint of the Taylor & Francis Group, an informa business

© 1989 John Dixon and Robert P. Scheurell

The right of John Dixon and Robert P. Scheurell to be identified as editor of this work has been asserted by him in accordance with sections 77 and 78 of the Copyright, Designs and Patents Act 1988.

All rights reserved. No part of this book may be reprinted or reproduced or utilised in any form or by any electronic, mechanical, or other means, now known or hereafter invented, including photocopying and recording, or in any information storage or retrieval system, without permission in writing from the publishers.

Publisher's Note
The publisher has gone to great lengths to ensure the quality of this reprint but points out that some imperfections in the original copies may be apparent.

Disclaimer
The publisher has made every effort to trace copyright holders and welcomes correspondence from those they have been unable to contact.

A Library of Congress record exists under LC control number: 89133160

ISBN 13: 978-1-138-94701-6 (hbk)
ISBN 13: 978-1-315-67032-4 (ebk)
ISBN 13: 978-1-138-94705-4 (pbk)

SOCIAL WELFARE IN DEVELOPED MARKET COUNTRIES

EDITED BY JOHN DIXON AND
ROBERT P. SCHEURELL

ROUTLEDGE
London and New York

First published in 1989 by
Routledge
11 New Fetter Lane, London EC4P 4EE
29 West 35th Street, New York NY 10001

© 1989 John Dixon and Robert P. Scheurell

Printed and bound in Great Britain by
Biddles Ltd, Guildford and King's Lynn

All rights reserved. No part of this book may be reprinted or
reproduced or utilized in any form or by any electronic, mechanical, or
other means, now known or hereafter invented, including photocopying
and recording, or in any information storage or retrieval system, without
permission in writing from the publishers.

British Library Cataloguing in Publication Data

Social welfare in developed market countries.
   — (Comparative social welfare series).
   1. Welfare services. Comparative studies
   I. Dixon, John, 1946– II. Scheurell,
Robert P. III. Series
361
   ISBN 0-415-00532-9

CONTENTS

ACKNOWLEDGEMENTS   vi

PREFACE   vii

CONTRIBUTORS   xiii

AUSTRALIA
John McCallum   1

CANADA
Donald F. Bellamy & Allan Irving   47

GERMANY, WEST
C. Wolfgang Muller   89

ITALY
Maurizio Ferrera   122

NETHERLANDS
Joop M. Roebroek   147

NEW ZEALAND
Stephen Uttley   190

NORWAY
Hildegunn M. Forsund   228

SWEDEN
Sven E. Olsson   264

UNITED KINGDOM
Jane Keithley   309

UNITED STATES OF AMERICA
Robert S. Magill   345

APPENDICES   387

INDEX   408

ACKNOWLEDGEMENTS

As this book goes to press we wish to acknowledge the help we received from a variety of quarters. A special debt is owed to Mr Hyung Shik Kim, a co-editor for the first volume in this comparative studies series - <u>Social Welfare in Asia</u> (1985) - for his crucial contribution to the conceptual framework that underlies the series.

To Mrs Cheryl Leeton go our thanks for typing the manuscript in its various drafts and in its final form. The artwork was done by Desktop Ink, to whom go our thanks.

Publication of this book, indeed the entire comparative series, would not be possible without the support received from the International Fellowship for Social and Economic Development Inc. (IFSED), a non-profit organisation. Further information about IFSED can be obtained from the Director, Mr John Dixon, PO Box 228, Belconnen, ACT, 2616, Australia.

To our wives, Tina and Sally, go our thanks for putting up with our idiosyncracies throughout the preparation of this manuscript.

For any errors of fact and for all opinions and interpretations, the authors and the editors accept responsibility.

John Dixon   Robert P Scheurell

PREFACE

This volume on <u>Social Welfare in Developed Market Countries</u> is one of six volumes which encompasses all of the regions of the World.

There are a variety of publications focussing on comparative public policy and in-depth studies of specific regions. What makes this series unique? Firstly, a similar model is used in each volume and for each country in order to develop as much consistency and uniformity in content as feasible; secondly, the system of co-editing attempts to develop consistency and uniformity in writing style; and, thirdly, the global perspective which encompasses the entire world. The 55 country profiles included in the series are primarily descriptive, but include evaluative summaries.

It is important to recognise that any comparative study must be placed in the context of the interlocking nature of the dominant social value or traditions, and of a variety of socio-economic and political forces, all of which interact with the prevailing patterns of social need and available resources to determine the fabric of particular welfare systems. Thus a comparative social welfare study, if it is to be useful, must place particular welfare systems in their particular cultural, social, economic, political and ideological environments. It must also acknowledge that different cultures create a different framework of reference from which to perceive human welfare and the institutions and programmes that have evolved to meet at least some human needs. It is pointless to attempt to compare countries that are fundamentally different, hence the regional focus of this tightly structured anthology.

Social security is defined as:

> the whole set of compulsory measures instituted to protect the individual and his family against the consequences of an unavoidable interruption or serious diminution of the earned income disposable for the maintenance of a reasonable standard of living (Rys 1966, p.242).

Thus it includes compulsory employer liability (with or without insurance); provident funds; social insurance (benefits subject to contributing conditions); social assistance (benefits subject to residence qualifications and an income or means test); and universal programmes (benefits subject only to residency qualifications). The social security boundary is, however, blurred in many countries, for elements of fiscal welfare (that is, a system of tax rebates or taxable income deductions that reduce the tax liability of particular target groups) and occupational welfare programmes (for example, occupational superannuation, non-statutory sick pay entitlements, free or subsidised health care for employees and their dependants) may impinge on social security in some instances. Where this is significant, details are included. Health insurance arrangements are also included.

The personal social services are characterised by service functions that have a major bearing upon personal problems, individual situations of stress, inter-personal helping or helping people in need, and the provisions of direct services in collaboration with workers from statutory and voluntary agencies. Accordingly, the term 'personal social services' will be used in such a way as:

- to distinguish them from cash benefits;

- to refer to various forms of services in kind that are provided, in the main, in response to recognised 'personal' needs; and

- to include service provisions that usually require the assistance and help of qualified personnel, such as social workers or probation officers.

The descriptive approach as used in this volume allows one to review a variety of countries and look for salient general trends. As we reviewed this manuscript, a number of general trends were present in all of the countries, although varying in degree. These themes can be classified into four broad areas, although there is some overlapping: economic, political, welfare policy and demographic.

ECONOMIC THEMES

It is interesting to note that whether the economic system is predominantly capitalist, democratic, socialist or a mixture, all of the countries in this volume have entered the post-industrial stage of economic development which is referred to as a service economy or, in some cases, service/information economy. With the development of the service economy there has been some stagnation of the industrial base of the economic system. There are many social and political implications of this trend towards a service economy, but the most immediate implication is rising rates of unemployment as labourers are dislocated from industrial employment.

POLITICAL THEMES

As the industrial base of the economies declined in the late 1970s and early 1980s one of the responses of the political system was a trend toward economic conservatism and fiscal restraint. These measures have resulted in reductions of money available for social security and personal social service programmes.

One implication of the political policies is that the benefits that the poor and the aged were receiving have decreased and resulted in less buying power for them. A second implication is that some reorganisation of the structure for providing services occurred and in about one-half of the countries this reorganisation resulted in more local control of programmes. All of the countries made a reference to a financial crisis for the welfare state.

WELFARE POLICY THEMES

With the political and fiscal conservatism, the immediate impact on welfare policy was decreased benefits and services. In addition, three structural changes were indicated: reorganisation of services for more local monitoring of programmes, an increase in proprietary or privatisation of some programmes; and an increased emphasis on self-help.

The local control and monitoring of programmes was clearly indicated as an attempt to enhance programme accountability. The privatisation of services in effect means proprietary services and not voluntary services. In almost every country there is debate about individuals paying more for services provided based upon various income levels, developing private pension plans and in some cases service to supplement public expenditures. All countries indicated a movement toward self-help groups as one means of reducing public expenditures for services.

Social welfare policy concerns which were common to all countries were the dependency ratio, care of the aged, and employment retraining. The dependency ratio refers to the fact that all of the countries are experiencing the aging of the population which means higher costs and potentially a reduced financial base. Care of the aged refers to who cares for them. In about one-half of the countries, it was clearly acknowledged that the care of the aged parent becomes a burden on the female children, who also have families. In those countries where this problem was acknowledged, there is debate about providing these female relatives with some financial support for their services. All of the countries were concerned with two aspects of the employment market: the increase of women in the work force and chronic high rates of unemployment. With the increase of women in the work force, there is a high demand for day care services, which in all countries is in short supply. Chronic unemployment is leading to debates on how to retrain labourers for the service economy and how to provide incentives to employers to develop programmes.

DEMOGRAPHIC THEMES

All of the countries have expressed concern about the dependency ratio, rate of poverty and unemployment. All of the countries are experiencing an ageing of the population with current estimates ranging from 10-20 per cent and projections for the year 2000 of 15-25 per cent. The ageing of the population has implications for health care, social security benefits, independent living arrangements, non-independent living arrangements and social relationships.

The rate of poverty in all countries regardless of the specific type of programmes available is estimated at between 15 and 20 per cent of the population. What this figure represents is the chronic nature of poverty and the seeming inability of the welfare state to eliminate poverty. In effect, using the concept of relative poverty, there will always be someone who is poor.
Unemployment in all countries is chronic and is highest amongst young people. The combination of an ageing population and unemployment significantly adds to the financial burden of public programmes.

OTHER OBSERVATIONS

It was interesting to note variations among the countries as to their perceptions of significant issues. In about half of the countries minority groups and concerns are a high priority for social policy, as is equality between men and women. In about one third of the countries juvenile delinquency is a high priority policy issue, as is immigrants and refugees.

It is clear that some broad generalisations can be made which indicate that most, if not all, of the post-industrial societies have common problems to be resolved.

MONETARY UNITS

All monetary units are expressed in natural currency units. No attempt has been made to convert these into a common unit by means of official currency exchange rates. The currency units for the countries included in this anthology are:

Australia	:	Dollar
Canada	:	Dollar
Germany, West	:	Deutsche mark
Italy	:	Lira
Netherlands	:	Guilder
New Zealand	:	Dollar
Norway	:	Krone
Sweden	:	Krona
United Kingdom	:	Pound
United States of America	:	Dollar

REFERENCE

Rys, V. (1966), 'Comparative Studies in Social Security: Problems and Perspectives', <u>Bulletin of the International Social Security Association</u>, 19, 7-8 (July-Aug), 242-68.

CONTRIBUTORS

Professor Donald F. Bellamy is in the Faculty of Social Work at the University of Toronto, Canada.

Dr Maurizio Ferrera is Associate Professor of Italian Politics in the Department of Political and Social Studies at the University of Pavia, Italy.

Ms Hildegunn M. Forsund is in the Planning Division of the Ministry of Social Affairs, Norway.

Dr Allan Irving is an Assistant Professor in the Faculty of Social Work at the University of Toronto, Canada.

Dr Jane Keithley is a lecturer in the Department of Sociology and Social Policy at the University of Durham, England.

Dr John McCallum is a Research Fellow in the Department of Sociology in the Research School of Social Sciences at the Australian National University, Australia.

Dr Robert S. Magill is an Associate Professor in the School of Social Welfare at the University of Wisconsin-Milwaukee, United States of America.

Professor C. Wolfgang Muller is Professor of Social Work at the Technical University of Berlin, West Germany.

Professor Sven E. Olsson is in the Swedish Institute for Social Research at the Stockholm University, Sweden.

Professor Joop M. Roebroek is in the Department of Social Security Science at Tilburg University, the Netherlands.

Mr Stephen Uttley is a Senior Lecturer in the Department of Sociology and Social Work at the Victoria University of Wellington, New Zealand.

For

Tina, Piers and Aliki

and

Lynn and Laura

AUSTRALIA
John McCallum

THE WELFARE SYSTEM ENVIRONMENT

Ideological Environment

The recent American Brookings Institute study of the Australian economy (Caves & Krause 1984, p.400) observes in many areas, including social welfare, that '... Australia's public policies are greatly influenced by the national distrust of market outcomes and a strong belief in equality'. Some half a century earlier Sir Keith Hancock (1930, pp.63-4) made a similar argument, with elaborations, as follows:

> This, then, is the prevailing ideology of Australian democracy - the sentiment of justice, the claim of right, the conception of equality and the appeal of Government as the instrument of self-realisation.

Notions of 'fairness' and 'equality' were clearly central to the process of nation building from pluralistic immigrant groups. Just as clearly they remained as ideologies or values which existed alongside widespread, actual inequalities. For one example, aboriginal Australians and Asians were excluded from full participation in mainstream Australian life, including social welfare and politics, in the first half of this century. Whilst aborigines and immigrants suffered disadvantages in the past, both these population groups now attract socially empowering labels and public subsidy. Because of high rates of post Second World War migration, considerations of fairness and equality remain as central values in a multicultural society.

Australia

The egalitarian values of Australians originally created, and now sustain an extensive range of flat-rate, means-tested pensions and benefits[1] financed from general revenues. This conception of equality is different from countries like the United States of America, where it is expressed as equal returns for equal contributions. Thus, in those countries welfare perpetuates pre-existing income differences. Another example of equality, which is not traditionally 'welfare' in its origins, can be seen in tariff protection of industries employing low wage, low skill workers. There is, as well, federal intervention in wage fixing to ensure 'living' and 'minimum' wages since the Harvester Judgement of 1907. Finally federal tax revenues are provided to the States by the Commonwealth on the principle of equalizing their abilities to provide the same level of service without having to raise extra revenues. This radical, geographic egalitarianism matches the egalitarian cast of Australian public policy in general.

There is, however, a strong countervailing emphasis on thrift, self-help, self-reliance and the value of work. One of Australia's more colourful Federal politicians W.C. Wentworth - Minister for Social Services in 1969 - outlined the two fundamental principles of income security, namely:

> ... to raise the general standard of pensioners, directing special relief to the areas of greatest need, and ... to encourage thrift, self-help and self-reliance ...(Commission of Inquiry into Poverty 1975, p.5).

The emphasis on individual responsibility is underwritten with assurances of minimum income security and of a 'fair go' in opportunities for self-improvement. If an Australian contemplating

---

1. 'Pensions' are long-term forms of income support, like age and invalid pensions, and are subject to both income and assets tests. 'Benefits' are supposed to be short-term support, like unemployment and supporting parents benefits, and are subject to income tests not asset tests.

unemployment, sickness, single parenthood or retirement wishes to maintain a standard of living beyond the government assured minimum it is necessary to provide for themselves in investments and savings. In these activities retirement savings and housing are encouraged by tax provisions. The very first Commonwealth welfare initiative, namely the provision of old age pensions from 1909, set out these values of thrift alongside minimum security. Despite the fact that the Royal Commission on Old Age Pensions of 1905-6 strongly emphasised that the pension was to be 'a right not a charity', it was means-tested to the extent that less than a third of those eligible by age received it. Thus the stigma of 'charity' for the poor was retained. The attempt to legitimate citizenship in the newly formed Commonwealth through universal pensions was constrained by considerations of cost. Moreover, as Senator Dobson pointed out during the Senate debates of 1907, there were 'moral hazards' to the age pension '... the pension is going to cause the thrifty to pay for the thriftless - the industrious to pay for the loafer'. Thus the egalitarianism that developed in Australian welfare was one that emphasised only minimum support for the needy rather than universal or earnings related support.

Whilst the values of the Australian welfare system have not been formally set down as they have in New Zealand (Social Security Department 1970), they are clear in the structure of the system. The primary strategy for achieving social policy goals has been through the labour market in which minimum rates and differentials are set by the Commonwealth Arbitration Commission. Vulnerable sectors were protected by tariff and trade regulation, and fortuitously unemployment was relatively low and the age structure relatively young, at least immediately following the Second World War. Social security operated as a complementary system covering market failures and personal risks with flat-rate, means-tested benefits so that the primary mechanism for social policy, namely work, would not be interfered with. Ironically these means tests, at least at the narrow bands where benefits are cut off, actually reduce incentives to thrift and hard work. Thus strong emphasis on equality, seen in flat-rate benefits financed from general revenue and equal provision of services, was balanced by

3

Australia

an equally strong emphasis on individual thrift and hard work, seen in the pervasive means-testing (and work-testing) of benefits and assessments for the provision of services to those with specific needs. These values imply an accommodation between the competing social visions of liberalism and socialism which, at particular periods of Australia's history, have influenced welfare policy.

Historical Origins

At the formation of the Commonwealth of Australia in 1901, its citizens had little but their own resources to fall back upon, with the possibility of support from families and friendly societies. Some 80 years later, old and new hazards of life - unemployment, illness, invalidity, single parenthood, widowhood and old age - are all alleviated by social assistance pensions and benefits and personal social services, provided by governments. This development took place over four periods, namely prior to the First World War, between the Wars, after the Second World War and finally, after the oil crisis recession of 1974-5.

In the first stage of 'nation building', up to the First World War, Australia implemented forward-looking welfare provisions. It developed effective labour laws and a conciliation and arbitration system, age and invalid pensions and made advances in education and health. The establishment of the Commonwealth Conciliation and Arbitration Commission led to the setting of 'fair and reasonable' wages, based on needs rather than on subsistence levels in the Harvester Judgement of 1907. The trade-off for employers was the provision of tariff and other forms of protection. Then in 1909 a variety of State pension schemes were superseded by Commonwealth age and invalid pensions. Whilst federal health expenditure was miniscule until well into the twentieth century, a quarantine service was developed and public health was advanced by the appointment of public health commissioners. In 1912 the Commonwealth maternity allowances scheme was introduced.

After this period of welfare innovation came stagnation in the inter-war period split by the Great Depression. In income security there was the development of a repatriation scheme providing pensions, treatment and economic assistance for

Australia

ex-service personnel, and also pensions and allowances for widows and dependants. Otherwise there was some consolidation in health and education but little advance in developing the welfare vision of the early years of nationhood.

New extensions in income security began during the Second World War with the introduction of child endowment benefits by the Menzies Government in 1941, widows' pensions by the Curtin Government in 1941, and unemployment, sickness and special benefits by the Chifley Government in 1945. Allowances were given for wives of permanently incapacitated age and invalid pensioners in 1943, and supplementary assistance to help with rent in 1958. Much later in 1973 Supporting Mothers Benefit (extended to males in 1977 and renamed Supporting Parents Benefit) was paid. The Aged and Disabled Persons Homes Act of 1954 became the vehicle for funding a rapidly expanding nursing home sector for the elderly. Education, between 1950 and 1975, moved from being a State and religious concern to being a Commonwealth one - with the Commonwealth both funding and overseeing tertiary, technical, secondary, primary and preschool education in both government and private schools. There were State and Commonwealth initiatives in housing policy to develop some public housing but primary emphasis was placed upon encouraging private home ownership. Finally there was the introduction of universal health insurance by the Whitlam Government in 1975.

The most recent period of welfare policy is characterised by pruning of expenditures and constrained new growth. Age pensions, which had been expanded to near universality, were made more target efficient by the tightening of means tests and the re-introduction of an assets test in 1985. A system of child endowments and tax deductions and rebates dating from 1941 were reorganised into a universal system of family allowances in 1976 to target them more effectively to poorer and larger families. In May 1987 these were made subject to income tests for families earning over $A56,000 a year with measures to protect large families. Poorer families, also, were targeted by the Family Income Supplement in 1983 and, as part of a new family package introduced in 1987, a Family Allowance Supplement. But Class B widows' pensions (for women over 50 without children) were phased out beginning from 1987. The new Home and Community

Australia

Care Programme, announced in the 1984-5 Budget, is a three year, cost shared (between the Commonwealth and the States) programme covering services such as home nursing, home help, transport and meals. So pruning and restriction of target groups is matched by constrained new initiatives. Any further expansions of welfare, other than those which arise from social and economic changes, for example, increased rates of unemployment, marital breakdown and retirement, will probably be financed from cuts in other areas of the welfare budget. The summary of the most important historical developments is shown in Table 1.

Political and Socio-economic Environments

Since 1901 Australia has had a federal constitution and a parliamentary system of government. Legislative power is vested in a bi-cameral national Parliament, comprised of the Senate and the House of Representatives. Each of the six States, except Queensland, also has a bi-cameral Parliament. Executive power at the national level is formally vested in the Governor-General, who is the titular Head of State. In practice, the Prime Minister, who is the leader of the majority party in the House of Representatives, and his cabinet of Ministers, who are also members of Parliament, exercise that power. At the State level the titular head is the Governor, but executive power rests with the Premiers, the leaders of the majority parties in the lower house in State Parliaments, and their Ministers, who are also Members of Parliament. Federal general elections take place every three years and all citizens 18 and over must vote.

The centres of gravity of the Australian welfare system are, then, the national capital Canberra for social security and for funding generally and the various State capitals for the personal social services, health, education and workers' compensation. The Departments of Social Security, Health, Community Services and Education all have central offices in Canberra where policy for national programmes is developed and negotiated with States. Unlike the British system, which provided models for many Australian institutions, there is a minimal role for local government - except in providing 'lifestyle' infrastructure like parks and walkways and so on.

Australia

TABLE 1: THE DEVELOPMENT OF AUSTRALIA'S MAIN COMMONWEALTH SOCIAL WELFARE PROGRAMMES

Specific Welfare Development	Expenditure 1985/6 $A million	No of Recipients 30/6/1986
Age Pension (from 1909) - wives allowance from 1943	5,897	1,324,600
Invalidity Pension (from 1910) - wives allowance from 1943	1,674	273,810
Veterans Programmes (from 1917)	3,545	813,294[1]
Maternity Allowance 1912/ Child Endowment 1941/ Family Allowance (from 1976)	1,538	(children) 4,191,373
Widows Pensions (from 1942)	925	155,623
Unemployment Benefits (from 1945)	3,122	569,761
Sickness Benefits (from 1945)	392	65,301
Special Benefits (from 1945)	108	18,579
Workers Compensation (from 1902)	1,024[2]	190,398[3]
Nursing Homes (from 1954)	1,056	75,793
Hostels (from 1972)	63	38,227
Supporting Parents Benefits (from 1973)	1,238	176,730
Health Insurance (from 1975)	6,701	total popn 15,913,900
Family Income Supplement (from 1983)	49	29,183
Home and Community Care (from 1984/5)	122	NA

Notes:
1. Disability and service pensioners only.
2. Cost of claims 1983-4 excluding disease cases for Western Australia (not available).
3. Total injury and disease cases 1983-4, excluding Western Australia (not available).

SOURCES: Budget Papers, Various Annual Reports and Australian Bureau of Statistics.

Australia

As Sir Keith Hancock (1930, p.140) tartly observed '... Perhaps it is a fraud to assert that there is such a thing as Australian Socialism. It would be truer to speak of Australian paternalism'. The dependence of citizens on State governments arose because they were the initial centres of colonial development. Only the new federal government was able to take over State government functions with the local government authorities relegated to minor roles. Initially only the States received tax revenues. With compliance from the States, the Commonwealth passed the Surplus Revenue Act in 1908 to finance Invalid and Old Age Pensions. The Commonwealth's struggle for control of taxation was later to take advantage of a unique opportunity. During the Second World War it took control of tax revenues 'in the national interest' and became the financier to the States from then onwards.

Federal-State relations have subsequently become a major political factor in Australian public policy formation. Whilst there is considerable consultation and cooperation, there can be points of tension between parties, particularly in contractionary times. States, for example, attempt to pass on health, workers compensation and other costs to the federal budget which the Commonwealth resists. There have been difficulties in negotiating the new cost sharing Home and Community Care Programme. Policies are slowed in their implementation and policy options may often not be considered because of potential State opposition, particularly when there are different political parties in power in States compared to the Commonwealth. Thus the quick introduction of a new national superannuation scheme, such as occurred in the mid-1970s under the Muldoon Government in New Zealand, could not be contemplated in Australia.

Australian politics is dominated by two parties: Labor on the Left, and Liberal and Nationals, separately or in coalition, on the Right at both State and federal levels. Generally the Labor Party has been the initiator of welfare programmes with the Liberal-National coalition being the consolidators and extenders of programmes. Only the Deakin Government's introduction of age pensions in 1909 and the Menzies Government introduction of child endowment in 1941 are exceptions to this rule of initiation by the Left. Whilst thrift and self-reliance tend

Australia

to be more emphasised by the right and equality by the Left, both parties have developed the welfare system. Both were in favour of universalisation of age pensions in the early 1970s, although it was the Whitlam Labor Government that removed means tests for all those over age 70 years. Similarly both parties restricted welfare targets in the present period of welfare policy.

The socio-economic environment restricting welfare and other Government expenditures is characterised by a high foreign debt, high unemployment, low growth and high inflation. Social changes have also led to higher rates of marital breakdown and single parenting and to increasing numbers and proportions of the aged. Currently the Australian foreign debt is $A81,000 million, over three-quarters of which was accrued by the non-government sector (that is neither Commonwealth or State governments), and the current account deficit stands at $A14,000 million. The unemployment rate is relatively stable at about eight per cent and the inflation rate hovers at a high level of about eight per cent. Social welfare takes a second place in policy debates behind tasks of lowering the national debt and improving international trade performance. Without improvement in these areas it is argued that the capacity to pay for future welfare would be further diminished.

THE WELFARE SYSTEM: AN OVERVIEW

Structure and Administration

Australian welfare is characterised by flat-rate, means-tested pensions and benefits (McAlister et al. 1981) and services provided equally (geographically) subject to assessment or screening. Governments, mostly States financed by the Commonwealth, have a prime responsibility in providing welfare with variable reliance on private organisations and the community. However, there is sometimes a tense relationship between Commonwealth and State levels of government in formulating policy. Because of the extreme variety in structures in the six States and two Territories and the prime position of the Commonwealth in policy-making only the Commonwealth structures will be dealt with in detail, as set out in Figure 1.

Australia

FIGURE 1: COMMONWEALTH ADMINISTRATIVE STRUCTURE FOR WELFARE

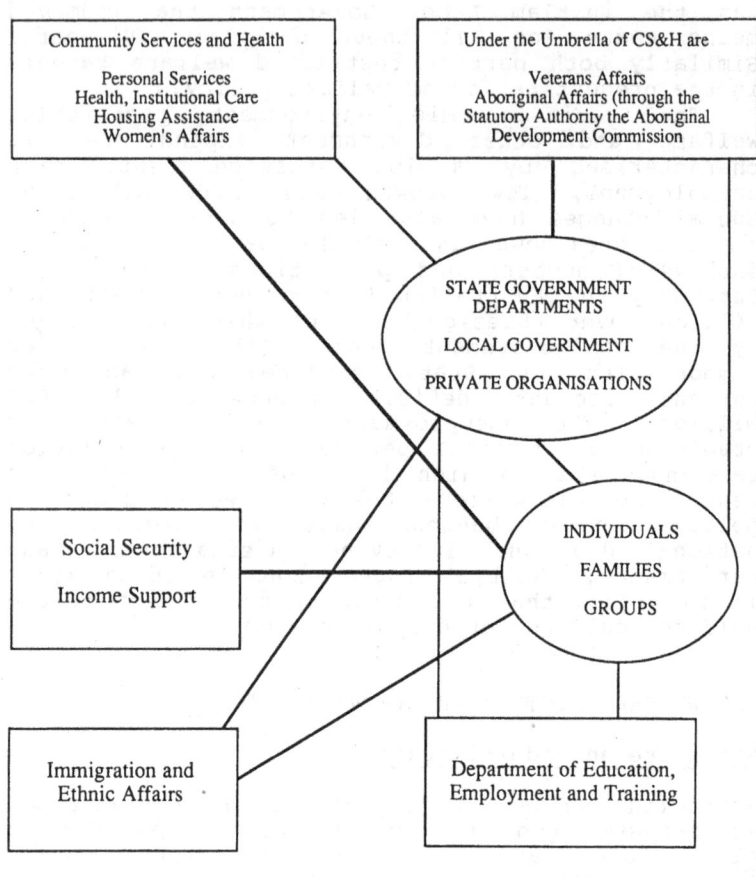

SOURCE: Based on Policy Coordination Unit, <u>Annual Report 1985-86</u>, p.8.

Australia

The three prime welfare Departments are Community Services, Health and Social Security. In 1984-5 the Department of Community Services was separated from Social Security and Health to implement a range of services for needy groups. This left the Social Security Department to specialise in income transfers and the Health Department in medical services. In 1987 a 'super' departmental structure re-combined Community Services and Health into one department but left Social Security as a separate ministry.

The Department of Social Security spends about a quarter of the Commonwealth budget to distribute funds either directly or through families to nine million people or about two-thirds of the population. Its pensions are designed as regular, minimum, means-tested payments for contingencies like retirement, invalidity, widowhood and single parenthood. On the other hand, benefits are intended as temporary cover for risks such as unemployment, sickness and special needs. The increase in duration spent in receipt of benefits, particularly through unemployment, has challenged this strategy for social security.

Paralleling the roles of these three departments is the repatriation system for veterans of war deemed to have had overseas service administered by the Department of Veterans Affairs. It is a system within a system providing parallel benefits earlier or more liberally than the national system. Its motivation is to honour Australia's debt to veterans and their dependants through programmes of care, commemoration, income support and housing assistance. As one commentator (Mendelsohn 1979, p.215) observes about this peculiar Australian development:

> ... The repatriation block has been a notable exception to the political ineptitude and powerlessness of welfare beneficiaries ... The temper of Australian politics was predominantly conservative, and the executives of the Returned Servicemen's League belonged to the same groups who provided a high proportion of politicians ...'

The success of this lobby is evident in the total programme expenditure of $A3,545 million for 1985-6 or about five per cent of the total budget expenditures. It survives as a separate department after the 1987 re-organisation but

Australia

headed by a junior minister answering to the Community Services and Health Minister.

The Department of Community Services was established in December 1984 to place in a single department the development and delivery of community services. The Department is responsible for programmes for people with disabilities, the aged, families with children, the homeless and others in special need. This Department works and shares responsibility for community care with broadly comparable State Departments and local governments, traditional service organisations, and community and self-help groups. The Department spends $A1,552 million or two per cent of the budget outlays in 1985-6. It will soon be a part of the 'super' Department of Community Services and Health.

The Commonwealth Department of Housing shared responsibility for housing with State Departments and will be incorporated into the new 'super' Department of Community Services and Health after 1987. Australians have a high rate of home ownership as a consequence of 'middle class' aspirations and policies directed to that end. The Commonwealth expenditure estimates for 1985-6 were $A988.9 million, a fraction of that spent on social security and welfare. The reason for this relatively low expenditure is the concentration on private housing, unlike British and other countries' policies for public housing.

Two other Departments, Aboriginal Affairs and Immigration and Ethnic Affairs, also have welfare roles in Australia's multicultural society despite not formally being in the welfare portfolios. In 1985-6 the Department of Immigration and Ethnic Affairs had an expenditure of $A212.26 million or 0.3 per cent of total budget outlays. Over half of these expenditures, $A123 million was spent on teaching English and another $A47 million was spent on television and radio media for migrants. There are also costs involved in obtaining migrants but, as well, there are considerable contributions and savings in the longer term from their labour.

The 1981 Census showed there were around 160,000 Aborigines and Torres Strait Islanders (by self-definition) in Australia. Some $A227 million in 1985-6 was spent in programmes administered by the Department of Aboriginal Affairs, and another $A212.4 million was expended by other Departments in programmes specifically for Aborigines. This,

Australia

in total, accounts for 0.6 per cent of the total budget expenditures,. Education, housing, health, employment and legal aid are the primary areas of activity for Aboriginal programmes.

Other activities of the Department of Education, Employment and Training will be discussed where appropriate in what follows. There are other private elements to the system which do not directly involve government nor are they compulsory. They will be discussed under the topic of financing because they can be generally categorised as fiscal welfare.

Financing Social Welfare

With the exception of Medicare which is financed by a tax levy, welfare in Australia is financed from general revenue not by contribution. Most social security payments, excepting family allowances and, generally, invalid pensions, are also subject to tax. As shown in Table 2, total social welfare expenditures are over two-thirds of the Commonwealth budget outlays, of which social security and other welfare are the largest, accounting for around a quarter of the budget outlays. The 1985-7 budget formulation process involved detailed examination of outlays in an attempt to restrain the rate of growth of government spending in a climate of fiscal austerity. As shown in Figure 2, non-Health social welfare function outlays fell by 1.55 per cent as a proportion of total outlays over the period 1982-3 to 1986-7. However, health outlays more than offset the fall in other social welfare portfolios. Over this period the balance has shifted away from the provision of income support payments to individuals to the provision of subsidies to or for individuals to obtain specific goods and services. This process is a direct consequence of the Hawke Labor Government's introduction of Medicare to replace a regressive health services financing programme with a progressive system. This was achieved by the abolition of a tax rebate for health insurance expenditure and the introduction of the Medicare tax levy of one per cent of salary above a minimum level.

The budget formulation process involves submissions from specific departments with the oversight of the Expenditure Review Committee, a phenomenon of economic recession created in the

Australia

TABLE 2: ACTUAL AND ESTIMATED COMMONWEALTH OUTLAYS ON SOCIAL WELFARE FUNCTIONS AS A PERCENTAGE OF TOTAL OUTLAYS BY PORTFOLIO 1982-83 to 1986-87

Portfolio	1982-83 Actual	1983-84 Actual	1984-85 Actual	1985-86 Actual	1986-87 Estimated
COMMUNITY SERVICES (DCS)					
Assistance to Aged	0.30	0.27	0.29	0.30	0.36
Assistance to Disabled	0.22	0.22	0.22	0.23	0.20
Assistance to Families	0.13	0.15	0.19	0.21	0.27
Nursing & Paramedical	1.55	1.55	1.52	1.48	1.47
Other	0.15	0.16	0.18	0.18	0.16
TOTAL	2.35	2.35	2.40	2.40	2.46
HOUSING & CONSTRUCTION (DHC) TOTAL	1.04	1.36	1.47	1.29	1.22
SOCIAL SECURITY (DSS)					
Income Support					
. Aged	9.97	9.41	8.85	8.43	8.45
. Sick & Disabled	2.89	2.99	3.05	3.13	3.26
. Widows & Supporting Parents	3.04	3.04	3.07	3.09	3.10
. Families	2.83	2.73	2.43	2.28	1.91
. Unemployed	4.61	5.16	4.68	4.47	4.76
Other	0.88	0.97	0.96	0.98	1.10
TOTAL	24.22	24.30	23.04	22.38	22.58
VETERANS' AFFAIRS (DVA) TOTAL	4.98	4.93	4.85	4.91	4.89
TOTAL SOCIAL WELFARE FUNCTIONS (FOUR PORTFOLIOS)	32.59	32.94	31.76	30.98	31.15
HEALTH (DH) Benefit Expenditure	3.79	4.89	7.03	7.31	7.38
Plus Tax Expenditure for Private Health Insurance	0.85	0.00	0.00	0.00	0.00
Less Medicare Levy	-0.00	-0.65	-1.84	-1.95	-2.25
TOTAL	4.64	4.24	5.19	5.36	5.13
TOTAL SOCIAL WELFARE FUNCTIONS (FIVE PORTFOLIOS)	37.23	37.18	36.95	36.34	36.28

SOURCE: Policy Coordination Unit, Annual Report 1985-86

Australia

late 1970s by the Fraser Liberal-National Government. There are many processes of consultation built into the budget process with State governments, business and trade union groups and various representatives of welfare recipients like the Australian Council of Social Services, the Australian Council on the Ageing and so on. Such welfare groups are, however, very minor players in this process.

FIGURE 2: SOCIAL WELFARE FUNCTION OUTLAYS AS A PERCENTAGE OF TOTAL COMMONWEALTH OUTLAYS

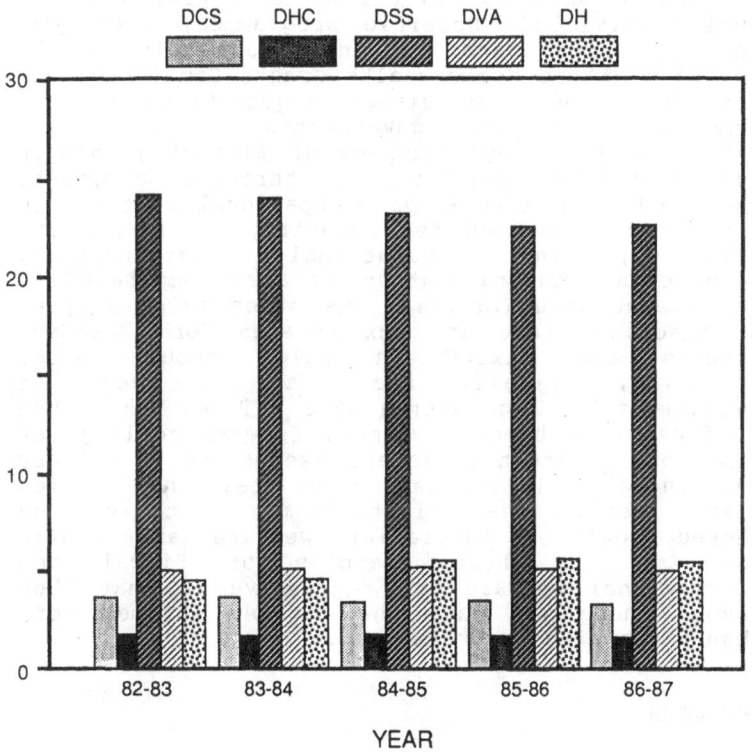

SOURCE: Policy Coordination Unit, <u>Annual Report 1985-86</u>.

Australia

The federal-State transfer process is monitored by the Commonwealth Grants Commission. Specifically it undertakes regular reviews of the general revenue grants to States, to calculate factors which adjust shares around the basis of a pure population share. Victoria has a factor of one, Western Australia 1.46 and Northern Territory 5.889 reflecting different social composition, degree of urbanisation and so on. The principle guiding this process is 'geographic equity', namely, that each State should be able to provide the same service at the same level without having to raise extra revenue. The general revenue available to States will be spent in cost-shared welfare programmes including the provision of health services. Specific programmes, like Home and Community Care, do not fall within the interest of the Commonwealth Grants Commission and are the subject of direct negotiations between Commonwealth and State governments.

There are other examples of financing through tax rebates and deductions or through employment. The two key programmes of occupational welfare are workers compensation for industrial accidents and illnesses, and occupational superannuation. Occupational superannuation is also encouraged by tax exempt accumulation. The other main examples of fiscal welfare are tax rebates for dependent spouses and laxity in rules about income splitting. Finally there are a range of incentives for acquisition of a private home, such as first home buyers schemes, federal ceilings of home loan interest rates and exemptions of primary residences from capital gains tax and pension means tests. The private home is truly 'the sacred cow' of Australian welfare and public policy. All these examples of fiscal and occupational welfare are regressive in that they favour those who have the highest incomes more than those with lower incomes.

THE AGED

Between now and the year 2000 the absolute numbers of persons aged 75 years and over will double and between 2000 and 2020, as the baby boom reaches retirement age, the numbers aged 60 to 75 years are expected to double as shown in Figure 3.

Australia

Whilst the aged of Australia are more likely to be contributors to their families, in terms of income and services, than recipients, and are subject to taxation, they face an increasing risk of low income, ill health and physical dependence as they age.

FIGURE 3: NUMBERS OF PERSONS AGED 60 AND OVER AND 75 AND OVER, 1981-2021

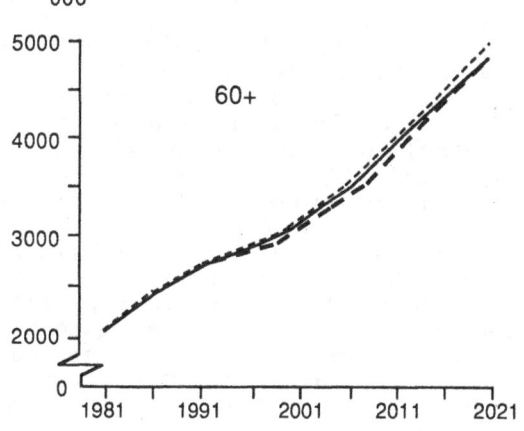

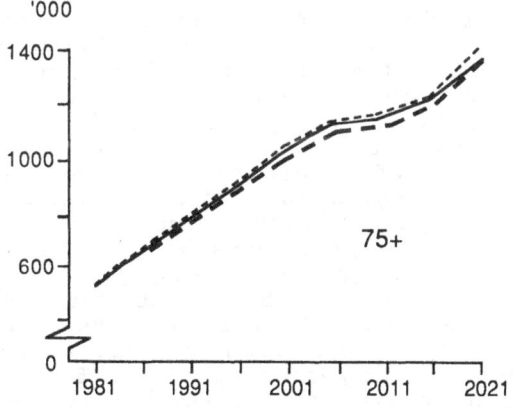

——— Australian Bureau of Statistics Series A/B, low fertility, medium migration.
- - - - - - - Australian Bureau of Statistics Series C, low fertility, high migration.
— — — Dept. of Immigration Series, low fertility, low migration and different mortality to ABS

SOURCE: Kendig & McCallum 1986.

Australia

Social Security

The first risk is low savings and accumulated income for old age and the absence of opportunity to supplement income through work. Since 1909, elderly Australians have lived with the security of a publicly provided minimum income being available in old age if they need it. Only recently, from 1968, has the age pension been made sufficient to live on - prior to this it was intended to supplement private savings. Actually pensions now provide an adequate minimum income only if people own their homes.

Women aged 60 or more and men aged 65 or more may qualify for an age pension, subject to income and assets tests, provided a person has been resident in Australia for ten years. War veterans are eligible for pensions earlier than these ages. Pensions are subject to twice yearly indexation in June and December in line with increases in the Consumer Price Index between the previous June and December quarters, and the previous December and June quarters respectively. The standard rate of pension is about one-quarter of the average weekly earnings. The maximum rate of pension is reduced to $A1 for every $A2 of non-pension income in excess of a defined limit which increases for each dependent child. Under the assets test the maximum rate of pension is reduced by $A1 a week for each $A500 of assessable assets above the allowable amounts. Blind people are paid the maximum rates regardless of income and assets and people aged 70 years are subject to slightly more generous income testing. Married pensions are paid to spouses as individuals and were 83 per cent of single rates, as of 30 June 1986. The age pension is subject to income tax. However, a special pensioner income tested tax rebate ensures that pensioners with little or no other income are not required to pay tax.

Currently some 67 per cent of retired Australians over age 45 years receive whole or part pensions as their main source of income. This take-up rate increases with age, for example 77 per cent of those over 65 years have pensions as their main source of income. Occupational superannuation is a main source of income for nine per cent and other sources for about 25 per cent of retired persons average 45 years. Low coverage of the workforce, lack of portability and a high proportion of payouts as lump sums rather than

Australia

regular payments, accounts for the poor performance of occupational superannuation. For most Australians their only significant saving is in their private home. Increasing pressure is being put upon the retirement income system by the trend to early retirement of the increased numbers of the elderly.

Personal Social Services

A significant risk in old age is the loss of some functional abilities and, as a result, people need help to live independently at home. Some 90 per cent of Australians over age 65 own their homes or are in public housing and another three per cent live in other private dwellings in the community. It is estimated that around 80 per cent of all forms of assistance to older people comes from family and friends (Kendig & McCallum 1986). The new Home and Community Care Programme will provide some assistance with home nursing, home help, transport, meals and respite care for people (not exclusively aged) who are at risk of premature or inappropriate long-term residential care. It costs the Commonwealth Department of Community Services over $A100 million per year which is shared with the States. This programme will be subject to review after three years and can be only a minor provider of services to the aged.

The next stage of risk for the aged occurs when the aged person is no longer able to remain at home and needs temporary or permanent institutionalisation. Intensive forms of care in nursing homes became the only option for care through the 1960s and 1970s to the detriment of home and community care and less intensive forms of institutional care - such as hostel accommodation. With the total cost of institutional care in nursing homes nearing $A1,000 million for a mere 76,000 residents, a ceiling has been placed on the growth in numbers of beds and strict assessment procedures have been set down for admission. The current alternatives to intensive institutional care are hostels and home and community care. Currently some 38,227 beds are available in hostel accommodation and some $A58,960,000 was paid out over the year 1985-6 for personal care, respite and normal hostel subsidies. The demand for residential care in some areas exceeds supply and maintenance of the quality of care whilst containing cost is a

Australia

current problem area. There has been some 'de-institutionalisation' as a consequence of stricter assessment for nursing home admission. For the future it is planned that there will be 100 residential care places provided per 1,000 people aged 70 or over of which a maximum of 10 per cent of new beds will be in nursing homes.

The minimum payment for nursing home care is set at 87.5 per cent of the basic pension and rental assistance. Over half of the publicly funded nursing home beds are provided by private, for-profit organisations with another quarter provided by 'not-for-profit' religious and ethnic organisations. The remaining beds, around 20 per cent, are provided by State governments. There is no purely private nursing home sector in Australia that is not public funded. Despite a period of constraint, particularly in nursing home funding, there will be improved congruence fit between individual need and institutional setting for support of the aged in Australia.

Evaluation

As the recent Brookings Institute study of the Australian retirement income system (Caves & Krause 1984, p.362) observed:

> ... the Australian system is probably more generous to the aged workers who have had low earnings than is the US system. In contrast the Australian system gives far less to those at the middle-income levels than do US and other social insurance systems. The average US social security recipient receives more, and those who had above average earnings receive much more, than they would receive from age pensions in Australia ...

In personal social services the special concerns of an 'ageing society' have only recently been recognised. Policies are, then, just developing and will be subject to evaluations over the next five years.

THE DISABLED AND HANDICAPPED

When Thomas Waddell, the Treasurer of the State of New South Wales spoke for the new Invalidity and

Australia

Accidents Pension Bill in 1907, he claimed: "As far as my knowledge goes, there has been no legislation of this kind in any other country" (NSW Parliamentary Debates, 4 December 1907, 1630). It was at least true that other countries' existing schemes had either more limited scope or different principles. The NSW Act was largely incorporated into the Commonwealth Invalid and Old-age Pensions Act of 1908. Whilst these Acts followed the German social insurance legislation of 1889, they provide an example of early entry of Australia into another area of welfare.

Since the 1940s the rates of grant have tended to rise, with the lowest rates coming in the 1950s and the highest rates in the late 1970s as shown in Figure 4. There are high rates for 16 to 19 year olds because of sufferers of congenital diseases first reaching pensionable age. Rates, also, rise steadily from about age 40 indicating the correlation of ageing with assessed invalidity. It is not plausible that the health of the population has worsened over the last 40 years. Rather the increases over time are likely due to the increased probability of persons suffering a degree of disability being granted a pension in more recent years. Over that time the causes of invalidity have also changed. For example, infectious diseases like tuberculosis, poliomyelitis, syphilis and rubella changed from being major to being negligible causes of invalidity.

Social Security

People aged 16 years or over who are blind or assessed as not less than 85 per cent of total incapacitation for work may be paid an invalid pension if the incapacity occurred in Australia or even if it occurred overseas, provided people have been a resident for 10 years. From 1987 it is required that 50 per cent of the incapacity for work be due to physical or mental impairment. These pensions are paid at the same rate as age pensions and are subject to the same income and assets tests - except for the blind. Prior to age pensions ages these benefits are not subject to income tax. Normally an invalidity pension is transferred to an age pension at ages 60 for women or 65 for men. There were 273,810 invalid pensioners in Australia as at 30 June 1986. War veterans have a parallel system of disability

Australia

FIGURE 4: RATES OF GRANT OF INVALID PENSION 1942-1983

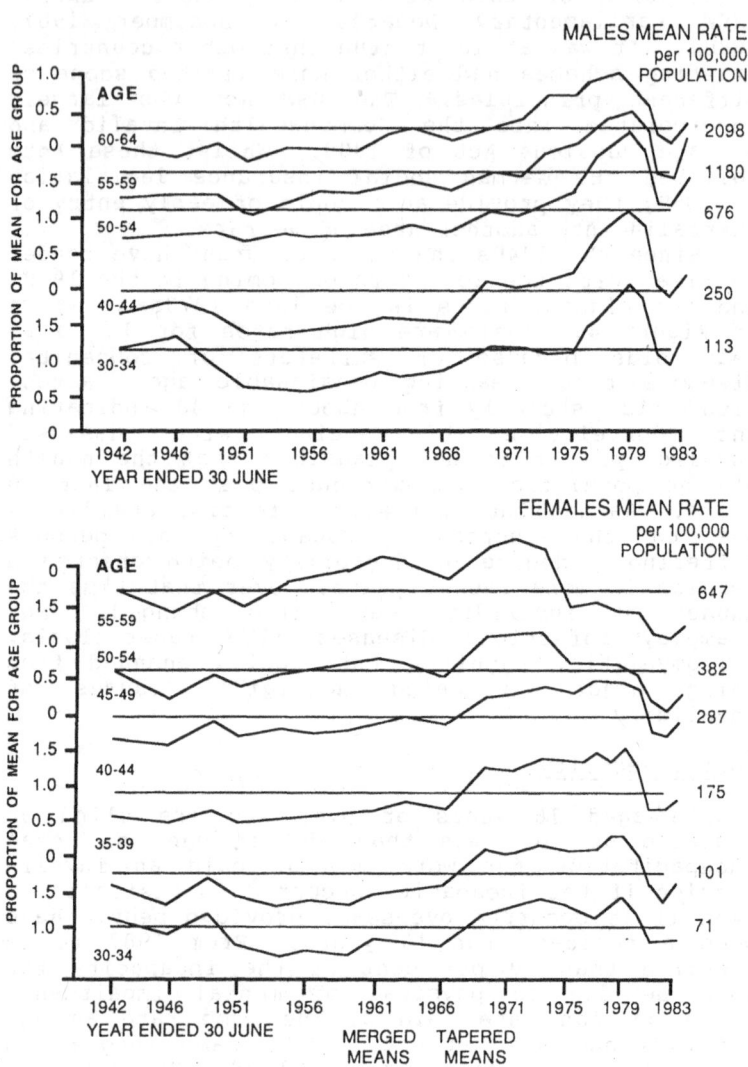

SOURCE: Permanent Incapacity and Invalid Pension in Australia, Department of Social Security, Research Paper No. 23, 1984.

Australia

pensions with the added advantage of special programmes compensating for loss of physical or mental well-being which affects lifestyles, including employability.

There are various allowances available to disabled and handicapped persons. Sheltered employment allowance may be paid as an alternative to invalid pensions if people work in approved sheltered employment services. There were 10,041 recipients as of 30 June 1986. A rehabilitation allowance is payable to persons who receive treatment or training through the Commonwealth Rehabilitation Service and who are eligible for social security pensions or benefits. There were 3,227 recipients of rehabilitation allowances as of 30 June 1986. Finally, wives pensions are available to wives of invalid pensioners and carers pensions to those who care for a severely handicapped relative. Some 83,212 wife's or carer's pensions were being paid at the end of June 1986 to wives of invalid pensioners.

Personal Social Services

Disabled and handicapped persons are the targets for a range of personal social services in particular the Disability Services Programme of the Commonwealth Department of Community Services. The services provided are: sheltered employment, activity therapy, training, residential accommodation, recreation, rehabilitation and holiday accommodation, the print handicapped scheme and aids for disabled people including home modifications, wheelchairs, orthoses, domiciliary oxygen, surgical wigs and mammary prostheses. The services are generally aimed to maximise individual potential and to facilitate integration into the general community.

The new home and community care programme is targeted to persons who are at risk of premature or inappropriate long-term residential care. These may be either frail aged or younger disabled persons, with moderate or severe disabilities. Due to the considerably greater risk of disability for the aged, these services will predominantly go to the aged. They enable the disabled person or their carers to provide for themselves in their home environment. Again most services of this kind, around 80 per cent as an estimate, will be provided by family and community persons rather than by governments.

Australia

Evaluation

As the variable rates of award of invalid pensions during the 1970s indicate, there is no real possibility of getting a uniform basis for the assessment of 85 per cent incapacity. Moreover, in a tight labour market, this assessment is changed by higher level requirements from employers. Older beneficiaries of sickness, unemployment and service benefits are more similar to invalid pensioners than not, although their incapacity for work is largely due to age and labour market conditions. More attractive sickness and unemployment benefits and conditions are needed so that these people are treated similarly to invalid pensioners. This problem is more general, with groups at all ages who are sick, but not 85 per cent incapacitated, and not necessarily available for work. They, therefore, are ineligible for both invalid pensions and unemployment benefits. In dealing with this gap in provision, the rights of the sick and incapacitated to work need to be carefully maintained.

CHILDREN AND YOUTHS

A range of government programmes are directed at children through families, including various forms of income support, education assistance, child care and health insurance. There is an emphasis on the primary responsibility of parents in providing for their own children. However, in areas like education and health professionals are the main service providers as they are in special situations when children are put at risk by parental failures or mishaps. Assistance for families is based upon the belief that children are a highly valued resource, on which the future living standards of the society depend. Parents are, therefore, responsible for the welfare of the future society, as well as for their children, and in this they are deserving of support.

Social Security

In providing income support to families with children three different concepts of equity are distinguished (Cass 1986, p.5). Horizontal equity is the aim of providing a fair share for all

Australia

families whilst vertical equity is the aim of providing adequate support for low income families. Within families there is further a concern to provide resources to the parent primarily responsible for children's care with the proviso that assistance does not discourage parents' workforce participation and potential for earning income. Again, as with other benefits, it is not expected that benefits will cover the full costs of rearing children except in the case of very low income families.

Since 1941 Australian families have received payments for children as well as enjoying tax deductions to 1975 and thereafter rebates. In 1976 child endowments and tax rebates for children were amalgamated and renamed as family allowances. Since the Second World War support for families was seen as a central part of welfare. Child endowment then family allowances were provided universally for children and were untaxed but since October 1987 they are subject to income testing. Originally 'family needs' had been part of the calculation of the basic wage, however, in 1974 and 1977 the Commonwealth Conciliation and Arbitration Commission determined that family needs should not be part of wage negotiations. Rather that concern was argued to be the proper domain of government family support programmes.

People who have one or more children under 16, or one or more full-time students aged 16 to 17 inclusive, who are wholly or substantially dependent on them, receive family allowances. The allowance may also continue for full-time dependent students aged 18 to 24 years living in low income families. As at 30 June 1986 there were 2,153,670 families receiving family allowances for 4,181,064 children and students. There were also 168 families with triplets and seven families with quadruplets receiving special additional family allowances costing about $A0.2 million in 1985-6. Family allowance cost $A1,538 million in 1985-6 and was the last vestige of universalism in Australian welfare. Since 1987 however, those with joint family incomes above $A56,000 are subject to means-tested allowances with special provision for larger families.

Australia

Personal Social Services

In addition to income support there are a range of services delivered through the Department of Community Services over which its Office of Child Care has jurisdiction. The primary objective of this office is to ensure that parents and children have access to quality childrens' services appropriate to their needs, regardless of their income, cultural background, disability or geographical location. Childrens' services cover child care and neighbourhood centres, family day care, services outside school hours, family and child assistance, family support services and so on. These programmes cost $A167 million in 1985-6.

Children and youth in Australia also benefit from free, universal and compulsory (until age 15) education services unless they choose private education which also attracts substantial public subsidy. They also benefit from universal health insurance under which, for 1.26 per cent of parents' taxable income above a minimum, they receive 85 per cent return of the scheduled fee. Where a doctor bills the government direct there is no charge to the service recipient. Some 40 per cent of a $A40 million supported accommodation assistance programme of the Commonwealth Department of Community Services goes to youth who are temporarily or permanently homeless. Finally, one area of responsibility remaining with the States is adoption and foster care services.

Youth attract special services to enable further education and the transition from school to work or to counter the negative effects of unemployment. Students who progress to tertiary or post-secondary level education are eligible for AUSTUDY grants subject to means-testing of parents unless the child has lived away from home for two years or more. They also enjoy education without fees but with a yearly administration fee.

Youth unemployment has been high in Australia over the last decade. This reflects in part low rates of participation in schooling by adolescents. Around 40 per cent of Australians aged 16 to 18 participate in schooling compared to rates of 75 per cent for Japan and the United States. In June 1986 the unemployment rate of youth (ages 15 to 19) was 18.5 per cent compared with 9.8 per cent amongst 20 to 24 year olds and 7.5 per cent for all age groups. Almost half

Australia

those individuals registered with the Commonwealth Employment Service of the Department of Employment and Industrial Relations are under 25 years of age.

To deal with these problems of youth the federal government initiated the Priority One Project with the following goals:

- to increase the attractiveness of completing secondary education,
- to extend the opportunities of job based training for early school leavers,
- to aid young unemployed under a range of labour market programmes, and
- to provide information on labour market, education and support opportunities.

The Commonwealth Employment Service works through the Local Schools Liaison programme which provides career education and information about jobs, careers, job search, interviews and employers needs and attitudes. Youth Access Centres for people aged 15 to 19 are situated in Commonwealth Employment Service Offices and at outreach locations to provide advice on careers, employment, training and income support opportunities.

Some $A53 million will be spent on vocational training for youth in 1986-7 of which $A35 million goes to the Australian Traineeship System. This provides structured on-the-job and off-the-job training in occupations which are not trades. A further $A290 million was spent in 1985-6 on the Community Employment Programme which funds approved jobs with community groups which provide work experience for the long term unemployed. Job Start is a wage subsidy scheme for persons six months unemployed in the last nine months or belonging to specially disadvantaged groups which cost $A115 million in 1985-6. In both these programmes there is substantial youth participation. Finally the Community Youth Support Scheme, costing $A32 million in 1985-6, funds local groups which assist unemployed people aged 15 to 24 years to obtain or retain employment or to take on further education and training or to become more self reliant while unemployed. These programmes reflect an interest in facilitating young people's socialisation for a self-sufficient working life.

Australia

Evaluation

With increased rates of unemployment and family breakdown problems for children and youth remain despite these extensive provisions. The Hawke Labor Government, re-elected in July 1987, gave unusually strong emphasis to support for children in its election campaign policy speech at the Sydney Opera House on 23 June 1987:

> For our next term, we are setting achievable new goals for Australia's future in the world. At the head of those goals is the future of all our children. So we set ourselves this first goal:
>
> By 1990 no Australian child shall be living in poverty.

A new programme of family help was proposed to help achieve this laudable goal. The Family Allowance Supplement was to be paid to mothers on the basis of family income and family size. Just what this election promise would mean and how it might be achieved are not yet clear. New programmes for children will, however, be appearing to help achieve this goal.

NEEDY FAMILIES

Needy families have long been recognised as requiring extra support, over and above basic assistance like family allowance. Such families need not be eligible for Government pensions or benefits and thus they become difficult to capture in the security net. In recent years high rates of unemployment and marital breakdown have led to the development of special benefits for sole parents in 1973 and for poor families not in receipt of pensions and benefits in 1983.

The percentages of families with dependent children headed by sole parents has increased from nine per cent in 1974 to 14.4 per cent in 1985. This trend matches patterns of social change in the United Kingdom, Europe and the United States. Sole parents, most of whom are female, are less likely to gain financial independence because they have low educational qualifications and interrupted working careers. Problems like access to child care, and its costs, and problems of

Australia

caring for children when sick, after school and during holidays, affect job prospects of sole parents. Women also face lower wages as a disincentive to working. Female sole parents have the lowest educational qualification of all parents. Some 45 per cent of married mothers have attended highest levels of secondary schooling compared to 37 per cent of single mothers (Cass 1986). These groups are, then, among the most disadvantaged by declining opportunities in the labour market.

Social Security

As well as the extensive system of family allowances, income-tested payments for pensioners and beneficiaries with children have been provided since the 1940s. These include an additional pension/benefit for children and a mothers/guardians allowance paid to sole parent pensioners and beneficiaries all of which will be replaced by the new Family Allowance Supplement introduced in 1987. Since 1983 family income supplement has been provided to low income families not in receipt of a pension or benefit. The purpose of all these payments is to augment the basic family allowance payment in low income families. The tax system also provides rebates for a dependent spouse and children, and for sole parents with dependent children and students, but they only benefit those with taxable income above the appropriate threshold.
Certain low income families, not in receipt of pensions or benefit, are eligible for Family Income Supplement (FIS), an income-tested, non-taxable allowance for dependent children under 16 years or full-time students aged 16 to 24 years. FIS ceases at the point when income goes above the limit set for eligibility for the Health Care Card for low income families. As of 30 June 1986 some 83,109 children received FIS at a cost of about $A50 million. These supplements go to 29,183 families of which 28,266 are married couples. As well as FIS, outlays on additional benefits for children of pensioners and beneficiaries totalled $A204 million for some 256,906 children.
Sole parents who have a dependent child under 16 years, or full-time student aged 16 to 24 years, may receive supporting parent's benefit if they do not receive any other pension or benefit.

Australia

They may also receive a Class A widow's pension. Some 74,180 Class A widows' pensions were paid out in 1985-86 at a cost of $A519. There were 176,730 supporting parent beneficiaries as of 30 June 1986 (166,660 women and 10,070 men), an increase of 5.2 per cent from the previous 12 months. This involved outlays of $A1,238 million, an increase of 16 per cent from the previous year. In 1986 sole parents constituted 14.4 per cent of all families with children as shown in Figure 5. Of all sole parents only 16.3 per cent were not in receipt of social security pensions and benefits. The residency requirements on supporting parents' benefits requiring only birth in Australia, has led to some concern about high rates of ex-nuptial births amongst New Zealand women in Australia. Generally support for sole parents, other than de jure widows, is more controversial than support for the elderly or widows.

Evaluation

Whilst the total number of supporting parents has been growing rapidly in the last 10 years, the numbers of de jure widows has not, as shown in Figure 6. The majority of sole parents, 85 per cent, are widowed, separated or divorced, indicating the role of marital breakdown in this benefit escalation (Cass 1986). Most stay on benefits for short periods, 2.8 years for divorced or separated women compared to 5.7 years for widows. Further, only four per cent are teenagers. Despite concerns about the benefit encouraging teenage pregnancy this figure has actually declined since the benefit began. Nonetheless the provision remains controversial. The prime question asked is why this status attracts benefits when its characteristics are all manageable without special provision, for example through unemployment provisions, support for children and needy families. The supporters argue it is an effective means of targeting a special need, its opponents see it as a political benefit designed to gain support from more radical women's groups.

The continuing problem of needy families is amply demonstrated by new poverty research analysis of the 1981-2 Income and Housing Survey using the detailed Henderson Poverty Line (before housing equivalent disposable income) which found 1.9 million of Australia's 15 million population were in poverty (Gallagher 1985). Of these

Australia

FIGURE 5: FAMILIES WITH DEPENDENT CHILDREN, 1986

Panel A

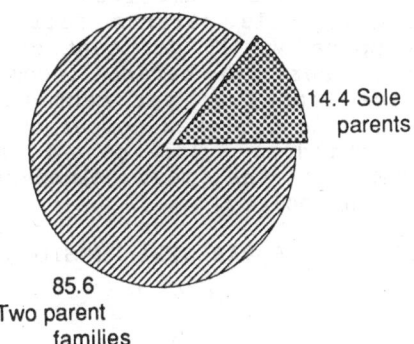

14.4 Sole parents

85.6 Two parent families

Sole parents with dependent children, 1986

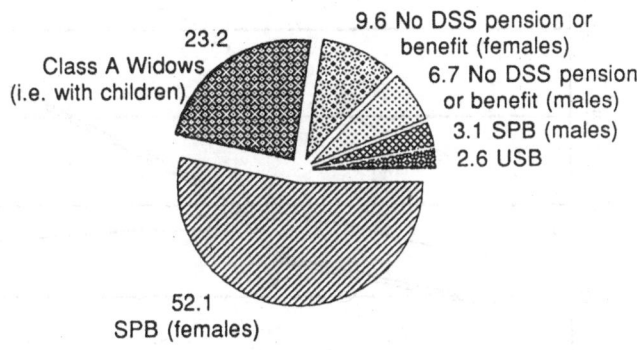

23.2 Class A Widows (i.e. with children)

9.6 No DSS pension or benefit (females)
6.7 No DSS pension or benefit (males)
3.1 SPB (males)
2.6 USB

52.1 SPB (females)

Note: USB - Unemployed, sickness and special beneficiaries
SPB - Supporting parent beneficiaries
DSS - Department of Social Security

SOURCE: Based on ABS data published in the bulletin 'Labour Force Status and Other Characteristics of Families', July 1985, from Department of Social Security, Annual Report 1985-86.

Australia

370,000 lived in sole parent income units and 840,000 were children. The highest risks for poverty were children in one parent families and for sole parents themselves. Some 54 per cent of children of sole parents fell below the poverty line compared to 15 per cent of children with two parents. For two parent income units the risk increases from five per cent to 33 per cent for those with no children compared to those with four or more children. Sole parents and their children are some of the most disadvantaged groups in Australian society.

FIGURE 6: SOLE PARENTS' PENSIONS, 1976-1986

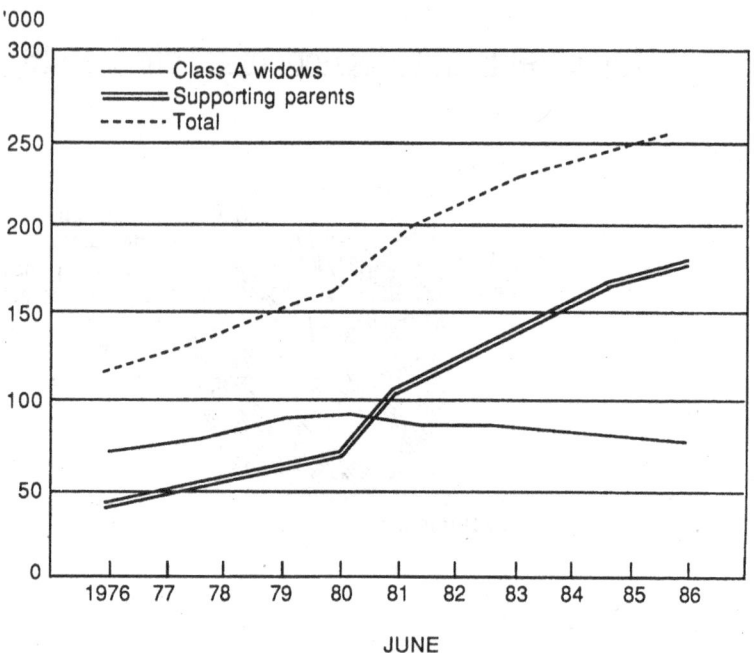

Note: Class A widows were those with dependent children.

SOURCE: Department of Social Security, <u>Annual Report 1985-86</u>.

Australia

THE UNEMPLOYED

Near the end of the Second World War the Commonwealth enacted the Unemployment and Sickness Benefits Act 1944, which had been promised when the National Welfare Fund was established in 1943. Like age and invalid pensions the benefits were flat-rate and paid from general revenue, however, unlike age pensions, they were not subject to assets testing, only to an income test. A further test is applied however, namely that persons register at the Commonwealth Employment Service and be willing to undertake suitable work if offered. Insurance style schemes consequently have not developed in Australia.

The assumption of the benefit system was that it was a transitionary support for job changers. This was a workable assumption whilst the national unemployment rate was around one or two per cent which it was through the post Second World War era to the oil crisis recession. However, as shown in Figure 7, between 1976 and 1986 the numbers of unemployment beneficiaries trebled and the Labour Force Surveys of those actively looking for work and available to start in the week of survey (the unemployed) show a doubling from 292,700 in August 1976 to 595,600 in August 1986. The proportion of unemployed seeking benefits has increased over the period as has the workforce participation rate of women.

The extent of the problem of unemployment is understated by rates of beneficiaries and of those defined as unemployed. Only about 45 per cent of non-employed persons who wanted to work technically fall within the definition of unemployed. The Surveys of Persons Not in the Labour Force show over half those wanting to work are not actively seeking it and about 80 per cent of these are available to start work within four weeks. Increasing workforce participation along with declining economic conditions have produced high, persistent rates of unemployment which cannot be expected to decrease in the near future. Given the centrality of employment to the Australian welfare system this change has shaken it to its roots.

Social Security

Flat-rate income-tested and taxed unemployment benefits are paid fortnightly, after a seven day waiting period, to people aged at least 18 years

FIGURE 7: UNEMPLOYMENT BENEFICIARIES BY AGE, 1976-86

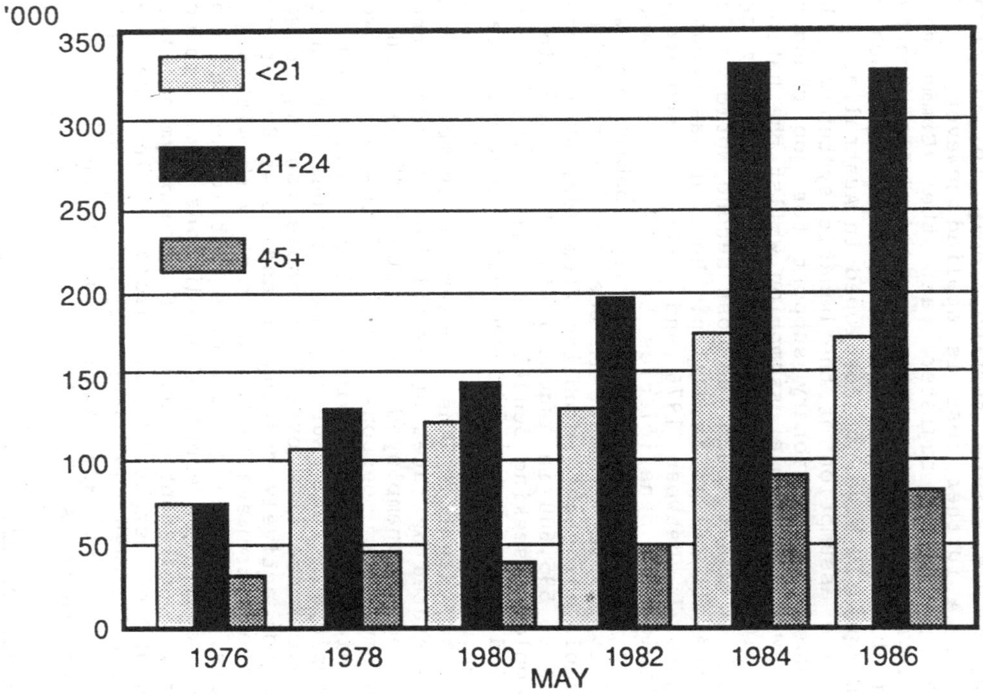
'000
350
300
250
200
150
100
50
0
<21
21-24
45+
1976
1978
1980
1982
1984
1986
MAY

SOURCE: Department of Social Security, _Annual Report, 1985-86_.

Australia

but less than 60 for women and 65 for men. School leavers, however, are subject to a 13 week waiting period. There is no limit on the length of time over which these flat-rate unemployment benefits can be received. Youths aged 16 and 17 years receive a flat-rate job search allowance which requires them to undertake training or active job search. Recipients must have lived in Australia for at least one year prior to claiming a benefit or intend to remain in Australia permanently. To be eligible for unemployment benefit a person must:

- have been unemployed for the period covered by the benefit;
- be capable of undertaking and willing to undertake suitable paid work (the work test is administered by the Commonwealth Employment Service);
- not be unemployed due to being, or having been, engaged in industrial action; and
- not be unemployed due to industrial action by other members of a trade union of which the person is a member.

A special tax rebate for beneficiaries ensured that persons wholly or mainly dependent on unemployment benefit would not have been liable to pay income tax in 1985-86.

As of 30 June 1986 there were 569,761 persons in receipt of unemployment benefit, an increase of 1.5 per cent during the year. The estimated average number of unemployment beneficiaries at the end of each week of 1985-86 was 559,237, a decrease on average of 3.9 per cent from 1984-85. The total outlays for this benefit in 1985-86 were $A3,122 million. Over the last 10 years unemployment rates have more than trebled. Since the Second World War, unemployment rates were relatively low in the range of one to three per cent of the work force.

Personal Social Services

The Commonwealth Department of Employment and Industrial Relations outlayed for 1985-86 some $A667 million on Labour Market Programmes and Services primarily directed to the unemployed. These programmes are in addition to the services for job search provided by the Commonwealth Employment Service. The Commonwealth Department provides a range of training assistance for adults

Australia

including the Skills in Demand (SID) Programme, General Training Assistance (GTA), Labour Adjustment Training Arrangements (LATA) as well as special training programmes for the disabled and job seekers with special needs. At the beginning of 1986 these programmes were incorporated into the Adult Training Programme which is primarily directed to support disadvantaged job seekers. For example, LATA addresses the special problems of workers affected by large scale retrenchments in designated industries or areas undergoing extensive restructuring. Industry sectors receiving assistance under LATA in 1985-6 were:

- the steel industry cities of Newcastle, Wollongong and Whyalla;
- firms supplying the steel industry in these regions;
- the New South Wales coal industry; and
- the passenger motor vehicle industry.

During 1985-6 there were 5,118 job seekers approved for General Skills Training including GTA, LATA and formal training for the disabled, with an outlay of $A14.4 million. Separate funding is provided for training and employment assistance associated with restructuring the heavy engineering industry.

Evaluation

The current situation of unemployment rates around eight per cent has seriously challenged the rationale for benefits as a temporary measure. As of August 1986 the median duration of benefit receipt was 30 weeks. However, the median duration for persons aged 45 and over was more than a year, being over 18 months for persons aged 60 to 64 years. Some two-thirds of those unemployed amongst 60 to 64 year olds have been on benefits for more than a year compared to a quarter of those aged under 25. In 1977, 27 per cent of unemployment beneficiaries aged 55 or more had been on benefit for more than a year which rises to 59 per cent in 1986. This is a consequence of both the rates of outflow and inflow to benefit being lowest for older individuals.

Unemployment is a major cause of increased poverty rates in Australia both directly and indirectly, for example, through increases in

Australia

hidden unemployment, that is, people who are out of the workforce. The flat-rate benefits do not maintain consumption levels and have become more than transitional support on the way to another job. The programmes for needy families, youth, children, disabled and handicapped are all aimed to deal with some of the consequences of unemployment.

THE SICK AND INJURED

Some 121 million medical services were delivered in 1985-86 (see Table 3).

A universal system of health insurance began in 1975 with the Medibank programme administered

TABLE 3: NUMBERS OF MEDICARE SERVICES PROCESSED 1984-86

	1984-85	1985-86	Change %
Total Number of Services Processed	113,010,760	121,352,958	7.4
Average number of services per head of population	7.129	7.054	5.3
- male	5.570	5.585	5.2
- female	8.673	9.139	5.4
Broad Type of Service			
General Practitioner attendances	64,038,654	67,866,425	5.9
Specialist attendances	10,475,651	11,228,548	7.2
Obstetrics	582,943	589,975	1.2
Anaesthetics	1,824,601	1,944,511	6.6
Pathology	22,144,962	23,907,763	8.0
Radiology	4,721,475	5,336,559	13.0
Operations	3,209,458	3,679,115	14.6
Assistance at operations	161,030	178,845	11.1
Optometry	1,487,877	1,683,956	13.2
Dental	2,478	2,704	9.1
Miscellaneous	4,341,631	4,934,558	13.7

SOURCE: Health Insurance Commission, Annual Report 1985-86.

Australia

by the Health Insurance Commission. Since then the system has been through many changes, the most recent being in 1983 with the enrolment and registration of the entire population in the Medibank programme through the issue of 7,500,000 Medicare cards.

This was financed by a one per cent levy on taxable incomes above a minimum level, but has been increased to 1.25 per cent. This covered all Australians to the level of 85 per cent of the scheduled fee for medical services. Some doctors direct-bill patients and accept the Medicare benefit as the full payment for the service. Public hospitals provide free hospital services but there are delays due to queuing. To avoid queues or exercise choice of doctors and facilities, private insurance is necessary. This new system overlays pre-existing provision of social security, namely Commonwealth Sickness Benefits and Workers Compensation.

Social Security

Flat-rate, income-tested and taxed sickness benefits are paid fortnightly, after a seven day waiting period, to people who have been temporarily incapacitated for work because of sickness, accident or incapacity. The age and residence requirements are the same as for unemployment benefits. A special tax rebate for beneficiaries ensured that most did not pay income tax in 1985-86.

As of 30 June 1986 there were 65,301 people receiving sickness benefit, an increase of 3.6 per cent over the previous year. The estimated average number of sickness beneficiaries at the end of each week of 1985-86 was 63,481 which was an increase of 1.7 per cent over the previous year. The total number of sickness beneficiaries has doubled from 30,000 since 1976 and durations have also increased. The steepest increase occurred between the years 1979 and 1983 at the same time as increases in unemployment rates. This indicates that the labour market became a decreasingly hospitable place for anyone with an illness or disability. This was exacerbated by more stringent assessment for invalid pensioners and also perhaps by health consequences of unemployment. Whereas such people would have been acceptable for jobs previously, employers were no longer willing to regard them as acceptable

Australia

employees in the late 1970s. While, in fact, health surveys show slight improvements in health, the rates of sickness beneficiaries increased because of changed perceptions of employable persons due to changes in the economic climate.

Employers are also liable for accident or work illness of employees. The central principle of Workers Compensation legislation in the various States is that, regardless of fault, employers must accept some part of the losses of employees who might suffer injury in the course of employment. Employees may, in some States, also pursue negligence action or seek benefits in the general social security system. Compensation schemes are by far the most important source of income for those injured at work. They began in Western Australia in 1902 and spread to the other States. However, with schemes being different in all States and some having a number of schemes, the situation is appropriately described by one commentator (Kewley 1977, p.568) as '... largely an uncharted wilderness'. An estimate using comparable figures for 1983-4 is that Australia wide, there were 167,384 injury cases and 23,014 disease cases (excluding Western Australia) which involved 2,180,590 weeks lost and payout of $A1,034 million in compensation.

Weekly earnings-related benefits are provided in respect of both temporary and permanent and total disabilities. There is no waiting period. Dependents' supplements are also paid. In addition, each scheme includes schedules which stipulate lump-sum payments in respect of specified permanent injuries. In the case of death, compensation is payable to dependent members of the deceased's family, typically as a lump-sum. In some States there is an upper limit upon weekly payments; in others, a maximum indicates the total amount that is payable; and there are differences in the payments due to variations between the States' medical benefits and funded grants are also paid. In Queensland, Victoria and the Northern Territory government schemes operate, under the auspices of a Workmen's Compensation Board or Commission, whilst elsewhere there is a mix of public and private providers with claims settled in court. As legal costs have taken larger bites of compensation premiums, employers have found costs prohibitive and State governments have pushed through reforms. Such reforms are generally designed to reduce legal

Australia

costs, put more emphasis on rehabilitation, reduce premiums and direct more benefits to injured workers. An Inquiry in 1974 (National Committee of Inquiry 1974, p.91) estimated that it cost 40 cents or more to deliver each dollar in benefits. New schemes are attacking that problem and improving the efficiency and effectiveness of the programmes.

Personal Social Services

The Medicare Programme finances the private provision of services by medical practitioners to private citizens except where they choose to insure privately. Some 121,352,968 services were processed in 1985-86, an average of seven and a half per person, worth an average of $A21.50 per service or $A161.31 per person. The type of services provided are shown in Table 3, and about half, 48.5 per cent, were direct-billed, that is, involved no cost to claimants. Children aged 0-4 have high rates of receipt of services but women from age 25 years and men later in life, at age 55 years, exceed them in the average value of benefit received as shown in Figure 8. Prescribed pharmaceuticals are also provided free to families who exceed a set amount of expenditure on these items over a year.

Evaluation

Medicare has provided a simple and effective system of providing medical and hospital services on an equitable basis. It has had problems controlling costs of medical practitioners and disputes with doctors over fees have become commonplace. Queues are a cause of concern to the sick but urgent cases are always given priority. Medicare is generally viewed as a considerable improvement on previous tax exemptions for medical costs. The balance between dis-incentives to overuse and provider over-servicing will become more difficult to hold under the dual pressures of cost increases and population ageing.

EVALUATION OF THE AUSTRALIAN WELFARE SYSTEM

The Australian social security system evolved alongside a strong wages policy and protectionism. Australia was an early starter in

FIGURE 8: AVERAGE VALUE OF MEDICARE BENEFIT Processed by Age and Sex, 1985-86

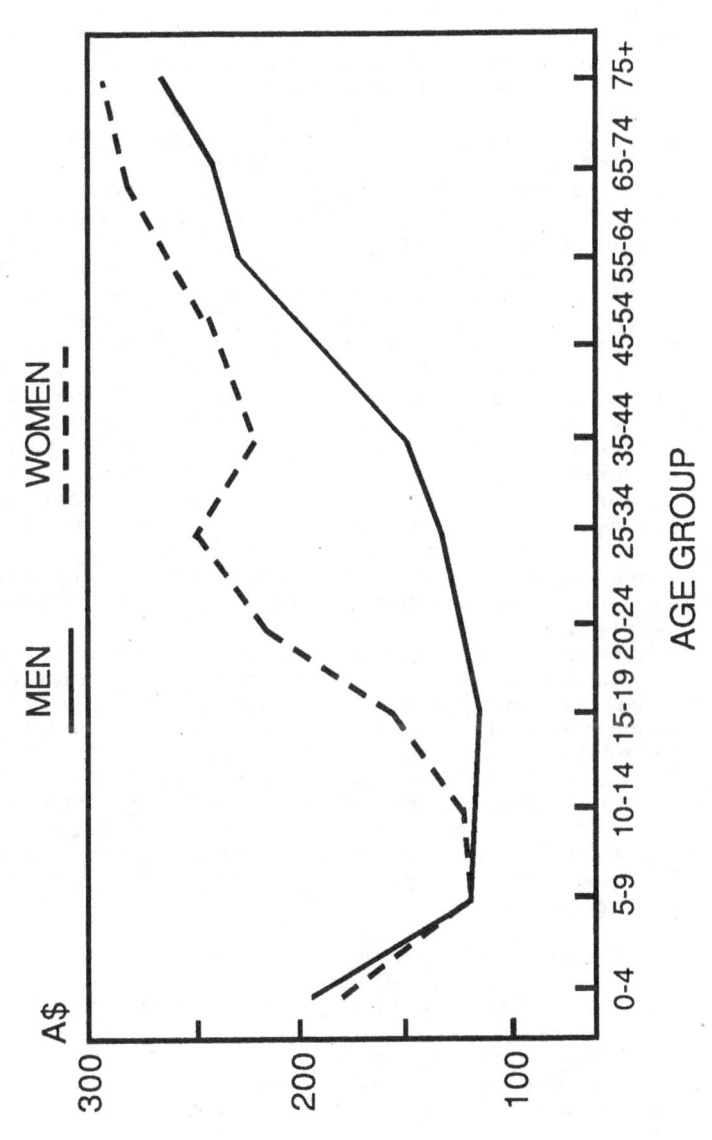

SOURCE: Health Insurance Commission, Annual Report 1985-1986

Australia

many areas of welfare and did not introduce later new thinking in social security policy because it already had a workable system and because change was difficult in a federal system. Consequently it is unique in providing flat-rate, means-tested, social security payments financed out of general revenue. After the Second World War Australia enjoyed very low rates of unemployment and had a young demographic structure. Consequently work incomes were satisfactory as the prime source of 'welfare' and the social security system was roughly in harmony with labour markets and the control of imports to local industry.

The fundamental premises of the system were shaken in the 1970s and 1980s with the decline in the Australian economy and with other social changes. Unemployment is relatively high, the population is ageing, and a rapid increase in sole parenting has created new risks to be addressed. There is disorder in the international market place and Pacific rim country imports are making moral claims to bypass protectionism of low wage and low skill industries. Finally, government expenditures are historically high whilst willingness to pay more tax is low. This situation is exacerbated by high foreign debt and declining terms of trade. The argument is that economic improvement must now come not from increased spending on government services but from investment in export or import-replacing industries.

Whether the Australian society would have been better prepared if it had extensive Scandinavian-type welfare programmes, in particular if it had earnings-related retirement pensions and unemployment benefits, is open only to conjecture. That the costs of the breakdown of the system are borne by the unemployed, the aged, single parents and those, in general, not in the workforce is indisputable. As Gallagher (1985, p.14) found, the percentage in poverty is highest for the following groups:

- children in one-parent families;
- sole parents themselves;
- children in families with four or more dependents;
- children with two parents;
- one-person income units; and
- married couples without children.

Australia

The cause of poverty can be directly linked to unemployment or other forms of absence from the workforce.

Whilst the work-oriented welfare system cannot deal adequately with the problems of the aged, unemployed and single parents into the future, the options for reform are constrained by fiscal restraints on the public sector. The Social Security Review was established by the Minister of Social Security '... to provide long-term perspectives on principles for the Australian social security system and to identify priorities for reform in the short-term'. It is currently examining three major aspects of the social security system, namely:

. income support for families with children,
. social security programmes related to the labour force, for long-term unemployed, older unemployed, sole parents, disabled and other unemployed;
. income support for the aged and retired.

Radical reforms cannot be expected, even if recommended by this review board. The general strategy will be to introduce new means-tested payments for special problems and tighter targeting of existing benefits, as well as better overall coordination of benefits and pensions. People out of the workforce and those on low incomes cannot expect an improvement in their circumstances in the foreseeable future.

There can be expected a new emphasis on private saving and occupational schemes. The Australian Council of Trade Unions is seeking the development of industry superannuation schemes to extend the coverage of occupational superannuation. Progress in this and other areas is going to be slow as Australians change their perceptions that the Government can provide all welfare.

In summary, new major public sector involvement in welfare cannot be expected until the year 2000. At best humane management of the welfare system, increasingly limited to those in real need, will be seen. In this state of affairs those not able or willing to enter the workforce will have a life spent on minimum income and consumption levels. The hope of improvements in welfare will be dependent upon improvement in performance of Australian producers at home and in

Australia

the international market place. The major effort of public policy will be directed toward that primary goal.

ACKNOWLEDGEMENT

The author acknowledges the extensive editorial advice received in preparing this chapter and the input of the Social Policy Division, Department of Social Security, in particular the help of Karen Wilson.

REFERENCES AND FURTHER READING

Cass, B. (1986), Income Support for Families with Children, Social Security Review, Issues Paper No.1, Canberra: Australian Government Publishing Service.

Castles, F.G. (1985), The Working Class and Welfare, Sydney: Allen & Unwin.

Caves, R.E. & Krause, L.B. (eds) (1984), The Australian Economy: A View from the North, Sydney: George Allen and Unwin.

Commission of Inquiry into Poverty (1975), Values in Australian Income Security Policies, Canberra: Australian Government Publishing Service.

Department of Community Services (1986), Annual Report, Canberra: Australian Government Publishing Service.

Department of Employment and Industrial Relations (1986), Annual Report 1985-6, Canberra: Australian Government Publishing Service.

Department of Social Security (1986), Annual Report 1985-6, Canberra: Australian Government Publishing Service.

Dixon, J. (1977), Australia's Policy Towards the Aged: 1890-1972, Canberra: Canberra Series in Administrative Studies, 3, Canberra College of Advanced Education.

Australia

_____ (1978-9), 'The Evolution of Australia's Social Security System 1890-1972: The Social Insurance Debate', <u>Social Security Quarterly</u>, 5(2) (Summer), 1-10.

_____ (1983), 'Australia's Income-Security System: Its Origins, Its Features and Its Dilemma', <u>International Social Security Review</u>, (1), 19-44.

_____ & Scheurell, R. (1987), 'Social Security in Australia and the United States: A Comparison of Value Premises and Practices', <u>Journal for International and Comparative Social Welfare</u>, 3(1&2), 1-20.

Gallagher, P. (1985), 'Targetting Welfare Expenditure on the Poor'. An unpublished paper presented at the NSW Council of Social Services, 'Welfare Services for the Most Needy', Public Meeting, Sydney, 25 June.

Graycar, A. (1979), <u>Welfare Politics in Australia</u>, London: Macmillan.

Hancock, W.K. (1930), <u>Australia</u>, London: Ernest Benn.

Health Insurance Commission (1986), <u>Annual Report 1985-86</u>, Canberra: Australian Government Publishing Service.

Kendig, H.L. & McCallum, J. (1986), <u>Greying Australia: Future Impacts of Population Ageing</u>, Canberra: Australian Government Publishing Service.

Kewley, T.H. (1977), <u>Social Security in Australia 1900-72</u>, Sydney: Sydney University Press.

McAlister, C, Ingles, D. & Tune, D. (1981), 'General Revenue Financing of Social Security: The Australian Minimum Income Support System', <u>Social Security Journal</u>, December, 24-38.

Mendelsohn, R. (1979), <u>The Condition of the People: Social Welfare in Australia 1900-1975</u>, Sydney: George Allen and Unwin.

Australia

Policy Coordination Unit, *Annual Report 1985-86*, Canberra: Australian Government Printing Service.

Repatriation Commission (1986), *Annual Report 1985-86*, Canberra: Australian Government Publishing Service.

Report of the National Committee of Inquiry (1974), *Compensation and Rehabilitation in Australia Volume One*, Canberra: Australian Government Publishing Service.

Social Security Department (1970), *Main Values Underlying Income Maintenance Programme*, Paper No.2, Wellington.

CANADA
Donald F. Bellamy & Allan Irving

WELFARE SYSTEM ENVIRONMENT

Ideological or Dominant Value Environment

There is a lively and continuing debate among Canadian scholars as to just what constitutes Canadian political culture or ideology (Horowitz 1968; Christian & Campbell 1974; Marchak 1975; Manzer 1985). It is now generally accepted that five ideological thrusts have combined historically to create the Canadian public political philosophy: 'traditional conservatism, anti-democratic liberalism, protective liberal democracy, developmental liberal democracy, and non-Marxist social democracy' (Manzer 1985, p.180). Tackling the thorny question of which of these strains is the dominant one in the formation of Canadian political culture, political scientist Ronald Manzer has carefully examined how the central and provincial governments have, from the early nineteenth century to the present, gone about promoting economic development, alleviating poverty, structuring the market, controlling crime, building schools and assuring the protection of human rights. His unqualified conclusion is that 'liberalism is not just the core, it is the essence of the Canadian public philosophy' (Manzer 1985, p.180).

C.B. Macpherson has suggested that there are two central themes running through the liberal tradition from Locke to the present: a capitalist market economy and a class-divided society (Macpherson 1977). Certainly both of these characteristics define Canadian society; as well as the liberal values of free enterprise, competition, individualism and self-reliance underlie a social welfare system that has attempted to mitigate the worst excesses of a market society.

Although liberalism is the predominant political paradigm in Canada, political scientist Gad Horowitz has suggested that Canada, unlike the United States (US), contains an important non-liberal element, what is referred to as a Tory fragment or strong Tory touch. This stems from the country's original patterns of settlement and from its non-revolutionary past. In essence Canada's political culture has collectivist elements that are largely absent in the United States. It has been argued for example that the presence in Canada of universal family allowances and national state health insurance reflects a more collectivist political culture than that of the United States which does not have these income security measures (Irving 1980).

Canada's French settlers brought with them the Tory conception of society as organic and hierarchic. The state took precedence over the individual and was seen as having responsibility for guiding the new society, particularly its economic development. There is as well a deep strain of Toryism in the British areas of Canada, harking back to the Family Compact and to Prime Minister John A. MacDonald's national policy of 1879, which emphasised the strong role of the state by publicly subsidising the Canadian Pacific Railway monopoly, promoting settlement and immigration, and protecting industry from competition through tariffs. As historian W.L. Morton points out, unlike the founding charter of the United States, which emphasised the liberal-individualistic values of 'life, liberty, and the pursuit of happiness', the Canadian Tory-influenced British North American Act (1867) stressed the goals of 'Peace, Order and Good Government' (Morton 1972, p.111). British Toryism is deeply rooted in the Canadian political culture. Canadian historian Viv Nelles notes:

> At a time when American conservative intellectuals were freeing the individual for the progressive Darwinian struggle, Canadian thinkers, owing more to Burke than to Darwin, insisted that the state should provide some measure of moral direction for the society. For them, loyalty to the British Crown signified more than just a choice of

particular representative institutions; it implied as well an organic view of society within which the Crown and the institutions of government moulded the character of the individual, measured wealth against commonwealth, and presided over just and orderly social change (Nelles 1974, p.41).

The collectivist elements in the Canadian political culture have given rise to a strong democratic socialist party in Canada originally called the Cooperative Commonwealth Federation and now called the New Democratic Party. This party has often been referred to as the idea given in Canadian politics, more sarcastically by some as 'liberals in a hurry' (Young 1969). From the 1930s on this party has been at the forefront of championing social welfare reform at both the national and provincial level and often has been instrumental in moving political opinion to the left as in the case of old age pensions and health insurance.

Both British and US liberal policy examples have been influential in the development of social welfare in Canada. The influence of Keynes and Beveridge on intellectuals and civil servants in the formative period of Canada's welfare state in the late 1930s and early 1940s was crucial (Owram 1986).

Historical Origins

The development of the Canadian welfare state can be divided into four main periods (Moscovitch 1982).

1867-1914. This was a time when the residual view of social welfare was predominant. It has been referred to as the period of the regulatory state. Initially social welfare was considered to be a matter for local responsibility, usually under private-voluntary auspices. The maritime Provinces did have a version of the poor law in effect whereas the Province of Ontario never enacted a Poor Law (Splane 1965). Social legislation in this period centred around regulating hours of work, improving working conditions and such reforms as proper treatment of neglected children (Jones & Rutman 1981; Sutherland 1976). Provincial governments did provide some funds for charitable agencies and established structures for inspecting charitable social institutions.

1914-1940. This was a time of intense activity in social reform and the development of social welfare (Brown & Cook 1974; Thompson & Seager 1985). During these years the federal government was forced, more and more by changing social and economic circumstances, to enter the field of social welfare (Struthers 1983). In 1908 the provinces of Quebec and Newfoundland introduced Canada's first Workmen's Compensation schemes, which were also Canada's first piece of compulsory insurance legislation. Most provinces passed mothers' allowance legislation between 1916-1920 and in 1927 the federal government introduced means-tested old age pensions. In the 1930s Canada reeled from a severe social and economic breakdown which brought a series of federal-provincial unemployment relief acts culminating in the passage in 1940 of a federal Unemployment Insurance Act (Struthers 1983; Thompson & Seager 1985). By 1940 it was beginning to be generally accepted in Canada that the residual nineteenth century idea of the family and the market providing for all needs was simply no longer adequate.

1941-1975. This period saw the full flowering of the Welfare State in Canada and has been dubbed the interventionist period. By the end of the Second World War Keynesian ideas had taken hold and a consensus emerged that decisions about investment ought to be left in private hands while the state would, through social and economic policy, act as a stabiliser in the country. The lessons of the 1930s were deeply imprinted on the minds of policy-makers and it was agreed that a social contract for peaceful co-existence between business, labour and government was desirable. This period saw the introduction of universal family allowances (1944), old age security (1951) and the introduction of national health insurance (1957 and 1966) and the Canada Assistance (1966) and Canada Pension Plans (1966) (Taylor 1978; Naylor 1986; Bryden 1974; Guest 1985; Hum 1983).

Since 1975. Canada and a number of other countries have experienced the rise of a neo-conservative ideology reflected in government cutbacks in social spending, restraint, privatisation and repeated claims that welfare state expenditures are impeding economic progress (Calvert 1984). During the twentieth century in Canada there has been a dramatic expansion in the size and responsibilities of the Canadian state. The more rugged individualism of the nineteenth century has been replaced by a sense of more collective responsibility for one another. The modern welfare state in Canada was forged out of war, depression, secularisation and industrialisation (Owram 1986).

The Political and Socio-Economic Environments

Federalism. Canada is the second largest country in the world with a total area of 16.5 million square kilometers. It is a federal system made up of a central government in Ottawa, ten provincial and two territorial governments. At confederation in 1867, the powers and responsibilities of the central and provincial governments were split, with provincial governments having jurisdiction over social welfare matters and the central government allocated most of the taxing power. Over time, of course, this division has created tremendous strains on the system, which reached crisis proportions in the 1930s when it was recognised that the federal government would have to take considerably more responsibility for social welfare (Banting 1982). The bargaining that has occurred and continues to occur between and among the central and provincial governments over social welfare (resources and responsibility) is a major factor in welfare policy formation. Social welfare in Canada has developed and has been shaped largely by the politics of federal-provincial relations (Irving 1987).

At present the federal parliament is made up of a large majority of the ruling Progressive Conservative Party (traditionally the party of business) with an opposition formed by a more middle of the road Liberal Party and the socialist New Democratic Party. Major policy issues confronting the federal government are the funding of a national system of child care; whether universal programmes (Family Allowance and Old Age Security) should be maintained; and whether unemployment insurance should be radically reformed as a recent report has suggested.

Dependence on the United States. The Canadian economy is enormously dependent on the US. No other developed country has the same high level of trade with one other nation as Canada has with its southern neighbour (about 80 per cent of total trade). Most of Canada's larger firms are simply branches of US multinationals and transnationals. Many trade unions too are branches of larger US labour organisations although recently there have been successful movements to create more autonomous Canadian unions.

Recently there have been intense negotiations with the US over a free trade agreement and there is some concern that this may have an adverse affect on Canadian social policy.

Income Distribution, Unemployment and Poverty. Over the past three decades the pattern of income distribution in Canada has remained virtually the same: 4.2 per cent of all income goes to the poorest 20 per cent of income units; 42.3 per cent of all income goes to the top 20 per cent of all income units (Djao 1983, p.71). The National Council of Welfare in Ottawa has documented that the number of people living in poverty in Canada increased by some 500,000 in 1981-2; it is estimated that there are well over four million poor people in Canada (population 25 million) (Riches 1985, p.112). In 1983 the number of officially unemployed in Canada was 1.5 million, giving an unemployment rate of 11.9 per cent in a labour force of 12.1 million; however, it has been argued that the real unemployment rate is much higher if a number of other factors are taken into account (discouraged workers, underemployed) and is about two million unemployed or 16.1 per cent (Social Planning Council 1984b).

Demographics. Canada's population distribution is 76 per cent urban and 24 per cent rural (total population 25 million); overwhelmingly the population is concentrated in a band at the south on an east-west axis. Two cities, Montreal and Toronto, have nearly 25 per cent of the total population.

Another important demographic feature of Canada is that almost 25 per cent of the population is French-speaking and largely concentrated in the province of Quebec. Historically, and in the present, Quebec has been awarded special treatment in the federation and this has caused many stresses and strains in the development of social welfare (Smiley 1976).

Canada

THE WELFARE SYSTEM: AN OVERVIEW

The Structure and Administration of the Welfare System

The acquisition by the federal authority of a direct interest in social welfare, through constitutional amendments and financial inducements of cost sharing, guarantees a measure of national uniformity and increased spending on social welfare. Locating the administrative accountability for delivering public personal social services and overseeing incorporated non-governmental services in the ten provinces and two territories has led to a complex set of arrangements. Some provinces, such as Ontario, from the beginning delegated major responsibilities to local governments (Banting 1987; Ismael 1985). Reliance on non-governmental services, many of them rich and powerful, others small and emerging have added to the fragmentation.

Social security instruments include demogrants, contributory social insurance, status payments (veterans), social assistance (including supplementary allowances), and tax benefits. Despite the achievement of major universal income benefit systems, the persisting values of residualism in social assistance and personal services are found in income or needs-testing for eligibility (Guest 1985).

Two popular developments in recent years have been the indexation of social security payments (excluding social assistance) to cost of living increases (Battle 1987), and the use of tax credits to redistribute incomes in favour of lower income groups.

Adding to the piecemeal development of policy and complex implementation are major regional variations, particularly economic and demographic, which affect the level of employment-yielding private investment and the affordability of social programmes. Since the bulk of Canada's population is concentrated in a narrow band along its border with the United States, social services in the sparsely populated northern regions are largely in the hands of senior levels of government and many essential local services are lacking. Some provincial laws permit Indian bands, most of them in the north and the western provinces, to administer their own services.

Canada

The administrative structure is tri-partite: government, voluntary agencies, and proprietry agencies. The government functions at the federal, provincial and local municipal levels. The federal share of expenditures is the largest because it covers universal income security programmes for children and the elderly and compensation for the unemployed. In addition, the federal authority contributes nearly half of provincial spending on social assistance and personal social services.

Provinces are responsible for social assistance, a wide range of personal social services in the community, and also, under semi-independent public boards, workers' compensation for work-related disabilities. Some provinces, notably Ontario, pass on part of the cost of implementing social assistance and service programmes to their municipalities. Social security spending (including health care) for the three levels of government for 1982 was federal $C31.7 billion, provincial $C19.7 billion, and municipal $C0.7 billion (Canada 1985a, p.223).

The voluntary (or non-profit) sector comprises incorporated agencies, special interest and self-help groups, and offers an array of personal social services. The total number of voluntary organisations of all kinds was about 100,000 in 1983; 53,000 of these were registered charities, which entitled donors to deduct their contributions from their income tax liability (Morrison 1986, p.18). This sector includes counselling, institutional care of individuals with special needs, community care (which includes support services for large numbers of people affected in recent years by deinstitutionalisation), rehabilitation centres and workshops, and child day care centres. Many are government-approved programmes in which services to needy individuals, families or communities may be purchased by government agencies or subsidised through grants.

The proprietary sector originally existed to meet needs that were not accepted as an appropriate public charge and catered to the more affluent. Notable examples today are commercial child day care centres, nursing homes, and retirement homes for the aged. All of these have expanded dramatically, particularly as a result of governmental purchase-of-service arrangements on behalf of needy persons. Standards may be set and enforced under provincial legislation. A sizeable proportion of these profit-making services are operated by multi-national corporations and conglomerates. The subsidisation of commercial interests in the provision of essential human services is an increasingly controversial public issue (see Social Planning Council 1984a).

Financing Social Welfare

Canada's Gross Domestic Product (GDP) for 1985 was $C476.361 billion in current dollars. The balance of international payments for 1986 was a negative amount, $C8.805 billion (Canada 1987a, pp.8-10).

Major revenues at the three levels of government are shown in Table 1.

TABLE 1: GOVERNMENT REVENUES IN CANADA BY TYPE OF TAX, 1985 ($C billion)

	Federal	Provincial	Local
Direct Taxation			
Persons	42.419	26.749	
Corporate & Government Business Enterprise	11.649	3.916	
Other direct taxes	13.241	3.423	0.188
SUBTOTAL	67.309	34.088	0.188
Indirect Taxes	18.904	24.612	15.348
Investment	8.349	15.871	1.261
Transfers from:			
Federal		21.253	0.502
Provincial			17.964
Local		0.165	
TOTAL REVENUE	94.562	81.699	35.263

SOURCE: Canada 1987a, pp.23-5

The federal authority uses general tax revenues for its two demogrants and an income conditioned pension supplement for the aged.

In the case of unemployment insurance, the federal government imposes a tax deductible employer/employee wage-related tax on employers and their employees. As of April 1987, to be covered in any week, an employee must work for 15 hours or earn $C105; the maximum earnings are set at $C530 weekly (or $C27,560 annually). The programme also requires heavy federal subsidies in order to meet recurring deficits. As a result of numerous incremental changes the programme has moved far from its intended social insurance character (Pal 1985). A three year official study recommended a return to a much stricter actuarial basis (Forget 1986) but this was found politically unpalatable and the programme may continue in essentially its present form.

Canada's national contributory wage-related pension programme is referred to as the Canada/Quebec Pension Plan (C/QPP) because the Province of Quebec has a programme comparable to the national scheme under a contracting-out arrangement in the legislation. The C/QPP is financed in two ways: firstly, equal tax deductible employer/employee contributions of 1.9 per cent of contributory earnings, or 3.8 per cent for self-employed. Contributory earnings, adjusted annually, exclude workers who earn below $C2,500 in 1987. The maximum earnings basis is the year's national average industrial wages, $C25,900 in 1987; secondly, interest on the partially funded reserves. Most of the reserves in the national system, $C29 billion in 1985 (Canada 1986b), are loaned to the provinces for social investment; the Quebec counterpart also invests heavily in the private sector. The contribution rates of both are scheduled to rise in order to meet sharply rising long-term pension commitments as the population ages.

Generous use of tax expenditures subsidises additional benefits by private means. To encourage a level of income replacement after retirement which is higher than government income security will provide, the federal tax system permits individuals with earnings and other specified income to set aside tax deductible savings in registered tax sheltered plans. The first are occupational Registered Retirement Pension Plans in which the maximum employee contribution is $C3,500 annually (Frenken 1986). The second type consists of personal Registered Retirement Savings Plans. Mainly intended for self-employed people, these plans are concentrated in higher income groups. For instance, in the income range $C10,000 to $C13,999, 17.3 per cent of taxpayers contributed an average of $C347; from $C30,000 to $C34,000, 54.2 per cent of taxpayers saved an average of $C1,403 (National Council of Welfare 1984b, p.84).

Total contributions under the retirement saving measures were in excess of $C20 billion in 1983 (Frenken 1986), consisting of:

Canada/Quebec pension Plan contributions	$C4.6 billion
Registered Retirement Savings Plan	$C5.0 billion
Registered Retirement Pensions	$C10.5 billion
TOTAL	$C20.1 billion

Both the federal and provincial governments give other benefits through the income tax system to achieve income redistribution, with mixed success. For example, federal child tax exemptions reduce the tax liability of families with children according to family size. Since the tax savings are greater in higher income groups, the horizontal equity which is built into the exemptions is achieved at the expense of vertical equity. A selective child tax credit is designed to have a progressive effect on family incomes: the credit paid to families is reduced progressively above an annual income of about $C26,000 (Canada 1985e, p.781). In a recent year the total net annual benefits per child from receipt of Family Allowances (after tax), child tax exemption, and child tax credit, amounted to $C702 at a family income of $C10,000, compared with $C538 at an income level of $C80,000 (Canada 1985b, p.17). Similar special federal tax exemptions and provincial property and sales tax credits provide income benfits to the aged from general revenues.

Under the Canada Assistance Plan, also financed from general revenues, the federal government provides the provinces with open-ended equal cost sharing for social assistance and services delivered to persons who are, or are likely to be, in need (see Hum 1983).

Provincial workers' compensation benefits are funded by employer payroll taxes. These are actuarially based on the risk of work injury or illness modified by experience ratings.

Canada

Coordinated fundraising for voluntary organisations is conducted by local United Ways or Community Chests. Total campaign contributions across Canada were $C155 million in 1986. These provide funds for many local personal social services available within the particular jurisdiction. Charitable contributions to organisations approved by federal tax authorities are deductible from corporate and individual income taxes. Of the estimated 53,000 organisations of all types in 1983, the aggregate of revenues was about $C6 billion or two per cent of GNP (Robichaud p.29). Personal service user fees scaled to income are also an important source of voluntary agency funds as are government subsidies for persons in need. Sizeable profits from government-run lotteries are used for social spending including the support of demonstration projects and innovations. Philanthropic foundations, very small in Canada, tend to contribute to research projects and capital expenditures rather than core budget items.

NEEDY FAMILIES

Family Policy. One of the central issues confronting Canadian social policy-makers in the decade ahead is to attempt to redress the gap that exists between family policy and family needs. There are now many more women working outside the home (well over 50 per cent), many more families headed by single parents, usually female (10 per cent), and percentages of poor families headed by women (35 per cent) than even ten years ago. Forty-six per cent of single mothers with jobs in 1984 only achieved at best poverty-level incomes.

Social Security

Social Assistance. At confederation in 1867 each province was assigned responsibility for social assistance. Since 1966 the federal government under the Canada Assistance Plan shares half the costs of provincial social assistance (Hum 1983). Provincial social assistance is granted to individuals and families on the basis of a needs test or budget deficit method which looks at persons' or families' budgetary requirements and financial resources (Canada 1986f).

Canada

The majority of social assistance recipients fall into four major categories: the aged, disabled, unemployed employables, or single-parent families. In the province of Ontario, for example, about 13 per cent of the caseload consists of single-parent families. As a condition of eligibility for social assistance a number of provinces require applicants to initiate proceedings against an absent spouse. Some provinces consider single parents as employable and therefore require them to seek work once their children have reached a certain age.

Those who own their own homes are not required to sell their principal residence as a condition of eligibility for assistance. In determining elegibility all sources of income are examined with some exemptions in determining amounts of social assistance. The budgetary items covered by provincial social assistance include food, clothing, shelter (including utilities), household and personal needs and in some provinces what are deemed special needs. The overall system is an extremely complicated one since no two provinces use the same method of calculating social assistance benefit levels.

Maternity Benefits. Maternity benefits are provided as part of unemployment insurance, which covers 95 per cent of all workers. The benefit payable is the same as that paid for unemployment, namely 50 per cent of the persons average weekly insurable earnings, up to $C297 a week (in 1986). This benefit is payable for 15 weeks.

Personal Social Services

Day Care. Day care is emerging as one of the central social policy issues in Canada during the last half of the 1980s. At the end of March 1987 a federal parliamentary task force on child care recommended, among other things, that millions of dollars a year in tax credits be given to parents to help defray the costs of day care. Under the proposed plan parents would be eligible for tax credits up to a maximum of 30 per cent of their day care costs. It is estimated that 10-15 per cent of the estimated $C700 million annual expenditure would be directed to provinces to pay for the operating and capital costs of both for-profit and non-profit day care centres. Currently the federal government spends $C255 million per year on day care; the extent of the problem is illustrated by the fact that currently in Canada there are only 192,374 day care spaces for about two million children of working parents. In making its proposals the committee did not accept the principle that child care like education is an essential service (institutional versus residual view) that should be available to all regardless of income (Toronto Star, 30 & 31 March 1987).

Battered Women. In 1980 the Canadian Advisory Council on the Status of Women revealed in a report, Wife Battering in Canada: The Vicious Circle, that 10 per cent of Canadian women who are in a relationship with a man are assaulted each year. To deal with this growing problem a number of transition houses have been established usually under voluntary auspices, with some support from public funding. Shortages of funds often makes it very difficult for follow-up services to be provided and hence problems often continue to be unresolved (Canadian Council on Social Development, p.57; Canada 1987c).

Housing. Adequate housing for families, particularly single-parent families on social assistance, is a major problem in Canada. It is especially acute in large urban centres like Toronto where housing prices increased by about 75 per cent in the 1985-86 period. In the Province of Ontario, for example, the Ontario Housing Corporation is a provincial agency which makes available rental units for qualified lower income families (where the parents are over 18 with at least one dependent child). There are over 84,000 public housing units in the Province with about 48,500 allocated to families (Ontario Social Development Council 1987, p.141).

Food Banks. In the past several years Canada has witnessed the establishment of food banks across the country to assist in feeding Canada's poor. The first food bank was established in 1981 and currently there are at least 75. Two types of food banks have been established: the voluntary/charitable model and the labour/union model. The voluntary/charitable model follows the traditional pattern of using the church and the voluntary agency sector to provide services and operates by having the community (for example, supermarkets,

Canada

churches, individuals) collect surplus food and making it available for distribution either themselves or through other local organisations. The labour/union model follows the same pattern but also engages in advocacy on behalf of those needing food. Figures for 1984 indicate large numbers are using food banks which some policy analysts have seen as an indication of the collapse of 'the public safety net' (Vancouver: 308,000; Regina: 50,000; Edmonton: 57,000). The rise of food banks has occurred within the context of neo-conservatism and 'are another example of government's intent to shift public responsibilities back to the community and thereby further erode social rights', comments Professor Graham Riches (1986, p.54).

Counselling Services. There are a host of voluntary non-profit organisations in Canada that provide family counselling centres.

Services to Canada's Native Population. As well there are services in various provinces directed towards the Canadian native population. In Ontario, for example, there are over 30 day nurseries operating on Indian reserves; child welfare services too are now managed locally on many reservations.

Evaluation

The phenomenon of the working poor family is one that Canadian social policy-makers have had difficulty addressing. A number of solutions have been put forward for these families: a national policy of full employment, some version of a guaranteed income, further reforms and refinements in Canadian divorce law; more progressive housing policies, and universal day care (Ontario Social Development Council 1987).

THE UNEMPLOYED

During the first years of the 1980s, despite mounting unemployment rates, still fluctuating between 10 or 11 per cent of the labour force, some 1.5 million people, there was a marked absence of any political or corporate strategy targeted at this group.

Canada

Social Security

Unemployment Insurance. In existence since 1940 the central purpose of the federal unemployment insurance programme is to provide income protection for those workers experiencing temporary interruptions in their employment. Benefits available to workers include regular payments to replace loss of income due to unemployment. Those attending approved job training courses or job creation projects or participating in work-sharing arrangements are eligible as well. Administration of the programme is by the federal department, Employment and Immigration Canada, while another federal department, Revenue Canada, Taxation is responsible for collecting premiums, determining insurable employment and making the payment of benefits. Local Canada Employment Centres, established throughout the country, process applications for benefits.

Approximately 95 per cent of all workers are covered by unemployment insurance (UI). The self-employed or those over age 65 cannot insure their earnings. To be eligible for benefits a person needs to have worked in what is called the 'qualifying period': 10-14 weeks of insurable employment. The number of qualifying weeks required varies according to the unemployment rate of the local region. To continue receiving UI persons must be able to work and satisfy a work test.

Those who qualify for regular UI benefits are paid one week of UI for every week worked in insurable employment during the last year to a maximum of 25 weeks. After this period another formula is applied with benefits extending to 50 weeks; for those over 55 a lump sum payment of three weeks' benefits is available upon application.

For those receiving these various UI benefits the payment rate is currently 60 per cent of a person's average weekly insurable earnings with the maximum benefit in 1986 being $C297 per week.

In 1985 the average number of monthly beneficiaries was 1.6 million, with gross benefit payments that year being well over $C10 billion (Canada 1985a; 1985a).

Both employers and employees contribute premiums. In 1986 workers paid $C2.35 for every $C100 of insurable earnings while employers paid $C3.29.

Canada

Personal Social Services

Throughout the 1980s local voluntary social service agencies (as they had in the 1930s) attempted the impossible task of coping with unemployed workers and their families. Local and provincial welfare caseloads have sky-rocketed.

Finally in September 1985 the federal government announced a plan of action in what it called Canadian Jobs Strategy (CJS) consisting of a seven-part thrust to tackle the seemingly intractable problem of joblessness (Daenzer 1987).

Job Entry. School drop-outs over the age of 16 are the particular focus of this part of the CJS with the goal being to ease school-to-work transitions for those with minimal educational qualifications. Those involved in the programme are to spend 26-52 weeks in a combination of both educational and direct employment situations. Financial aid during this period of intensive training was to be either through unemployment insurance or federal training allowances. The desired outcome is for trainees to be hired by the employers they worked for during the period of training.

Job Re-entry. The goal here is to prepare women for more than low paying entry level jobs. Training allowances and other costs are to be provided by the federal government.

Job Development. This is aimed at grappling with the needs of the long-term unemployed, a particularly intractable group. Employees are given wage subsidies to hire and train workers for future anticipated needs. The emphasis here is on a cooperative partnership between government and industry in training workers for the future. As with other parts of CJS employers are under no obligation to provide permanent employment once the training period ends.

Skill Investment. This is seen as largely preventative and provides employers with federal subsidies up to a maximum of three years to retrain workers for anticipated labour force changes. The idea is to prevent lay-offs arising from outmoded skills.

Canada

Skill Shortages. This aspect of CJS makes financial assistance available to employers to develop training programmes for their workers in particular skill areas. Employers are expected to develop training plans for their future human resource needs with the federal government subsidising the cost. The expressed overall goal is to foster productivity and competitiveness.

Innovations. This part of CJS is intended to stimulate creative solutions for Canada's labour market problems. Financial support is available to employers for pilot programmes and projects that empirically examine new approaches and solutions to the problem of unemployment and inadequate training and to those employers who see opportunities to develop Canada's work force potential.

Community futures. This provides special assistance for local communities hit especially hard by major lay-offs and plant closures as well as those communities constantly confronting chronic unemployment and economic decline.

Evaluation

Unemployment is one of Canada's most intractable social welfare problems. Since the early 1920s the Canadian state has grappled with how best to develop social policies for the unemployed. Recently it has been suggested that the welfare state in Canada is undergoing a major transition in its stance towards unemployment, from one with an emphasis on income security to one that now places job creation programmes at the centre of social policy for this group. The 1985 Report of the Royal Commission on the Economic Union and Development Prospects for Canada (the Macdonald Commission Report) strongly suggested that this redirection from income security to job creation should take place. This represents a significant change in the evolution of the Canadian welfare state (Ismael 1987, p.xi).

THE SICK AND INJURED

In 1957 the federal government passed the Hospital Insurance and Diagnostic Services Act which provided for the federal government to share on a

Canada

50/50 basis the costs of provincial hospital insurance plans. Services to be covered included acute, convalescent and chronic hospital care. In 1964 a federal Royal Commission on Health Services recommended the extension of the 1957 arrangements to a comprehensive, universal system of health care (hospital and medical care insurance) that would be cost-shared by the federal and provincial governments (Guest 1985, pp.147-8 & 160-2).

Social Security

Health Insurance. Acting on the recommendations of the 1964 Royal Commission the federal government introduced the Medical Care Act in 1966 which specified that all services provided by a physician were to be insured. The federal-provincial cost-sharing arrangement was that the federal government would reimburse provinces 50 per cent of the national per capita expenditure, multiplied by the number of insured persons in each province. By 1972 the Act had been accepted and implemented in all provinces and territories. In order to share in federal funding for both hospital and medical care insurance, provinces were required to meet four basic criteria:

- provincial plans had to be administered on a non-profit basis.

- comprehensive coverage for all services provided by doctors was required.

- plans had to be universally accessible to all provincial residents on equal terms and conditions.

- provincial plans had to be portable from one province to another.

By 1972, then, there was in operation throughout Canada a universal system of public hospital and medical care insurance often referred to as Medicare (Bennett & Krosny 1981).

In 1977 with the enactment of the Established Programmes Financing Act by the federal government, the financing mechanism of cost-sharing was replaced by what is known as 'block' funding. A most complicated formula (consisting of four components) was arrived at to determine the amount of money each province would receive under block funding from the federal government. Certainly one of the intentions of this change in the funding formula was to control and limit increases in health care costs. In 1984 the federal government passed the Canada Health Act which replaced both the Hospital Insurance and Diagnostic Services Act and the Medical Care Act. One of the central points of this Act was that it allowed the federal government to withhold funds from provinces that did not comply with certain conditions in the practice of medicine. The Canadian Health Act mandated the provinces to put an end to extra-billing by physicians (charging patients more than the public insurance system allowed) and user fees for hospital care. This has proven to be a most controversial piece of legislation and is being legally contested by the Canadian Medical Association as unconstitutional.

Provincial Workers' Compensation. Each province or territory in Canada has workers' compensation legislation to protect workers and their dependents against wage loss stemming from occupational injury or disease and to help with the costs of medical care and rehabilitation. In addition federal legislation protects federal government employees, seamen not covered by provincial legislation, and discharged inmates injured in a federal penitentiary. It is a scheme whereby employers in given classes of industry or occupation are jointly liable for the overall costs of all injuries in that class (Canada 1986d).

Each provincial administration establishes a Compensation Board whose primary responsibility is to assess whether an injured worker is eligible for compensation. Compensation rates are based on an injured worker's earnings at the time of injury. In all jurisdictions a ceiling is placed on annual amounts of earnings that are considered insurable. Awards can be based on temporary or permanent disability and whether or not the disability is considered to be total or partial.

Surviving dependents of a worker (work-related death either by accident or from illness) are entitled to cash compensation. Usually benefits continue to a surviving spouse until death or remarriage. Orphans also receive a benefit. The workers' compensation system makes physical and vocational rehabilitation services available to injured workers. The basic philosophy is to return workers to the work force as soon as possible. The system is funded entirely by contributions from employers.

Sickness benefit. Sickness benefits are paid under the auspices of Unemployment Insurance on the same basis as maternity and unemployment benefits.

Personal Social Services

Visiting nurse and homemaker services are available throughout Canada, providing trained personnel to assist families in the home in the event of severe illness. The Victorian Order of Nurses (VON) for example, is a voluntary, non-profit, health agency whose main function is to provide nursing on a home-visit basis to individuals and families. The service is available seven days a week, 24 hours a day. In the Province of Ontario, which is served by 33 VON branches, it is available to practically the entire population. Often, in addition to the basic nursing programme, local VON branches co-ordinate and administer other programmes, such as friendly visiting, senior citizens counselling, homemaking service and meals-on-wheels.

Evaluation

The Canadian health care system continues to be organised around the individual physician and fee-for-service payments, all within the framework of universal state health insurance. It is considered to be in a state of almost continual crisis. Escalating costs, particularly payments to physicians, has been the major contributing factor to this crisis. The high cost of high-tech equipment constitutes a further burden to a health care system already under severe strain. Recently it has been suggested that other structural arrangements, such as community clinics, may need to be developed much more widely than at present.

THE AGED

The age structure of the Canadian population is youthful, compared with the structure in other industrial societies. According to the 1981 census the proportion of the population aged 65 and over was only 9.8 per cent, or 2,495,000 persons (Canada 1985a, p.56). This figure represented a 23 per cent increase over the previous 10 years. As for the future, 'medium projections' indicate that 15.4 per cent of the population will be aged in 2021, or 20 per cent using 'old population' projections (Economic Council of Canada 1979, App.C, Table C-3).

Gender differentiated life expectancy is a continuing trend: in 1985, 56 per cent of the aged were female.

Although the aged are over-represented as a percentage of population in rural Canada, where they are underserved, the impact of absolute numbers is more significant in urban centres where three-quarters of Canadians live.

Increasingly healthy longevity, with declining family supports to sustain the aged at home, has led to growing interest in developing informal and formal community supports (see Marshall 1980).

The income position of families headed by the aged has improved steadily during the last two decades. The estimated incidence of poverty (based on 1985 family expenditure and income data differentiated by area of residence and family size) for families with aged male heads was 9.0 per cent, compared with 9.5 per cent for families headed by males under age 65, whilst for families with aged female heads it was 15.9 per cent, compared with 46.4 per cent for families headed by females under age 65 (Canada 1986c).

Economic disadvantage is much more severe among the unattached aged, and is especially serious for women. An estimated 33.2 per cent of unattached men age 65 and over had low income status compared with 30.0 per cent for younger males; the comparable figures for women were 50.1 per cent and 36.3 per cent respectively (Canada 1986c).

Social Security

Parallel public and private retirement income systems have developed, with public policies instituted after 1950 providing almost all of the impetus for programme development.

Government Measures. A tiered set of complementary programmes provides the principal incomes of the aged (see Guest 1985). Old Age Security (OAS) is a near-universal demogrant which requires a 20 year residency to qualify for a full flat-rate benefit at age 65 ($C300 in April 1987). The pension is indexed quarterly to cost of living increases. In February 1987, 2.692 million aged received the maximum pension; another 11,000 having less than full residence received a reduced pension. Pensions were payable outside Canada and totalled 40,000 (Canada 1987b). The 1987 payout for the pension from federal general revenues is an estimated $C9.7 billion, some of it recoverable since the pension is subject to income tax.

The Canada/Quebec Pension Plan (C/QPP) is a compulsory contributory wage-related pension plan with supplementary survivor, disability, and lump sum death benefits. The plan takes the place of occupational pensions for the bulk of the Canadian labour force. In addition to providing a modest supplement to the demogrant, the C/QPP has been required to lend the bulk of its reserves to the provinces for economic and social development projects.

The modest benefits of the Canada Pension Plan (CPP), 25 per cent of contributory earnings after age 18, are a maximum of $C521 monthly for 1987. Automatic cost of living adjustments apply. Adjustments in the event of delayed or early retirement, credit splitting in the event of marriage breakdown, pension splitting on retirement, a child drop-out provision, and continuation of survivor benefits after remarriage are new features (Canada 1986c). Coverage of homemakers under the pension plan is an issue; the National Council on Welfare argues that 'the best way to provide better pensions for homemakers is to provide better pensions for everyone' (National Council of Welfare 1984b).

The Guaranteed Income Supplement (GIS) is an administratively simple income-tested federal supplement to needy OAS recipients. GIS was introduced in 1965 along with the C/QPP; although intended to exist only during the ten year maturation of the contributory pension programme, it proved so popular and essential as an income source that it has remained.

Quarterly cost of living escalation is automatic. The full amount of $C5,580 (April 1987) guarantees an aged couple with Old Age Security a pension income of $C12,780 a year. Single or unattached aged may receive a combined total of $C7,884 a year (Canada 1987c). The majority of single beneficiaries of the GIS are women.

Canada

As an indication of the dire straits affecting many of the aged a half of all Old Age Security recipients also receive the GIS payment, the majority at the maximum rate. In addition, a number of provinces operate income-tested programmes for the low income elderly to supplement their OAS/GIS pensions. The rather sizeable payments vary widely among the provinces. In addition a special tax deduction effective at age 65 allows the first $C1,000 of pension income to be deducted from taxable income (see National Council of Welfare 1984b).

A Spouse's Allowance (SPA) was designed to lessen the financial hardship of couples after one of them turned 65 years of age. This income-tested benefit supplements the incomes of spouses from age 60 to 64 where the other receives OAS; it may continue in the event of widowhood during the five year period before 65.

Table 2 shows federal social security recipients and payments as of February 1987.

TABLE 2: FEDERAL SOCIAL SECURITY PAYMENTS TO THE AGED (FEBRUARY 1987)

	Number	Gross Amount ($C'000)
OLD AGE SECURITY	2,743,744	811,678.1
SPOUSE'S ALLOWANCE	144,251	40,936.1
GUARANTEED INCOME SUPPLEMENT	1,345,375	294,496.6
CANADA PENSION PLAN[1]		
Retirement	1,307,426	25,535.8
Disability		
Disability Pension	148,745	9,821.3
Child Benefits	46,342	1,023.4
Survivors	441,047	787.6
	89,369	464.3
Death Benefits	(5,747)	10,275.0

NOTE: 1 Quebec Pension Plan (QPP) not included. CPP cost $4.4 billion and QPP $1.6 billion (1984-85 estimates) (Canada 1985e, p.782).
SOURCE: Canada 1987b, Table 3.

All provinces reduce property and/or school taxes for aged persons by means of tax credits.

Property tax credits or rebates vary according to shelter costs. Rental assistance or housing allowances, free health insurance coverage and drug benefits have much financial value for the aged (Ontario 1981a, p.20).

Occupational Pension Plans. Less than half of all paid workers are covered by tax assisted employer-sponsored pensions plans; in 1982, 15,000 plans were registered (Frenken 1986). Many plans cover higher income workers; in public service employment coverage is virtually 100 per cent. Despite government encouragement of private sector development, which would lessen the strain on the public pension sector, the private sector has been slow to respond. Current provincial legislative reforms are expected to include earlier vesting and portability of credits, inflation protection, survivor benefits and improvements to control siphoning off 'excess' earnings from investing the employer's share of contributions. As in the case of the C/QPP many part time employees are excluded from coverage (Frenken 1986).

Tax sheltering under personal Registered Retirement Savings Plans allows conversion of the funds to income when the individual reaches age 60, but requires it no later than the 71st birthday. Federal expenditure on subsidies in regard to retirement income benefits for the aged in 1984 totalled $C5.1 billion, with the provinces contributing a further $C2.5 billion.

Personal Social Services.

Numerous services are available to help the aged to remain in the community as long as they can (see, for example, Ontario 1981a; Marshall 1980). These services may be provided on a self-help basis: by organised local volunteers through churches, fraternal and other bodies, or under governmental auspices. Generally the more formal and complex the service, the less likely it seems that the lonely and isolated and marginally eligible will be reached. This applies not only in rural and thinly populated areas, but also in urban centres where the aged may drop out of sight. Costs are often defrayed through federal/provincial funding agreements under the Canada Assistance Plan.

Canada

Domiciliary services. The available supports range from simple contact activities by telephone or friendly visiting to 'meals-on-wheels' programmes in which volunteers deliver hot meals to frail people weekly, or more often, for a small charge.
At more frail or dependent levels of functioning, public or private homemaker and visiting nurse services are available in many communities. Professional coordinated home care service is much less readily available; in a few places multidisciplinary teams are being tested. Home care services have become increasingly important in this country, whose state health care system is plagued by excessive use of active treatment hospitals for chronic care.

Subsidised accommodation. Most urban communities have subsidised (or below-market) rental accommodation available in purpose-built apartments under government, non-profit, or cooperative auspices. Federal, provincial, and municipal subsidies are available in different mixes across the provinces. The numbers of units are small and long waiting lists the rule. Especially in metropolitan centres, poor planning, design and location have frequently combined to produce ghettos for the aged and poor.

Day care. some residential care institutions, community centres and clubs have day care programmes to assist families and help the aged to socialise.

Residential care. Long term care of the frail and infirm aged is available in publicly or philanthropically funded institutions and commercial establishments (see Social Planning Council 1985a). These programmes provide varying amounts of bed care, but not sufficient to meet the demand. For this reason proprietary nursing homes have multiplied across the country; what were once small, financially marginal operations, have in many instances been replaced by commercial chains. The assurance of heavy government subsidies for individual residents under Canada's health insurance programme has provided much of the incentive for corporate investment and expansion; public policies of privatisation facilitate these developments (Social Planning Council 1984a).

Canada

Evaluation

Canada has evolved a multi-faceted social security system that provides a broad income maintenance safety net.

Reluctant provincial authorities are being forced by effective advocacy group pressure to improve and enforce standards of residential care through inspection and audit. Disclosures of abuse and neglect of persons in residential care have precipitated opposition to commercialisation, much as in the case of child day care. Unfortunately housing and residences, each of the latter specialising in a different level of care, evolved as separate systems in Canada. Progressively frail and infirm aged are often moved several times between unfamiliar surroundings to get the care they need. A few integrated care facilities under one auspice have come to public attention as models, but are difficult to emulate in decentralised and fragmented systems.

THE DISABLED AND HANDICAPPED

Resources are available to eligible handicapped persons on the basis of age, status, cause of handicap and personal resources, and under governmental, voluntary non-profit, as well as commercial auspices.

Social Security

Workers' Compensation. Virtually all employers and self-employed pay a compulsory payroll tax (or pay the costs of claims directly in the case of certain major organisations) to cover their employees under provincially operated compensation programmes (see Weiler 1980). Workers' compensation is based on agreement between employers and worker representatives to prohibit litigation in exchange for universal coverage of workers regardless of liability in the genesis of the injury or industrial disease. All costs associated with the medical and hospital treatment and rehabilitation of the worker claimant are paid, and in addition partial replacement of lost income and monthly pensions for surviving dependents in the event of a fatality from an injury or disease. After a short waiting period, totally disabled workers receive 90 per cent of net lost earnings or 75 per cent of gross lost earnings, depending on the province, up to a maximum amount. The income replacement is non-taxable. Permanent disability pensions are based on the level of medically determined permanent physical or mental disability and the previous earnings level. In 1981, minor claims for medical care only were made by 622,208 workers across the country; disabling injuries and diseases accounted for 585,410 claims including 967 fatalities. The payout was $C1.67 billion (Canada 1985a, p.188).

Canada/Quebec Pension Plan. Disability pensions are a supplementary benefit (Canada 1985a, p.208). Applicants must have contributed during five of the last ten years and be unemployable as a result of a 'severe and prolonged' physical or mental disability. The benefit contains a flat-rate component and a variable component based on the person's retirement benefit; the maximum for 1986 was $C598 a month.

Social Assistance. Each province provides income tested assistance and services to disabled adults, cost-shared with the federal government under the Canada Assistance Plan. The Canada Employment and Immigration Commission is responsible for paying the cost of training, including training allowances, on behalf of persons who may enter the labour force. Socially disadvantaged groups are also assisted under special programmes, for example, immigrants for language training, and women out of the labour force for long periods who need basic skills assessment and training.

Personal Social Services

For veterans, a wide array of supportive services is available such as counselling, medical, dental and prosthetic services, attendant care, residences and funds for post-secondary education of children (Canada 1985a, pp.205-6). Rehabilitation services for veterans spearheaded programmes for other disabled groups in the population.

Vocational Rehabilitation. Provincial workers' compensation boards provide vocational rehabilitation services where the continuing disability prevents returning to the former occupation and the worker can benefit from training. Job placement is an important function of the boards. Worker compensation programmes have come under criticism for not reflecting the true losses of either income or economic and social opportunities (Weiler 1980; Ontario 1981b). On the other hand, the boards are often under pressure to extend benefits beyond a strict interpretation of 'arising out of and in the course of employment'. Such pressure might lessen if Canada had universal income benefit programmes covering accident and sickness.

A National Health Grants programme in 1948, designed initially to enable the provinces to develop a health care infrastructure, included a system of provincial rehabilitation services. Major provincial programmes of vocational rehabilitation originated in the 1950s under federal coordination. The advent of federal-provincial hospital insurance in 1957 and especially medicare in 1964, 'brought physical rehabilitation into the twentieth century' (Watt 1981, p.38). Some provinces have developed a social rehabilitation component.

<u>Vocational Education, Training and Testing</u>. These are provided through a variety of resources: basic academic, technical and professional education (when warranted at university level); and numerous locally operated sheltered workshops. These offer a range of government subsidised services such as work testing, training and long-term sheltered employment for physically, mentally and developmentally handicapped people. Vocational rehabilitation cannot be fully effective in a society with a high rate of unemployment, particularly one that does not require employers to hire disabled and handicapped people. This has created a bottleneck in programmes such as sheltered workshops, which tend to be regarded as places of terminal employment. According to a Toronto journalist, 'An estimated 50 to 80 per cent of the disabled population are unemployed' (Orwen 1987). Nearly a third of cases before the Canadian and Provincial Human Rights commissions are concerned with disability.

<u>Subsidised Housing</u>. Disabled persons are also over-represented on waiting lists for subsidised housing which is in very short supply. Assistance with home remodelling and modifications for the

Canada

disabled is available on the basis of financial need under social assistance programmes (in contrast to veterans and injured workmen for whom it is disability determined).

Attendant Care Programmes. These are under expansion across the country.

Disabled and Handicapped Children. These are integrated whenever possible in the regular public school system, but often in separated special education classes or classes for the developmentally handicapped. A comprehensive range of rehabilitation services is available at some governmental and private (non-profit) centres (a notable example is the Easter Seal Society in Ontario) for children with severe physical disabilities such as cerebral palsy and congenital malformations.

Other Support Services. Numerous national, provincial and local voluntary agencies such as the March of Dimes, Associations for the Developmentally Handicapped, the Canadian Paraplegic Association, and the Canadian National Institute for the Blind contract with government agencies to provide much of the service to disabled people. Advocacy for more and better government support for programmes is an important function of these bodies. New causes arise frequently, such as a growing movement to alleviate the socio-economic handicap experienced by functionally illiterate people, who comprise a significant proportion of the population (Arnoti 1987).

Evaluation

The emotional appeal of certain conditions or circumstances, often combined with the ability to attract substantial financial support, has created inequities. For instance it has been argued that physically disabled children do not have the same access to the range of services available to other children with special needs (Easter Seal Society 1982). Few Canadians would deny their war veterans a right to the best available treatment; fortunately other groups of disabled and handicapped that have been quite disadvantaged by comparison with veterans generally receive excellent services today.

Canada

CHILDREN AND YOUTHS

Canadians expect families to be economically productive and self-sufficient and to ensure healthy development of their children as preparation for becoming independent, caring and contributing adults. Many of Canada's more than 4.3 million families with children (1981 Census) are unable to achieve these aims successfully because supportive family policies and programmes are weak.

The young generation is experiencing some major consequences of rapidly changing family life brought about by social and economic forces. Expanded labour force participation of women; reformed family laws affecting divorce, parenthood, and child custody; and changes in the status and treatment of children are three of many environmental forces affecting children and youths. As a proportion of the population, children are declining, yet still constitute one-fifth of the total population. Of the number of children living in lone-parent families with low incomes, two-thirds were members of female headed lone-parent families, the majority of whom were in the child-bearing age group (Arnoti 1986, p.20).

Social Security

Approximately 3.6 million families with children receive child benefits in the form of cash payments and tax benefits (Canada 1987b). A demogrant is paid to all families (usually to the mother) with one or more children under the age of 18 years who are Canadian born or landed immigrants. Standard amounts of about $C32 in 1987 (formerly, but no longer, indexed) are paid monthly except in Alberta and Quebec which have different arrangements with Ottawa. Allowances are indexed and taxed as income except in Quebec; this province also provides from its own resources a substantial variable supplement to the Family Allowance (Canada 1985b).

Child Tax Credit. Middle and low income families are eligible for a refundable income-tested Child Tax Credit, indexed to increases with the Consumer Price Index. The refunds are payable to families that pay no taxes. Above an income of about $C26,000 a year, they are reduced by $C5 for each additional $C100 of income. The parent who is the designated beneficiary receives a single annual payment through the federal tax system.

Child Tax Exemptions. This is a third form of benefit; the value of the exemption increases progessively with income.

Maternity Leave. This is recognised as an important employee benefit. Unemployment compensation is payable for a total of 17 weeks around the time of delivery. Some labour relations contracts permit adoption leave, generally for the adoptive mother.

Personal Social Services

Most services for children and youth are either partially or fully government subsidised based on financial need of the parent(s).

While the majority of children under the age of six are cared for by persons other than their parents, a high proportion attend nursery schools and kindergartens. Proportionately few children not cared for at home are in supervised or governmentally-regulated day-care centres. Low income families may have subsidised care in regulated day-care centres, but long waiting lists are the rule. Most families requiring day care meet the full charges of private, often substandard, day care or baby-sitting arrangements in commercial centres or in unsupervised family homes.

The responsibility for child care services including protection and care at home, foster care, residential care and adoption resides at the provincial level (see Levitt & Wharf 1985). In most provinces a provincial department implements the legislation; in some (such as Ontario) authority is delegated to quasi-governmental children's aid societies. Indian agencies provide services to families and children of Indian ancestry in many communities (see Hudson 1987).

The court may order children in need of protection to be made wards of the province (crown wardship), either temporarily or permanently. The latter normally expires at the eighteenth birthday. Anyone performing professional services or official duties with respect to a child is legally required to report any actual or suspected child abuse (see for example Ontario 1984).

Canada

Approved agencies may operate under provincial licence. This includes private child adoption agencies, which have taken over much of the adoption work formerly done by government or quasi-government agencies (see Sachdev 1984). Numerous scattered small residential institutions and group homes under licence treat disturbed or delinquent children. Children in care are enabled to participate in decisions that concern their future care. In Ontario, whether in voluntary placement or as crown wards, children over the age of 12 years can take part in reviews of their cases. If dissatisfied with their placements, they can request hearings by impartial tribunals and be represented by legal counsel.

Children with developmental handicaps have been placed with community resources through aggressive implementation of deinstitutionalisation policies. Numbers of developmentally handicapped children continue to be cared for alongside adults in nursing homes and similar institutions. Public concern underlies resolve at the official level to move such children into segregated facilities.

Youthful offenders, children age 12 or over up to age 18, are dealt with under the federal Young Offenders Act, 1984 (see Weiler & Ward 1985). Matching provincial legislation may vary the upper age limit, as Ontario's, where the age of 16 is normally applied. Depending on the seriousness of the charge, a young person may be kept in temporary open or secure detention, in medium security custody, or in maximum secure custody. Probation services are available. 'Alternative measures programmes' allow young offenders to avoid stigmatising court records and to participate in community activities instead of being dealt with under regular judicial proceedings. In a number of provinces, these young people are being dealt with alongside children in need of protection under child welfare authorities. In Ontario and Prince Edward Island alternative measures are not available; in the latter instance, the province claims its resources are too limited to comply. In Ontario, non-compliance is based on the principle that child offenders have a right to be dealt with judicially. The federal authority is in the process of challenging the provincial ruling under the Canadian Charter of Rights.

Canada

Evaluation

The net effect of the combination of three child-related social security benefits is that low income families receive less than middle income families. In high income categories the net benefit declines only slightly (Canada 1985b, p.17).

AN ASSESSMENT OF THE CANADIAN WELFARE SYSTEM

Canadians have near-universal access to social security programmes, with assurance of non-discriminatory provision under the Canadian Charter of Rights. Universal transfers, social insurance and income-tested benefits processed through the tax system are simple and non-discriminatory means of income redistribution. The take-up rate in the case of tax-related benefits (income-conditioned pensions and tax credits) is determined by the filing of a tax return or claim, which may be seriously hampered by a lack of information or understanding of the benefits. Despite the high level of effective coverage, certain groups are disadvantaged and discriminated against; for instance, part-time workers who earn below the set weekly minimum covered earnings (as in C/QPP and Unemployment Insurance) are left to their own resources or social assistance.

Despite improvements in the economic circumstances of the aged, benefit structures and provisions favour aged couples whose income benefits are double the amounts for single persons. Lone parent families headed by males are disadvantaged by policies that employ a stereotypical view of roles. Regardless of great expenditures on a complex and illogical array of income security programmes, the extent of poverty remains steady. The income gap between the poor and middle and high earners has enlarged. Simply, efforts to eliminate poverty by the introduction of new programmes and frequent ad hoc adjustments have failed. A myriad of studies and reports on social security in the last 20 years has produced no clear consensus among either the experts or the general public on how to manage the problem and no political mandate to reform the patchwork that has developed in the post Second World War period has emerged. There are intimations that Canadians

Canada

will again hear the arguments for a guaranteed annual income (Social Planning Council of Metropolitan Toronto 1986), but the readiness to proceed with a policy will be affected by various understandings and ideological interpretations of the concept and the political priority attached to deficit reduction and fiscal concerns. Forces external to the country, such as trade incentives and barriers and the impacts of international finance, will also shape the future Canadian welfare state. If the power of the federal government is eroded, as appears likely, there will be 10 Welfare States, one for each of the provinces.

From the standpoint of personal social services, too few services and the provision of inadequate services for the poor are serious issues. The trend toward commercialisation raises important questions about the social purpose of human services and the extent to which the public purse can be expected to meet the social needs of citizens, particularly those in lower income or especially disadvantaged target groups. The trend is in the direction of local community based services with a high degree of initiative provided by participation in self-help activity. Given the national and international context of many problems there is no single way to cope with the need for social support in a stressful society.

REFERENCES AND FURTHER READING

Arnoti, Brigitta (1986), 'Children in Low-Income Families;, Canadian Social Trends, Ottawa: Statistics Canada, Winter.

_____ (1987), 'Low Educational Attainment in Canada, 1975-85', Canadian Social Trends, Ottawa: Statistics Canada, Spring.

Banting, Keith (1982), The Welfare State and Canadian Federalism, Kingston: McGill-Queen's University Press.

Battle, Ken (1987), 'Indexation and Social Policy', Canadian Review of Social Policy, No.16 & 17, January.

Canada

Bennett, James E. & Krosny, Jacques (1981), 'Health Care in Canada' in David Coburn et al (eds), *Health and Canadian Society*, Toronto: Fitzhenry and Whiteside.

Brown, R.C. & Cook, Ramsay (1974), *Canada 1896-1921: A Nation Transformed*, Toronto: McClelland and Steward.

Bryden, Kenneth (1974), *Old Age Pensions and Policy-Making in Canada*, Montreal: McGill-Queen's University Press.

Calvert, John (1984), *Government, Limited*, Ottawa: Canadian Centre for Policy Alternatives.

Canada (1985a), *Canada Year Book*, Ottawa: Queen's Printer.

_____ (1985b), *Child and Elderly Benefits: Consultation Paper*, Ottawa: Health and Welfare Canada.

_____ (1985c), *Equality for All*, Ottawa: Queen's Printer (Parliamentary Committee on Equality).

_____ (1985d), 'Privatisation in the Canadian Health Care System', (a paper prepared for Health and Welfare Canada by Greg L. Stoddart & Roberta J. Labelle), Ottawa: Ministry of Supply and Services.

_____ (1985e), *Report of the Royal Commission [Macdonald Commission] on the Economic Union and Development Prospects for Canada*, Vol.2, Ottawa: Ministry of Supply and Services.

_____ (1986a), *Basic Facts on Social Security Programs*, Ottawa: Ministry of Supply and Services.

_____ (1986b), *Canada Pension Plan: Report for the Year March 31, 1985*, Ottawa: Ministry of Supply and Services.

_____ (1986c), 'Information on Low-Income and Income Security Programs', Ottawa: Health and Welfare Canada (mimeo). (From 'Income Distribution by Size in Canada, Statscan Cat. No.13-206, September 1986.)

Canada

―――― (1986d), *Inventory of Income Security Programs in Canada, July 1985*, Ottawa: Ministry of Supply and Services.

―――― (1986e), *Services to the Public: Canada Assistance Plan*, (Study Team Report to the Task Force on Program Review [Neilson].) Ottawa: Ministry of Supply and Services.

―――― (1987a), *Canadian Statistical Review*, Ottawa: Statistics Canada, April.

―――― (1987b), *Monthly Statistics: Income Security Programs*, Ottawa: Health and Welfare Canada.

―――― (1987c), 'News Release, March 23, 1987', Ottawa: Health and Welfare Canada.

―――― (1987d), *Sharing the Responsibility*, Ottawa: Ministry of Supply and Services. (Special Committee on Child Care.)

Canadian Mental Health Association (1983), *Unemployment: Its Impact on Body and Soul*, Toronto: Canadian Mental Health Association.

―――― (1984), *Work and Well-Being: The Changing Realities of Employment*, Toronto: Canadian Mental Health Association.

Charter of Rights Educational Fund (1985), *Report on the Statute Audit Project: Background Paper*, (rev. ed.), Toronto: The Fund.

Christian, W. & Campbell, C. (1974), *Political Parties and Ideologies in Canada*, Toronto: McGraw-Hill Ryerson.

Cook, Terry (1983), 'The Canadian Conservative Tradition: An Historical Perspective', *Journal of Canadian Studies*, 8(4), November.

Coutts, Jim (1987), Toronto *Star*, April 12.

Daenzer, Pat (1987), 'Canadian Job Strategy: In Support of a Buyer's Market', *Canadian Review of Social Policy*, 18, 58-64.

Djao, Angela (1983), *Inequality and Social Policy*, Toronto: John Wiley and Son.

Canada

Easter Seal Society of Ontario (1982), 'The Unmet Needs of Physically Handicapped Children in Ontario, A discussion Paper to the Government of Ontario', Toronto: The Society.

Economic Council of Canada (1979), *One in Three: Pensions for Canadians to 2030*, Ottawa: Ministry of Supply and Services.

Forget, Claude (1986), *Commission of Inquiry on Unemployment Insurance*, Ottawa: Queen's Printer.

Frenken, Hubert (1986), 'Retirement Income Programs in Canada' in *Canadian Social Trends*, Ottawa: Statistics Canada, Winter.

Grant, George (1970), *Lament for a Nation*, Toronto: McClelland and Stewart.

Guest, Dennis (1985), *The Emergence of Social Security in Canada*, (2nd ed. rev.), Vancouver: University of British Columbia Press.

Horowitz, Gad (1968), *Canadian Labour in Politics*, Toronto: University of Toronto Press.

Hudson, Peter (1987), 'Manitoba's Indian Child Welfare Services in the Balance', in Jacqueline S. Ismael & Ray J. Thomlison (eds), *Perspectives on Social Services and Social Issues*, Ottawa: Canadian Council on Social Development.

Hum, Derek (1983), *Federalism and the Poor: A Review of the Canada Assistance Plan*, Toronto: Ontario Economic Council.

Irving, Allan (1980), 'The Development of Income Security in Canada, Britain and the United States, (1908-1945): A Comparative and Interpretive Account', Toronto: Faculty of Social Work, University of Toronto.

_____ (1987), 'Federal-provincial Issues in the Development of Canadian Social Welfare Policy', in Shanker A. Yelaja (ed.) (2nd rev. ed.), *Canadian Social Policy*, Waterloo: Wilfred Laurier University Press.

Canada

Ismael, Jacqueline S. (ed.) (1985), *Canadian Social Welfare Policy: Federal and Provincial Dimensions*, Kingston: McGill-Queen's University Press.

───── (ed.) (1987), *The Canadian Welfare State: Evolution and Transition*, Edmonton: University of Alberta Press.

Jones, Andrew & Rutman, Leonard (1981), *In the Children's Aid: I.J. Kelso and Child Welfare in Ontario*, Toronto: University of Toronto Press.

Levitt, Kenneth & Wharf, Brian (eds) (1985), *The Challenge of Child Welfare*, Vancouver: University of British Columbia Press.

Lightman, Ernie (1984), 'Canada's Tax System and the Poor: A Background Paper and Pre-budget Submission to the Minister of Finance', Ottawa: National Anti-poverty Organization.

MacPherson, C.B. (1977), *The Life and Times of Liberal Democracy*, Oxford: Oxford University Press.

Manzer, Ronald (1985), *Public Policies and Political Development in Canada*, Toronto: University of Toronto Press.

Marchak, Patricia (1975), *Ideological Perspectives in Canada*, Toronto: McGraw-Hill Ryerson.

Marshall, Victor (1980), *Ageing in Canada*, Toronto: Fitzhenry and Whiteside.

McKenna, Frances (1985), 'Corporate Welfare - Alive and Well in the '80s', *Perception*, May/August.

Morrison, Ian (1986), 'A New Era for Voluntarism: An Overview', in United Way of Metropolitan Toronto, *A New Era for Volunteerism, Proceedings of a Conference*, June 1-3, Toronto.

Morton, W.L. (1972), *The Canadian Identity*, (rev. ed.), Toronto: University of Toronto Press.

Moscovitch, Allan (1982), 'The Rise and Decline of the Canadian Welfare State', *Perception*, (November).

Canada

National Council of Welfare (1984a), *Better Pensions for Homemakers*, Ottawa: The Council.

───── (1984b), *A Pension Primer*, Ottawa: The Council.

Naylor, C. David (1986), *Private Practice, Public Payment: Canadian Medicine and the Politics of Health Insurance, 1911-1966*, Kingston: McGill-Queen's University Press.

Nelles, H.V. (1974), *The Politics of Development: Forests, Mines and Hydro-Electric Power in Ontario, 1849-1941*, Toronto: Macmillan of Canada.

Ontario (1981a), 'The Elderly in Ontario: An Agenda for the '80s', Toronto: Secretariat for Social Development, Task Force on Ageing.

───── (1981b), *White Paper on the Workers' Compensation Act*, Toronto: Ministry of Labour.

───── (1984), 'Child and Family Services Act', Statutes of Ontario.

Ontario Social Development Council (1983), *The Province of Ontario, Its Social Services*, Toronto: The Council.

───── (1987), 'Government and the Canadian Family: New Directions', *The Reporter*, 32:1 (Winter).

Orwen, Patricia (1987), 'The Struggle for Independence', Toronto *Star* (second of a three-part series), 24 March.

Owram, Doug (1986), *The Government Generation: Canadian Intellectuals and the State, 1900-1945*, Toronto: University of Toronto Press.

Pal, Leslie A. (1985), 'Revision and Retreat: Canadian Unemployment Insurance, 1971-1981', in Ismael, Jacqueline (ed.), *Canadian Social Welfare Policy: Federal and Provincial Dimensions*, Kingston: McGill-Queen's University Press.

Canada

Riches, Graham (1985), 'Social Services in Canada in the 1980s: Fragmentation, The Status Quo, and Growth', in Jenkins, John R.G. & Yelaja, Shankar (eds), The Allocation of Social and Economic Resources in Canada in the 1980s, Waterloo: Wilfrid Laurier.

_____ (1986), Food Banks and the Welfare Crisis, Ottawa: Canadian Council on Social Development.

Robichaud, Jean-Bernard (1986), 'Issues of Government Funding', United Way of Metropolitan Toronto, A New Era for Volunteerism, Proceedings of a Conference, June 1-3, Toronto.

Sachdev, Paul (ed.) (1984), Adoption: Current Trends and Issues, Toronto: Butterworth.

Smiley, Donald (1976), Canada in Question: Federalism in the Seventies, (2nd ed.), Toronto: McGraw-Hill Ryerson.

Social Planning Council of Metropolitan Toronto (1984a), The Commercialization of Human Services in Ontario, (C. Freiler, Project Director), Toronto: The Council.

_____ (1984b), Hidden Unemployment, Toronto: The Council.

_____ (1986), A Guaranteed Annual Income: A New Look at an Old Idea, Discussion paper No.4, Toronto: The Council.

Splane, Richard B. (1965), Social Welfare in Ontario, 1791-1893, Toronto: University of Toronto Press.

Struthers, James (1983), No Fault of Their Own: Unemployment and the Canadian Welfare State, 1914-1941, Toronto: University of Toronto Press.

Sutherland, Neil (1976), Children in English-Canadian Society: Framing the Twentieth Century Consensus, Toronto: University of Toronto Press.

Canada

Taylor, Malcolm G. (1978), *Health Insurance and Canadian Public Policy*, Montreal: McGill-Queen's University Press.

Thompson, John Herd & Seager, Allen (1985), *Canada 1922-1939: Decades of Discord*, Toronto: McClelland and Stewart.

Watt, Susan (1981), 'Canadian Rehabilitation Policy and the Social Work Role', Browne, J.A., Kirlin, Betty & Watt, Susan (eds), *Rehabilitation Services and the Social Work Role: Challenge for Change*, Baltimore and London: Williams and Wilkins.

Weiler, Paul (1980), *Reshaping Workers' Compensation in Ontario*, Toronto: Ministry of Supply and Services.

Weiler, Richard & Ward, Brian (1985), 'A National Overview of the Implementation of YOPA. One Year Later', *Perception*, May/August.

Young, Walter (1969), *The Anatomy of a Party: The National CCF, 1932-1961*, Toronto: University of Toronto Press.

GERMANY, WEST
C. Wolfgang Muller

THE WELFARE SYSTEM ENVIRONMENT

Ideological Environment

The Federal Republic of Germany (FRG) is a highly developed capitalist country. It ranks among the top half dozen countries in the world in terms of production and standard of living. Ideologically the FRG is on the path from a bourgeois 'constitutional state' towards a post-bourgeois 'social welfare state'. Since the 1880s the statutory social security agencies and their insurance benefits have reduced the material risks of increasingly larger proportions of the population (health insurance, accident insurance, old age insurance and old age care and unemployment insurance). Three socio-political traditions compete for priority in the shaping of social welfare programmes in regard to the personal social services. Christianity (both Protestantism and Catholicism) claims for itself and for the other private welfare agencies a prerogative in the care of individuals and groups with social problems; they acknowledge the right of intervention by political administrations in municipalities and states only where and if the non-statutory organisations are not active ('Subsidiarity Principle'). Bourgeois liberalism assumes that the state is not required to intervene in the structure of individual life; care for personal existence is much more the concern of each individual and should be left to the laws of the 'free market' ('the night watchman state'). Trade unionism, on the contrary, wants the protection of the population against 'reproduction risks' to be the responsibility of the political community, anchored in legislation and independent of individual efforts and social differences.

Charity. Care for the physical and spiritual well being of one's fellow man is an ancient Christian commandment. This is illustrated by the parable of the good Samaritan and still is considered as an important Christian duty. The practice of this duty has assumed differing forms in the course of history.

Work Education. In the eighteenth century and thereafter the capitalist development of production required massive mobilisation of the workforce of men, women and children. To insure the willingness to work of those portions of the population who found no work initially (the 'industrial reserve army'), those living in poverty were divided into 'worthy' and 'unworthy' cases. Only the 'worthy' were granted exactly calculated poor relief. The general goal of worker education was to free mankind from the traditional ties of feudal dependence and to replace them with the 'ideal' of the 'free wage labourer' (Karl Marx).

Solidarity. The working class movement approved of the mobilisation of attitudes toward work. It viewed socially useful work as an important element in the social and political development of people. It rejected, however, the Christian principle of individual charity and advocated instead the collective principles of 'class solidarity' and 'international solidarity'.

Subsidiarity. According to Catholic social ethics people in distress should be assisted first by those persons who are closest to them. This leads to a sequence of responsibility from the family to the parochial community. Communal or state help may be granted only when the former cannot help (Enzyclica Quadrogesimo Anno 1931).

Contract of Generations. The solidarity concept of the socialists was reformulated by the conservatives as the 'Contract of Generations' through the insurance legislation adopted under the rule of Kaiser Wilhelm I and his Chancellor Otto von Bismarck (1883, 1884, 1889). Payment into the insurance system by the younger generation of workers was to provide a financial guarantee for the old age of parents and grandparents. The modalities of this statutory social security were regulated through legislation.

Right to Education. During the first German (Weimar) Republic (1919-33) Catholics, liberals and socialists formulated for the first time the 'right of every German child to education for physical, spiritual and societal soundness' (Juvenile Welfare Law 1922) as being equivalent to the right of private education in the family. Thus kindergarten care, residential child care, school social work, youth services, recreation and probation services were established and expanded as mandatory tasks of the local community; private as well as communal organisations were charged with these tasks.

Right to Life in Human Dignity. The obligation of the local community to provide material assistance to people in need was recognised already in the past century. This obligation was not, however, linked to a right to assistance for those concerned. It was only through passage of the Social Assistance Act of 1961 that every citizen of the FRG was guaranteed the 'right to lead a life in accordance with the dignity of man' (Federal Social Assistance Act (1961) and Social Code 1975).

Welfare State. The concept of a 'Welfare State' in the FRG combines the principle of individual freedom and the principle of social justice and fair and free access to social opportunities and public services. Most public services in the fields of general education, vocational training, university education, personal assistance and counselling are free of charge and financed by general taxation.

Self-Help. The guiding principle of any financial and personal assistance is to enable the recipient to live independent from the help of others (individual self-help). The guiding principle of the statutory social security systems is the collective responsibility of a given generation for the succeeding generations (collective provision). The rapid growth of funds and institutions of the Welfare State has fostered a tendency towards bureaucracy and alienation from individual needs, interests and problems. To counteract this tendency countless local initiatives and self-help groups have mushroomed in the fields of health, education, social problems, environmental protection, disarmament and local employment initiatives in the last 20 years.

Historical Origins

The contemporary welfare system of the FRG has developed in the course of centuries as a synthesis of sequential, parallel and competitive endeavours on the part of church welfare, philanthropic efforts, the working class movement, state legislation and the activities of social movements (especially the women's movement and the youth movement).

Churches. Some church congregations traditionally have supported their active members in case of undeserved hardship. In the nineteenth century welfare agencies developed beyond the realm of parochial communities and regional boundaries. They encompassed a wide range of institutions for the disabled and handicapped, orphans and youth with special problems, homeless and aged. Other non-denominational welfare agencies followed, but to this day the two large Christian welfare agencies (Diakonisches Werk and Caritas) occupy more than a million volunteers and professional workers.

Philanthropic Movements. Since the beginning of the nineteenth century many representatives of the wealthy and educated middle class were concerned with children's pre-school education as a supplement to and a corrective for education in the family. They mistrusted the educational ideology of the churches and they practised secular education based upon the theories and methods of German progressive education (Reformpaedagogik).

Municipalities. Traditionally the local communities in Germany were responsible for public assistance within the limits of their financial means: initially in the native community of those seeking assistance, after 1924 in the community of 'usual residence'. After passage of the statutory social security laws in the 1880s, the local communities were responsible only for the needy without rights to insurance benefits, those whose insurance benefits had expired, those with insurance benefits below the legally established minimum for existence or those in a particularly acute state of hardship.

Working Class Movement. From the very beginning the working class movement fought for the right of each citizen to public assistance in case of need. In the nineteenth century the trade unions established funds to assist members and their families during wage disputes and in the event they were fired. Bismarck's social security legislation also was intended to take the wind out of the sails of the Social Democrats. In 1919 the Social Democratic Party created its own welfare agency (Arbeiterwohlfahrt). Its activities, however, were limited to the care of veterans and to the exemplary development of pilot projects for personal and institutional care.

Women's Movement. The bourgeois women's movement which had its origin in the philanthropic movement of the German middle class developed institutions and methods as supplements to or substitutes for family education in nursery schools (Henriette Schrader-Breymann), school social work (Anna von Gierke), family welfare (Alice Salomon, Marie Baum) and youth welfare (Gertrud Baeumer). The women's movement laid the foundation for the development of a methodology for the personal social services (Alice Salomon, Siddy Wronsky).

Youth Movement. At the beginning of the twentieth century, both the bourgeois and the proletarian youth movement discovered the peer group as a decisive medium for self-education of children and youths. In the first German Republic education in schools and other institutions was influenced by this concept of autonomous group education.

Fascism. In the 13 years of fascist rule (1933-45) the achievements of progressive education and the democratic structures of the welfare system were liquidated although part of the basic welfare legislation formally remained in force. However, the socialist and other progressive welfare agencies were forbidden. Democratic social educators and social workers were arrested, tortured and murdered or driven

Germany, West

into exile. Public assistance was granted only to worthy, genetically healthy, arian families. All others seeking assistance were left without help or sent to forced labour camps and some were annihilated in concentration camps. The developed system of communal welfare was misused to identify 'non-arians', 'congenitally diseased', and 'shirkers' and to deliver them to the arbitrary actions of fascist officials.

Federal Republic of Germany. After the total defeat of the fascist Third Reich the old German welfare system was re-established and further developed progressively in the occupation zones of the French, British and Americans. As the standard of living increased in the 1950s and 1960s ('German economic miracle') the social security laws were expanded and methods of the personal social services were further developed and refined, in part linked to Anglo-American standards and in part developed independently.

New social movements. The student movement, social work movement, alternative movement, new women's movement and self-help movement provided numerous methodological and institutional impulses to the social welfare system. The increasing centralisation and bureaucracy of the system of public assistance and personal social services were challenged by the principle and practice of decentralisation, debureaucratisation and grass roots orientation. This new practice did not remain without influence upon the work of the large, established welfare agencies and upon public allocation practice.

Political and Socio-economic Environment

Contrary to the multi-party system of the first German Republic, as well as the one-party system of the fascist Third Reich, since 1949 the FRG developed a political system consisting of three major parties: Christian Democrats (conservatives); Social Democrats (progressive), which were roughly equal in strength; and the Free Democrats (liberals), a small mid-stream party that often tipped the scale when coalition governments were constituted. A new radical-democratic party with an ecological orientation emerged in the 1980s (Die Gruenen).

Germany, West

The FRG is a federation of 11 States. The former capital Berlin has a special status under the auspices of the Second World War allies. The political coalitions in the State governments frequently differ from that of the federal government.

The constitution defines the duties and obligations of the federal government (for example, foreign affairs, defense), the State governments (for example, education, cultural affairs, law enforcement) and the local communities (districts and counties).

The federal legislature of West Germany consists of two chambers: the <u>Bundestag</u> (the Lower House) or federal cabinet, and <u>the Bundestrat</u> (the Upper House) or federal council. The nominal head of state is the President, who is elected for five years. The actual executive head is the Chancellor, who is appointed by the President from among the leaders of the majority party in the <u>Bundestag</u> and it must be approved by the <u>Bundestag</u>. The Chancellor appoints his cabinet, comprising Ministers who head the various departments of government.

Each of the States has its own executive and elected legislature. Each State is divided into districts and communes. The smallest independent unit of public, social, and political life in the FRG is the so-called commune, with its own parliament and an independent administration. A certain number of communes form a rural or municipal district ('Kreis, Kreisfreie Stadt'). The district again has an independent parliament and offices of public administration. A certain number of districts form a state within the federation.

The population of the FRG is approximately 56 million; almost 50 per cent live in urban areas. The number of people engaged in agriculture has diminished continually in the past decades to the current level of 10 per cent, while agricultural production continues to rise. The importance of the traditional basic industries (coal and steel) in the northwest of the FRG has diminished in the past 10 years. In their place chemical and microelectronic industries in the south and southwest of the FRG now determine economic growth.

In the 1980s economic rationalisation and a temporarily increased birth rate lead to a hard core unemployment rate of nearly 10 per cent of the workforce. Youths, women and persons living in the northern and northwestern regions were particularly affected. A declining birth rate and an increasing proportion of aged persons are anticipated in the period until the end of the century. Nevertheless, until now the Gross National Product (GNP) has continually grown through the effects of economic rationalisation and significant sales growth on the international market, even though the annual economic growth increases of the 1960s diminished which, in turn, damaged the 'social security net' - critics have termed this a 'dismantling of the social state' and a 'redistribution of resources from the bottom to the top'.

THE WELFARE SYSTEM: AN OVERVIEW

Structure and Administration

There are four dominant features shaping the social welfare system of the FRG:

- The <u>social security system</u> is centrally supervised by the Federal Ministry of Labour and Social Affairs, through the Federal Salaried Employees Insurance Institute, the Federal Insurance Institute and the Federal Institute of Labour, but locally administered by networks of specialist funds.

- Most <u>personal social services</u> are financed and administered or supervised by local district authorities and/or private welfare agencies with municipal grants.

- <u>Services in kind</u>, institutional care and professional counselling are provided mainly by private welfare organisations with municipal grants.

- <u>Public assistance</u> benefits are highly standardised by generally accepted norms (<u>Richtsaetze</u>). Public assistance benefits are administered by municipal public welfare offices, personal social services are supervised by municipal health and youth offices.

Districts are responsible for services like general education, vocational training, libraries and museums, hospitals, kindergarten care, homes for children, juveniles and adults, and other social and recreational facilities.

Communes and districts have the right to collect certain local taxes, but in general they depend financially on allocations provided by the State (<u>Land</u>) and the Federal government (<u>Bund</u>).

Social rights, social benefits and public allowances have been developed over a period of 100 years. A multitude of laws and regulations with social security and social welfare provisions are assembled in the Social Code (<u>Sozialgesetzbuch</u>), which comprises ten volumes; the first volume was adopted in 1975. The Social Code contains a catalogue of social rights which are identical to the rights of the European Social Charter; they guarantee access to a number of social benefits and allowances in different situations:

- aid for education, training and employment
- social insurance
- public compensation for injury to health
- financial aid for the family
- housing allowances
- youth services
- public assistance
- integration and rehabilitation of the handicapped

(Flamm 1983, pp.90-6).

The term 'Social Welfare' (<u>Soziale Arbeit</u>) is used in the FRG for the totality of institutions and services which, over and above the private, individual efforts to provide for oneself, guarantee life in human dignity protected against the risks and distress in the cycle of life and the process of work. Emerging from this totality, the benefits of the social security system have become in a 100 year process a firm element of a collective, state-controlled and guaranteed basis for human existence. And beyond that, in the more limited sense of the term 'Social Work' (<u>Sozialarbeit</u>), institutions and services have been expanded and further developed, particularly by private welfare agencies, municipalities and self-help groups of the social movements. They provide personal social services (in kind benefits and counselling) for particular groups of children, youths, adults and aged citizens. Fully trained social workers and, to the extent that

Germany, West

specific educational activities are offered, fully trained social educators (especially in nursery schools, day care centres, homes for children and juveniles, youth clubs and recreational centres) work in these facilities. Both professional groups are trained at college and masters level. Altogether the number of full time workers in social work has risen from 40,000 in 1950 to 182,000 in 1982, half of them are graduates of professional programmes (Brauns/Kramer 1986, p.194).

Financing Social Welfare

Since 1968 the Federal Ministry for Labour and Social Affairs publishes usually every second year a 'Social Report' and a 'Social Budget', which:

> describes in comments and figures the manifold aspects of social security, gives a breakdown by uniform criteria and relates the figures to overall economic data. One of its characteristics is that benefits and financing are forecast in accord with the medium-term assumptions of the Federal Government on economic and financial trends (Sozialbericht 1978, p.66).

Table 1 shows the social budget from 1980 to 1990 (projected) as a percentage of Gross National Product (GNP).

TABLE 1: THE SOCIAL BUDGET AS A PERCENTAGE OF GROSS NATIONAL PRODUCT: 1980-1990

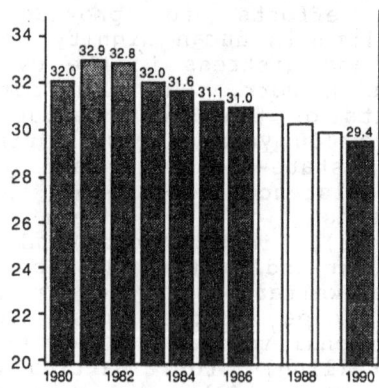

SOURCE: Sozialbudget 1986, p.99.

Germany, West

Between 1980 and 1985 the rate of social expenditure in relation to GNP stabilised at the level of 30 per cent, the absolute figures rising from 475 billion DM (1980) to 572 billion DM (1985). According to the latest forecast it will be 654 billion DM in 1990. In 1978 social expenditure amounted to 6,590 DM per capita of which 2,080 DM, i.e. one third, was spent on health benefits (Sozialbericht 1978, p.76). Table 2 shows social expenditure for 1985.

TABLE 2: FEDERAL REPUBLIC OF GERMANY SOCIAL BUDGET 1985

	Expenditures (in million DM)	Percentage
Pension insurance for workers and salaried staff and servants of public administration	220,200	38.5
Statutory health insurance	114,500	20.0
Accident insurance	11,700	2.0
Public health system	1,900	0.3
Unemployment insurance	15,300	2.7
Promotion of jobs and job creation	24,700	4.3
Public assistance and housing allowances	24,800	4.4
Youth services	7,800	1.4
Others	151,100	26.4
Total	572,000	100.0

SOURCE: Sozialbudget 1986, pp.98-158.

The major burden for expenditures in the framework of the 1985 Social Budget is carried by

Germany, West

the government with 39.1 per cent, business provides 31.8 per cent and the insured employees contribute 28.3 per cent. Table 3 shows the sources of funding the social expenditures in 1985.

TABLE 3: FEDERAL REPUBLIC OF GERMANY SOCIAL BUDGET 1985

	Percentage
Federal	20.6
States	10.9
Districts	7.6
Employers	31.8
Social Security Fund	0.2
Private Organisations	0.6
Employees	28.3
	100.0

SOURCE: Sozialbudget 1986, p.158.

AGED

Services and care for the aged, unemployed, sick and/or injured are provided (or guaranteed) by the federal social security agencies on the basis of social insurance principles. Public assistance allowances will be granted only in cases in which insurance benefits are not or are no longer paid at or above poverty level.

Social Security

Old age pensions have a tradition in Germany of more than one hundred years. They emerged from the miner's self-help initiatives in the late Middle Ages (Bruderbuechsen) and since the 1870s were extended to ever larger segments of the population. These programmes became obligatory and were financed by matching monthly contributions from employers and employees. In 1984 the contribution to the old age pension insurance amounted to 18.5 per cent of monthly income.

Germany, West

Retirement age is 63, with 35 years' insurance coverage, or 65, with 15 years coverage. It is possible to retire at 60 provided the insured person either has been unemployed for one year in the last 18 months, is a women with ten years coverage in the last 20 years, or disabled and 35 years' coverage. An income test applies if retirement occurs before age 65.

The old age pension is a wage substitute payment. The amount is based upon the duration of coverage and 'assessed wages' (the ratio of workers' earnings to the adjusted national average over the period of coverage). In 1985 blue collar male workers received an average monthly pension of 1,490 DM (1,043 DM for females) and 1,932 DM for white collar male workers (1,506 DM for females). These differences result from differing types of work in economic life and the still existing lower valuation of women's labour for comparable work (Sozialbudget 1986, p.121). The average pension amounts to about 75 per cent of the net income for comparable professions. Some 80 per cent of the male and 75 per cent of the female population are covered by pension insurance which in 1982 amounted to 30 million people.

Self-employed persons may join the old age pension insurance on a voluntary base or join an independent private insurance programme which may turn out to be more expensive. Servants of the public administration in districts, States and the federal government are covered by separate programmes.

The level of pensions is adjusted on the basis of changes in wages and salaries in regular, legally determined intervals. Pensions amount at present to the largest single expenditure (38 per cent) in the framework of the FRG social security budget. This sum also includes pensions for victims of war and victims of fascist injustice at home and abroad. It does not include supplementary benefits from employers in the form of pension and benefit programmes of individual enterprises; these amounted to 11 billion DM in 1985 (Sozialbudget 1986, p.141).

Pensions are financed in the following manner. The generation actively working finances through its social security contributions the pensions of the generation no longer employed and, in turn, expect that their pensions will be provided later by the subsequent working generation. This contract of generations will be rendered difficult in the future through changes in the demographic structure of the population. By the end of the millenium the number of employed persons will decrease in proportion to the number no longer actively employed. This is related to:

- a decreasing birth rate;
- the increase in long-term unemployment, part-time work and a reduction in the total period of employment through extended professional training and early work inability due to illness and invalidity; and
- the increase in life expectancy in the third life phase.

On the other hand, the productivity per working hour still increases by leaps and bounds. The 1960 GNP required 56 billion working hours; the 1982 GNP was double that of 1960 but required only 45 billion working hours. Only part of this increase in productivity was reflected in increased income and only to this extent augmented contributions to the pension insurance scheme. So far the bottlenecks in pension payment have been compensated by temporary increases in the federal allocations of about 20 per cent of all payments regulated by legislation and/or through increases in the monthly contributions from employers and employees.

Public Assistance. Public assistance is available to elderly people who are unable to pay the cost of institutional care.

Personal Social Services

Many of the aged are not only old but at the same time sick, disabled and needy. Therefore they appear as a target group in other areas of social work activity. The private welfare agencies and the communal social welfare offices provide special personal social services for the aged (such as day centres, meals-on-wheels, visiting services, recreation and fitness programmes). The control of public standards for running a private old age home or hostel is the responsibility of these offices at the state level.

Germany, West

Evaluation

In the course of time the public image of old people has changed. The idea that they are needy, passive and grateful has been replaced by the concept of an active life in the third period of the life cycle. Special social programmes are now developed to encourage the aged to share their lifelong experiences and professional skills with the younger generation.

THE DISABLED AND HANDICAPPED

A person who is physically, mentally or emotionally handicapped or who is threatened by such disability, is entitled to the assistance required to avert, remove, improve or prevent the worsening of the handicap or to reduce its consequences, and to assistance to secure for the handicapped person a place in society in accordance with his inclinations and abilities, above all in working life (Flamm 1983, p.180).

The cause of the individual disability, the time of its origin and the degree to which it affects living and working possibilities are factors determining which of the differing institutions of the social security system is responsible for the material expenditures and efforts necessary for the recovery of physical and social health in order to lead an independent life: health insurance, accident insurance, pension insurance, work promotion and public assistance.

Social Security

Invalidity pensions are available to insured employees who are incapacitated for any gainful activity (general invalidity) or who suffer a 50 per cent reduction in earning capacity in their usual occupation (occupational invalidity), provided they have 60 months' contributions.
The amount of the general invalidity pension is determined identically to that provided to retirees. A reduced proportion of assessed wages applies in respect of occupational invalidity. If invalidity occurs before age 55 then, provided an insured employee has paid contributions for 36 of

the last 60 months (or for 50 per cent of the months since he entered insurance), a full invalidity pension is payable. A child's supplement is also payable. Pensions are adjusted annually according to wage changes.

In 1983 13 billion DM (2.5 per cent of the social budget) were expended for the rehabilitation of disabled and handicapped persons; the largest part was financed by the pension insurance and public assistance. Specific action programmes of the federal government were implemented to facilitate the reintegration of disabled and handicapped persons in work and society. Under the Rehabilitation Adjustment Act of 1974 priority was given to the rehabilitation of health and renewed employment; this was considered to be more meaningful and financially sensible than long-term payment of pensions or public assistance. In 1984 the Federal Institute of Labour paid for professional retraining activities for disabled and handicapped 65-75 per cent of previous net wages during the period of retraining. The Severely Handicapped Persons Act of 1974 required private and public employers to make at least six per cent of their jobs (800,000) available to this group of people. Any dismissal of a severely handicapped person from employment requires special permission from the local welfare authority.

Personal Social Services. The disabled and handicapped have been offered a variety of services by non-statutory welfare agencies, particularly churches and individual church congregations for a protracted period of time, and increasingly in recent times by small, regional self-help groups in which the disabled and handicapped come together to overcome their individual isolation, and to take collective action towards the goal of better integration in social life. These personal social services include individual counselling, cultural and recreational activities in integrated groups and transportation.

Evaluation

Increasing attention has been given to the group of emotionally disturbed and handicapped persons. It became necessary to discriminate between emotionally disturbed children and young people, drug addicts, and emotionally sick aged people. Classical treatment through institutional care and psychotherapy proved to be expensive and ineffective in many cases:

> Apart from the efforts to extend professional psychiatric and psychotherapeutic ambulatory and community services and to reform stationary and part-stationary care, the urgent need to expand the supplementary ambulatory and part-stationary socio-psychiatric services to form a basis for providing integration assistance is of crucial importance (Flamm 1983, p.182).

For this reason the federal government financed a six-year pilot project in the 1970s to extend communal psychiatric services and to link the different local ambulatory and part-stationary psychiatric facilities.

CHILDREN AND YOUTHS

According to the Constitution, marriage and family are under the special protection of the political community. The care and education of children are natural rights of parents as well as their primary responsibility. Children may be removed from the family against the will of their guardians only on the basis of law, when the guardians fail to meet expectations or when the children are in danger of neglect. Each mother is entitled to the protection and the care of the community. Legislation dating from 1970 guarantees illegitimate children identical conditions for physical, spiritual and social development as legitimate children (Grundgesetz A.6).

Social Security

Child Benefits. Families with children and one-parent families in the FRG are granted tax reductions, child-related tax exemptions and family allowances. Child benefits are paid by local employment offices according to the number of children (30 DM a month for the first child, 70 DM for the second child and 140 DM for each subsequent child).

Low income families receive somewhat higher allowances. Partial allowances are payable to pensioners. Foreign workers with children are also entitled to these benefits.

Since 1985 one of the parents of a newborn child may take leave from work for one year and is entitled to a monthly educational allocation of 600 DM. For each child raised at home the responsible parent also is credited with one year of pension insurance coverage. In the case of divorce, the pension rights acquired during the period of marriage are divided equally between the two parties (since 1977), and expenditures for child education receive special consideration.

Limited paid leave is also provided by sick funds when an insured employee is required to care for a sick child.

Personal Social Services

Youth Welfare and Youth Service. Under the Youth Welfare Act of 1922 which was amended several times, youth welfare was removed from the general welfare administration of the local community. Special youth welfare offices were established at the local level. They are responsible for the duties and services provided by the Youth Welfare Act. These include:

- protection of foster children and arrangement of adoptions;
- public guardianship and supervision of private guardians;
- juvenile court assistance and probation;
- supervision of the application of laws to protect children and juveniles at work and in public life;
- placement of neglected and deprived children and juveniles in private or public educational homes outside of the family and supervising the standards of such homes;
- counselling in questions of care and education within the family and child guidance;
- maternity care;
- public health care;
- children and family recreation;
- promotion of recreational activities, citizenship education and international exchange of young people; and
- guidance in vocational education and training.

Germany, West

The Youth Welfare Office is headed by a Youth Welfare Committee consisting of men and women experienced in youth affairs and youth services. It is a link between the statutory youth service and the independent youth organisation which have - being part of the autonomous youth movement - a long and vital history.

Children's Rights. The Youth Welfare Office acts as a mediator between the interests of parents and the - sometimes divergent - interests of children and juveniles. The office is obliged to respect the parents' decisions on the fundamental religious and ideological principles to guide individual education but also to recognise the priorities and decisions of the children and juveniles themselves. In the last decade the right of children to self-determination has been strengthened in law and jurisdiction.

Kindergarten Care. The kindergarten is a traditional German educational institution dating back to 1844 (Friedrich Froebel). In the last 20 years the number of day-care kindergartens (up to the age of six) and day-care centres for school children (up to the age of 10-12) has rapidly increased. Approximately 80 per cent of all pre-school children and six per cent of all school children regularly attended a kindergarten or day-care centre for school children in 1982. There has been a long dispute whether kindergarten should be part of the school system or remain under the supervision of the youth authority. The final decision was to keep it as part of the extra-family and extra-school education of the younger generation.

Guardianship Courts. The FRG has special guardianship courts to regulate the guardianship system. The local Youth Welfare Office co-operates with the guardianship court in the event of a divorce of the parents, in adoptions and so forth. In former times statutory official guardianship was applied to any child born out of wedlock. After a reform of 1970 parental authority over the child born out of wedlock was granted to the mother:

> Until the child is 18, the father must pay for the child born out of wedlock a standard amount to cover (the child's) maintenance in

accordance with the provisions of the regulation on Standard Maintenance of 1970 and 1976. An official trustee or guardian must arrange for and supervise this payment. If it becomes necessary, the Youth Welfare Office must guarantee the maintenance from public funds by means of maintenance advances or social assistance (Flamm 1983, p.152).

Juvenile Courts. Since 1924 there are special juvenile criminal courts which have principles different from those of other criminal courts. These courts are characterised by educational and correctional measures. In criminal proceedings the Youth Welfare Office provides juvenile court assistance and probation services if the execution of a sentence is suspended.

Youth Promotion Schemes. Since 1950 the Federal Youth Plan is an important instrument in the promotion of education of children and juveniles apart from family and school. It supports and finances primarily the autonomous youth associations, political educational activities for young people and international youth exchange as well as pilot projects for the promotion of socially underprivileged youth.

In 1985 about 86 billion DM (15 per cent of the social budget) were expended - or accepted as tax reductions through exemptions - for measures and institutions of family promotion, out-of-school education for children and juvenile promotion. The expenditures in the framework of the Youth Welfare Law were financed largely by the districts and the States.

Evaluation

The personal social services for children and youths have a long tradition in Germany. They involve a wide range of activities, programmes and institutions, all of which support the development of social responsibility and self-determination in young people. Critics of the old Youth Welfare Act of 1922 argue that it should be adapted to meet current contemporary demands. Attempts to reformulate it failed however, because of the high costs implied and because of memories of the government-induced political indoctrination of youth that occurred under the rule of German fascists.

Germany, West

NEEDY FAMILIES

The material support of needy individuals and families was initially the responsibility of parochial communities, monasteries and private charity. It was provided within the municipality in which the recipient was born and well known. The mobility of the population forced by industrialisation shifted this support to the place of 'customary residence' and entrusted the local community with the administration of poor relief. Parochial communities provided additional help for their active members in accord with their financial means.

Social Security

In 1924 the traditional poor relief was replaced by a new welfare relief. A personal right to public assistance in case of need came into existence through the Federal Public Assistance Act of 1961. It can be granted in the form of 'ongoing assistance for personal maintenance' or as 'assistance in particular emergencies'. It should permit conducting life that 'reflects the dignity of man'.

The type and amount of public assistance (personal assistance, monetary and material benefits) depends upon the particularity of the individual case, takes into account the support obligations of immediate family members and relates to the nature of the need and to local conditions. The amount of ongoing payments for maintenance is determined by 'standard allocations' by the States of the FRG; these allocations are periodically adjusted to reflect changes in the cost of living index. The assistance should be granted in a manner which, to the extent possible, enables the recipient again to become independent of public assistance. It may also be granted as a preventive measure prior to an emergency or as follow-up after it has been eliminated. The standard allocations are, however, so modest that they always fall below the lowest wage groups in order 'to permit the willingness to work to grow weak.'

Survivors' Pensions. Survivors of deceased insured persons with 60 months' contributions or of deceased pensioners receive a pension equal to 100 per cent of the deceased's pension for three

Germany, West

months, subsequently reducing to 60 per cent of the widow aged 45, when invalid or caring for children, otherwise 60 per cent of the occupational invalidity pension payable in respect of the deceased. These are payable to widowers. Additional benefits are provided in respect of orphans, including students up to age 25 or invalids and, subject to an income test, to apprentices up to age 25. The maximum survivor's pension is 100 per cent of the deceased's general invalidity pension entitlement.

A death grant is also payable.

Survivors of work injury victims receive 40 per cent of the deceased's earnings at age 45, invalid or caring for children, otherwise 30 per cent. Payable to all widows and dependent widowers. Additional pension is payable in respect to orphans, parents or grandparents. The maximum survivor's pension is 80 per cent of the deceased's earnings.

A death grant is also payable.

Maternity Benefits. Pregnant insured women with 12 weeks' insurance or employment between the tenth and fourth month preceding confinement, working or excused for working from six weeks prior to expected confinement, qualify for a maternity benefit, equal to full wages, for 14 weeks. Both minimum and maximum benefits are specified. A lump-sum payment of 150 DM is paid to ineligible insured women.

A maternity grant is also provided after each birth.

Some sick funds provide lump-sum maternity grants to female dependents of insured members.

Housing Allowance. The majority of people in the FRG do not own a house but rent a flat. The rents have become more and more expensive in the course of reconstruction of metropolitan areas, towns, and villages after the Second World War. For a certain period rents were generally frozen at a pre-war level. But with the 'liberalisation' of the housing market many rents doubled within ten years. The Federal Government launched a comprehensive public housing programme, but since construction prices also increased this programme did not succeed in bringing the 'free rents' down again. To ensure that people are not forced to move from their accustomed neighbourhood there is a special Housing Allowance Act (1960), which enables a local District Office for Housing Allowances to subsidise the actual rent up to certain limits, depending on the number of persons in the dwelling and the character of the area. This allowance is also paid to owners of private houses with low income and to foreign workers. In the FRG in 1975 housing allowances were received by some 1.67 million households, particularly pensioners, recipients of public assistance and families with three and more children (Social Report 1978, p.51).

Personal Social Services

Needy families with dependent children are taken care of by social workers of a special public counselling agency ('Familienfuersorge'), which is part of the Youth Welfare Office and is guided by a more or less explicit case work approach. In special cases of educational problems public and private child guidance agencies offer specialised psychological, educational and practical help free of charge. But only few of them reach the hard core of multi-problem families who have, over the generations, become dependent on public assistance. To meet their special needs a new kind of personal service was developed in the 1970s. A qualified social worker spends - if the family co-operates - up to 19 hours per week counselling the family and giving active assistance in matters of housekeeping, home economics, education and family communication ('Familienhilfe'). This new approach, which combines practical assistance and family counselling, has proved to be effective in more than 50 per cent of multi-problem families.

Evaluation

The net of social security incorporated in the statutory social security agencies is close knit in the FRG in comparison with other industrialised countries. Most emergency situations arising from illness and invalidity, unemployment and old age are covered by the social insurance programmes. Their payments generally are coupled with long-term employment and the corresponding contributions into the insurance programmes. In times of long-term mass unemployment and for high risk groups (younger unemployed persons, refugees, foreigners and asylum applicants, single mothers) insurance payments do not exist or are insufficient to permit leading a life that reflects the dignity of man. Such cases are entitled to public assistance and/or housing allowances which should guarantee dwellings suitable for families that have less than average income.

In the ten years between 1976 and 1985 public assistance payments (including housing allowances) climbed from 9.6 billion DM to 24.8 billion DM and amounted to about four per cent of the social budget. Funding is provided by the municipalities and districts (80 per cent) and the States (20 per cent).

Three factors are responsible above all for the increases in the public assistance budget:

- long-term unemployment;
- cost increases in stationary care for the elderly; and
- above average increases in rent in the past years.

For this reason there have been repeated demands for a basic monthly pension of approximately 1,000 DM for each citizen.

This demand has been countered with arguments that the principle of a pension based on contributions and the principle of examination of need in the individual case may not be relinquished. The parliamentary opposition criticised in 1986 that the benefit balance of the social state has been weakened by a multitude of state interventions and that a 'new social policy' was becoming increasingly manifest which entailed massive redistribution of the social product to the advantage of the profits of employers and to the detriment of employees, pensioners and public assistance recipients (Deutscher Bundestag, Drucksache 10/6704, p.5). The opposition further criticised that recipients of ongoing maintenance payments can be drafted for work of public benefit for which they receive only a limited additional payment and not insurance protection. This is a relic of the traditional 'workhouse test' used to test the willingness to work of recipients.

Germany, West

THE UNEMPLOYED

Following the reconstruction period of the war-damaged German industry, the long period of full employment in the 1950s and 1960s ('German economic miracle') enabled the integration of millions of citizens and their families from the German Democratic Republic into an ever-expanding labour market. Millions of housewives were persuaded to enter the workforce. Millions of foreign workers from the south and southeast Europe were also attracted to Germany. In sharp contrast, unemployment became a familiar feature of economic, social and political life in the early 1980s. Most severely affected were juveniles, who found it more and more difficult to enter into the labour market and qualified but older persons who lost their jobs before reaching retirement age. This was initially viewed as a transitory feature, but it has now become a permanent structural phenomenon.

Social Security

In 1927 Parliament passed the Unemployment Insurance Act, the last piece of social legislation Bismarck put through. It was replaced in 1969 by the Labour Promotion Act. This legislation surpasses the framework of a classical, obligatory and legally regulated unemployment insurance and is part of a general, state economic and social affairs policy. The Federal Institute of Labour in Nurnberg is charged with the administration and implementation of this policy. Any person who works or wants to work has free access to the personal and financial services of the Federal Institute of Labour and its agencies in different parts of the country; career counselling, grants and loans for basic and advanced training and retraining, public information on job openings, financial compensation for short-time and bad-weather-jobs, unemployment benefits, and unemployment relief.

Unemployment Benefits. Any person who has worked for at least 60 consecutive months and has contributed to the unemployment insurance fund (2.1 per cent of income, another 2.1 per cent is paid by the employer) may claim unemployment benefits for up to 312 working days averaging 63 per cent of net income plus family supplements.

Germany, West

Unemployment Relief. After this period unemployment relief averaging 56 per cent of net income is paid. It includes social health insurance contributions. It is paid if the claimant is unable to maintain himself/herself or has no means and resources from his/her family.

Personal Social Services

Federal Institute of Labour. A federal institute is responsible for the administration of employment promotion, vocational training, vocational counselling and unemployment benefits. The institute and its offices throughout the country is governed by representatives of employers, employees and public institutions. It is financed by matching contributions from the individual employee and his/her employer; each contributes between two and four per cent of the wage total. If these contributions are not sufficient to cover the expenses the federal government is required by law to assist (Bundesgarantie).

The total expenditure for labour promotion amounted to 22.8 billion DM in 1980 (five per cent of the social budget); the comparable figure for 1985 was 39 billion DM (6.8 per cent of the social budget) of which 14 billion DM went for unemployment insurance benefits. These figures would be significantly higher if all unemployed persons registered claims or if they could enjoy insurance protection without time limits. Since only part of the unemployed register is 'seeking work' (unemployed youths, married women and migrant workers often do not register) and since this part is no longer eligible after one year, the burden of the long-term unemployed falls upon the federal government (unemployment assistance), the municipalities and districts (public assistance) or their families.

Evaluation

Whether and how the current unemployment level of about 10 per cent (1986) can be corrected on a long term and lasting basis is a matter of political dispute. The CDU-FDP Federal Government has confidence in the positive impact of a general policy of industrial and investment promotion with increasing tax exemptions and investment aids for successful entrepreneurs. The opposition supports occupational programmes and taxes to create new jobs, particularly in the fields of ecology and energy conservation; these programmes should be financed by credits and taxes to be independent of economic growth. The Opposition argues that through new technologies and the rationalisation effects linked to them more jobs are being destroyed currently than could be created by possible (but uncertain) economic growth.

A long-term solution to structural unemployment, given the current circumstances, will be attained only through a radical redistribution of working time in the entire society and through a falling birth rate.

THE SICK AND INJURED

A statutory Social Health Insurance was founded in Germany by federal law in 1883 for certain groups of qualified workers in the big industries. Over time most branches of blue and white collar workers and employees were included, nowadays also students, trainees, pensioners and their families are included. Self-employed persons and other freelance professions may join on a voluntary basis. Today 90 per cent of the total population of the FRG and their dependents are members of this collective form of self-provision. Additional private health insurance agencies offer services for upper echelon employees on an optional basis. They are all part of a 'contribution and benefit community'. The statutory social health insurance agencies throughout the country and the private but state-controlled health insurance agencies ('Ersatzkassen') are part of a comprehensive social health conservation system anchored in federal law of December 1976. Their boards are elected by free and secret ballot for a period of six years; employers and employees are represented on an equal basis.

Social Security

The statutory social health insurance provides medical attention in the event of illness for the insured and his/her family, including early diagnosis and comprehensive maternity care and sick benefits as a substitute for (up to 80 per cent) wages after the first six weeks of the onset of illness. Until this time the employer is required to continue paying the normal wage or salary. The insurance also provides medical treatment, such as drugs, artificial limbs, therapy and hospital treatment and the bills of private doctors. These bills as well as the pharmacy bills are payed directly by the agency.

The statutory health insurance funds are administered under public law. Contributions usually are borne half by the employer and half by the employee. In 1986 they amounted to 13 per cent of the monthly gross earnings.

The public health insurance expenditures rose 290 per cent between 1970 and 1982; in the same period wage costs increased only 140 per cent. In 1985 health insurance payments totalled 114.5 billion DM accounting for about 20 per cent of the total social budget and were, following old age care provided through the pension insurance, the largest single entity of social expenditure. An additional sum of two billion DM was expended for public health services. The cost explosion of the past 15 years was a result of several factors:

- An over-supply of practising doctors and hospitals, which resulted in a certain 'over care' of the population;
- The income of doctors and daily cost of hospital care also rose above the national average;
- The drug industry had a rapid and unfounded expansion of the market for pharmaceutics and psychopharmaceutics that are particularly expensive in the FRG in comparison to other European countries;
- The indirect payment system for doctors, hospitals and pharmacies has induced doctors, hospitals and patients to 'behave uneconomically' and to demand more services for longer periods of time than necessary.

The federal government attempted to check the cost explosion in health services through cost legislation. A structural reform of health insurance will become effective in 1989; it provides for patient participation in covering the costs of doctors and pharmaceutics.

Work Injury Insurance. Insured employees suffering a temporary disability due to a work injury receive full pay for six weeks, paid for by the employer, after which by one of the 52 industrial or agricultural accident insurance funds. This is payable until recovery or certification of permanent disability.

If total permanent disability occurs as a result of a work injury then insured employees receive two-thirds of their last year's earnings. Supplementation occurs for the generally disabled (earnings capacity loss of 50 per cent or more) with no other pension, and if a child is being cared for.

A pro rata payment is made in the event of a partial permanent disability (involving a loss of earnings capacity of 20 per cent or more). Complete medical care, rehabilitation and appliances are also provided by either a sick fund or an accident fund.

Total expenditure on work injury insurance in 1985 was 11.7 billion DM (some two per cent of the 1985 Social Budget).

Sickness Benefit. Insured employees (members of sick funds) receive full pay for the first six weeks of illness from their employer, thereafter from their sick fund at the rate of 80 per cent of wages for up to 78 weeks in every three years.

Medical benefits are provided to insured employees by doctors, hospitals and pharmacists under contract with and paid by the sick funds.

Personal Social Security

Health Welfare Office. In addition to the social and private health insurance systems there are health welfare offices in each district of the FRG located in the vicinity of youth welfare offices and public assistance offices. Their services are free of charge. They offer pregnancy consultation, counselling for young mothers and fathers on infant care, health care in schools, special assistance for the handicapped, emotionally disturbed and addicted. Each health welfare office employs or works together with medical doctors who have the responsibility to consult but not to treat patients.

Evaluation

The comprehensive statutory social health insurance system of West Germany has taken away the anxiety from nearly all the population about coping with the financial burden of sickness, injury and long-term hospital isolation. On the other hand, this comprehensive system has to accommodate a nearly unrestricted supply of medical services, pharmaceutic drugs and a comparatively large capacity of more and more expensive public (and private) hospitals. Many experts say that the effectiveness of this mixed system is no longer guaranteed.

ASSESSMENT OF THE WEST GERMAN WELFARE SYSTEM

The professionalisation of social work in Germany was early and extensive. The first schools of social work were founded at the turn of the century. Social workers and social educators are trained currently in some 50 specialised professional schools and 40 universities. Fully trained social workers and social educators occupy the bulk of the positions in municipalities and private welfare agencies. Generally they have been trained in one of the classical methods of social work or have participated in integrated courses in 'methodological approaches'. Supervision has been adopted as a necessary feature of professional work.

In Germany group education was developed as early as the turn of the century by the autonomous youth movement. Between 1920 and 1930 it was taken over in school teaching; after the military defeat of fascism it was reinstituted as 'social group work'. In the mid 1920s case work was introduced into welfare practice by Alice Salomon and Siddy Wronsky drawing upon the work of Mary Richmond; in the 1950s social case work received new impetus with the help of American, British and Dutch experts. Community organisation has no specific tradition in Germany. It was developed at the end of the 1960s by social workers because methods of social case work and social group work turned out to be inadequate in new developments, new cities and redevelopment areas of traditional urban centres.

In the 1970s social action was introduced particularly by autonomous citizen action and self-help groups as a means to mobilise the public. At the same time the methodological approach of social case work was refined and supplemented by new approaches such as Gestalt therapy.

Germany, West

Building on history and tradition the FRG has developed different facets of an interesting welfare mix in the fields of fund-raising, welfare organisation and service administration. The enormous amount of social security benefits (two-thirds of the social budget of 572 billion DM in 1985) is financed in equal amounts by private households, employers and the taxpayer. Nearly every citizen of the FRG - including resident foreign workers - is a member of this collective provision community with regulations laid down by law and safeguarded by federal authority. In the field of welfare organisations there is historical competition between traditional welfare service organisations, newly emerging local initiatives and self-help groups sponsored by new social movements - which may develop into big welfare organisations in the future or disappear from the field - and communal service agencies which offer their experience and services to target groups free of charge and with public grants. These grants authorise public authorities to supervise and control the professional standards of the services and the adequacy of their infrastructure. Social work education has a broad and pluralistic base without adhering too closely to the 'three classical methods of social work'; it produces a sufficient number of well-trained social workers with a general and generic methods orientation by following a more pragmatic line of professional performance.

The main criticism of this welfare mix system comes from the right as well as the left side of the political spectrum. Conservatives complain that the heavy burden of the social welfare and security system makes the average working hour in the FRG too expensive for effective competition of German products and services on the international market. Socialists are worried that this system is not rooted deeply enough to survive an economic depression comparable to the Great Depression of 1929, which paved the way for the Third Reich of German Fascists.

Germany, West

REFERENCES AND FURTHER READING

Brauns, Jans-Jochen & Kramer, David (eds) (1986), Social Work Education in Europe. A Comprehensive Description of Social Work Education in 21 European Countries, Frankfurt: Eigenverlag des Deutschen Vereins.

Der Bundesminister fuer Arbeit und Sozialordnung (1978), Sozialbericht 1978, Bonn.

───── (1984), Sozialbericht 1983, Stuttgart: Kohlhammer.

Eyferth, Hanns (ed.) (1984), Handbuch Sozialarbeit/ Sozialpadagogik, Neuwied: Luchterhand Verlag.

Flamm, Franz (1983), The Social System and Welfare Work in the Federal Republic of Germany, Frankfurt: Eigenverlag des Deutschen Vereins (2nd English edition translated from the 3rd German edition Frankfurt 1980).

Kreft, Dieter & Mielenz, Ingrid (ed.) (1980), Woerterbuch Soziale Arbeit, Weinheim: Beltz Verlag.

Landwehr, Rolf & Baron, Ruedeger (ed.) (1983), Geschichte der Sozialarbeit. Hauptlinien ihrer Entwicklung im 19. und 20, Jahrhundert. Weinheim: Beltz Verlag.

Mollenhauer, Klaus (1986), Einfuehrung in die Sozialpaedagogik, Weinheim: Beltz 1964.

Mueller, Wolfgang C. (1986), Wie Helfen zum Beruf wurde. Band 1: Methodengeschichte der Sozialarbeit 1883-1945, Weinheim: Beltz.

───── (1987a), Wie Helfen zum Beruf wurde. Band 2: Methodengeschichte der Sozialarbeit 1945-1985, Weinheim: Beltz.

───── (ed.) (1987b), Einfuehrung in die Soziale Arbeit, Weinheim: Beltz.

Projektgruppe Soziale Berufe (ed.) (1981a), Sozialarbeit: Ausbildung und Qualifikation. Expertisen I, Muenchen: Juventa Verlag.

Germany, West

_____ (1981b), <u>Sozialarbeit: Problemwandel und Institutionen. Expertisen II</u>, Muenchen: Juventa Verlag.

_____ (1981c), <u>Sozialarbeit: Professionalisierung und Arbeitsmarkt. Expertisen III</u>, Muenchen: Juventa Verlag.

Sachsse, Christoph & Tennstedt, Florian (1980), <u>Geschichte der Armenfuersorge in Deutschland. Vom Spaetmittelalter bis zum 1, Weltkrieg.</u> Stuttgart: Kohlhammer.

Sozialbericht (1986), <u>Deutscher Bundestag</u>, 10/5810 vom 1.7.

Deutscher Verein fuer oeffentliche und private Fuersorge (ed.) (1980), <u>Fachlexikon der sozialen ARbeit</u>, Frankfurt: Eigenverlag d.Dtsch.Vereins.

ITALY
Maurizio Ferrera

THE WELFARE SYSTEM ENVIRONMENT

Ideological Environment

The first pillars of the Italian welfare system were posed during the era of liberalism - the six decades between the unification of the country in 1861 and the Fascist take-over of 1922. The liberal principles of individual insurance and employers' liability, in the context of a watchful but minimal state, moulded the first welfare schemes, that is, the Occupational Injury Insurance and the Old Age (voluntary) Insurance introduced in 1898 (Jocteau 1987).

This first lay (non-church) imprint on Italian welfare was soon overwhelmed, however, by Catholic activism. Starting with the papacy of Leo XIII (1878-1903) the church greatly increased its attention towards social questions and mobilised its resources to counterbalance the 'secular' approach of the liberal elite. The social doctrine of the Catholic Church imposed itself as the most prominent ideological force behind Italian welfare policies and its influence lasted throughout the twentieth century - a doctrine centred on the principles of social harmony, of collaboration between classes and groups and of christian charity. According to this doctrine, external (and especially public) interventions in response to social needs ought only to play a 'subsidiary' role with respect to the self-reliance of primary social groups. This 'subsidiarity' criterion has prevented the development of universalistic policies within the Italian welfare system (at least until recently), but has allowed for the proliferation of special programmes targeted to single groups and/or contingencies (especially in the 1950s and 1960s) and is thus responsible for the marked fragmentation which still characterises the Italian welfare state (Cherubini 1977).

The socialist tradition has played an important, but ambiguous role with respect to social policy. Ideas of workers self-help had a short-lived diffusion in the last decades of the nineteenth century (Paci 1984). The maximalism of the socialist party kept it largely aloof from the early politics of welfare before the advent of Fascism. In the first two post-war decades, the orthodox Marxist-Leninist leanings of the Italian Left pushed it to pursue a strategy of short-term defence of the core industrial workers' interests, in a substantial destruction of social democratic reformism (and in a hope of a capitalist collapse) (Regini & Regonini 1981).

In the course of the last 15 years, a new ideological mix has, however, gradually emerged with respect to social problems. The 1970s was an important decade for Italy, one that witnessed a process of substantial modernisation and secularisation. Major changes have occured, which have drastically modified the character of Italian society. Divorce was introduced in 1971 and retained after a referendum promoted by the Catholic Church in 1974. Family law was thoroughly reformed and fully modernised in 1975; the age of majority was lowered in 1975 to 18. Equal treatment between men and women with respect to work was introduced in 1977 and abortion was legally authorised in certain circumstances in 1978. As the Catholic Church was loosing its influence on Italian society, the Left was toning down its anti-capitalist and Marxist dogmatism. It was gradually embracing a more 'social-democratic' approach, centred on welfare reformism. As a result of these developments, a number of important steps were taken to rationalise the welfare system. There was also the emergence of a new 'populism', stemming from the convergence of Christian democratic and communist interests, towards welfare <u>largesse</u>, heedless of financial implications, which was conducive to serious budgetary strains. As a reaction to this, a 'neo-liberal' approach has gained ground in recent years, stressing the need for (and the merits of) a more austere social policy and advocating, at least, a partial

Italy

retrenchment of the state from the provision of social welfare support.

Historical Origins

As shown in Table 1, the origins of the Italian Welfare State can be traced back to the last decade of the nineteenth century, when the first social insurance scheme was introduced, covering work accidents. The liberal phase of welfare development witnessed also the establishment of two other social insurance schemes, covering old age and invalidity, and unemployment. A number of proposals were also put forward after the First World War for the introduction of a sickness insurance scheme. By the early 1920s, a system of social security had fully emerged in Italy, in line with the European trend.

The advent of Fascism (1922-45) marked the beginning of a second phase. In order to curb the strength of the organised working class, the new regime quickly restrained the expansion of insurance programmes. With the creation of a corporatist state in 1927, however, fascism started to view and use the welfare system as an instrument of social control (Terranova 1975). Thus the 1930s witnessed a large expansion of social programmes, especially for mothers, children (more generally, the family) and the poor. A number of minor occupational categories were granted special privileges in order to secure their political support (particularly public employees). At the beginning of the 1940s the Italian state already appeared as an articulated and pervasive complex of institutions characterised by a high degree of fragmentation (Cherubini 1977).

After the war, a thorough debate was initiated on the desirability of restructuring the liberal and fascist legacy. A parliamentary commission proposed the replacement of the various occupational insurance schemes with a single unitary insurance covering all workers (a sort of Italian 'Beveridge Plan') (Commissione per la Riforma della Previdenza Sociale 1948). Due to financial difficulties and political opposition, this proposal was not supported by parliament and the traditional framework of social policy was restored, with only minor changes and improvements (see Table 1). The 1950s and 1960s were a period of rapid expansion. Social programmes witnessed

TABLE 1: MAJOR EVENTS IN THE HISTORY OF THE ITALIAN WELFARE STATE

1898	Introduction of insurance against occupational injuries and voluntary insurance against old age and invalidity.
1919	Introduction of insurance against old age, invalidity and unemployment.
1928	Introduction of tuberculosis insurance; all employment contracts should foresee sickness insurance.
1936	Introduction of family allowances to all employees.
1945	Introduction of survivors insurance.
1946-48	Rationalisation of sickness insurance.
1950	Introduction of maternity insurance.
1952	Pension reform: improvement of pension formula and introduction of pension minima.
1968	Reform of financial and administrative regulation for hospitals. Improvement of unemployment benefits.
1969	Pension reform: introduction of earnings-related and social pensions; cost-of-living indexation.
1972	Jurisdiction over social assistance and services transferred to regions.
1974	Hospital assistance transferred to regions.
1977	Social assistance agencies and funds liquidated; jurisdiction transferred to local authorities.
1978	Establishment of the National Health Service.

real growth (see Table 2), resulting in some benefit improvements, but above all in massive coverage extensions (particularly to the self-employed) (Ferrera 1986). The inauguration of a Centre-Left government and the inclusion of the Socialist party into the governing coalition in 1962 gave a new impulse to welfare development and initiated a rigorous commitment to social reformism (Centorrino 1976; Delogu 1967). As Table 2 shows, during the Centre-Left period (1960-75) income maintenance and health almost doubled their share of the GDP. Major institutional innovations were introduced between 1968 and 1972, changing the structure of many social policies. Thus the first half of the 1970s really represented the heyday of the Italian Welfare State. Around the mid 1970s, however, a new phase of development began inaugurating a process of thorough-going restructuring of both social security and social services. At its beginning this process was predominantly intended to promote a further improvement and the modernisation of these sectors, via the transfer of jurisdiction over social services to local authorities and the creation of a National Health Service (NHS). The worsening of the economic crisis gradually shifted the emphasis from these objectives to that of restraining welfare expenditure in response to growing fiscal problems. As Table 2 shows, the rhythm of expansion of social expenditure indeed slowed down in the 1975-85 period, but fiscal imbalances are still severely straining Italy's public budget.

TABLE 2: SOCIAL EXPENDITURE IN ITALY BY MAJOR COMPONENT, 1955-1985 (of GDP)

	1955	1960	1965	1970	1975	1980	1985
Income Maintenance	6.6	7.7	9.8	10.0	13.8	13.7	15.9
Health	1.2	2.2	3.0	4.0	5.9	5.8	5.7
Social Assistance	2.4	2.1	1.8	1.8	1.5	1.3	1.5
TOTAL	10.2	12.0	14.6	15.8	21.2	20.8	23.1

SOURCE: Instituto Centrale di Statistica, Rome

The Socio-Economic and Political Context

At the beginning of the 1950s, Italy was to a large extent still an agrarian country, with widespread unemployment. In the three and one-half decades since, the Italian occupational structure has rapidly evolved towards the pattern typical of an advanced economy (Brunetta 1982). The shift from agriculture to the industrial and tertiary (service) sectors, and the relative growth of the self-employed have put heavier burdens on social security programmes, since industrial and tertiary employees normally enjoy better entitlements (Ferrera 1984). Economic growth has been rapid, but unevenly distributed: the North/South cleavage has not been overcome and the economic backwardness of many regions still calls for continuous and active support from the central government. Southern underdevelopment has always been, and still is, a major preoccupation and target of Italian social policy (Becchi Collida 1979; Boccella 1982; Forte 1978).

Significant pressures have also resulted from demographic changes. The proportion of the aged (60 and over) has risen from 12.2 to 17.4 per cent in the period 1951-81. The ageing of the Italian population has had immediate repercussions on the pension and health systems (Ferrera 1986; Ferrera & Zincone 1986).

Italy's constitution dates from 1948. It provides for a President, chosen for a seven year term by the members of the Italian national assembly, a two chamber body: Chamber of Deputies and the Senate. The President is empowered to dissolve the national assembly and to nominate the Premier. The executive power rests with the Council of Ministers or Cabinet, comprising the Premier and, and as a rule, other members of the national assembly.

The judiciary is constitutionally independent of the executive.

There are 20 autonomous regions in Italy, divided into 94 provinces, but the major unit of local government is the commune, of which there are more than 8,000.

Italy has a multi-party system characterised by a high degree of fragmentation (multiplicity of parties), factionalism (factions within parties) and polarisation (high ideological distance between parties, especially between Opposition and Government parties). The participation in highly fragmented and ideologically divided coalitions has made it difficult for each partner to promote and implement its own social policy fully. The Italian Welfare State has thus developed through a proliferation of minor laws for selected problems and clients, each of which a single party has had a specific interest in promoting but no party a specific interest to oppose. This is particularly true in the case of pensions (Regonini 1984). Moreover, all important reforms involving structural change have been systematically delayed, in a roll-over process of small counter-adjustments needed to integrate the interests of all the coalition partners (Ferrera 1987).

Italy

THE WELFARE SYSTEM: AN OVERVIEW

Organisation

From an institutional and administrative view-point, the Italian welfare system is sub-divided into three distinct sectors: social insurance (<u>prevedenza</u>), health and sanitation (<u>sanita</u>) and social assistance (<u>assistenza</u>). Social insurance includes six major schemes: pensions, unemployment, tuberculosis, family allowances, sickness and maternity, occupational injuries and diseases. These schemes are administered by a number of separate agencies and funds associated with selected occupational categories. The central position is, however, occupied by two agencies created during Fascism, namely the INPS (National Institute for Social Insurance) and INAIL (National Institute for Occupational Injuries Insurance). INPS represents the institutional and administrative core of the Italian welfare state. It pays more than 90 per cent of all benefits to private sector contributors. This agency is governed by a board which includes representatives of the unions, the employers' association, the self-employed associations and the Ministry of Labour. Since 1969 the administration of INPS has been gradually decentralised. It is now sub-divided into 18 separate funds, each with local branches.

Until the establishment of the National Health Service (NHS) in the late 1970s, the health sector was institutionally fragmented, being dispersed among a number of separate funds and agencies.

The largest of these was the National Institute for Health Insurance (INAM), which operated a general scheme for employees and their dependents. With the creation of the NHS, all occupational funds and agencies, including INAM, have been liquidated. The administrative structure of the NHS is broadly decentralised. At the central level, it is co-ordinated by the Ministry of Health, in collaboration with a National Health Council comprising representatives from the regions, various ministries, a number of experts and the Higher Institute for Health (a technical research centre). The Ministry develops the guidelines for the National Health Plan which must be presented to Parliament for approval every third year.

Italy

The regions have extensive powers in organising their own health services. They develop their own regional health plans. Local governments take care of the basic administration of health services through special units called Local Health Units which provide all services, including public hospitals (there must be one unit for every 50,000-200,000 inhabitants). The local health units are run by an executive board nominated by the general assembly of the respective local government.

A high degree of fragmentation characterised also the third sector of the Italian welfare system - social assistance - until the early 1970s. This was in fact provided by a variety of public charity institutions, a few social security agencies and local governments. Numerous reforms have, however, thoroughly restructured this sector in the second half of the 1970s. The basic unit for the provision of social assistance and social services is now the commune, which operates according to a legislative framework established by the central government and the regions. The commune has wide organisational and administrative autonomy and normally coordinates the provision of social services with that of health services through the local units of the National Health Service.

The Italian welfare system rests very heavily on the public pillar. Private provision of benefits and services has traditionally played only the marginal role of supplementing public provisions. The last few years, however, have witnessed a clear growth of private insurance in the pension and health fields (Ferrera & Zincone 1986; FOR 1986). The voluntary sector has long been monopolised by the Church, but there seem to be signs of an accelerating secularisation and re-vitalisation (Rossi & Donati 1982).

Financing Social Welfare

The main source of financing for the Italian welfare system is social security contributions. This is especially true for the sectors of income maintenance and health, although the reforms of the 1970s (especially the 1978 reform) have gradually increased the importance of general revenue financing of health services. Social assistance and services have always been financed largely out of general revenues.

Italy

The greatest share of social security contributions is paid by employers, who pay the entire cost of unemployment, maternity, TB and family allowance insurance. The rate of contributions for these schemes varies according to the economic sector and the type of scheme (in 1985 the range was 0.53 per cent - 6.5 per cent of the payroll). For pension insurance the employers pay two-thirds of the contribution, the remaining one third is paid by the employees. In the case of health insurance, employees pay very little share (one per cent) and the rest is borne by the employers (17 per cent).

The self-employed pay flat-rate yearly contributions to the schemes to which they belong. The state pays statutory 'solidarity' contributions to the pension fund for agricultural self-employed. It also pays a statutory contribution to the fund which provides social pensions to the aged poor. The state participates in the financing of social insurance in two other ways: through ad hoc interventions, aimed at relieving the employers of part of their contributions in order to reduce labour costs in periods of economic crisis; and through ad hoc interventions in order to cover the deficits between receipts and expenditures of the various funds. This second type of interventions has been increasing enormously since the 1970s, particularly with respect to pension funds. Given that these funds have access to the Treasury for their financial requirements, their growing deficits are held as largely responsible for the fiscal imbalances of Italy's public sector.

The 1980s have witnessed the emergence of serious financial strains within the health budget. The state has increased the rate of contributions and its own ad hoc interventions. Two other channels of financing have been inaugurated: user charges and an ear-marked supplementary tax on personal incomes, with a rate of 4-7 per cent (depending upon the income bracket).

THE AGED

The Italian social security system provides relatively generous retirement benefits to the aged population. Old age and survivors pensions are offered by a number of occupational schemes

Italy

covering dependent workers (blue collar workers since 1919 and white collar workers since 1939); the self-employed (small farmers, share-croppers and tenant farmers since 1957, artisans since 1959 and small traders since 1966) and civil servants (since the last century); and a variety of minor schemes providing benefits to special professional groups.

Social Security

Pension insurance is compulsory for all the economically active (dependent and self-employed); the unemployed in receipt of insurance benefits are also eligible for pension rights, whilst housewives can join a voluntary scheme. In 1969 a special scheme was introduced to provide a social pension for the aged with very low incomes and not eligible for benefits under any other scheme.

Italian pension insurance aims at providing a sizeable proportion of the retiree's previous earnings by means of earnings-related pensions. It also aims at guaranteeing to all the aged at least a subsistence income, regardless of their previous occupational status, by means of pension minimum and social pensions. The structure of benefits varies greatly from one scheme to another. The standard old age pension for private employees insured under the general scheme amounts to 80 per cent of previous earnings, up to a ceiling, after 40 years of contributions. The age threshold is 55 for women and 60 for men. Public employees must retire at 65, but a pension may be claimed, regardless of age, after 20 years of service. The self-employed are not entitled to earnings-related pensions. They receive benefits which are based on the actuarial revaluation of their contributions. No pension however can be lower than the minimum applying to all pensions. Survivors pensions are granted to widows, invalid widowers, children up to the age of 18 (26 if students) and siblings. The level of benefits ranges from 60 per cent to 100 per cent (depending on the number and type of survivors) of the pension to which the deceased member would have been entitled. All pensions are indexed to the cost of living and to the minimum contractual wage in the industrial sector.

Italy

Personal Social Services

A wide range of welfare benefits is offered to the elderly, especially those falling beneath a minimum income threshold. These benefits are of a selective and discretionary nature. They fall under the jurisdiction of regional governments and are administered by communes with a variety of different formats. These include cash supports for aged needy and personal social services such as domiciliary help, meals-on-wheels, homes for the elderly, holiday centres, 'open' structures for permanent, temporary, daily accommodation and recreation and so forth. Given the local character of this type of assistance, there exist large inter-regional and intra-regional variations. In general, it can be said that social services are much more developed and advanced in the North and Centre regions than in the South, where this sector is still heavily moulded by the old tradition of 'institutional' social assistance.

Evaluation

Despite the relatively generous pension regulations (by international standards), and the array of services provided by communes, the aged are still a social group facing a high risk of economic poverty (Sarpellon 1982). The majority of Italian pensioners receive a minimum or social pension. In fact the beneficiaries of earnings-related benefits, matured during a regular working career, are still relatively limited in number. Social and minimum pensions are unable to guarantee a decent standard of living when they are the sole source of family income. Old age and widowhood may thus lead to impoverishment when other family resources fail. The inadequacy of the minimum or social pension exerts a pressure on the pension system, in the direction of further increasing benefits. A pressure in the opposite direction stems, however, from the very 'generosity' of the pension formula: the earnings-replacement rate is the highest of Western Europe, whilst age thresholds for pension benefits are the lowest. Thus the 'maturation' of the pension system (as well as demographic trends) is causing serious financial strains to the public budget. A broad reform plan is currently under discussion, aimed at slightly improving the amount

Italy

of basic flat-rate pensions and at curbing high earnings-related benefits provided by the public insurance scheme, leaving room for private and/or occupational supplementations on an actuarial basis (FOR 1986).

THE DISABLED AND HANDICAPPED

Recent surveys of the health status of the Italian population have revealed that the number of people affected by a serious disability or handicap amounts to some 1,700,000, of which 750,000 are considered severe. The breakdowns by nature of disability are as follows: 183,000 blind; 80,000 deaf and dumb; 146,000 mentally retarded; 683,000 affected by other movement disabilities. Considering that one person's disability or handicap tends to have significant consequences for the whole household, it can be estimated that the number of people coping with this problem amounts to some five million, almost nine per cent of the Italian population (CENSIS 1983).

Social Security

Cash support to the disabled is provided through invalidity pensions and occupational injury benefits. Compulsory invalidity insurance (which is part of the general pension insurance) covers all the economically active population. In principal, it offers earnings-related benefits, or contribution-related benefits in the case of the self-employed. The vast majority of invalidity pensioners are granted flat-rate minimum pensions - a minimum which is somewhat lower than the old age minimum. The number of invalidity pensioners has always been extraordinarily high in Italy in comparison with other Welfare States. Since 1971, invalidity pensioners have constantly been more numerous than old age pensioners. This has little to do with the disability rate of the Italian population. Rather, invalidity benefits have been extensively used as an indirect subsidy for underdeveloped areas with limited employment opportunities (most typically, the agricultural south) supplementing (or more often substituting) for a very low, flat-rate unemployment indemnity (Ferrera 1986; Gardner 1977).
    The insurance scheme covering occupational injuries and diseases protects workers in the

Italy

industrial sector and self-employed workers in the agricultural sector. This scheme offers earnings-related benefits for both temporary and permanent disability. It also provides in-kind assistance for the disabled and those affected by occupational diseases, as well as rehabilitation programmes.

General medical care for the disabled and the handicapped is provided by the National Health Service.

Personal Social Services

The NHS also runs local centres for daily care of the severely handicapped (sheltered workshops). Communes organise, in turn, training programmes for those handicapped who can enter the labour market (labour regulations provide specific incentives for the hiring of the handicapped). Discretionary cash support is offered to low income families with handicapped children. The blind and the deaf also receive a means-tested allowance. A special mention must be made in this context to the mentally ill. In 1978 a law was passed which promoted the de-institutionalisation of psychiatric patients. Asylums were 'opened' and a large number of their patients returned to their families. Special 'protected homes' and open centres of care were to be created for temporary help and custody; and infirmary staff and social workers were supposed to assist the mentally ill in their family contexts, in an effort to integrate professional and family care. At a decade's distance it is now recognised that this integration has not materialised to a satisfactory extent and that the closure of asylums has created more problems than it has solved. Alternative 'open' structures have remained very few; infirmary vigilance has not provided sufficient assistance to families and the trend (at least de facto) is now towards a partial re-institutionalisation of the mentally ill in specialised wards of public hospitals.

Evaluation

The distorted use of invalidity pensions has come under increasing attack in recent years due to the wide opportunities of client manipulations and even frauds which it has long permitted. A thorough review of the scheme is currently under

Italy

way, in conjunction with the unemployment insurance scheme. As to the personal social service provisions for this target group, the Italian situation in the 1980s can be described as one of 'unequipped ambitions', of grand designs and important innovations not accompanied, however, by the necessary organisational arrangements.

CHILDREN AND YOUTHS

Like almost all European countries, Italy has witnessed a constant decline of the birth rate since the early 1960s. Mainly as a consequence of this the relative weight of the young age cohorts within the population has fallen from 24.5 per cent in 1961 to 21.6 per cent in 1981.

Social Security

Parenthood is supported by the social security system through a maternity insurance scheme covering all economically active women. Female employees are entitled to an earnings-related indemnity amounting to 80 per cent of earnings while on their maternity leave, which starts two months prior to confinement and extends for three months after. An extra six month period of leave during the first year of life of the child, with job security and an indemnity equal to 30 per cent of earnings is also available. Female employees are entitled as well to paid leave in order to care for their sick child during the first three years of the child's life. Maternity insurance also covers self-employed women in the agricultural, artisan and commercial sectors, to whom a flat-rate natality allowance is paid when a child is born. Maternity and paediatric care (as well as counselling) are provided by the NHS.

Personal Social Services

Various forms of discretional support to needy mothers and children (including orphans) used to be offered until the mid-1970s by a National Institute for Maternity and Childhood (established in 1934 by the Fascist regime). Since 1975 the functions of this Institute have been transferred to communes. Single parent families receive a discretionary allowance.

Italy

In the last decade, the traditional institutional care of orphans has been increasingly paralleled by foster care - at least on an experimental basis. Adoption of orphans is regulated by the legal authorities. Before adoption can be legally finalised, a period of informal fostering is foreseen, supported by social workers.

Communes provide recreational and sporting facilities as well as holiday centres for needy children. Since the early 1970s, all children are entitled to nursery care in public nursery centres and kindergarten, run by communes.

From the age of three, children may enter voluntary pre-school education, provided by public institutions in every local jurisdiction. Compulsory education begins at six and extends until the age of 14. It comprises primary education (five years) and lower secondary education (three years). Voluntary upper secondary education lasts five years and leads to higher education at universities. Education is largely provided by state institutions, and is compulsory. It is free and special assistance is offered to pupils from poor families (free books, transportation and meals; after-school care and so forth). Enrolment fees are minimal for upper secondary education and relatively modest for higher education. A very limited number of scholarships are available for university students and a small allowance is granted annually to university students with incomes below a given level. Empirical research on all these compensation policies has, however, shown that their efficacy has been modest, if not altogether absent (Trivellato 1982).

Evaluation

Children and youth have been a prime target of local authority activism in the last decade. The number and quality of services is now considered to be largely satisfactory, especially in the North and Centre of the country. The supply of infra-structures, especially kindergarten, still falls short of fully satisfying the demand; but constant and rapid decline of fertility is gradually improving the situation. The strengthening of maternity insurance, the legalisation of abortion, the family and parental counselling offered by the NHS have all promoted

Italy

the emergence of more responsible and less burdensome child-bearing and child-rearing in Italian society.

NEEDY FAMILIES

According to a thorough and recent survey (Sarpellon 1982), 9.4 per cent of Italian families still live in destitution and another 11.4 per cent are to be considered in need, according to average national consumption standards.

Social Security

The main social insurance benefit specifically targetted to the family is the family allowance. This consists of a monthly flat-rate payment to all employees, to the unemployed in receipt of unemployment benefits, to pensioners and to the self-employed in agriculture. During the 1950s and 1960s, regulations regarding eligibility to this type of benefit and its amount varied across occupational and economic sectors. In the 1970s, regulations were fully standarised and family allowances became a single flat-rate benefit. In the 1980s, however, state policy turned towards selectivity. Entitlement to allowances has been tied to income, with families of employees earning 28-34 million lira per year (that is about 1.5 times the average household income) losing one or more allowances according to the number of children, and employees earning above 34 million lira losing all entitlements.

The Italian fiscal system takes family size into account and offers tax credits for family dependents. These take the form of income tax deductions of an amount which varies according to the number and type of dependents (children, spouse, parents, and so forth).

Personal Social Services

Discretionary support in cash and in-kind to needy families is provided by communes. The NHS runs local units for family counselling.

Evaluation

Poverty is much more evident in the South than in the North and Centre. Poor families in the South

Italy

tend to be large (six members or more), earning an income which is insufficient to guarantee a relatively decent standard of living. In the North and Centre poor families tend to be much smaller, one or two members living on a low (social or minimum) pension. Although undeniable progress has been made in combating family poverty since the early 1950s Italy is still amongst the highest rates of family poverty in Western Europe. Family supplements and allowances, and ad hoc local interventions, do not seem adequate instruments to cope with this problem. The idea of a 'guaranteed social minimum' has been put forward but the overall political and economic context does not offer much prospect for such a programme (Gorrieri & Guerzoni 1982).

THE UNEMPLOYED

Unemployment has always constituted a severe problem for the Italian economy, especially in the South.

Social Security

The social security system covers the risks of both full and temporary or partial unemployment. A single scheme (established in 1919) provides insurance benefits for full unemployment to all employees. Benefits consist of flat-rate daily allowances (of very modest amounts) for a maximum of 180 days per year. Earnings-related benefits, in case of full unemployment, are only granted to special categories and/or in special circumstances. Two other schemes provide benefits for temporary and partial unemployment, one for industrial workers (since 1941) and one for agricultural workers (since 1972). These benefits are earnings-related. Their duration and replacement rate is normally negotiated by unions, employees and the Ministry of Labour.

Until the early 1960s, the modest, flat-rate full unemployment indemnity constituted the prevailing form of cash support for jobless workers. Since the mid-1960s, however, the strong unions have pressed for an extensive resort to more generous temporary/partial unemployment benefits, which now represent the most common form of protection within the 'strong' sections of the labour market (typically in the industrial

Italy

North). The problem of unemployment within the 'weak' section (typically in the agricultural South) has been increasingly coped with in an indirect way, by resorting to invalidity insurance (Becchi Collida 1979). Through a relaxation of the eligibility criteria and of the medical controls for invalidity insurance, this type of benefit has in fact become a substitute for the flat-rate unemployment indemnity. In the early 1970s, the link between invalidity pensions and unemployment was even institutionalised. It was in fact decided that, in order to establish the extent of an applicant's invalidity, the socio-economic conditions of the area of residence - and in particular the available chances of finding a job - should be taken into account (this norm has been recently abolished and controls have become tighter).

Personal Social Services

Besides unemployment (invalidity) benefits, the Italian state has tried to cope with the problem of unemployment through a public monitoring of the labour market, aimed at easing entry into it. The traditional instrument used has been a network of local labour offices responsible for the allocation of available jobs, the organisation of waiting lists, training courses and so forth. Since the mid 1970s an array of new policy instruments have been experimented with (under the responsibility of regional governments), such as the creation of special employment programmes for young people in search of first jobs, coupled with vocational training initiatives; labour retraining schemes in connection with industrial restructurations and reconversions; and monetary incentives to encourage labour mobility.

Evaluation

Despite these recent efforts, however, state unemployment policy is still faulty and ineffective. Unemployment insurance displays a dual character: it grants full and strong protection only to a core group of workers, whilst providing only weak and often indirect support to peripheral or marginal groups in the labour force. The economic crisis of the early 1980s has aggravated this dualism and has exacerbated its perverse effects. The generous benefits offered

Italy

to strong workers have posed severe constraints on economic performance (for instance, discouraging labour mobility and encouraging absenteeism) and have generated trade-off problems between security and efficiency; the inadequate protection offered to weak workers has been a factor of impoverishment for families living in backward areas. Poverty due to unemployment is still quite prevalent in the South. A debate is currently going on regarding the appropriate policy interventions to standardise the unemployment insurance system and to bring about a more equitable distribution of protection opportunities throughout the working population (for example, through the establishment of a minimum social wage replacing unemployment benefits). More active measures for youth and Southern unemployment are also widely advocated.

THE SICK AND INJURED

During the 1970s health became a major target of Italian welfare policy. The old social insurance system, based on a variety of occupational schemes with different regulations, was widely accused of being economically inefficient and incapable of guaranteeing adequate and equitable standards of care. Moreover, it had many coverage gaps, thus leaving some sectors of the Italian population without medical protection. In 1978, after almost two decades of heated discussions, a National Health Service was created, with a single general scheme covering all citizens regardless of their occupational status. This scheme replaced all previous schemes (except for a smaller TB insurance) (Ferrera 1987).

Social Security

The NHS provides health assistance at three different levels: firstly, basic care, offered free of charge by family practitioners in their own small ambulatories; secondly, specialist and diagnostic care, offered for a small fee by specialised physicians in larger public ambulatories or in private treatment centres under contract with the NHS; thirdly, hospital care, provided free of charge in public hospitals or in clinics under contract with the NHS. Pharmaceuticals are supplied for a small charge at

Italy

the two first levels of care; no fee is requested for the consumption of drugs during hospital stays. A system of fee exemption applies depending on the social-economic conditions of users and the gravity of their illness. Low income users, invalids, handicapped and people affected by a number of serious illnesses (such as cancer, renal insufficiency, glaucoma and so forth) do not pay fees for pharmaceuticals, diagnostic treatments and specialised care.

Besides the provision of medical services, cash sickness benefits are paid to all employees, generally from the first day of sickness.

Personal Social Services

Special rehabilitation programmes are available for the disabled and the injured, in combination with the occupational injuries and diseases insurance. A great emphasis is placed within the NHS (at least in principle) on prevention. Local sanitation offices monitor environmental conditions and carry out sanitary controls on workers exposed to special environmental or work related risks. Local health units carry out epidemiological surveys in their jurisdiction and a number of groups (such as the aged, pregnant women, children) are selected as special targets for policy by the National Health Plan.

Evaluation

The establishment of the NHS certainly represents an important and tangible improvement over the previous situation. By introducing universal health care the reform of 1978 filled the serious coverage gaps of the old social insurance schemes. The standardisation of benefits and servces has, in turn, overcome the often absurd disparity of treatment across socio-economic categories. At almost a decade's distance from its creation, the balance sheet of the NHS is, however, regarded as highly unsatisfactory (Cavazzuti & Giannini 1982; Ferrera & Zincone 1986; Freddi 1984; Piperno 1986). The new service has failed, so far, to bring about a territorial standardisation of opportunities for care. The transfer of responsibilities to regional governments seems to have aggravated pre-existing disparities between North and South. Another unattained goal is the re-orientation of the

Italy

health system from high-cost, hospital-centred care to more effective community care, emphasising sanitation and prevention services. The administration of the NHS is chaotic. Both politicised and consumer dissatisfaction is widespread. There is an ongoing debate about the best possible ways of improving the quality of a well devised, but badly implemented, reform.

AN ASSESSMENT OF THE ITALIAN WELFARE SYSTEM

The expansion of social welfare represents one of the most significant developments in post-war Italian society. Income maintenance, health, education and the other social services have played a major role in the real improvement of living standards over the last 35 years and constitute, today, an essential element of the population's well-being.

The social security net has greatly extended its coverage. For some risks (most notably, illness) it protects virtually all citizens. Benefits have substantially improved in both real and relative terms, thus providing a more effective economic security for workers. It is important to note that benefit improvement did not slow down during the 1970s, thus showing that the Welfare State has been able to at least maintain its protection in times of serious economic recession. Transfer payments have grown to become an important component of the income of Italian households. Indeed they constitute the main or even the only source of income for a sizeable part of these households. Social policies have certainly contributed to the alleviation of poverty, at least understood in the sense of absolute destitution (which was still widespread in the early 1950s).

The data on inequality is more ambiguous. There seems to be some evidence that fiscal policies and family transfers have tended to mitigate earnings differentials. It must be emphasised, however, that the Italian social security system has always been oriented (at least institutionally, if not ideologically) less towards the equalisation of market incomes than towards their preservation in the public transfer system.

On the basis of these aggregate indicators and in a medium term, diachronic perspective, the success of the Italian Welfare State thus seems undeniable.

Behind the magic of percentages and averages, the picture is somewhat gloomier. Welfare benefits are real and substantial, but their distribution is far from being even and equitable.

In the first place, social security has manifestly failed some groups. Institutional regulations still bar in many ways access to welfare (for example, to underemployed and unemployed in backward sectors/areas or to those not yet employed); basic benefit levels are inadequate to guarantee a decent living standard to the impoverished elderly, widows, single parents, disabled, large households without adequate market incomes. To those who have been unable to share in the general economic progress of the post-war period the Welfare State has only distributed meager subsidies.

Furthermore, social security benefits and contributions are characterised by marked redistributive distortions. In a 'vertical' direction, in the case of both transfer payments (for example, pensions) and public services (for example, education) there seems to be some evidence of a high share of expenditure flowing towards (lower) middle income groups rather than to poorer ones; in a 'horizontal' direction, some occupational categories seem to be clearly favoured in comparison with others (for example, the self-employed versus the employees, and within the latter, public versus private employees).

Finally, the quality and efficiency of the services provided by the welfare system - despite recent efforts of rationalisation - remains rather poor if compared to that of other advanced countries. The high degree of consumer dissatisfaction, especially in the health sector (Piperno 1986), and even the frequent discovery of fraudulent behaviours of welfare administrators testify that the system does not perform according to the 'good' standard set by the ambitious reforms of the past decade.

It remains to be seen if the vast debate currently occurring on welfare reform, and centred on the themes of a 'higher efficiency' and a 'return to selectivity' (Ferrera 1986), will be capable of producing adequate institutional and organisational changes, in the present context of political instability and financial stress.

Italy

ACKNOWLEDGEMENT

The research on which this article is based has been financed by a grant from the Italian Ministry of Public Education.

REFERENCES

Ascoli, U. (ed.) (1984), <u>Welfare State all Italiana</u>, Bologna: Il Mulino.

Becchi Collida, A. (1979), <u>Politiche del Lavoro e Garanzia del Reddito</u>, Bologna: Il Mulino.

Boccella, N.M. (1982), <u>Il Mezzogiorno Sussidiato</u>, Milano: Angeli.

Brunetta, R. (1982), 'Marginalita e Precarieta nel Mercato del Lavoro Italiano', in Sarpellon, G. (ed.), <u>La Poverta in Italia</u>, Milano: Angeli.

Cavazzuti, F. & Giannini, S. (1982), <u>La Riforma Malata</u>, Bologna: Il Mulino.

Centorrino, M. (1976), <u>Consumi Sociali e Sviluppo Economico in Italia</u>, Roma: Coines.

Centro Studi Investimenti Sociali (CENSIS) (1983), <u>Spesa Publica e Politica Sociale</u>, Milano: Angeli.

Cherubini, A. (1977), <u>Storia della Previdenza Sociale</u>, Roma: Editori Riuniti.

Commissione per la Riforma della Previdenza Sociale (1948), <u>Rapporto sui Lavori della Commissione</u>, Roma: Ministero del Lavoro.

Delogu, S. (1967), <u>Samite Publico, Sicutezza Sociole e Programmatione Economica</u>, Tonino: Einaudi.

Ferrera, M. (1984), 'I Sistemi Previdenziali: Crisi e Prospettive', in Fondazione Agnelli, <u>Atlante di Futurama</u>, Torino: Fondazione Agnelli.

_____ (1986), 'Italy', in Flora, P. (ed.), <u>Growth to Limits. The West European Welfare States Since World War II</u>, Vol.2, Berlin & New York: De Gruyter.

Italy

---- (1987), 'The Politics of Health Reform: Origins and Performance of the Italian Health Service in a Comparative Perspective', in Freddi, G. & Bjorkmanm, J.W. (eds), <u>Controlling Medical Professionals: the Comparative Politics of Health Governance</u>, London: Sage.

---- & Zincone, G. (eds) (1986), <u>La Salute che Noi Pensiamo: Domanda Sanitaria e Politiche Pubbliche in Italia</u>, Bologna: Il Mulino.

Forte, F. (ed.) (1978), <u>La Redistribuzione Assistenziale</u>, Milano: Etas.

Freddi, G. (ed.) (1984), <u>Rapporto Perkoff: Salute e Organizzazione nel Servizio Sanitario Nazionale</u>, Bologna: Il Mulino.

Futuro Organizzazione Risorse (FOR) (ed.) (1986), <u>La Sfida dei Fondi Pensione</u>, Roma: FOR.

Gardner, C.M. (1977), 'Previdenza Sociale e Esodo Agricolo in Italia', <u>Rivista di Economia Agraria</u>, 3, 679-95.

Gorrien, E. & Guerzoni, L. (1982), <u>Il Salano Sociole Famiglia e Reddito nella Crisi della Stato Assistentiale</u>, Roma: Edizioni Lavoro.

Jocteau, G. (1982), 'Le Origini della Legislazione Sociale in Italia. Problemi e Prospettive di Ricerca', <u>Movimento Operaio e Socialista</u>, 2, 289-303.

Paci, M. (1984), 'Il Sistema Italiano di Welfare tra Tadizione Clientelare e Prospettive di Riforma', in Ascoli, V. (ed.), <u>Welfare State all Italiana</u>, Bologna: Il Mulino.

Piperno, A. (ed.) (1986), <u>La Politica Sanitaria in Italia</u>, Milano: Angeli.

Regini, M. & Regonini, G. (1981), 'La Politica delle Pensioni in Italia: il Ruolo del Movimento Sindacale', <u>Giornale di Diritto del Lavoro e di Relazioni Industriali</u>, 10, 217-42.

Regonini, G. (1984), 'Il Sistema Pensionistico: Risorse e Vincoli', in Ascoli, U. (ed.), <u>Welfare State all Italiana</u>, Bologna: Il Mulino.

Italy

Rossi, G. & Donati, P.P. (eds) (1982), <u>Welfare State: Problemi e Alternative</u>, Milano: Angeli.

Sarpellon, G. (ed.) (1982), <u>La Poverta in Italia</u>, Milano: Angeli.

Terranova, F. (1975), <u>Il Potere Assistenziale</u>, Roma: Editori Riuniti.

Trivellato, U. (1982), 'Le Diseguaglianze Sociali nella Partecipazione e nella Riuscita Scolastica', in Sarpellon, G. (ed.), <u>La Poverta in Italia</u>, Milano: Angeli.

NETHERLANDS
Joop M. Roebroek

THE WELFARE SYSTEM ENVIRONMENT

Ideological Environment

Two ideological perspectives have dominated the history of social welfare in the Netherlands: firstly, the demarcation of responsibilities between church authorities, private initiative and public institutions; and secondly, the specific character of public social security arrangements. Should they obtain a more Bismarckian or a more Beveridgean outlook?

The first ideological dispute concerned poor relief. Originally support of the poor was a privilege of the church authorities who interpreted poverty as a moral problem: 'the needy are not able to live according to the laws of God'. In the sixteenth century this privilege was contested by the first generation of entrepreneurs, who were convinced that church charity deprived the upcoming working class of the coercion to perform their daily labour at the weaving looms. Charity became a social question, in which several social institutions, church authorities, private initiative and public institutions, for centuries competed with each other in order to gain control over the living conditions of the poor.

Until the middle of the nineteenth century the religious interpretation and practice dominated. Since that time, partly because of the strengthening of more secular economic views, and partly because of the actual deficiencies of existing provisions, the call for public social policy gained ground. In 1851 a first attempt to strengthen the role of the state failed. The

Catholic and Protestant churches appealed fiercely against the proposed Poor Law. In a second attempt, three years later, the state acquired its first, however restricted (residual) tasks. In principle local authorities had to leave the poor relief to the church and private initiative; only in case of 'absolute and inevitability' they were allowed to act themselves. This point of departure, the 'absolute inevitability', was linked with the Catholic principle of 'subsidiarity' (<u>subsidiariteit</u>) and the Protestant principle of 'sovereignty in own circle' (<u>soevereiniteit in eigen kring</u>): social policy should appeal to the own responsibility of people and social organisations; and only in case they fail, the state has the moral right, and even duty to intervene. The Poor Law (<u>Armenwet</u>) of 1912 in fact elaborated further on the principles of the 1854 Law and lasted until 1963 with the acceptance of the General Public Assistance Act (<u>Algemene Bijstandswet</u>) when the state obtained a central position in poor relief. Immaterial relief, partly financed by the state, remained in the joint hands of the church, private initiative and the state.

This fundamental discussion on the relation between state and society also marked the development of social insurance programmes since the end of the nineteenth century. It was not the introduction of social insurance programmes that exercised the minds, but rather the questions of coverage and administration. Until the 1950s the employers' organisations, the Conservative and Confessional political parties and Confessional labour unions opted for a Bismarckian interpretation of social security: the programmes had to be restricted to wage-earners, aimed at compensation and income replacement, financed by contributions of employers and employees, and administered by industrial insurance boards (<u>Bedrijfsverenigingen</u>) under control of employers and employees. The Social-Democratic party and labour union opted for a Beveridgean approach: programmes for the whole population, pointed at safeguarding from want for all citizens and some degree of income redistribution, mainly financed through taxation and administered by state institutions. During the interbellum and the first post-war years the Bismarckian option dominated the discourse and determined the development of the social insurance programmes.

Netherlands

Since the 1950s, the time the social security system acquired its present form, both options went hand in hand. And it was only since the economic crisis that new options were launched in the direction of a more selective system, in which the state only guarantees a minimal level of security and the above-minimal section is privatised.

Historical Origins

Initially, and that goes back to the middle ages, the church, private and, to a lesser extent public poor relief accounted for the essence of social welfare. The first origins of social welfare as a social security system can be traced back to the middle ages. Within the guilds, arrangements existed that supported members who fell into needy circumstances because of sickness, old age or death of family members, called the bussen or bossen. They covered not only artisans, but also the journeymen and apprentices. In the nineteenth century these funds extended their range and the risks they covered (for example into the field of health insurance), and new funds, especially mutual labour union sickness and unemployment funds (ziekenkassen and werkloosheidskassen) emerged. These social security arrangements, originally private, voluntary and without broad engagements, constituted the predecessors of the social security programmes of the twentieth century.
    The first compulsory social security programme was enacted with the Industrial Injuries Insurance Act (Ongevallenwet) in 1901. In 1919 a compulsory invalidity scheme (Invaliditeitswet) and an old age insurance scheme (Ouderdomswet) for workers was introduced and later on, in 1930, followed by a compulsory sickness insurance scheme (Ziektewet) for workers. Besides these new social security programmes other social welfare provisions, mainly for the unemployed, came into being: state contributions to voluntary unemployment funds, out-of-work payments, public provision of work and labour mediation. During the Second World War two important insurance acts were enacted: under pressure from the German occupation authorities the Sickness Fund Decree (Ziekenfondsbesluit), according to which all workers (and their employers) insured under the Sickness Act were obliged to pay contributions to the Sickness Funds

(Ziekenfondsen) 1941, and the Family Allowance Act (Kinderbijslagwet), passed in late 1939, and coming into effect in 1941. The Sickness Fund Decree of 1941 was replaced by the Health Insurance Act (Ziekenfondswet) in 1964.

Until the mid-1950s the social security system developed along pre-war lines. In 1947 the Old Age Pensions Emergency Provisions Act (Noodwet Ouderdomsvoorziening) was enacted, providing means-tested pensions for all persons over 65 irrespective of their previous employment record, and in 1949 a compulsory Unemployment Insurance Scheme (Werkloosheidswet) was enacted. The period of 1955 until the mid 1970s was probably the most salient phase of the development of the Dutch social security system. Not only because the system has fundamentally been extended and rounded off during that time, but also because that development has been combined with the aspiration to transform the more or less restricted (in terms of coverage, compensation and income replacement as main objectives) right to social security to a fundamental social right, laid down in the Dutch Constitution, and defined as the right to self-realisation and equality of rights. Three elements characterised that development. Firstly, the introduction of five national insurance schemes (Volksverzekeringen). These schemes covered the total population, had a flat-rate benefit and were administered by the state. Secondly, the 'causality principle' was eliminated. This led to the disappearance of the difference between disability caused by an industrial accident and disability as consequence of another origin. That was the result of the enactment of the Disablement Insurance Act (Wet op de Arbeidsongeschiktheidsverzekering) in 1966, and in 1975 the General Disablement Benefits Act (Algemene Arbeidsongeschiktheidswet). Thirdly, since 1963, in several, rather more incrementalist steps a social minimum was introduced as a floor within the different social security schemes, and the wage building in order to protect the income of families and single persons within the total framework of income relations, that is wages, social insurance and other social provisions. In 1974 net benefits for households according to the General Public Assistance Act were fixed at 100 per cent of the minimal wage for a married worker aged 23 and over. This was definitely settled in the Adjustment Mechanism Act (Wet Aanpassings-

Netherlands

mechanismen Minimumloon en Sociale Uitkeringen) in 1980. Figure 1 gives a summary of the social security legislation in the Netherlands.

FIGURE 1: EARLIER AND EXISTING SOCIAL SECURITY CORE LAWS

Social Security Law	Since	Until
Invalidity/Sickness		
Industrial Injuries Insurance Act	1901/1921	1967
Maritime Industrial Injuries Insurance Act	1919	1967
Agricultural & Horticultural Industrial Insurance Act	1922	1967
Invalidity Act	1919	1967
Miners' Invalidity Act	1936	1967
Interim Invalidity Pensioners Act	1963	1967
Disablement Insurance Act	1966	
General Disablement Benefits Act	1975	
Sickness Benefits Act	1930	
Old Age Pensions		
Old Age Pensions Act	1919	1978
Old Age Pensions Emergency Provisions Act	1947	1957
General Old Age Pensions Act	1956	
General Widow's and Orphan's Benefits Act	1959	
Health Insurance		
Sickness Fund Decree	1941	1964
Health Insurance Act	1964	
Exceptional Medical Expenses Act	1967	
Family Allowances		
Family Allowances Act	1940	1980
Temporary Family Allowance Act for the Self-employed	1951	1980
General Family Allowance Act	1963/1980	
Unemployment		
1917 Unemployment Decree	1917	1952
Unemployment Insurance Act (Old)	1952	1986
Social provisions for the Unemployed	1952	1965
Unemployment Provisions Act	1964	1986
Unemployment Insurance Act	1986	

Netherlands

Social Assistance

Poor Law	1894/	
	1912	1963
General Public Assistance Act	1963	
Government Unemployed Assistance Regulation	1963	
Incidental Payment Act	1981	
Additional Allowances Act	1986	
Income Provision Act for Elderly & Partially Disabled Unemployed Employees	1986	

Within the context of this historical overview four further themes should be mentioned. Firstly, along with the compulsory social security programmes several occupational social security schemes came into being, especially pension schemes. They cover approximately 20 per cent of all social security expenditure. Secondly, apart from the social security programmes in stricto sensu, there exist two programmes that deliver financial support to citizens, rent subsidies, mainly the Individual Rent Subsidy (Individuele Huursubsidie) since 1967, and State Study Allowance (Studiebeurzen) since 1951. Thirdly, the Dutch welfare system is predominantly a transfer system. The relation between social security transfers, health care (mainly transfers), and personal social services in terms of costs is 67.7, 26.3 and 6.0 per cent in 1985. The provision of public (financed) personal social services is relatively underdeveloped. There exist many small private institutions that provide personal social services. These services, based on the principle of giving support where individuals and family fail in providing the necessary relief, are located in several fields: health care, old people's homes, sick, child, old age and family care, social counselling, alternative assistance for youth, handicapped persons, centres for drug and alcohol problems. These activities are partly financed through the social security schemes and state subsidies as well as contributions of clients. This wide range of institutions originated from the earlier poor relief organisations and developed, especially since the Second World War, in diverse directions. Finally, since the end of the 1970s the economic crisis, accompanied by mass

Netherlands

unemployment and changes in the political power relations resulted in a reconstruction of the social security programmes. That reconstruction resulted in some far-reaching changes since 1 April 1986, and especially since 1 January 1987. In April 1986 the sub-systems of the Health Insurance Act (Ziekenfondswet) were brought together, and on 1 January 1987 three new acts came into force: the (new) Unemployment Insurance Act (Werkloosheidswet) as a replacement of the (old) Unemployment Insurance Act and the Unemployment Provisions Act (Wet Werkloosheidsvoorziening), the Additional Allowances Act (Toeslagenwet), and the Income Provision Act for Elderly and Partially Disabled Unemployed Employees (Wet Inkomensvoorziening Oudere en Gedeeltelijk Arbeidsongeschikte Werkloze Werknemers).

Political and Socio-Economic Environments

The Dutch political system is in a strict institutional sense based on proportional representation. The seats of the First Chamber of the Parliament (75 members) are indirectly assigned by the members of the Provincial States; the members of the Second Chamber (150 members) are each chosen for four years by direct elections. The Second Chamber is the main parliamentary institution that provides the government with a parliamentary majority, shares the legislative tasks with the government, and controls the public authorities.

For a long time Dutch politics was strongly influenced by its pillarisation. Besides the two Confessional 'pillars', the Catholic and the Protestant, there existed also a Socialist one. These pillars formed social, political and ideological entities, that had their own political parties, labour unions, press, charitative and social organisations. Concerning religious dichotomies an explicitly socio-political segregation between the different 'pillars' remained until the end of the 1960s. In 1954 this segregation culminated when the Catholic episcopacy interdicted by the so-called Mandement their church-members to join the Social Democratic party and the social democratic labour union. Since the end of the 1960s a fast process of 'deconfessionalisation' and 'depillarisation' has taken place. The Catholic and Social Democratic labour unions even merged in 1976. In a more general sense of 'belonging to', the religious cohorts in the population stayed relatively stable: Catholics in 1947, 38.5 per cent of the population, in 1981 37.5 per cent; the Protestants in 1947, 40.8 per cent, in 1981, 30.6 per cent, and 'no religion' in 1947, 17.1 per cent, in 1981, 26.8 per cent (Centraal Bureau voor de Statistiek 1984, p.79). Since the mid 1960s, the advent of prosperity, industrialisation, and mass communication eroded the tenacious group of religion and the churches over Dutch society, and weakened the influence of 'pillarisation'.

This depillarisation was reflected in a weakening of the parliamentary position of the Confessional political parties since 1963. Since the establishment of universal suffrage at the end of the First World War, Confessional parties had always kept a majority of the votes in the elections. In 1963 they still had a majority of seats in the second Chamber, but thereafter they slipped into rapid decline (in 1981 they had only one-third of the seats in this Chamber). This decline, however, was not reflected in composition of the Cabinet. Since the Second World War the Confessional parties formed a constantly dominant component of government (with the exception of the Den Uyl Government between 1973 and 1977). Between 1946 and 1958 they governed together with the Partij van de Arbeid (Social Democratic party). Since that time, with the exception of a brief intermezzo in 1965-66, the Netherlands has been governed by a series of weak Right-of-Centre cabinets, dominated by the Confessional parties. In 1973 the Social Democrats returned into the government until 1977. Since then Confessional-Liberal governments were in office, except for some months in the winter and spring of 1982.

The demographic parameters of the Netherlands reveal a process of population ageing. Between 1950 and 1980 the percentage of the population older than 65 grew from eight to 11 per cent, and the percentage of the people of the age of 80 and more from one to two per cent respectively. For the period until 2010 these figures are expected to grow to 16 and four per cent. This development was accompanied by a decline of the number of persons of 19 years and younger. The average figure between 1950 and 1970 was 37 per cent. Since 1970 the percentage of the population 19 years and younger declined to 31 per cent in 1980, and it is expected to decrease to 23 per cent in 2010. The total population of the Netherlands in 1984 was 14.1 million, and is expected to stabilise around the 15 million at the beginning of the twenty-first century (Sociaal en Cultureel Planbureau 1984, p.27).

Two important changes took place in the employment pattern of the Dutch population since the Second World War (see Table 1). Firstly, a relative shift of employment from the primary (agriculture and fishing) and secondary (industrial production) to the private service (transport, banking and trade) and the public sector appeared.

TABLE 1: EMPLOYMENT PATTERNS OF THE DUTCH POPULATION IN 1950-1980 (PERCENTAGE OF THE WORKING POPULATION

Sector	1950	1960	1970	1980
Agriculture/Fishing	15.4	11.1	7.6	6.2
Industrial Production	39.6	41.0	37.1	32.6
Industrial Services	34.6	36.2	43.2	46.7
Public Service	10.4	11.7	12.1	14.5
	100.0	100.0	100.0	100.0

SOURCES: Own calculations based on: 1950-70: CBS, Tachtig jaren statistiek in tijdreeksen, The Hague, 1979, p.68; 1980: CBS, Statistisch zakboek 1981, The Hague, 1981, p.128.

Secondly, the employment situation of the Dutch population deteriorated quite drastically, a process that started in the mid 1970s. Total employment as a percentage of the population between 15 and 65 years was quite low in the Netherlands. In 1980 it was 54.3 per cent falling to 51.9 per cent by 1983. An important aspect of that development is unemployment, and besides that a large number of persons that live with a disablement benefit (in 1984 772,000 persons got a disability benefit in the Netherlands, and 50 per cent of that disability can be ascribed to the labour market situation). The official

Netherlands

unemployment figure for 1984 is 14 per cent, but if one takes into account the 'unemployment-component' of disability regulations, it would probably exceed 20 per cent.

The number of welfare beneficiaries grew fast from 1.85 million in 1970 to 3.38 million in 1984. This development led to a strong expansion of social and public expenditure. Public expenditure as percentage of Gross Domestic Product (GDP) in the Netherlands increased 37.2 per cent in 1960, 47.4 in 1970 to 63.9 per cent in 1982; and social expenditure from 12.9 per cent in 1960, 22 per cent in 1970 to 36 per cent in 1982.

This development can be placed in a broader context of changing socio-economic forces. A conjunction of the high level of public expenditure, the international economic crisis, and, some years later, the growing demographic and economic constraints on the labour market, brought the Dutch welfare state into an uneasy position. More concretely, although inflation has been restrained since the beginning of the 1980s (see Table 2), economic growth was low, unemployment high and the budget deficit grew about 10 per cent of the GDP in 1983.

TABLE 2: ECONOMIC GROWTH, UNEMPLOYMENT AND INFLATION, 1966-1984

Year(s)	Economic Growth Percentage per annum	Unemployment Percentage of Employment	Inflation Percentage per annum
1966-70	5.5	1.3*	4.1
1971-75	3.2	2.7	9.3
1976-80	2.7	5.5	6.0
1981	-0.7	8.5	6.7
1982	-1.7	11.4	6.0
1983	0.6	13.7	2.8
1984	1.7	14.0	3.3

* 1967-70

SOURCE: economic growth 1966-70: OECD, <u>Historical Statistics 1960-1980</u>, Paris, 1982, p.40 (table 3.1); 1971-1983: OECD, <u>Historical Statistics 1960-1983</u>, Paris, 1985, p.44 (table 3.1); 1984: OECD, <u>National</u>

Accounts 1960-1984, Volume I, Paris, 1986, p.55; unemployment: 1966-1970: OECD, Historical Statistics 1960-1980, Paris, 1982, p.37 (table 2.15); 1971-83: OECD, Historical Statistics 1960-1983, Paris, 1985, p.41 (table 2.20); 1984: OECD, Employment Outlook, Paris, 1986, p.140; inflation: 1966-1970: OECD, Historical Statistics 1960-1980, Paris, 1982, p.77 (table 8.11); 1971-1983: OECD, Historical Statistics 1960-1983, Paris, 1985, p.83 (table 8.11); 1984: CBS, Statistisch zakboek 1985, The Hague, 1985, p.293.

A socio-economic environment has developed which places severe pressure, in terms of moderation and economisation of expenditure, on the future development of social security programmes and personal social services.

THE DUTCH WELFARE SYSTEM: AN OVERVIEW

Social Security Structure

Dutch social security is composed of national insurance schemes, social insurance schemes, for employed persons, social assistance provisions, and occupational programmes.

National Insurance Schemes. These programmes (Volksverzekeringen) are compulsory, and designed to cover the community as a whole. In principle, any person resident in the Netherlands is covered by the various forms of the national insurance provided under the General Disablement Benefits Act (Algemene Arbeidsongeschiktheidswet (AAW)), the Exceptional Medical Expenses Act (Algemene Wet Bijzondere Ziektekosten (AWBZ)) the General Old Age Pensions Act (Algemene Ouderdomswet (AOW)), the General Widows' and Orphans' Act (Algemene Weduwen-en Wezenwet (AWW)) and the General Family Allowances Act (Algemene Kinderbijslagwet (AKW)).

Employed Persons Insurance Schemes. These schemes are also compulsory. The relevant ones are: the Unemployment Insurance Act (Werkloosheidswet (WW)), the Sickness Benefits Act (Ziektewet (ZW)), the Disablement Insurance Act (Wet Arbeidsongeschiktheid (WAO)), and, only for reimbursement, the Health Insurance Act (Ziekenfondswet (ZFW)). Under the Health Insurance Act an earnings limit is set above which employees are not insured.

Social Assistance Provisions. These include: Public Assistance Act (Algemene Bijstandswet (ABW)), with its most important administrative regulation being the Government Unemployment Assistance Regulation (Rijksgroepsregeling Werkloze Werknemers (RWW)), the Additional Allowances Act (Toeslagenwet)), and the Income Provision Act for Elderly and Partially Disabled Unemployed Employees (Wet Inkomensvoorziening Oudere en Gedeeltelijk Arbeidsongeschikte Werkloze Werknemers (IOAW)). These provisions are means-tested.

Occupational Programmes. These refer mainly to pensions payments, unemployment payments, sickness and, to a lesser extent, disability payments. The supplementary occupational pensions schemes are organised either on an enterprise (Ondernemingspensioenfondsen), or an industry-wide basis (Bedrijfspensioenfondsen). Separate funds exist for doctors and medical specialists. Approximately 85 to 90 per cent of all private sector employees are members of one of the occupational pensions schemes.

Social Security Administration

Social Security Programmes. The administrative structure of the system is quite complex, partly the result of the historical development of the system, partly a consequence of the tension between central government on the one hand and organised industry on the other concerning the question whether central government should administer the insurance schemes or whether this responsibility should be in the hands of the employers' and employees' organisations.

The National Insurance Schemes, with the exception of the AAW and AWBZ, are executed through 22 public bodies, the Labour Councils (Raden van Arbeid), supervised by the Social Security Bank (Sociale Verzekeringsbank). Three of the social insurance schemes for employed persons (WW, ZW and WAO), and the Additional Allowances Act are administered by 26 Industrial Insurance Boards (Bedrijfsverenigingen), in which employers and employees cooperate. They are controlled by the Social Insurance Council (<u>Sociale Verzekeringsraad</u>), that represents employees, employers and the government. The WAO scheme is partly administered by the Joint Medical Office (<u>Gemeenschappelijke Medische Dienst</u>), which gives medical advice to the Industrial Insurance Boards. The same administrative framework is used to administer the National Insurance Scheme AAW. The Health Insurance Act, and the General Medical Expenses Act, as far as reimbursement of medical expenses is concerned, are administered by the Health Insurance Funds (<u>Ziekenfondsen</u>), private health insurers designated under the Act, and bodies operating the medical insurance schemes for civil and public servants.

The administration of the social assistance schemes and the Income Provision Act for Elderly and Partially Disabled Unemployed Employees is through the Ministry of Social Affairs and Employment; application in individual cases is entrusted to the authorities in the municipality, the Local Social Offices (<u>Sociale Diensten</u>). The daily routine of Dutch social security evokes an image of decentralised, and fairly autonomous practice. An image that is correct as far as the execution of policy-lines is concerned. However, the formulation and prescription of these policy-lines is a strongly centralised proceeding.

<u>Health Care</u>. The health system contains two forms of health insurance: the compulsory insurance schemes, according to the Health Insurance Act, and the General Medical Expenses Act, for people below a certain wage ceiling (70 per cent of the population), and private schemes for the higher income groups. Furthermore, there are ambulatory care and stationary care programmes. Most general practitioners in ambulatory care work are in single practice. They receive their fees from the Health Insurance Funds and the private health insurance organisations. District nurses take care of home nursing. They are employed by private - charitable - cross-societies, <u>kruiserengingen</u>, organised on a pillarised basis. Initially, these societies obtained their revenues from membership contributions. As time went by, they became more and more dependent on state subsidies, which were replaced by social insurance contributions in 1978. In spite of their growing dependency on public revenues they maintained their private and confessional character. Most

Netherlands

stationary and ambulatory institutions are private foundations (80 per cent). 60 per cent of the institutions have confessional administrative bodies.

Personal Social Services Administration

These services are provided by some 4,300 small institutions, which have emanated from (pillarised) private initiative. 1,800 of these institutions are old people's homes. These old people's homes are still strongly pillarised. In 1977, 60 per cent were confessional. Within family care, however, there has been a strong 'de-pillarisation'. In 1968, 77 per cent were confessional, while only 29 per cent were in 1977.

Social Security Finance

The various social welfare programmes are differently financed. And even within the general categories of programmes sometimes several methods of financing are used.

National Insurance Schemes. They are mainly financed on a pay-as-you-go basis through (earnings-related) contributions of employers and employees. The AAW, AKW and AWBZ are financed by the employers, who pay 6.2, 2.65 and 4.55 per cent of the wage (on 1 January 1987); the AOW and AWW are based on contributions of employees, respectively 11.75 and 1.25 per cent of the wage. All these contributions are paid up to a maximum income ceiling above which no additional contributions are required. That ceiling was 64,550 HFL on 1 January 1987. The AOW is also supported by a small central government subsidy.

Employed Persons Insurance Schemes. The financial basis of the insurance schemes for employees are also (earnings-related) contributions of employers and employees. These contributions are paid over a maximum of 262 HFL a day, except the ZFW with a maximum of 161 HFL a day (on 1 January 1987). They pay both the WW (0.7 and 0.7 per cent), the ZW (5.35 and 1.0 per cent), and the ZFW (4.9 and 4.9 per cent). The contributions for the WAO are only paid by the employees (14.4 per cent). This percentage holds only above a certain wage-level. There exists a premium-free base of 91 HFL (a day) on 1 January 1987.

Netherlands

TABLE 3: THE FINANCIAL SOURCES OF SOCIAL INSURANCE PROGRAMMES (MILLIONS OF GUILDERS)

	Employers	Households	State	Interest
1950	605	199	60	39
Per cent	67.6	22.6	6.0	4.0
1960	1,478	1,900	199	120
Per cent	39.3	52.2	5.3	3.2
1970	7,530	9,234	1,145	294
Per cent	41.4	50.7	6.3	1.6
1980	27,438	33,806	11,690	980
Per cent	37.1	45.6	15.8	1.3
1985	32,600	52,294	2,923	760
Per cent	36.8	59.0	3.3	0.9

SOURCES: 1950-1970: CBS, Tachtig jaren statistiek in tijdreeksen, The Hague, 1979, p.187; 1980: CBS, Statistisch Zakboek 1981, The Hague, 1981, pp.336-7; 1985: CBS, Statistisch Zakboek 1986, The Hague, 1986, pp.350-1.

Social Assistance Provisions. These are paid out of general revenues (90 per cent from central government and 10 per cent from municipal government, except the Additional Allowances Act, that is completely financed by central government). The voluntary occupational schemes are financed either by employers, or by both employers and employees.

These schemes have four financial sources (see Table 3): contributions of employers, contributions of households (employees), state subsidies and interest. The relative weight of the various sources changed over time. Especially the influence of the crisis and the growing financial problem of the central government cannot be overlooked.

The employers' contributions decreased steadily since 1970. Public financing increased between 1970 and 1980, but since then as the public debt has increased, state contributions have diminished as dramatically as the

Netherlands

contributions of households have increased. It looks like the financial burden of the economic and financial crisis, as far as social insurance is concerned, has been unloaded on the households.

TABLE 4: THE FINANCIAL SOURCES FOR HEALTH CARE AND PERSONAL SOCIAL SERVICES (MILLIONS OF GUILDERS)

Source	1981	Percentage	1983	Percentage	1985	Percentage
Health Insurance Act	13,015	36.7	14,389	36.1	14,981	36.5
Exceptional Medical Expenses Act	8,070	22.7	9,122	22.9	9,583	23.3
State	3,259	9.2	3,921	9.8	6,294	15.3
Consumers	8,783	24.7	9,981	25.1	10,284	25.1
Other	2,361	6.7	2,439	6.1	-81	-0.2
TOTAL	35,488	100.0	39,852	100.0	41,061	100.0

SOURCE: Ministerie van Welsijn, Volksgezondheid en Maatschappelijk Welzijn, Financieel overzicht gezondheidszorg en maatschappelijk welzijn 1986, Leidschendam, 1985, p.9.

Health care and personal social services. The financing of the health system (see Table 4) is partly based on contributions from the ZFW and the AWBZ, and partly on state subsidies and own contributions. Finally, social work is paid out of several sources, the AWBZ, the ABW and contributions of members of various non-profit organisations such as the cross-societies.

The largest part of the health and personal social services is financed by the two social insurance acts, the Health Insurance Act and the Exceptional Medical Expenses Act (59.8 per cent in 1985). Consumers contributed about 25 per cent, while the state contributions raised between 1983 and 1985 from 9.8 to 15.3 per cent.

Netherlands

So, more in general, social welfare in the Netherlands is mainly financed by contributions from employers and households (employees). Public financing is relatively low for the social security programmes, and only slightly higher for health and personal social services.

WELFARE BENEFICIARIES

Before the specific position of the different target populations is treated, two aspects of the more general position of the Dutch welfare beneficiaries are mapped out: the number of welfare beneficiaries and recent changes in income position of beneficiaries. The number of welfare beneficiaries almost doubled between 1970 and 1985 (see Table 5).

TABLE 5: THE NUMBER OF BENEFICIARIES OF THE DUTCH WELFARE STATE (x '000)

	Pensions	Sickness	Disability	Unemployment	Social Assistance	Total
1970	1,203	204	287	59	99	1,851
1980	1,494	268	662	239	125	2,788
1985	1,630	224	713	653	180	3,400
Percentual Share of Total Growth Between						
1970-75	27.5	1.3	27.5	38.3	5.2	
1975-80	31.2	6.8	40.0	19.2	2.8	
1980-85	22.2	-7.2	8.3	67.6	9.0	

SOURCE: Ministerie van Sociale Zaken en Werkgelegenheid, Financiele nota sociale zekerheid 1987, The Hague, 1986, blz.8.

In the 1970s a quite solidary attitude prevailed concerning the income position of welfare beneficiaries related to the position of the working population, strongly supported by the income policy of the Den Uyl Social Democratic Government (1973-7). However, this solidary attitude disappeared at the end of 1970s. Since

Netherlands

the early 1980s the relatively strong position of the welfare beneficiaries has been undermined, as a result of several Centre-Right governments being unable to maintain the relative position of welfare beneficiaries.

THE AGED AND SURVIVORS

In 1950 309,000 persons received an old age pension, in 1960 814,000, in 1970 1,061,000, and in 1980 1,333,000 persons; in 1960 116,000 persons got a survivors pension, in 1970 155,000, and in 1980 174,000 persons. In 1985, on the base of the AOW and the AWW, 1,459,000 and 174,000 people respectively were entitled to benefits, amounting together to 26,681 million HFL, that is, 20.7 per cent of total expenditure on social security (inclusive all pensions), or 6.4 per cent of GDP. In 1985 total expenditure on old age and survivors pensions amounted to 44,170 million HFL, that is 34.4 per cent of total expenditure on social security, or 10.6 per cent of GDP (see table 6).

Social Security

The pension system consists of the basic pension provisions, the General Old Age Pensions Act (Algemene Ouderdomswet (AOW)), and the General Widows' and Orphans' Act (Algemene Weduwen- en Wezenwet (AWW)), covering all residents, special pensions schemes for public servants, and a variety of occupational pensions schemes for private employees, and to some extent also for the self-employed.

Since 1957 all residents receive according to the AOW a flat-rate pension at the age of 65 which is related to the number of insured years (two per cent per year), and is supposed to provide a basic social minimum. Until April 1985 married women did not have an individual entitlement to a pension. Since that time they have an equal right to an old age pension. Man and wife receive a 50 per cent AOW benefit. If one of the partners is not yet 65, then he/she gets an additional allowance equal to the 50 per cent AOW benefit. This allowance is until 1 April 1988 independent of the partners earned income. After that date the additional allowance will be income-tested. From 1962 on, widows between the age of 40 and 65, and widows younger than 40 years of age, who are unfit

Netherlands

to work, or have one or more children under the age of 18, were entitled to a pension. Widows not qualifying for a pension under these conditions received temporary benefits. Since 1977 a number of early retirement schemes (<u>Vervroegd Uittreden</u> (VUT)) were introduced on the initiative of the government in collaboration with employers' and employees' organisations.

TABLE 6: PUBLIC EXPENDITURE IN 1985 ON PENSIONS

	Expenditure (Millions of Guilders)	Percentage
General old age pensions (AOW)	23,094	52.5
Early retirement pensions (VUT)[1]	895	2.1
Public servants' superannuation	7,025	16.0
Other public servants' pensions[2]	1,689	3.9
Enterprise pensions[3]	2,529	5.8
Industry-wide pensions[4]	1,960	4.6
Collective insurance pensions	3,880	8.8
Other occupational pensions	226	0.1
General widows' and orphans' pensions (AWW)	2,692	6.2
TOTAL	43,990	100.0

Notes:

1   Inclusive of government early retirement regulations.
2   Military pensions, pensions for ex-Indonesian public servants, and pensions for railwaymen.
3   <u>Ondernemingspensioenfondsen</u>
4   <u>Bedrijfspensioenfondsen</u>

SOURCE: Ministerie van Sociale Zaken en Werkgelegenheid, <u>Financiele nota sociale zekerheid 1987</u>, The Hague, 1986, p.84.

Netherlands

In addition to this general provision, there are various private sector supplementary pensions schemes, organised either on an enterprise (Ondernemingspensioenfondsen) or an industry-wide basis (Bedrijfspensioenfondsen). Separate funds exist for doctors, medical specialists and so forth. The industry-wide Pensions Funds Act of 1949 (Wet op de verplichte deelneming aan een bedrijfspensioenfonds) empowered the Minister of Social Affairs to make membership of such schemes compulsory, if requested to do so by employers' and employees' representatives. In 1980 there were 83 industry-wide funds in existence, 62 of which had compulsory membership. Pension schemes organised on an enterprise basis are also subject to some statutory control, under the 1952 Pensions and Savings Funds Act (Pensioen- en spaarfondsen wet), which covers the organisation and administration of pension and savings funds. In 1980 there were about 1,000 enterprise pension funds in existence, in addition to which 20,000 pension contracts were made on a collective basis with an insurance company. Approximately 85 to 90 per cent of all private sector employees are members of one of the occupational pension schemes. Occupational pensions funds bear risks either on their own, or by means of reinsurance with a life insurance company. However, no exact data are available concerning this reinsurance.

In 1985, expenditure on occupational pension scheme benefits amounted to 8,595 million HFL, 6.6 per cent of total expenditure on social security, or 2.1 per cent of GDP.

General pensions provide universal flat-rate benefits. The net old age pension for a married couple, or a couple living together, today equals the net minimum wage which is linked to a special wage- and price-index (Index van Regelingslonen). On 1 January 1987, this pension amounted to 1,106.21 HFL a month for single persons (with 67.76 HFL holiday allowance), and 799.47 HFL for the individual members of a couple, married or living together (with 48.40 HFL holiday allowance). For a couple that is about 53 per cent of average net earnings of households, and 79 per cent of national income per head of the population; for a single person that is about 67 per cent of average net earnings of individual persons, and 55 per cent of national income per head of the population. Widows with a child under the age of 18 are provided with a full pension.

Netherlands

Other widows receive the same amount as single pensioners, that is 70 per cent of a full pension.

Public servants receive a special old age pension which is co-ordinated with their AOW-benefits at a wage-and-service-years basis. Occupational pensions are also supplementary to AOW benefits. They differ from one industry or enterprise to another.

Personal Social Services

Within Dutch social welfare there exists a broad spectrum of personal social services for the aged. They cover housing facilities for the aged living on their own, old people's homes, family care, nursing-homes, cross-work, health care, socio-cultural, recreative and extra-mural provisions. A very rough estimation of total costs is about 12,000 million HFL, about three per cent of GDP in 1984.

The housing facilities for the aged living on their own consist of three kinds of subsidies. Firstly, and above all, the rent subsidies to lower income tenants, the Individual Rent Subsidies (Individuele Huursubsidies). In 1984 about 254,000 aged persons, received such a subsidy amounting to some 490 million HFL. Secondly, there is a rent habituation subsidy (huur-gewenningsbijdrage) for tenants who are suddenly confronted with a sharp rent increase, for example, people who had to move from a slum district to a new suburb. Finally, there exist special provisions for houses, in order to make them more suitable for aged persons.

In 1983, 134,733 aged people were living in 1,499 old age homes, that is about eight per cent of the total population over 65 years of age. On 1 January 1984, there further existed 150 nursing-homes for somatic patients, 85 homes for psycho-geriatric patients and 96 combined nursing homes. These homes account for about 48,000 beds, of which 27,000 are in the somatic sector and 20,500 in the psycho-geriatric sector. That is a capacity of about 1.2 beds per 100 aged persons. Total costs of age and nursing homes in 1984 were 7,471 million HFL.

Family care mainly concerns domestic help in case of sickness, handicap, the death of a partner or psycho-social problems, while cross-work (especially district nursing) provides help and services that allow the aged to live as long and as healthy as possible on their own. The total costs for 1984 came to 950 million HFL.

Finally there exist several socio-cultural, recreative and surveillance provisions: reductions for travelling, provision of meals, gymnastics, alarm-systems, telephone-circles, district homes and so forth.

Evaluation

The old age pensions arrangements improved since the Second World War. The replacement ratio increased from about 45 per cent in 1960 to 68 per cent in 1980 for a standard worker. The redistributional effects of the AOW and AWW are quite strong. Measured through the 'Theil-coefficient', these acts led in 1981 to a reduction of income inequality of 40 per cent (Muffels, Nelissen & Nuyens 1986).

The buying power of the AOW benefits has since 1973 grown faster than the minimal and modal wage, 22.7 per cent against 18.1 and nine per cent respectively. However, since 1979 the buying power of the AOW benefits has decreased strongly by 13.5 per cent, a 1.1 and 2.5 per cent faster decrease than the minimal and modal wage respectively over that period. This decrease of buying power since 1979 brings many of the aged and especially the 40 per cent that receive no or hardly any supplementary pension, into needy circumstances. The aged are over-represented in the category of people living on a minimal level of subsistence.

There exists at least one other major problem concerning the development of pension rights, the so-called 'pension-break', the fact that an interruption of the pension-building in consequence of job alteration, disablement or unemployment leads to lower (supplementary) pension-claims. The government and the social partners are working on proposals to overcome this 'pension-break' in the near future.

Some problems exist in the personal social services. Firstly, there are the rather selectivist policies of the various governments since 1980 which reduced the level of expenditure of the personal social services for the aged. Secondly, there are some shortcomings that should be improved in the near future: a better tuning-in of the several services; a better attainableness and accessibility of services; more decentralisation of planning (to regional and local governments) and harmonisation of the financial structure; and a higher degree of participation of the aged within the institutions that provide services.

THE SICK, DISABLED, INJURED AND HANDICAPPED

The distinction between sick, disabled, injured and handicapped disappeared in 1967 with the elimination of the 'causality principle' in social security arrangements. According to that change persons unfit for work owing to physical or mental illness and those whose incapacity is caused by an accident or industrial disease are treated equally.

Social Security

Sickness cash benefits according to the Sickness Benefits Act (Ziektewet (ZW)) are provided for a maximum period of one year, after which time general invalidity pensions based on the General Disablement Benefits Act (Algemene Arbeidsongeschiktheidswet (AAW), which may be supplemented by special invalidity pensions according to the Disablement Insurance Act (Wet Arbeidsongeschiktheid (WAO)) for employees, are paid. In 1950 61,000 persons received a sickness benefit, in 1960 93,000, in 1970 204,000 and in 1980 268,000 persons; and in 1950 121,000 persons received an invalidity pension, in 1960 161,000, in 1970 294,000 and in 1980 680,000. In 1985, on the base of the ZW, inclusive of the Public Servants' Sickness Benefits (Doorbetaling Salaris Overheidspersoneel (DSO)), the WAO, inclusive of the Invalidy Act, and the AAW 226,000, 565,000 and 218,000 people respectively were entitled to benefits, together amounting to 28,634 million HFL, that is 22.3 per cent of total expenditure on social security, or 6.9 per cent of GDP (see table 7).

Since the introduction of the Sickness Benefits Act in 1967 all employees, except the public servants that have their own scheme, are insured for sickness. Benefits are paid after a statutory period of two days, but large groups of the insured receive non-statutory benefits from the first day on from the Industrial Insurance Boards (Bedrijfsverenigingen), that administer the sickness insurance schemes. Sickness benefits are paid up to a maximum period of 52 weeks, after which the disablement schemes come into operation, and go up to the age of 65. Public servants' salaries are continued for a maximum period of 18 months, in case of temporary unfitness to work. After that period they receive a disablement pension.

TABLE 7: PUBLIC EXPENDITURE IN 1985 ON SICKNESS AND INVALIDITY

	Expenditure (Millions of Guilders)	Per Cent-age
Sickness Benefits (ZW)	7,555	26.4
Public Servants' Sickness Benefits (DSO)	3,730	13.0
Invalidity Pensions (IW)	162	0.6
General Invalidity Pensions (AAW)	10,893	38.0
Employees' Invalidity Pensions (WAO)	6,294	22.0
TOTAL	28,634	100.0

SOURCE: Ministerie van Sociale Zaken en Werkgelegenheid, <u>Financiele nota sociale zekerneid 1987</u>, The Hague, pp.84 & 86.

Sickness cash benefits are earnings-related up to a certain maximum wage ceiling. Until 1987 insured persons received 75 per cent of previous earnings. Since 1 January 1987 the benefits cover only 70 per cent. For persons or families who fall below the (monthly) social minimum of 1,103.97 HFL (for a person of the age of 23 and more) and 1,577.11 HFL for a family (on 1 January 1987), the benefit is supplemented according to the Additional Allowances Act (<u>Toeslagenwet</u>). That supplement is income-tested. So the minimal benefit according to the ZW for a couple is about 53 per cent of average net earnings of households, and 79 per cent of national income per head of the population; for a single person that is about 58 per cent of average earnings of individual persons, and 63 per cent of the national income per head of the population. For large groups of insured persons the statutory benefit of 70 per cent is supplemented by non-statutory regulations up to 100 per cent.

The system of invalidity pensions is based on two acts: the Disablement Insurance Act and the General Disablement Benefits Act. Both schemes insure against the financial consequences of lasting illness, disablement or occupational injuries, and provide pensions after a waiting period of 52 weeks during which time insured people are entitled to claim sickness benefits. The General Disablement Benefits Act provides a basic pension to all citizens between the age of 18 and 65, and with a certain income prior to disablement, and for at least 25 per cent invalidity. For so-called early-handicapped this income qualification for entrance naturally does not hold. The Disablement Insurance Act pays (also up until the age of 65) supplementary pensions to all employees, except public servants and railway employees, who are covered by their own schemes.

Invalidity benefits according to the Disablement Insurance Act correspond to the degree of the claimant's incapacity and previous earnings up to a certain maximum wage ceiling. Starting with a 15 per cent incapacity, there are seven benefit grades between 14 and 70 per cent of previous earnings up to the maximum, corresponding to different degrees of disablement. When the beneficiary is totally disabled, and requires regular attendance and nursing, the pension is increased to 100 per cent of previous earnings. Some of the beneficiaries are entitled to non-statutory supplementary benefits, which increases the 70 per cent benefit, sometimes even up to 100 per cent for a limited period.

Invalidity benefits according to the General Disablement Benefits Act are also based on a scale of invalidity. The benefits are flat-rate, not related to previous earnings. According to the degree of incapacity (six degrees) the beneficiary receives a benefit between 21 and 70 per cent of a standard daily amount. As per 1 January 1987 the standard daily amount was 91.74 HFL for persons aged 23 and older (for younger persons that amount decreases for each year). Since the implementation of the AAW in 1976, the WAO benefits have become supplementary. The WAO scheme defines maximum benefit to which a beneficiary may be entitled, and provides the difference between the AAW benefit and this maximum benefit. For persons or families that fall below the (monthly) social minimum of 1,103.97 HFL (for a person of the age of 23 and more) and 1,577.11 HFL for a family (on 1 January 1987), the benefit is supplemented according to the Additional Allowances Act (<u>Toeslagenwet</u>). That supplement is income-tested.

New since 1 January 1987 is the fact that the 'discount-regulation' is abolished. According to that regulation persons that were only partially disabled received, in case they were unemployed for the rest of the time, a full disablement pension. In the new situation the disabled will, in case they worked in the period before becoming disabled, for the remaining part be treated as if they were unemployed. In case they fall under the social minimum they can appeal to an income-tested extra allowance. After the unemployment benefit is ended (a maximum of three years), or in case the beneficiary does not have a labour past, the disabled person receives an income-tested (especially the income of the partner) benefit according to the Income Provision Act for Elderly and Partially Disabled Unemployed Employees (<u>Wet Inkomensvoorziening Oudere en Gedeeltelijk Arbeidsongeschikte Werkloze Werknemers</u> (IOAW)). That benefit is (on 1 January 1987) at the level of the social minimum of 1,495.80 HFL with a holiday allowance of 81.31 HFL for a family, 1,346.25 HFL with a holiday allowance of 73.18 HFL for a single-parent family and 1,047.05 HFL with a holiday allowance of 56.92 HFL (for a person aged 23 and more), and paid up until the age of 65. So here the minimal benefits in relation to average earnings and national income per head of the population are the same as for the Sickness Insurance Act.

<u>Health insurance arrangements</u>. The public health system is mainly financed through the health insurance systems, and some direct public expenditure. In 1965 8.8 million people (71.4 per cent of the total population) were insured, in 1975 9.4 million people (68.8 per cent), and in 1985 9.6 million people (66.5 per cent). In 1986 public health expenditure amounted to 29,237 million HFL, that is 22.8 per cent of total expenditure on social security, or seven per cent of GDP.

There are two major health insurance schemes.

Netherlands

Firstly, a scheme based on the 1964 Health Insurance Act (<u>Ziekenfondswet</u> (ZFW)), providing ordinary medical benefits, including in-patient and out-patient treatment, dental care and medicines; this scheme contained until 1986 four sub-systems: the compulsory scheme, the old people's schemes, the voluntary scheme and the supplementary scheme. On 1 April 1986 the sub-schemes were abolished, and since then there exists only one compulsory scheme.

All private employees and beneficiaries of social transfer payments, below a certain income ceiling (that is, an annual income of not more than 49,150 HFL in 1987), are compulsory insured. Family members without income are automatically covered (without an additional contribution). Public employees have their own comparable schemes, and in all other cases one has to insure through an insurance corporation with private or public legal status. The Health Insurance Act provides its members with so-called third-class free medical benefits. Additional contributions entitle the beneficiary to a higher class of benefits, but the real difference between the classes is relatively insignificant.

Secondly, a scheme providing special medical benefits, in particular, long-term treatment in institutions, based on the 1967 Exceptional Medical Expenses Act (<u>Algemene Wet Bijzondere Ziektekosten</u> (AWBZ)).

The Exceptional Medical Expenses Act covers all residents. The scheme reimburses exceptional medical care costs, in particular for long-term and special in-patient treatment. Since 1980 the services of the non-profit cross-organisations (<u>kruisverenigingen</u>) have mainly been paid through this scheme.

Personal Social Services

Services in the field of health care are provided by the cross-organisations, which provide nursing services, district nursing, family help and information services. Other facilities are ambulatory mental health care and school medical (especially dental) services.

The Handicapped Workers Labour Act (<u>Wet Arbeid Gehandicapte Werknemers</u> (WAGW)) of 1 July 1986 is meant to improve the position of the (partly) handicapped within the labour force. The Government forced the employers' organisations and

Netherlands

labour unions to take action in order to preserve and to enlarge the possibilities for the handicapped to work in a normal job.

For the handicapped there are nursing homes, centres for the deaf and blind, homes for the handicapped, and full-time home-care in special cases. The costs are covered by the Exceptional Medical Expenses Act. Further, several services are provided: special housing programmes, rehabilitation, social-pedagogic help, holiday camps and holiday mediation, information and documentation centres, and all kinds of specialised help for the handicapped.

Evaluation

The position of the sick, injured, disabled and handicapped did certainly improved with the reorganisation of the invalidity pensions and sickness cash benefits, the abolition of the 'causality principle', and the introduction of the General Disablement Benefits Act. The redistributional effects of the ZW, WAO and AAW are less than in the case of the pensions. Measured through the 'Theil-coefficient', these acts led in 1981 to a reduction of income inequality of 10 per cent (Muffels, Nelissen & Nuyens 1986). That lower figure is the result of the fact that the benefits for the ZW and the WAO are earnings-related. The buying power of the minimal sickness/disablement benefits grew faster until 1979 than the minimal and modal wage, 23.5 per cent against 18.1 and nine per cent; the above-minimal benefits stayed somewhere in between with their 16.8 per cent. However, since 1979 the buying power of the benefits decreased strongly with 13.7 and 22.4 per cent. For the above-minimal benefits the decrease is even stronger (5.6 per cent) than the increase between 1973-79. That was the result of the reconstruction of the social security system which began in 1983. The level of the benefits was decreased step-by-step from 80 to 70 per cent, a development that mainly affected the above-minimal benefits. It is too early to assess the full consequences of the abolishment of 'discount-regulation' since 1 January 1987. It is, however, quite clear that this regulation leads to a heavy loss of income in the case where the disabled person has an income earning partner.

Netherlands

The accessibility of health services through the insurance regulations is, in general, quite good and does not depend on income since almost 70 per cent of the population is covered by the Health Insurance Scheme. However, clear differences in treatment still exist between the treatment of privately and publicly insured people.

CHILDREN AND YOUTHS

Less than one third of the Dutch population are 19 years or younger and by the year 2010 it is expected to be a quarter.

Social Security

In 1980 a radical simplification of the legislation and administration of family allowances took place. The existing schemes for employees, the self-employed, civil servants, and a general scheme were incorporated into a single new General Family Allowances Act (Algemene Kinderbijslag Wet (AKW)), under which all residents became entitled to allowances for the first and subsequent children. In 1985 7,672 million HFL were paid under the AKW, that is 6.0 per cent of the total expenditure on social security, or 1.8 per cent of GDP.

As a basic and general rule, allowances are payable to insured persons (all residents, father or mother) in respect of their own children, stepchildren and adopted children aged under 16, and under more specific conditions of children aged between 16 and 27.

The level of the allowance is dependent upon the age of the child and the number of children in a household. At 1 January 1987 the amounts per child are shown in Table 8.

For children aged under five two percentage rates are given. The 75 per cent rate applies for children who were born before 1 January 1983 and are not the eldest child of the family, and have never been the eldest child. The 70 per cent rate applies to all other such children. In view of the introduction of a new system of education allowances, the family allowances for children between aged 18 and 27 are abolished. Only in case a child of this age has no right to an education allowance can there exist a right to a family allowance.

Netherlands

TABLE 8: THE AMOUNT OF CHILD ALLOWANCES (IN GUILDERS PER QUARTER)

Age	0-5 (70%)	0-5 (75%)	6-11 (100%)	12-17 (127.5%)	18-26
Families with					
1 child	202.69	217.27	289.56	369.18	298.02
2 children	265.85	284.83	379.78	484.22	390.88
3 children	284.66	305.00	406.66	518.50	418.55
4 children	310.94	333.15	444.20	566.35	457.18
5 children	326.70	350.03	466.71	595.05	480.35
6 children	343.88	368.44	491.25	626.34	505.61
7 children	350.15	381.59	508.79	648.70	523.66
8 children	370.81	397.29	529.73	675.40	545.21
9 children	382.21	409.51	546.02	696.18	561.98
10 children	391.34	419.29	559.06	712.80	575.40

An orphan's pension is according to the General Widows' and Orphans' Act (Algemene Weduwen-en Wezenwet (AWW)) granted to full orphans up to 16 years of age. In certain cases (for example if the child is disabled) an orphan's pension is payable up to the age of 27. A public servants' orphan's pension amounts to one-seventh for 'half' orphans and two-seventh for 'full' orphans of the old age pension of the father. However, these pensions are reduced, as public servants' orphans are in receipt of AWW-benefits.

Maternity allowances are according to the Sickness Benefits Act (Ziektewet (ZW)) paid six weeks before and after the date of confinement.

Personal Social Services

Since 1 October 1986 a new system of educational allowances was introduced. In principle all persons between 18 and 30 years who study, have a right to this allowance. Persons living on their own get (for the period 1986-7) a monthly allowance of 604.22 HFL; persons living with their parents receive 265.96 HFL. Underlying the allowance is a low interest bank loan guaranteed for students dependent on the income of their

Netherlands

parents and the kind of education they receive. The maximum monthly amount is 822.65 HFL for persons living on their own, and 404.37 for persons living with their parents.

For young persons there are day-care centres, residential schools, homes for single parents and their children, centres for advice, foster-help, and centres for drug-help. Cross-organisations provide maternity care, baby-care and consultation, family care and help. Further, there are private nursery schools and child day care institutions partly subsidised by the state. Disabled children attend special state subsidised schools.

Evaluation

The redistributional effects of the allowances based on the General Family Allowances Act are rather modest. Measured through the 'Theil-coefficient', the benefits according to this act led in 1981 to a reduction of income inequality of only 4.0 per cent (Muffels, Nelissen & Nuyens 1986). The most striking shortcoming of the Dutch system of family allowances is the fact that they only cover a small part of the costs of raising children. That leads to the fact that families with children, living on a minimal income or social security benefit, fall under the minimal level of subsistence.

NEEDY FAMILIES

About 10 per cent of the Dutch households live below the official poverty line, with an over-representation of single-parent families (Wiebrens 1981). And about 40 per cent of these housholds expressed that they do not have enough money to provide the food necessary for healthy nutrition.

Social Security

The Dutch social security system has, since the introduction of the General Public Assistance Act (Algemene Bijstandswet (ABW)) in 1963, a social minimum financial floor within its social security structure. Any Dutch citizen or family without sufficient means to provide for his or her essential needs is entitled to assistance. This

Netherlands

consists of a monetary payment, commensurate with the applicant's circumstances and capabilities, and on the degree of responsibility to provide for his or her subsistence. The assistance is designed to enable the individual or family, where possible, to provide for themselves. The assistance granted under the General Public Assistance Act is complementary to all other subsistence allowances and is provided as a last resort. On the one hand, this means that assistance is given to the extent that the applicant's own resources (income, assets) are not sufficient to provide for essential needs. On the other hand, it serves as a safety net if and to the extent that the help provided under other legislation and schemes (for example social insurance) is inadequate.

The General Public Assistance Act explicitly refers to essential needs, thus excluding a subjective interpretation from the outset. The term covers the costs of food and drink, clothing, housing, heat, furniture, and recreation. These things are regarded as 'necessary to enable the individual or family to live a life worthy of a human being'.

Social assistace expenditure for 1985 amounted to 5,909 million HFL, that is 4.6 per cent of total expenditure on social security, or 1.4 per cent of GDP.

The level of assistance is governed by national rules, laid down in the National Assistance Rates Decree of 1974, which specifies the rates to be paid per month. There are standard rates for families, one-parent families, single persons (so called 'front-door sharers') and unemployed young people. The benefits are linked to the net minimum wage since 1980. The rates are:

- 100 per cent of the net minimum wage for married people; that is monthly net 1,495.80 HFL with 81.31 HFL holiday allowance (on 1 January 1987);
- 90 per cent of the net minimum wage for one-parent families; that is monthly 1,346.25 HFL with 73.18 HFL holiday allowance (on 1 January 1987);
- 70 per cent of the net minimum wage for single persons aged 23 and over; that is monthly 1,047.05 HFL with 56.92 HFL holiday allowance (on 1 January 1987);

60 per cent of the net minimum wage for 'front-door sharers' (single persons, not married or living officially together, who do not live alone); that is monthly 889.35 HFL with 56.92 HFL holiday allowance (on 1 January 1987).

Lower rates apply to unemployed young people aged 18 to 23, the rates increasing with age.

These rates are in the following proportion to average net earnings and national income per head of the population: for a couple that is about 49 per cent of average net earnings of households, and 73 per cent of national income per head of the population; for a one-parent family the figures are 45 per cent and 66 per cent; for single persons that is about 63 per cent of average net earnings of individual persons, and 51 per cent of the national income per head of the population; for a 'front-door sharer' the figures are 47 and 44 per cent.

As a general rule all earned income is deducted. An exception is made, however, in the case of income which may be regarded as 'secondary earnings' in view of the amount, nature and regularity of such earnings. One-third of these earnings is exempt up to a fixed maximum. That maximum is 224.35 HFL a month for families and single-parents families, and 157.05 HFL for a single person of 23 and over (on 1 January 1987); for younger people that amount is lower with a decreasing rate.

Since 1981 a lump-sum benefit is paid annually to the receivers of a minumum benefit in the social insurance and assistance schemes (the so-called 'real minimal beneficiaries', echte minima). That figure is annually fixed without a clear definition in order to protect, to a certain extent, the buying power of the minimal benefits. In 1984 a further differentiation of the real minimal beneficiaries was introduced. A part of the echte minima was labelled as meerjarige echte minima, (the long-term minimal beneficiaries; that is people that received a lump-sum benefit the year before), and also received an additional benefit. In 1985 and 1986 only this last group, the meerjarige echte minima got a lump-sum benefit, while the (new) echte minima were excluded. In 1985 a family with children received 685 HFL (830 HFL in cases where the family or

Netherlands

single person received the lump-sum benefit for the third time) plus 60 HFL (160 HFL) for each child; families without children 660 HFL (805 HFL); one-parent families 635 HFL (745 HFL) plus 60 HFL (160 HFL) for each child; and single persons aged 23 and over 460 HFL (505 HFL).

The number of echte minima increased strongly between 1982 and 1985 from 468,000 to 775,000. That is more than one-fifth of all welfare beneficiaries. The percentage of this group categorised as meerjarige echte minima increased from 47.9 to 67.2 over the same period.

Personal Social Services

There exist some private and public institutions that provide several services to needy families: (interest-free) loans, meals-on-wheels, advice, mediation, and family care (by cross-organisations).

Rent subsidies are paid to lower income tenants, through the Individual Rent Subsidies (Individuele Huursubsidies) programme. In 1984 approximately 584,400 people received such a subsidy (in 1970 only 31,000), receiving about 1,131 million HFL, on average 1,935 HFL a year each. In addition there is a rent habituation subsidy (huur-gewenningsbijdrage) for tenants who are suddenly confronted with a sharp rent increase.

Evaluation

The introduction of the General Public Assistance Act in 1963 contributed to a large extent in securing a minimal level of subsistence within the social security and wage building. That level is, compared with that of other western countries, fairly high.

THE UNEMPLOYED

In 1955 44,000 people received an unemployment benefit, in 1960 45,000, in 1970 103,000, in 1980 333,000 and in 1985 744,000 people. This figure for 1985 was composed of 82,000 people receiving benefits according to the WW, 175,000 according to the WWV, 404,000 according to the RWW, 80,000 according to the WSW, and 3,000 according to the BKR. In 1985 total unemployment expenditure amounted to 16,921 million HFL (that is 13.2 per cent of total expenditure on social security (inclusive of all pensions), or 4.1 per cent of GDP).

Social Security

Income maintenance for unemployed people was until 1987 based on three kinds of acts: the (old) Unemployment Insurance Act (Werkloosheidswet (WW)), the Unemployment Provisions Act (Wet Werkloosheidsvoorziening (WWV)), and the social assistance regulations, [the RWW, BKR and WSW are regarded as social assistance regulations] the Government Unemployment Assistance Regulation (Rijksgroepsregering Werkloze Werknemers (RWW)), the Scheme for State Aid to Artists (Beeldende Kunstenaars Regeling (BKR)) and the Sheltered Employment Act (Wet Sociale Werkvooziening (WSW)). Public servants have their own regulations: Public Servants Redundancy pay Scheme (Wachtgeldregeling Overheidspersoneel (WRO)).

TABLE 9: PUBLIC EXPENDITURE IN 1985 ON UNEMPLOYMENT

	Expenditure (Millions of Guilders)	Per Cent-age
Unemployment Insurance (WW)	2,403	14.2
Unemployment Provisions (WWV)	4,721	27.9
Unemployment Assistance (RWW)	7,073	41.8
Unemployment Assistance (BKR)	85	0.5
Unemployment Assistance (WSW)	1,779	10.5
Public Servants Scheme (WRO)	860	5.1
TOTAL	16,921	100.0

SOURCE: Ministerie van Sociale Zaken en Werkgelegenheid, Financiele nota sociale zekerheid 1987, The Hague, 1986, p.8.

Since 1 January 1987 the Unemployment Insurance Act and the Unemployment Provisions Act are joined together into the (new) Unemployment Insurance Act (Werkloosheidswet (WW)). This Act

Netherlands

covers all employees under the age of 65 and some self-employed with a similar status. Under the WW scheme, any insured person who has been working for at least 130 days in the same branch of industry or trade during the 12 months preceeding unemployment is entitled to a benefit for half a year. After that period the possibility exists that the benefit is continued. That depends on two further conditions. Firstly, the unemployed person has to have worked during three years in the last five years (at least eight hours a week). Secondly, the total labour record has to exceed the limit of five years. The duration of this extension is coupled to the total labour record according to the following scheme:

Total Labour Record	Duration of Extension
5 years	3 months
10 years	6 months
15 years	1 year
20 years	1.5 year
25 years	2 years
30 years	2.5 years
35 years	3.5 years
40 years	4.5 years

Since it is very difficult to trace a person's complete labour record the WW determines that the labour record has only to be calculated over the last five years; before that time age is taken as standard of the labour record (beginning at the age of 18).

Unemployment benefits according to the WW are earnings-related. The unemployed receive 70 per cent of their previous earnings. For persons or families that fall below the (monthly) social minimum of 1,103.97 HFL (for a person of the age of 23 and more) and 1,577.11 HFL for a family (on 1 January 1987), the benefit is supplemented according to the Additional Allowances Act (Toeslagenwet). That supplement is income-tested. So the minimal benefits according to the WW are for a couple about 53 per cent of average net earnings of households, and 79 per cent of national income per head of the population; for a single person that is about 63 per cent of average net earnings of individual persons, and 55 per cent of the national income per head of the population.

Netherlands

After the continued benefit, coupled to the labour record, there exists a possibility to receive a prolonged benefit for one more year under the condition that the unemployed worked during three years in the last five years. The benefits according to this supplementary regulation amount to 70 per cent of the minimum wage. In cases where the unemployed earned less than the minimum wage, they receive 70 per cent of that lower amount. Heads of households will in both cases get a benefit that is lower than the social minimum. In that case they receive a supplementary allowance according to the Additional Allowances Act (<u>Toeslagenwet</u>).

Persons that became unemployed at the age of 50 and over, but before they were 57.5 years old, and passed the complete WW track (the earnings-related benefit and the prolonged regulation), and persons that became unemployed at the age of 57.5 and over and could only claim a WW-benefit in the first half year, receive an income-tested (including the income of the partner) benefit according to the Income Provision Act for Elderly and Partially Disabled Unemployed Employees (<u>Wet Inkomensvoorziening Oudere en Gedeeltelijk Arbeidsongeschikte Werkloze Werknemers</u> (IOAW)). That benefit is (on 1 January 1987) at the level of the social minimum of 1,495.80 HFL with a holiday allowance of 81.31 HFL for a family, 1,346.25 HFL with a holiday allowance of 73.18 for a single-parent family and 1,047.05 HFL with a holiday allowance of 56.92 HFL for a person of the age of 23 and more (with a duration up until 65 years).

The unemployed who cannot claim a benefit according to the WW, or used their maximum rights to such a benefit, receive unemployment assistance under the Government Unemployment Assistance Regulation (<u>Rijksgroepsregering Werkloze Werknemers</u> (RWW)), the most important regulation within the General Public Assistance Act. Benefits are calculated on the basis of personal circumstances and are means-tested.

The Scheme for State Aid to Artists forms part of the social security system in as much as it is directed at maintaining and improving the artist's ability to work and his employment opportunities. The Sheltered Employment Act is intended for persons who are capable of working but are unable to find employment because of disablement or other personal factors. Sheltered employment offers

Netherlands

such people social security in the form of suitable work. The work is particularly aimed at maintaining, restoring or improving the individuals ability to work.

Public servants' WRO benefits are earnings-related and amount to 100 per cent of previous earnings during the first three months, 90 per cent in the next nine months, 80 per cent in the next four years, and 70 per cent thereafter. Benefits under the 1966 Allowance Regulation amount to 100 per cent of previous earnings in the first two months, 90 per cent in the next two months, 80 per cent in the next eight months, and 75 per cent thereafter, up to a maximum period of one-sixth of the service, with a maximum of two years. For those with a period of service of less than three years, 80 per cent benefits are provided during a 130 day period.

Personal Social Services

Some of the services for the unemployed are coupled with existing unemployment schemes, others are separate services.

Several services are provided according to the WW. There exist possibilities to attend retraining with maintenance of an unemployment benefit; some retraining activities are financed through the WW-scheme.

The Regional Employment Offices (<u>Gewestelijke Arbeidsbureaus</u> (GAB)) register both the unemployed and work vacancies offered. Where necessary, they organise retraining programmes and in a few cases they have started their own enterprises. The unemployed can take part in social work provision schemes, organised by public corporations, or start up an enterprise on their own with the continuation of their unemployment benefit for a limited period.

Finally, central government provides subsidies for (local) experiments with retraining, part-time jobs and for the creation of employment programmes within the public sector.

Evaluation

The redistributional effects of the WW and WWV are quite neglectable. The main cause is the fact that the benefits according to these laws are earnings-related. The 'Theil-coefficient' of the WW is only one per cent, and that of the WWV five

Netherlands

per cent. The conclusions concerning the development of the buying power of the unemployment benefits are the same as in the case of sickness and disablement. Before 1979 the buying power of the minimal sickness/disablement benefits grew faster than the minimal and modal wage, 23.5 against 18.1 and 9.0 per cent; the above-minimal benefits stayed somewhere in between with their 16.8 per cent. However, since 1979 the buying power of the benefits decreased strongly with 13.7 and 22.4 per cent. For the above-minimal benefits the decrease is even stronger (5.6 per cent) than the increase between 1973-9. That was the result of the reconstruction of the social security system which began in 1983. The level of the benefits was decreased from 80 per cent to 70 per cent, a development that mainly affected the above-minimal benefits. Finally, the structural character of unemployment (in 1985 54 per cent of the unemployed are out of work for more than one year) resulted in a relative de-entitlement of the unemployed, in the sense that people slipped off to relatively minor rights and lower benefit levels. For instance, in 1972 37.3 per cent of all the unemployed had a right to an earnings-related benefit according to the (old) Unemployment Insurance Act (WW), in 1980 that figure declined to 20.9 per cent, and in 1985 only 12.4 per cent. The number of unemployed receiving an (income-tested) unemployment assistance benefit grew from 9.9 per cent in 1972 to 61.1 per cent in 1985.

The personal social services consist mainly of employment and retraining provisions. It is quite clear that they had only a marginal effect on the development of unemployment since the end of the 1970s. However, without these services the unemployment rate would probably have been about two per cent higher than the 13 per cent recorded in 1986.

ASSESSMENT OF THE DUTCH WELFARE SYSTEM

Since the Second World War two general (ideological) options dominated the Dutch welfare system, a Bismarckian and a Beveridgean one. The Bismarckian option stressed the 'subsidiarity' (subsidiariteit) and the principle of 'sovereignty in own circle' (soevereiniteit in eigen kring): social policy should appeal to the own responsibility of people and social organisations; and only in case they fail, the state has the moral right, and even duty to intervene. The Beveridgean option asserted programmes for the whole population and pointed at safeguarding from want for all citizens and some degree of income redistribution, mainly financed through taxation and administered by state institutions. These options went hand in hand in moulding the Dutch system. It was only since the economic crisis that new options were launched in the direction of a more selective system, in which the state only guarantees a minimal level of security and the above-minimal section is privatised.

The sufficiency of social welfare is dependent on the coverage, the level of the benefits and the services. These indicators show the Netherlands had improved the level of sufficiency from the mid 1960s until the 1980s; especially the introduction of the system of national insurance schemes, the passing of the General Public Assistance Act (_Algemene Bijstandswet_ (ABW)) in 1963, and the introduction of the social minimum as a floor of a fairly high level of subsistence, almost 50 per cent of average income for a couple and 63 per cent of average income for individual persons. The effects of all social security schemes, together lifted about 18 per cent of Dutch households above the official poverty line (Kapteyn, et al. 1985).

However, some shortcomings should be noted. Firstly, insecurity of subsistence can be caused by more than one contingency. In complex situations of cumulated social problems the existing system of protection can be insufficient; secondly, the fact that the system has not adequately been geared to some new social problems, such as the growth of the number of long-term unemployed and one-parent families, or the growing number of the aged in society. Thirdly, the Dutch social security system did not succeed in breaking through the existing social stratification. It rather consolidated the prevailing relations. People with the highest socio-professional training and status face less risks if they get sick, disabled or unemployed and have the best welfare arrangements, while people with the lowest training and the hardest jobs lay the biggest claims on social welfare provisons. Fourthly, family allowances only provide minor contributions to the costs of rearing children.

That brings families with a low income under the minimal level of subsistence. Finally, from the beginning of the 1980s major retrenchments within social security arrangements and personal social services have been introduced. Concerning social security arrangements the adjustment mechanisms of benefits on the general development of the wages (through the minimal wage) have since July 1980 actually been undermined, and in 1983 the government proposed several decreases of the replacement ratio for sick, disabled and unemployed persons, proposals that were converted in concrete measures in 1984 and 1985.

In the realm of the personal social services the level of service is threatened by a decrease of the number of people working in those kind of services and a reduction of the financial sources.

One other problem of the Dutch welfare system is the relative inaccessibility of the system. Three major causes can be discerned: the intransparent character of many arrangements; the fact that (new) groups of welfare clients (aged, handicapped, divorced women, single parents) have not significantly influenced the policy-making process, administration and control of social security, and a lack of knowledge of social provisions. Certainly, several initiatives have been taken to improve this situation. Some of them failed, others were successful. On the positive side of the balance are: the foundation of an advice centre, the Voorlichtingscentrum Sociale Verzekering in 1967, the broadening of the informative function of the Social Security Council, the introduction of commissions of complaint of the Social Security Council and the National Health Board, and the regulations concerning the right of privacy and the right of access to personal dossiers. On the negative side: the stagnation of the process towards the removing of administrative obstructions, towards a simplification and codification of social security laws, towards an integration of existing laws and regulations, and towards a minimal representation of new groups of welfare clients within the administration.

Concerning the last evaluative aspect of the Dutch welfare system, the redistributive balance of the insurance schemes, four conclusions are drawn. Firstly, the redistributive effect of the social security system is quite large. Secondly,

Netherlands

the General Old Age Pensions Act has by far the largest redistributive impact, measured in terms of the 'Theil-coefficient', 40 per cent. Thirdly, the employed persons insurance schemes, the Sickness Insurance Act, the Disablement Insurance Act and the Unemployment Act have only, in contrast to the national insurance schemes, minor redistributive effects. That is the result of the fact that contributions as well as benefits are coupled with the earlier wage. Finally, in spite of the strong redistributive effects of social security benefits, the same system cannot save a relatively great deal (10 per cent) of households from falling below the official poverty line.

ACKNOWLEDGEMENT

The author would like to thank Dr John L.M. Schell for his very helpful juridical advice and comments.

REFERENCES

Bruyn Kops, J.L. de (1852), Over het beginsel van armenverzorging door den staat, Amsterdam.

Centraal Bureau voor de Statistiek (1984), Statistisch zakboek 1984, The Hague: Staatsuitgeverij.

Kapteyn, A., Kooreman, P., Muffels, R.J.A., Seigers, J.J., Van Soest, A., & Willemse, R.J.N. (1985), Determinanten van bestaansonzekerheid. Een vooronderzoek, The Hague: Ministerie van Sociale Zaken en Weikgelegenheid.

Ministerie van Sociale Zaken en Werkgelegenheid (1982), Social Security in the Netherlands, The Hague: Ministerie van Sociale Zaken en Werkgelegenheid.

Muffels, R.J.A., Nelissen, J.H.M. & Nuyens, W.F.I. (1986), 'De inkomensherverdelende werking van sociale overheidsregelingen', in Sociaal Maandblad Arbeid, nr.1.

Netherlands

Roebroek, J. & Berben, T. (1987), 'The Netherlands' in Flora, P. (ed.), <u>Growths to Limits. The Western European Welfare States Since World War II</u>, Volume 4, Berlin/New York: de Gruyter (pp.671-750).

Sociaal en Cultureel Planbureau (1984), <u>Collectieve uitgaven en demografische ontwikkeling, 1970-2030</u>, Rijswijk: Staatsuitgeverij.

Widbrens, C.J. (1981), <u>Inkomen en rondkomen</u>, The Hague: Staatsuitgeverij.

NEW ZEALAND
Stephen Uttley

THE WELFARE SYSTEM ENVIRONMENT

Socio-economic Environment

Population. New Zealand is an island country in the South West Pacific, about 1,200 miles South East of Australia. The population of New Zealand in 1986 was about 3.3 million. The population density is low relative to world standards, although this partly reflects the rugged landscape, which makes substantial areas of both main islands unsuitable for high density settlement. The population is a highly urbanised one, with about 84 per cent living in urban areas. There is a concentration of the population in the North Island and around the northern city of Auckland.
The average annual growth rate of the population for much of the 1940s to 1960s was about two per cent, however there has been a substantial reduction in more recent years, averaging 0.65 per cent since 1976. The reduced rate of population growth reflects changes in fertility levels and, to a lesser extent, variations in net migration.
According to the 1981 census just under 86 per cent of the population are of European descent. The New Zealand Maori population was 8.9 per cent, 2.8 per cent of the population were Pacific Island Polynesians and the remaining 2.3 per cent a variety of other groups including Indian and Chinese. There was a substantial migration of Pacific Islanders into New Zealand during the early 1970s. The Pacific Island community is concentrated in the Auckland area.

New Zealand

Economic Context. The Organisation for Economic Cooperation and Development's (OECD) economic survey of New Zealand for 1984-5 indicates the following:

> The performance of the New Zealand economy in the period since the first oil shock has been worse than in other OECD countries. Output growth has been lower, inflation higher, and serious economic imbalances have developed.
>
> From being one of the richest developed countries in the post-war period New Zealand is now one of the least well-off countries in the OECD. One of the contributing factors for the decreased economic level has been the rapid expansion of government expenditure (particularly the Welfare State expenditures) during the 1970s and 1980s producing a fiscal deficit of about nine per cent of the Gross Domestic Product (GDP) in 1983-4.
>
> Unemployment has increased since the 1970s peaking at 5.4 per cent of the labour force in 1982-3. The growth in unemployment is partly a consequence of increases in the size of the labour force and in participation rates.
>
> The Labor government elected at the end of 1984 has introduced major changes in economic policies generally aimed at reducing the degree of state intervention. These changes include devaluation of the currency, floating of the exchange rate, the removal of many import licensing controls, the removal of price and wage controls, reduction in the size of the fiscal deficit and changes in taxation policy, including substantial reductions in personal income tax and the introduction of a goods and services tax.

Political Environment

New Zealand has a single house parliament with elections taking place every three years. The New Zealand political stage has been dominated for much of this century by a two-party system; from 1911 to 1928 by the Liberal and Reform parties and from 1936 to the present day by the National and Labour parties. A variety of other parties have attempted to establish themselves politically over time but, despite commanding a sizeable percentage of the total vote, the 'first past the post' voting system has prevented this support being

New Zealand

translated into parliamentary seats. Although the National and Labor parties could be viewed as parties of the political Right and Left respectively, neither has as strong an ideological base as may be found in equivalent parties in many other countries. The differences between the parties are often questions of nuance rather than fundamentals. For example, for much of the 1960s and 1970s both parties advocated highly interventionist strategies and the present Labor government is implementing broadly 'free market' policies with the National party opposition trying to find distinctive policies within the same approach.

Historical Origins

Table 1 shows the major legislative changes in the historical development of the social security system and the framework of personal social services in New Zealand.

TABLE 1: THE HISTORICAL DEVELOPMENT OF SOCIAL WELFARE IN NEW ZEALAND

LEGISLATION	YEAR	BRIEF DESCRIPTION
Old Age Pensions	1898	Means-tested pension those aged 65 and over.
Workers' Compensation	1900	Employers required to insure against accidents to workers.
Widows' Pension	1911	Pension payable to widow.
Child Welfare	1925	Creation of separate childrens' and young persons' Courts.
Family Allowances	1926	Small allowance related to the size and income of the family.
Social Security	1938	Established a comprehensive system of cash and medical benefits. Income-tested payments for sickness, widowhood, orphanhood, unemployment. Income-tested age benefit at age

New Zealand

		60. Small universal benefit at age 65 irrespective of income. Social security tax of one shilling in the pound on personal and company incomes.
Family Benefit	1946	Universal payment for each child irrespective of income.
Mental Health	1969	System of care and treatment of mentally disordered.
Department of Social Welfare	1971	Merging of the Departments of Social Security and Child Welfare Division of the Department of Education.
Accident Compensation	1972	No-fault principle. Earnings-related payments. Equal status to earners and non-earners.
Social Security Amendment	1973	Statutory benefit available to all solo parents.
Children and Young Persons	1974	Establish Children's Boards for children in need of care, protection and control.
Disabled Persons Community Welfare	1975	Extensions in financial support. Assistance to organisations working with the disabled.
New Zealand Superannuation Scheme	1975	Compulsory contributory scheme-employer/employee payments. Earnings-related benefits.
National Superannuation	1976	Universal payment to all aged 60 and over. Payment linked to average wage level.

There have been two important Royal Commissions on income maintenance issues during recent years; the Royal Commission on Compensation for Personal Injury (1967) which led to the creation of the

New Zealand

Accident Compensation Scheme, and the Royal Commission on Social Security (1972), which reviewed the operation of the social security system. There have also been a number of reports, discussion documents and conferences examining major changes to the Children and Young Persons Act (see for example, New Zealand Commission of Inquiry into the Case of a Niuean Boy 1977; New Zealand Human Rights Commission 1982; New Zealand Advisory Committee on Youth and Law in our Multicultural Society 1983; New Zealand Department of Social Welfare 1984).

Ideological or Dominant Value Environment

New Zealand has been viewed at various points in its history as a leader in the development of the Welfare State. The reforms of a Liberal government at the end of the last century, the post-depression creation of the basic structure of the welfare system by a Labor government of the 1930s, and more recent innovations, such as schemes for dealing with accidental injury and income support for solo-parents, have all generated international interest. What ideological forces have influenced the New Zealand Welfare State? Commentators have tended to point to the apparent lack of ideological influences. Metin, for example, described the Liberal reforms of the 1890s as 'socialism without doctrine' (Castles 1985, p.12). Certainly political ideology has not been an accurate indicator of likely policy. A recent example of this in the 1970s was the introduction of a contribution-based variable-benefit system of income support for the aged by the party of the Left, which was quickly replaced by a generous, universal benefit by the party of the political Right.

What values have been reflected in New Zealand's Welfare State? The continued willingness to turn to central government for action since the early phases of colonisation may be seen as a reflection of the difficulties of developing a relatively large and isolated country with a small population and limited access to capital. The emphasis on the central government for services is also a reflection of the wish to provide security for citizens against the dual impact of physical isolation and economic reliance upon exports. Economic policies such as import controls, exchange controls, producer subsidies, government support of producer co-operatives and so on can be seen in this context. The development of the welfare system has been described as part of this 'quest for security' (Sutch 1966). This quest for security was early indicated in the establishment of access to free, secular education - the efforts to provide health care at zero or subsidised cost - and the provision of income support to cover a wide range of contingencies. Briggs quotes the International Labour Office (ILO) as describing New Zealand's 1938 Social Security Act as defining 'the practical meaning' of social security and being extremely influential outside New Zealand (1961, p.255).

The New Zealand social security system is unusual in its reliance upon flat rates of benefit which are financed through general taxation. There is a long history of rejection of proposals which involve contributory payments from citizens. Castles (1985) has argued that this reflects the continuing strategy of organised labour since the turn of the century to focus narrowly on wages and working conditions. The social security system represents the safety net beneath that wage system. Any move towards improved benefits through contributory schemes is rejected because of its potentially undermining effect upon wages.

The general level and range of social security benefits available within the present social security system suggest that New Zealand can no longer be viewed as a world leader. The system is under scrutiny for its high and growing cost at a time when constraint of government expenditure is regarded as necessary. Social security benefits are equally being scrutinised by those concerned about the adequacy of the benefits being paid. (Budget '85 Task Force 1985; Ministerial Task Force on Income Maintenance 1986).

The main thrust of the welfare system is to give citizens access to material resources, such as income, housing, health care and education. A wide range of personal social services is available but it is difficult to detect any specific coherent ideology or set of values underpinning these services. The services are organisationally disparate both within the government sector itself and the voluntary and for-profit sectors. Legislation is ineffective in identifying service goals for similar reasons and

New Zealand

tends to lag substantially behind current practice. Perhaps the greatest indicator of a lack of policy direction for the personal social services is the absence of any systematic collection of data on the activities and expenditures of government.

THE WELFARE SYSTEM: AN OVERVIEW

The Structure and Administration of the Welfare Services

Central Government. The welfare system as a whole is dominated by direct service provision by central government organisations. The Department of Social Welfare which is responsible for social security employs about 5,600 people and has an annual budget well in excess of NZ$4 billion which represents about 28 per cent of the total government income. The Department has developed a system of district offices and has recently committed itself to the creation of an intermediate organisational tier of regional offices. The accident compensation scheme is administered by a public corporation - the Accident Compensation Corporation. The annual expenditure of the Corporation is around NZ$300 million and the Corporation employs about 700 staff.
Many government departments are involved in the provision of personal social services including the Departments of Social Welfare, Health, Internal Affairs, Maori Affairs, Justice, Education, Labour and Police.

Local Authorities. Local authorities tend to be quite small, except in the urban areas where there has been development of regional authorities in recent years. There is no strong tradition of providing social services through these bodies. Some local authorities do provide housing (including pensioner housing), child care facilities, employment programmes and they employ community workers.

Voluntary or Non-profit Sector. This sector is important in the provision of personal social services but its diversity makes classification and description difficult. There are large nationally organised or federated agencies, both secular and church based. (Historically the churches have played a critical role in the development of social services, particularly personal social services.) These large voluntary organisations are major providers of services and receive substantial government funding. Beyond these relatively few large agencies are a multiplicity of regional and local agencies and self-help groups which focus on particular needs.

Privately Owned/for Profit Sector. The social security system and the accident compensation scheme have left only limited scope for the insurance industry. Companies do provide cover for weaknesses or gaps in statutory provisions, for example, lump-sum payments for disablement. Insurance companies have also developed new products in the pension and investment field aimed at income support in old age. Changes in both the tax treatment of policy premiums and the personal tax regime for those aged 60 and over have impacted upon the attractiveness of these products to consumers.

Private agencies are visible in two main areas of the personal social service programmes, first the residential care of the aged, and second child care centres for pre-school children. Both activities receive direct financial support from public funds through subsidies. Indirect support through income maintenance payments to the aged and tax rebates for child care fees have also played a part in the growth of these types of private sector provision.

Decentralisation. During the last decade arguments have been advanced for the decentralisation of power, particularly within the public sector. One of the reasons for the retention of a system closely controlled from the centre is the desire to achieve uniform standards of service throughout the country. Despite elaborate administrative procedures there is evidence to indicate that wide variations of service exist in the provision of social services (New Zealand Department of Social Welfare 1982). The remoteness of centrally planned and provided social services has been blamed for the lack of sensitivity to users and a general lack of public interest and involvement (New Zealand Council of Social Service 1978). For some commentators the issue of centralisation reflects more fundamental values in New Zealand society (Franklin 1985). Uniformity of service is equated with pressure towards conformity by the individual which in turn is aligned with an ideology of egalitarianism. (Despite the 'egalitarian tradition' the evidence is that New Zealand is, and has been, an unequal society, for example, Pearson & Thorns 1983.) The emphasis on uniformity through centralised control, which is reflected in the welfare system, may prevent the achievement of effective services by restricting options and discouraging creative responses to service needs (New Zealand Task Force on Economic and Social Planning 1976; New Zealand Planning council 1984; Franklin 1985). There have been some moves toward decentralisation of social services with radical attempts to change by the Department of Maori Affairs (Uttley 1983) and the creation of a regional organisational tier in the Department of Social Welfare.

Financing Social Welfare

Social Security. Historically New Zealand's social security system has, with one exception, been financed through general taxation. Insurance and contributory schemes were considered and rejected in the 1880s and since the 1898 Old Age Pensions Act the system has remained firmly based on flat-rate benefits financed through general taxation. A small social security tax was introduced in the 1938 Social Security Act but was abolished in 1958. The exception to financing through general taxation has been payments to those who suffer accidental injury. The present scheme for responding to accidental injury provides universal coverage to the victims irrespective of the cause of the accident or where it occurs. It has been financed through levies on employers and self-employed people and on the owners of motor vehicles, with a relatively small amount coming from general taxation to cover accidents which occur outside the workplace or the highway.

Table 2 describes the level of expenditures on social security and income support relative to gross domestic product over the last eight years.

New Zealand

TABLE 2: SOCIAL SECURITY EXPENDITURE 1978-85

Year	Social Security Benefits[1] ($NZ million)	National Superannuation[2] ($NZ million)	Total as Percentage of GDP
1978	507.9	926.5	9.3
1979	571.6	1,162.9	9.9
1980	693.8	1,334.1	9.6
1981	879.8	1,556.8	10.0
1982	966.3	1,895.8	9.8
1983	1,132.8	2,418.9	11.0
1984	1,321.1	2,526.1	11.0
1985	1,464.0	2,743.5	10.9

Notes:

1 War pension payments have been included. Expenditure on Accident Compensation is not included.
2 National Superannuation is a universal payment made to all those aged 60 and over.
   National Superannuation and some unemployment benefits are subject to personal income tax therefore net expenditure is substantially less than the gross figure.

SOURCE: Derived from the Report of the Department of Social Welfare for the year ended 31/3/85.

Personal Social Services

The lack of any coherent planning or monitoring of these services is reflected in the paucity of data and this certainly applies to information on financing. A recent discussion paper has been unable to provide expenditure data even for services provided by government departments (Ministerial Task Force on Social Welfare Services 1986). The only information available is for the Department of Social Welfare. Even this data is confined to total expenditure on social work services by the Department and to the proportion of this which is used to fund voluntary organisations.

The larger voluntary organisations produce annual reports which give indications of expenditure and sources of funding, however no attempt has been made to centralise data collection. There are indications that the larger voluntary organisations have become increasingly reliant upon government funding in recent years and that the mechanisms for providing that funding have become more complex as ad hoc responses are made to particular issues. The possibility that the total effect of the funding maze may work in such a way as to thwart the objectives of service programmes has been highlighted in a recent report. The same report also draws attention to the lack of any overall philosophy in funding allocation decisions (New Zealand Department of Social Welfare, Social Programme Evaluation Unit 1984, p.8).

THE AGED

The aged are defined as those 60 years and over since this is the age at which a universal social security payment is made. (There is a variation in the definition of the aged used in planning and delivering different social services.)

Table 3 shows the size of the actual and projected aged population from 1951 to 2011.

TABLE 3: ACTUAL AND PROJECTED AGED POPULATION: 1951-2011

Census (Year)	Number of Aged 60 and Over	Aged as Percentage of Total Population
1951	255,970	13.2
1961	294,904	12.2
1971	358,024	12.5
1981	445,800	14.0
Projected		
1991	539,400	15.4
2001	593,006	15.7
2011	719,300	18.3

SOURCE: Derived from New Zealand Social Advisory Council (1984), The Extra Years, Wellington: Government Printer, p.62.

New Zealand

The combined effect of a low birth rate during the 1930s depression and the Second World War with the high birth rates from 1946 to 1970 have placed New Zealand in a rather different position from many other developed countries in respect to the aged. The percentage of the aged in the population is not expected to increase significantly until the cohort born from 1946 to 1970 moves into the aged population from 2006 onwards. The ratio of aged to the full time labour force will remain constant until the next century and the overall 'dependency ratio' of young and old will be at its lowest level in 30 years. In these circumstances New Zealand is in the relatively fortunate position of having the opportunity to plan for the future demands on services in the early part of the next century, whilst in the short-term dealing with the increase in the absolute numbers of the aged and the ageing of that population.

Social Security

New Zealand was in the forefront of countries which developed some form of financial provision for the elderly in the latter part of the nineteenth century. The 1898 Old Age Pension Act gave a small payment to those over 65 years of age provided they passed a stringent means test, a residency requirement, various behaviour criteria and were not of Asiatic descent. Minor modifications were made in this scheme until the more radical reforms introduced by the Labour administration of the late 1930s. The 1938 Social Security Act introduced a means-tested benefit payable at 60 and a universal benefit payable to all aged 65 and over. Initially age benefit was paid at a substantially higher rate than universal superannuation but by 1960 the two benefits were paid at the same rate, although universal superannuation was taxable.

The Royal Commission on Social Security (1972) questioned the adequacy of benefit levels, particularly for the aged. The Labor government legislated in 1974 for a new superannuation scheme based on compulsory contributions from workers and employers which would entitle individuals to an earnings related pension. The issue of income support for the aged was an important factor in the 1975 general election in which the National party put forward a policy for a new universal

New Zealand

pension scheme. National won the election and quickly implemented their scheme. National Superannuation involves a payment to all citizens aged 60 years and over subject to a residency requirement. The level of payment is linked to wage levels and a married couple receive 80 per cent of the after tax average wage for full-time workers. The payment is subject to personal income tax (tax liability in New Zealand begins with the first dollar received). The scheme is financed through general taxation. Table 4 shows expenditure for the aged from 1945-85.

TABLE 4: EXPENDITURE ON INCOME SUPPORT FOR THE AGED

Year	Aged[1] (NZ$000)	Total[2] Benefits (NZ$000)	Expenditure on Aged as Percentage of Total	Expenditure on Aged as Percentage of GDP
1945	18,974	27,067	70.1	–
1955	58,002	106,934	54.2	–
1965	110,314	198,811	55.5	3.0
1975	365,808	617,694	59.2	3.6
1980	1,334,115	1,918,851	69.5	6.3
1985	2,743,512	4,081,058	67.2	7.1

Notes:

1. 1945-1975 Expenditure on Age Benefit plus Universal Superannuation. 1980-1985 Expenditure on National Superannuation.
2. Expenditure on all social security benefits paid through the vote for the Department of Social Welfare.

SOURCE: Derived from the 1985 Report of the Department of Social Welfare.

The cost of national superannuation on the one hand and the political constraints on modifying a scheme aimed at an increasingly important section of the electorate on the other, has seen income support for the elderly take a prominent place in political and social debates in recent years. Modifications to the scheme have been made in an attempt to constrain costs, the most recent being the introduction of a tax surcharge of 25 cents on the dollar for those with significant amounts of other income. The public debate tends to focus upon the gross cost of national superannuation which is rather misleading. The Department of Social Welfare (1985) estimates that 23 cents in the dollar is recovered through income tax and the tax income generated by the tax surcharge is in addition to this.

Fiscal Welfare. An allowance against income for tax purposes is available for contributions made towards a personal or employee pension scheme. The amount of the allowance depends upon whether the scheme is subsidised by an employer or not. There are two rebates within the personal tax system which are also relevant: first against payments made to support dependent relatives, and second a housekeeper rebate which can be claimed if someone is paid to look after the house for an infirm or disabled old person or their spouse.

Occupational Welfare. Both employers and unions are active in the formation of occupational pension schemes, however the information available from individual firms and unions has not been collated and present statistical reports do not identify the extent of coverage or the adequacy of benefits provided through such schemes. Government action is confined to a regulatory role in that superannuation schemes are subject to approval through the government actuary. The government itself is a major provider of occupational welfare and this is certainly true in the pension area. Just under 70 per cent of the permanent government workforce are members of the government superannuation fund. What was already an attractive scheme has recently been revised to include many improvements including indexation of benefits. Employee contributions during 1984-5 accounted for about 42 per cent of payments made during the year with the shortfall being made up by the government (New Zealand Government Superannuation Fund 1985).

Personal Social Services

As in other developed countries studies of the aged indicate that most live in one or two adult households, independent of other family members. These studies also show that contact between the aged and other family members, particularly children, is high and it is family members who provide the bulk of support and caring (for example Koopman-Boyden 1981; New Zealand Department of Statistics 1984).

<u>Home Support Services</u>. The majority of hospital services are run by 29 Hospital Boards although funding of the Boards comes from central government. Hospital Boards typically provide services for the aged such as community nursing, social work, physiotherapy, occupational therapy, meals on wheels, home help and a laundry service. Most of these services are provided free to the users but a small charge is made for meals on wheels and home help. Many voluntary organisations are involved in providing these types of services, especially social work, counselling services and home helps with the most prominent being church agencies.

The Department of Social Welfare offers support to those caring for the aged in their own homes. Section 12 of the Disabled Persons Community Welfare Act allows for meeting the cost of alternative care for up to four weeks in a year for families caring for a seriously disabled child or adult.

Help in maintaining the house and garden has been identified by the elderly as one of the most important forms of help they need (for example, Koopman-Boyden 1978; New Zealand Department of Health, Special Report Series No.59 1981; Wellington Old Peoples Welfare Council 1981). The size of the traditional New Zealand house, its wooden construction and the size of the building section mean that both house and garden require high levels of maintenance. It is not surprising to find this is a cause of considerable anxiety to elderly people in terms of the physical work or the cost of employing others to do that work. Despite the identification of this concern by the elderly little effort has been made which focuses on this significant service provision.

Another area of concern to the elderly is access to public buildings and transportations. Some progress has been made in making buildings and public places more accessible. Access to public transportation, particularly buses, remains a problem. The recent development of subsidised special transportation schemes which are operated through taxi companies using modified vehicles offers the prospect of substantial improvements in mobility for the aged and disabled (New Zealand Social Advisory Council 1984).

Community Services. There are a variety of community based clubs and centres catering to the elderly and offering companionship, leisure, education and social activities. The size and scope of such clubs is very much a reflection of the local situation. There are also day-care centres, usually attached to residential facilities, to which local people are brought on a daily or regular basis, however day care is only used by a very small percentage of the aged population.

Residential Care. An issue in relation to the care of the aged has been the rate of institutional care in hospitals and other institutions (67.2 per 1,000 population over 65 years, Wellington Old People's Welfare Council 1981). This pattern exists despite the evidence, over a number of years, that many people living in old people's homes run by hospital boards, voluntary organisations or privately run homes are inappropriately placed (New Zealand Department of Health 1976; Wellington Old Peoples Welfare Council 1981).

The main providers of residential care for the aged are voluntary welfare organisations, particularly those operated by religious groups, and private provision from small-scale operators perhaps running one or two rest homes. Hospital Boards also provide some residential home provision. A recent development has been the entry of a number of large firms which have invested considerable funds in the building of retirement villages. This development is seen by some as an undesirable innovation because of the segregation of the aged from the rest of the community. The apparent demand for this type of accommodation suggests that it may become important in the future.

Evaluation

One of the major difficulties for New Zealand in utilising the opportunity to plan for the impact of the growth of the aged population over the next 20 to 30 years is the lack of any clear overall responsibility in the total welfare system for policy toward the aged. The present divisions in responsibilities for financing, maintaining standards and service development represent an obstacle to coherent policy formation and implementation. Currently planning advice comes from a multiplicity of essentially ad hoc bodies. For example, there is an advisory committee to the Minister of Health on the care of the aged, a National Old Peoples Welfare Concil and 11 regional councils. There are signs of progress such as the requirement of the Department of Health that Hospital Boards produce service development plans and that these plans consider the linkage between public, private and voluntary sector contributions to health services. Despite these developments it would appear that some reorganisation at the central government level which identifies the responsibilities for the overall development of policy for the aged is required.

CHILDREN, YOUTHS AND NEEDY FAMILIES

The trends in New Zealand are similar to those in other developed countries. The overall fertility rate in 1984 was 1.9 which is below replacement level. There is an increase in two adult households without children, particularly in the younger age groups. There has been an increase in the average age at marriage and a substantial increase in the percentage of couples delaying the birth of their first child. There has been an increase in single parent families with dependent children and in 1981 they constituted 14 per cent of all families with dependent children. In 1984 one in four births were to parents who were not legally married. About 80 per cent of these children live with one or both parents with about half living with both natural parents.

The labour force participation rate for women, and married women in particular, has increased considerably over the last 20 years, although it remains lower than that for many other OECD countries (New Zealand Planning Council, Social Monitoring Group 1985).

Social Security

New Zealand was one of the first countries to introduce a payment to families in recognition of the costs of raising children. The 1926 family allowances scheme was means-tested and excluded many sections of the community as well as only being payable for the third child onwards. Small modifications were made to the scheme until 1946 when a universal family benefit structure was introduced and this scheme remains in force today. The rate at which family benefit is paid has only been increased three times since 1946. The cost of even quite modest increases in this universal benefit, combined with community and hence political resistance to modification or abolition of the benefit, has resulted in the gradual erosion of the benefit through leaving the rate unchanged.

The social security system makes provision for the main contingencies which may cause an interruption in family income - sickness, invalidity, unemployment, widowhood, old age and solo parenthood (a separate scheme covers those suffering accidental injury). Benefit levels are adjusted every six months in line with movements in the consumer price index. The structure allows for the payment of child supplements to beneficiaries with dependent children but the rate at which the supplements are paid is not indexed.

There are additional provisions to assist the families of beneficiaries and low income families to meet certain costs. A weekly payment towards accommodation costs is available to beneficiaries, subject to a means test. There is discretionary authority for the payment of Special Benefit to beneficiaries or low income families in the light of their essential commitments. A subsidy towards the costs of child care services can be made. Other forms of special assistance include exemption from prescription charges, higher rates of subsidy towards the cost of visits to a general practitioner, telephone concessions and transportation concessions.

A major component in providing financial support to needy families and children has been the development of a statutory benefit payable to single parent families. The Domestic Purposes Benefit (DPB) was introduced in 1973, although the discretionary emergency benefit system had been used to assist single parents prior to this. There has been a substantial growth in the number of DPB benefits paid and the level of expenditure on this benefit since 1973. Single parents are also paid a special child supplement in respect of their first child. This supplement brings their level of payment to the equivalent of that payable to a married couple without dependent children on a statutory benefit. This supplement is adjusted on a six-monthly basis. The higher rate of supplement is made in recognition of the cost of setting up a new household. Since its inception the DPB has been the focus for much public debate: on the one hand criticisms of the rationale for the benefit, its possible effect on marital breakdown and claimed benefit abuses; and on the other hand the continued evidence from available income data that shows that single parent families figure disproportionately in households with the lowest levels of household income.

<u>Fiscal Welfare</u>. The unit of assessment for personal income tax in New Zealand is the individual, not the family. Changes in the rebate structure within the tax system since 1976 have tried to provide income support to families and also change the relative positions of one and two income families. In 1976 a rebate for families caring for a child under five years of age was introduced. A single income family rebate programme was established in 1978 for those caring for a child under 10 years of age. This rebate programme was modified in 1981 so that payment was based on total family income. These rebates could be claimed either by the principal income earner or a single parent. In 1982 the young family rebate, low income family rebate and the longer established spouse rebate were replaced by a new rebate termed the family rebate. This, in turn, was replaced in 1986 by the Family Support Programme.

Other rebates in the tax structure such as the housekeeper rebate and charitable donations/school fees rebate provide some assistance to families in meeting the cost of pre-school care and school expenses. There are some special provisions for single parents in these rebates.

<u>Family Care</u>. The present Labor government introduced this scheme shortly after their election late in 1984. It involved a weekly payment for each dependent child to families on low or moderate incomes. The payment was available to wage and salary earners and self-employed people, but not to those in receipt of social security benefits. Parents must work a minimum of 30 hours a week between them to qualify

for family care and payment is subject to a means test. There was provision in the scheme for extra payment to ensure a minimum annual family income. An important feature of the programme was that payment is made to the primary carer of the children in the family. It was superseded by the Family Support Programme in 1986.

Family Support. One of the major changes to come from a review of benefits and taxes undertaken in 1985 was a restructuring of financial assistance to families. The family tax rebate and the family care scheme was replaced by a new programme called Family Support as of October 1986. A weekly payment is made for each child with a larger payment being given for the first child. As with family care the payment will be means-tested against family income so that family support represents a further move towards focusing assistance on families with low incomes rather than all families. One of the effects of family support is to guarantee a minimum family income related to family size. The guaranteed minimum income for a family with one dependent child is NZ$250 per week. When the scheme was announced at the end of 1985 this represented about 78 per cent of the average weekly wage. By the time of implementation in October 1986 the guaranteed minimum represented about 67 per cent of the average wage with the next annual wage round negotiations about to begin (Estimate based on New Zealand Department of Labour 1985, 1986; New Zealand Institute for Economic Research 1986). In a two parent household the family support payment is divided equally between the parents, with payment being made through the Inland Revenue Department where both parents are wage earners and through the Department of Social Welfare to a non-wage earning parent.

One of the main criticisms of Family Care had been the exclusion of beneficiaries from the scheme. Family support will be paid to beneficiaries by replacing the present child supplements in the benefit system with the family support payments. This has meant a complex change in benefit structures to incorporate the payment without increasing benefit expenditure. This was necessary given the government's view that the full effect of Family Support should not be passed on to beneficiaries, as this would worsen problems associated with the relativities between wage and salary earners and beneficiaries.

Personal Social Services

There is a lack of systematic description and analysis of the personal social services in New Zealand. It is certainly difficult to isolate services to particular groups such as adolescents from the more general categories of service.

Pre-School Services

In the past a distinction has been made between services provided by playcentres and kindergartens which have been viewed as educational and administered accordingly and child-care services which have come under the ambit of the Department of Social Welfare. The last 15 years has seen a growth in child-care services which has developed from three programme areas: Firstly, an increase in the provision of child-care centres (local authorities, voluntary organisations and for profit agencies) - in 1972 there were 376 registered centres offering 9,906 places, by 1984 there were 585 centres offering 15,470 places (New Zealand Social Advisory council 1985); Secondly, the development in the late 1970s of family day care services under the aegis of voluntary organisations and/or local authorities in which care-givers provide care in their own homes. The care-givers are recruited by the agency which also oversees the 'contract' between care-giver and parents; thirdly the Te Kohanga Reo programme which aims to provide education and care within a Maori family 'whanau' environment in which Maori language and culture predominate. By 1985 360 Te Kohanga Reo were in operation. How to respond to these innovations in terms of funding and administration has been a major issue in recent years. The subsequent impact upon primary and secondary education programmes of the Te Kohanga Reo is also a critical question.

Children and Young Persons Legislation. The 1974 Children and Young Persons Act delegates to the Department of Social Welfare the duty to promote family well-being and ensure the adequate care and protection of children. The pressure for change in the legislation has been constant since the 1974 Act was passed and a new Act is likely to be

New Zealand

introduced into Parliament in the near future. The impetus for change in this legislation is centred around the following:

- Child abuse - there has been strong lobbying from diverse but powerful interest groups (such as lawyers, doctors, police and voluntary organisations) for the creation of Child Protection Teams. At present such teams do exist in some areas as a reflection of local initiatives but what is proposed is the statutory requirement to establish team(s) in all areas. The composition of the teams would reflect that of the interest groups (Department of Social Welfare 1984). Included in the proposals on child abuse is mandatory reporting of suspected abuse.

- 'Care and control' - the pressure from interest groups appears intent on trying to re-establish the nineteenth century distinction between those in need of care as a result of abuse or neglect and those who have committed offences against the law. The proposals that have been advanced would create two distinct systems: one involving professional interventions and treatment through child protection teams and hearings in the family court; and the other for children aged 12 to 17 years who have committed offences where action will be determined by Youth Assessment Panels and the creation of a special Youth Division of the District Court.

- Residential care - the standard of residential care for children in homes run by the Department of Social Welfare has been under close scrutiny for a number of years in the light of allegations of ill-treatment. These allegations have concerned the use of secure units within residential homes, punishment regimes and the adequacy of staff and staff training (New Zealand Human Rights Commission 1982, 1986; New Zealand Committee to Report to the Minister of Social Welfare 1982). These issues, combined with a community care ideology, and the concern for cost containment in the face of heavy relative expenditure on residential care and many old buildings requiring substantial investment for replacement or upgrading, has contributed to the decision to close a number of residential homes.

New Zealand

> Cultural sensitivity - a recurring theme in the total debate about services for children and young people is the high numbers of Maori children who come into contact with these services and the numbers of Maori children in care and in residential care in particular (this issue is of course only one small aspect of the wider question of race relations and inequality in New Zealand society). Many proposals have been put forward and some initiatives taken. Possible actions include changes in the training of social service workers, programmes aimed at promoting the knowledge of Maori culture and language for children in care, special foster care programmes for Maori children to be cared for within the Maori community and the creation of management committees for residential homes which would be required to have a strong Maori representation (New Zealand Advisory Committee on Youth and Law in our Multicultural Society 1983; New Zealand Ministerial Advisory Committee on a Maori Perspective 1986).

Evaluation

The last decade has been characterised by experimentation in ways of delivering income support to families outside the conventional social security framework. The use of mechanisms within the fiscal system employed during the 1970s has given way to measures such as Family Care, and most recently Family Support, which supplement market incomes. The absence of indexation of such payments to prices and/or wages raises the fear of rapid erosion in their real value.

There can be no doubt of the need for change in the legislative framework within which services to children and young people are provided. There is, however, the concern that changes likely to be implemented in the near future will replicate service structures introduced in other countries which are increasingly the focus of critical review.

THE UNEMPLOYED

The size of the employed labour force in November 1984 is estimated at just over 1.15 million people with 73 per cent employed in the private sector

New Zealand

and 27 per cent in the public sector. The labour force participation rates for men and women based on the 1981 census are 79.4 per cent and 47.3 per cent respectively. The labour force participation rate for women continues to be lower than in many other OECD countries although this is partially a reflection of the age structure of the population. Table 5 shows estimates of employment and unemployment from 1976-85.

TABLE 5: ESTIMATES AND FORECASTS OF EMPLOYMENT AND UNEMPLOYMENT[1] ('000)

March 31	1976	1978	1980	1982	1984	1985
Registered Unemployed	5.0	19.8	29.0	47.0	68.3	58.3
Unregistered Unemployed	20.8	13.8	15.1	12.0	13.0	11.1
Registered Unemployed (%)	0.4	1.6	2.2	3.5	5.0	4.2
All Unemployed (%)	2.0	2.6	3.3	4.4	5.9	5.0

Note: 1 This Table gives the number of registered unemployed and estimates of those available for work but unemployed and not registered with the Department of Labour, that is, unregistered unemployed)

SOURCE: New Zealand Employment Promotion Conference, 'Employment and Unemployment in New Zealand. Conference Backgrounder' 1985, Table 2, p.33.

Unemployment tends to affect certain groups more than others. The incidence of unemployment for women is higher than for men and women tend to be unemployed for a longer period of time. The rate of unemployment amongst young people in the 15-19 year age group is 13.8 per cent with the rates for young women and young men being 16.5 per cent and 11.5 per cent respectively. The rates of unemployment amongst the Maori and Pacific Island population groups in 1981 are considerably higher than the rest of the population, 14.0 per cent and 10.3 per cent respectively in comparison to an overall rate of 4.5 per cent. The situation is

New Zealand

particularly serious for young Maori and Polynesian women in the 15-19 age group with unemployment rates of 41.3 per cent and 33 per cent.

Social Security

Unemployment benefits are paid to people aged 16 and over who are unemployed, but are actively seeking work or taking part in an approved work-related training programme. The fact that visible unemployment in New Zealand is very much a phenomenon of the last 10 years is reflected in the growth of expenditures on unemployment benefits which has grown from less than one per cent of the total benefits expenditures in 1975 to about seven per cent in 1985. On 31 March 1985 there were 34,825 unemployment benefits in force and during the year the average time spent on unemployment benefits was 18.1 weeks.

There are a number of features of the eligibility conditions for unemployment benefit which deserve to be noted. There is a 12 month residency requirement for the benefit which is a cause of concern for migrants from the Pacific Islands. The qualifying age for the benefit is 16 years rather than 15 years which is used for sickness and invalidity benefits. Single beneficiaries with no dependent children are paid at a lower rate of benefit until they reach 20 years of age (18 years for other benefits). There is a waiting period of seven days after wages stop before unemployment benefits are paid, but for single people without dependents the waiting period is 14 days. Since 1979 all unemployment benefits paid to those without dependent children have been subject to personal income tax.

As of 1 October 1986 all benefits are subject to personal taxation, however this will be done on the basis of increasing benefits so that the amount received will actually remain the same and the relative positions of different beneficiaries will not be altered. The only change specific to the unemployed was the introduction of a non-taxable allowance to encourage the long-term unemployed to move into the workforce.

Personal Social Services

The unemployed have not been singled out as a special group for the delivery of personal social services. The main thrust towards the unemployed has been the creation of training and subsidised work schemes. A multiplicity of schemes have emerged with different objectives and target groups within the unemployed. A major rationalisation of programmes for the unemployed was announced at the end of 1985 which places the primary focus upon training and education rather than a job subsidy to employers.

The high incidence of unemployment among Maori and Pacific Island communities has already been noted and a number of measures are in place to address this problem. The Department of Maori Affairs has, over the last decade, moved towards a developmental approach rather than one based on individual pathology. Emphasis on economic development for Maori people has been regarded as central to this approach. The government has allocated funding for a Maori Enterprise Development Scheme in which funds will be allocated from the Board of Maori Affairs to local level committees, usually based on tribal affiliation, for use in promoting employment. Funding has also been allocated for a Pacific Island Employment Scheme and a special board will be formed to manage this.

The Job Opportunities Scheme is aimed at severely disadvantaged groups such as the physically handicapped, mentally ill, gang members and ex-prisoners. A number of extensions have recently been made to the scheme which now has four components: firstly, a general wage subsidy available to those employing someone identified as severely disadvantaged by the Vocational Guidance Service; secondly, help is also available to set up self-employment schemes for this group; the assistance involves advice and financial aid; thirdly, a substantial subsidy of NZ$250 a week for 12 months and NZ$150 a week for a further 12 months is available to employers who will provide a disadvantaged person with a 'supportive work environment'; fourthly, a clear training or work experience programme.

One of the training schemes which is being phased out in the reorganisation of training programmes is the Voluntary Organisation Training Programme. This programme was established to enable voluntary organisations to play a part in providing employment opportunities for the unemployed. One of the concerns expressed about the way this programme developed was that

New Zealand

voluntary organisations were using the unemployed as labour to provide a wide range of social services. In effect the government has rejected the use of the unemployed to provide personal social services which would otherwise not be provided and give future career opportunities to the unemployed at the same time (Pearl & Reissman 1965). A special fund of $20 million has been set up to enable essential social services threatened by the removal of the previous scheme to continue. Whether this fund will be adequate to compensate remains to be seen.

Evaluation

Government action to respond to the needs of unemployed people has been far from convincing. The inability of successive governments to control and reduce the level of unemployment, along with harsher eligibility conditions for access to unemployment benefit, are a reflection of this but perhaps the greatest problem has been the numeracy and impermanence of training programmes which have been intended to assist unemployed people enter or re-enter the workplace.

THE SICK AND INJURED

The historical discrepancies in the treatment of those suffering from sickness, in comparison to those experiencing accidental injury, in New Zealand is a vivid illustration of the complex policy issues which are generated when two independent schemes evolve based upon the <u>cause</u> of need, rather than the <u>condition</u> experienced by an individual.

Social Security

There are two distinct mechanisms for providing income support which depend upon the cause of incapacity: sickness or accidental injury.

<u>Sickness Benefit</u>. A loss of earnings due to sickness entitles an individual to sickness benefit subject to a means test, a minimum age requirement of 15 years and a residency requirement of 12 months. There has been little variation in the number of sickness benefits payable over the last 10 years and expenditure

represents about five per cent of total benefit expenditure. The majority of sickness benefits are paid to men, because the means test tends to exclude married women from access to the benefit.

Almost a quarter of sickness benefit payments include payments for a dependent spouse or child (Ministerial Task Force on Income Maintenance 1986).

Accidental Injury Benefits. A loss of earnings as a result of accidental injury is covered by the Accident Compensation scheme. The scheme derives from the report of the Royal Commission on Compensation for Personal Injury (1967) and was implemented in 1974. The scheme rests upon two basic principles; first that the community as a whole should accept responsibility for accidental injury; and second that all citizens must be covered. All accidents are covered whether they occur in the workplace, on the road, in the home or in leisure activities. Payments are earnings-related payable at 80 per cent of normal earnings subject to a maximum weekly payment. Reimbursement of medical and other costs incurred as the result of accidental injury can also be claimed under the scheme. In the year ending 31 March 1984 there were 153,259 claims made under the scheme, about 71 per cent for accidents at work, 11 per cent for accidents on the road and 18 per cent for other accidents. Expenditure on compensation for the year was just under NZ$260 million.

Personal Social Services

For most people who experience interruption of work due to sickness or injury the medical services received are sufficient for them to be able to return to work within a relatively short period of time. There are a wide range of personal services available when this is not the case but these will be discussed in the section on disability and handicap. It is, however, important to note the responsibility of the Accident Compensation Corporation for the prevention of accidents. It discharges this responsibility through safety and hazard analysis courses for employers, a close monitoring of safety records and public education programmes on road safety, home safety and recreational safety in conjunction with other government departments and voluntary bodies.

New Zealand

Evaluation

A major issue in present considerations of benefit reform is the discrepancy between income support for the victims of sickness and accidental injury. This is a complex problem which involves many considerations, including: the implications of any changes in accident compensation, since the introduction of the scheme removed the legal right to seek damages; questions of individual entitlement if sickness benefit were to be brought into line with accident compensation; the impact of changes in sickness benefit on attempts to unify the overall benefit structure.

THE DISABLED AND HANDICAPPED

A detailed survey of handicap in the Wellington region (New Zealand Department of Health 1981) indicated that 8.7 per cent of the population have some form of physical disability and about 4.9 per cent have a handicap which severely restricts everyday living. The 4.9 per cent with severe handicap is made up of about 2 per cent with sensory handicaps, 2.6 per cent with other physical handicaps and 0.3 per cent who are mentally handicapped (Ministerial Task Force on Benefit Reform 1986). The rate of disability increases with age and the rates of disability are higher for women than for men at all ages. The vast majority of disabled people live in the community, with only about six per cent living in some form of residential care. Employment rates for those with sensory handicaps are about five per cent below the rates for the population as a whole. The unemployment rates for other forms of physical handicap are 22 per cent for men and 45 per cent for women. The majority of severely mentally handicapped people living in the community attend sheltered workshops rather than being employed in open employment.

Social Security

Those who suffer from long-term disability as a result of an accident are covered by the Accident Compensation Scheme. Those who experience disability through a birth condition or as a result of illness are covered by the social security system. An invalids' benefit is payable

New Zealand

to those with long-term incapacity subject to a means test and a residency requirement of 10 years. Expenditure in the 1984-5 year was just under NZ$106 million, about 4.3 per cent of total benefit expenditure. It is estimated that 62 per cent of those receiving invalids' benefit suffer from mental disorders or mental handicap. There will be people of working age who are not covered by either accident compensation or by social security (excluded by the means test) and there are estimated to be about 3,000 people in this position (Ministerial Task Force on Benefit Reform 1986). Other forms of direct financial assistance to disabled people and in some cases sick people and other social security beneficiaries are available.

Disability Allowance. A weekly payment in recognition of the additional costs arising from the disability and the nature and extent of the disability. The allowance is means-tested and relatively few people qualify for the payment.

Handicapped Child's Allowance. A weekly payment to persons caring for a child with a serious physical or mental disability who needs constant care for a period in excess of 12 months.

Domestic Purposes Benefit. This benefit mainly provides income support to solo parents caring for dependent children but the benefit is also payable to men and women over 16 years of age who give full-time care to a person, other than a spouse, who would otherwise have to be admitted to a hospital.

Alterations to Homes. Grants can be made for essential modifications to be made to a person's home where they are seriously disabled.

Relief Care. Families caring for seriously disabled children or adults can be eligible for a grant to cover the cost of providing alternative care for up to four weeks in any one year.

Other Assistance. There are a number of other forms of assistance available such as telephone concessions, travel and accommodation costs associated with medical treatment, purchase of appliances and the purchase and modification of motor vehicles.

New Zealand

Personal Social Services

The 1974 Disabled Persons Community Welfare Act gives the Department of Social Welfare the pivotal role in the planning and co-ordination of services for the disabled. In practice there is a complex web of agencies involved at various levels: at central government level Social Welfare, Education, Health and Labour are some of the more obvious participants - a public corporation in the Accident Compensation Corporation - a fully funded quasi-governmental agency, the Rehabilitation league - a number of large voluntary organisations - a myriad of voluntary and self-help groups some operating at a national level and others highly localised.

The main role of the Department of Social Welfare and the Accident Compensation Corporation in relation to personal social services for the disabled is in funding voluntary organisations to provide direct services, for example the Rehabilitation League is involved in the assessment of disabled people and in providing work experience and employment placement services. The Society for the Intellectually Handicapped provides similar services for adult mentally handicapped people and a wide range of services for children including residential services.

Evaluation

One might expect that disabled people living in their own homes would be receiving support from community health services and personal social services. A survey of physically handicapped people in Wellington (Department of Health 1981) found that only a third of disabled persons were receiving at least one community health or personal social service. The majority of these services were health orientated such as community health nursing, physiotherapy or chiropody. Private home-help services and regular assistance in the maintenance of house and garden were the most frequent forms of personal social services. Only 3.5 per cent of the 2,024 disabled persons interviewed were receiving help from voluntary groups in the community with churches appearing to play the major role.

The focus in the discussion of services for the mentally ill, and to some extent the mentally handicapped, tends to be on the adequacy of health services, both institutional and community based. There are many recent reports which document the deficiencies of these services (Committee of Inquiry 1983; Department of Health 1985; Department of Health 1986). In attempting to develop community-based rehabilitation programmes it is acknowledged that a major obstacle is the lack of resources to support community-based initiatives and its impact upon community input and involvement (Department of Health 1986, pp.9-11).

The problems of maintaining services in the face of growing competition amongst voluntary agencies for both government funding and donation income is an issue for large agencies but is also reflected throughout the diverse voluntary/self help sector. Small grants from government departments, local authorities or charitable trusts can be critical to the continued survival of programmes and indeed agencies in the voluntary/self-help sector in the present environment.

AN ASSESSMENT OF THE NEW ZEALAND WELFARE SYSTEM

At any one point in time there are many issues confronting the welfare system, however three issues seem to be particularly important in New Zealand.

<u>The Welfare System and the Maori People</u>. There is growing evidence of the existence and extent of disadvantage amongst the Maori population relative to the non-Maori population. This is reflected in the following areas: indicators of health (such as infant mortality rates, life expectancy rates and the incidence of particular illnesses); indicators of educational achievement (such as examination pass rates and involvement in tertiary education); indicators of economic status (such as income levels, unemployment rates and house ownership); and relatively high rates of admissions to institutions (such as children's homes and prisons).

The 1970s saw the beginning of a concerted effort by the Maori people to rekindle their culture and in particular to save their language and re-establish the traditional tribal basis of social organisation. The challenge presented by these developments extends into all aspects of New Zealand society. The institutions of the welfare system are viewed as having played a critical role in destroying traditional Maori care and support systems and in creating dependency. The demands for change do not stop at merely seeking to modify services but rather extend to demands for a direct say in decision-making and the transfer of resources to tribally based organisations (for example, Ministerial Advisory Committee Report 1986).

The movement towards decentralising social services which has appeared in many industrialised countries in recent years is apparent in the Maori critique of social services in New Zealand. Their demands are of a more radical nature in that they seek direct control over service planning and allocations at a local level by people outside the service bureaucracy. In a country like New Zealand with a long tradition of central government provision and extremely strong centralised bureaucracies this is indeed a radical challenge.

Expenditure on the Welfare System. The present government is committed to reducing the budget deficit and has already achieved some success in this respect. Welfare spending has been constrained and some relatively minor cuts in programme spending introduced, however the bulk of expenditure cuts and restructuring of government activities has occurred outside the welfare system. Any further progress in controlling the budget deficit will have to involve the major spending programmes of social security, health and education.

A 'Blueprint' for Policy-Making. The present Labor government came to power in 1984 promising a Royal Commission of Inquiry into the social security system. This intention has now been modified to allow for a much wider review through a Royal Commission on Social Policy. The membership of the Commission will be announced in the near future and they will be expected to report their findings by the middle of 1988. The need for such a review is based on the argument that the objectives and structure of the welfare system still broadly reflect the reforms made in the 1930s and that this system may no longer be appropriate in the light of social and economic change.

New Zealand

Conclusion. New Zealand faces a similar dilemma in relation to its Welfare State as other OECD countries. The government must respond to the immediate pressures for change stemming from both economic and social considerations, whilst at the same time addressing the need to redefine the value base of the Welfare State and devise an appropriate institutional framework within which to realise welfare objectives. As a recent OECD report observes:

> the 'economic crisis' of the Welfare State may have peaked, it seems likely that the process of major institutional reform has only just begun (OECD 1985, p.62).

REFERENCES AND FURTHER READING

Briggs, A. (1961), 'The Welfare State in Historical Perspective', European Journal of Sociology, 2(2), 251-8.

Castles, F.G. (1985), The Working Class and Welfare, Wellington/Sydney: Allen and Unwin.

Easton, B. (1980), Social Policy and the Welfare State in New Zealand, Sydney: Allen & Unwin.

Franklin, H. (1985), Cul De Sac. The Question of New Zealand's Future, Wellington: Unwin/Port Nicholson Press.

Koopman-Boyden, P.G. (1978), Families in New Zealand Society, Wellington: Methuen.

_____ & Scott, C.D. (1984), The Family and Government Policy in New Zealand, Sydney: Allen & Unwin.

New Zealand (NZ) Accident Compensation Corporation (1985), Report of the Accident Compensation Corporation, Papers of the House of Representatives, E.19, Wellington: Government Printer.

_____ Advisory Committee on Youth and Law (1983), Report of Advisory Committee on Youth and Law, Auckland: Race Relations Conciliator.

New Zealand

_____ Budget '85 Task Force (1985), <u>Benefits, Taxes and the 1985 Budget</u>, Wellington, Government Printer.

_____ Commission of Inquiry into Case of Niuean Boy (1977), <u>Report of Commission of Inquiry</u>, Wellington: Government Printer.

_____ Committee of Inquiry into Procedures at Oakley Hospital and Related Matters (1983), <u>Report of the Committee of Inquiry</u>, Wellington: Government Printer.

_____ Committee to Report to the Minister of Social Welfare on the Current Practices and Procedures Followed in Institutions of the Department of Social Welfare (1984), <u>Report of the Committee to Report to the Minister of Social Welfare</u>, Wellington: Government Printer.

_____ Council of Social Service (1978), <u>Sharing Social Responsibility</u>, Wellington: Council of Social Service.

_____ Department of Health (1976), <u>Accommodation and Service Needs of the Elderly</u>, Special Report Series No.46, Wellington: Government Printer.

_____ (1985a), <u>Caring, Curing and Controlling</u>, Special Report Series No.75, Wellington: Government Printer.

_____ (1985b), <u>Physical Handicap</u>, Special Report Series No. 59, Wellington: Government Printer.

_____ (1986), <u>Review of Psychiatric Hospitals and Hospitals for the Intellectually Handicapped</u>, Wellington: Department of Health.

_____ Department of Labour (1985a), <u>Report of the Department of Labour</u>, 1984-85, Papers of the House of Representatives, G 1, Wellington: Government Printer.

_____ (1985b), <u>Wages, Hours and Employment</u>, Wellington: Government Printer.

_____ (1986), <u>Wages, Hours and Employment</u>, Wellington: Government Printer.

New Zealand

_____ Department of Maori Affairs (1985), *Report of the Department of Maori Affairs, 1984-85*, Papers of the House of Representatives, E 13, Wellington: Government Printer.

_____ Department of Social Welfare (1984), *Review of Children and Young Persons Legislation*, Wellington: Department of Social Welfare.

_____ (1985), *Report of the Department of Social Welfare 1984-85*, Papers of the House of Representatives E 12, Wellington: Government Printer.

_____ (1982), Social Programme Evaluation Unit, *District Variations in the Use of Extended Substitute Care*, Wellington: Department of Social Welfare.

_____ (1984a), *Government Funding of Voluntary Welfare Agencies*, Wellington: Department of Social Welfare.

_____ (1984b), *The Implications of Social and Demographic Change for DSW*, Wellington: Department of Social Welfare.

_____ Department of Statistics (1984), *Report on the Social Indicators Survey 1980-81*, Wellington, Government Printer.

_____ Employment Promotion Conference (1985), *Employment and Unemployment in New Zealand*, Wellington: Government Printer.

_____ Government Superannuation Fund (1985), *Report of the Government Superannuation Fund, 1984-85*, Papers of the House of Representatives B 20, Wellington: Government Printer.

_____ Human Rights Commission (1982), *Report on Children and Young Persons Homes*, Wellington: Human Rights Commission.

_____ (1986), *Reply to Chairman of Miramar Girls Home Visiting Committee*, Auckland: Human Rights Commission.

New Zealand

_____ Institute of Economic Research (1986), *Quarterly Predictions*, Wellington: New Zealand Institute of Economic Research.

_____ Ministerial Advisory Committee on a Maori Perspective for the Department of Social Welfare (1986), *Puao-Te-Ata-Tu*, Wellington: Government Printer.

_____ Ministerial Task Force on Income Maintenance (1985), *Benefit Reform*, Wellington: Government Printer.

_____ Ministerial Task Force on Social Welfare Services (1986), *Social Welfare Services*, Wellington: Government Printer.

_____ Planning Council (1984), *Meeting Needs in the Community*, Wellington: Planning Council.

_____ (1984), Population Monitoring Group, *The New Zealand Population: Patterns of Change*, Wellington: New Zealand Planning Council.

_____ (1985a), *Young People, Education and Employment*, Wellington: Planning Council.

_____ (1985b), Social Monitoring Group, *From Birth to Death*, Wellington: New Zealand Planning Council.

_____ Royal Commission on Compensation for Personal Injury (1967), *Report of the Royal Commission*, Wellington: Government Printer.

_____ Royal Commission on Social Security (1972), *Report of the Royal Commission on Social Security*, Wellington: Government Printer.

_____ Social Advisory Council (1984), *The Extra Years*, Wellington: Government Printer.

_____ (1985), *Child Care Services. Impact and Opportunities*, Wellington: Government Printer.

_____ (1986), *Partnership. The Delivery of Social and Community Services*, Wellington: Social Advisory Council.

New Zealand

_____ Task Force on Economic and Social Planning (1976), *New Zealand at the Turning Point*, Wellington: Government Printer.

Organisation for Economic Co-operation and Development (OECD) (1985), *New Zealand, OECD Economic Surveys 1984/85*, Paris: OECD.

_____ (1985), *Social Expenditure 1960-1990*, OECD: Paris.

Pearl, A. & Reissman, F. (1965), *New Careers for the Poor*, New York: The Free Press. Collier/Macmillan.

Pearson, D.G. & Thorns, D. (1983), *Eclipse of Equality*, Sydney: Allen & Unwin.

Seymour, J.A. (1976), *Dealing with Young Offenders in New Zealand*, Auckland: Legal Research Foundation.

Sutch, W.B. (1966), *The Quest for Security in New Zealand*, Wellington: Oxford University Press.

Uttley, S.C. (1983a), 'Bridging the Divide: A Maori Initiative in Linking Formal and Informal Care' in Pancoast, D.L. et al. (eds), *Rediscovering Self Help*, Social Service Delivery Systems, 6, Beverly Hills: Sage.

_____ (1983b), 'The Welfare State and the Public Expenditure Crisis in New Zealand: Public Debate and Theoretical Speculation', in Dixon, J. & Jayasuriya, D.L. (eds), *Social Policy in the 1980s*, Canberra: Canberra College of Advanced Education in conjunction with the Australasian Social Policy and Administration Association.

Wellington Old Peoples Welfare Council (1981), *Accommodation Change in Old Age*, Wellington: Wellington Old Peoples Welfare Council.

NORWAY
Hildegunn M. Forsund

THE WELFARE SYSTEM ENVIRONMENT

Historical Origins and Ideological Environment

The modern Norwegian welfare system has primarily developed after the Second World War on the basis of an overall political consensus acknowledging the role of government in providing services. The social security system consists of a national insurance scheme based on universal rights and a social care system which provides means-tested economic assistance. The provision of various health and personal social services is viewed as a major public responsibility.

Humanitarian Paternalism. Acts for regulating care for the aged and poor people by the farmers existed from the eleventh century until the turn of the nineteenth century. The content of these laws was a humanitarian idea of not only providing care for the extended family but also for the poor and the aged who had no relatives to support them. In this period the Church and the guilds also took part in and initiated social aid activities.

Liberal Ideology. The impact of liberal principles of self-help and individual responsibilities on the early social policy increased as the industrialisation process expanded, but it was never particularly strong.

International Diffusion. The embryo of the Norwegian Welfare State is to be found at the turn of the century and the principles embodied the Bismarckian social insurance acts of the 1880s.

Norway

In comparing the development of the social security policies in the Nordic countries, Kuhnle (1983) found that Norway was the country most influenced by these acts as far as accident and sickness insurance were concerned. Similar external diffusion also occurred after the Second World War, when the 1942 British Beveridge plan further influenced the forming of the Norwegian social welfare policy (Kuhnle 1983; Kuhnle & Solheim 1985).

The Underlying Values of the Social Security System. The policy for poor relief was based on the principle of providing a minimum assistance for those poor people who were physically or medically unable to make their own living, the so-called deserving poor. These principles were manifested in the two Poor Laws from 1845 and 1900. Sociological knowledge about the structural reasons for poverty contributed a broader view of social assistance which was incorporated in the Social Care Act of 1964. The intention of this Act was to provide social services for all citizens and social assistance for people temporarily without income regardless of the reason. Social assistance is means-tested and is provided on an individual basis, not in accordance with a set of national standards. In practice, it is payable to people without any legal rights to insurance benefits, and constitutes a security system for a residual group of people with little or no income (Oeyen 1975).

The development of the Norwegian social security system may be viewed as the product of competing principles:

- universal rights based on national standards principle versus rights for particular groups based on the principle of means-testing;

- the insurance principle versus the taxation principle;

- compulsory participation principle versus voluntary participation principle; and

- the minimum standard principle versus the principle of income replacement.

The first social insurance acts passed at the turn of the century concentrated on social security issues relating to labour conditions for the industrial employed, (including occupational injury, unemployment and sickness). They required compulsory contributions and provided means-tested benefits. The important questions about the need for social security were first raised during debates on old age pensions in the 1930s. The Conservatives at first advocated the social insurance principle within the framework of an achievement performance model, where social needs are met on the basis of merit. The Social Democrats preferred the taxation principle aiming at a social security system based on the reallocation of resources. Due to pragmatic political alliances, the Old Age Pension Act enacted in 1936 was based on both the social insurance and the taxation principles. The scheme was compulsory with regard to contributions, and means-tested with regard to payments.

The social democrats have advocated universality as a basic principle of social security throughout the century. Before the Second World War, the Conservatives were eager to reduce the public expenditure but they supported social security for the needy. After the War there was no real disagreement about universality as a goal and in 1956-7 the Norwegian parliament enacted both a universal sickness insurance and an old age pension legislation.

After 1945 several social security reforms were passed including: childrens' pensions (1957), occupational injury (1958), extended disability pension (1960) and rehabilitation allowances and allowances for unmarried mothers and widows (1964).

The issue of contention in the 1950s and 1960s was the question of a united national insurance scheme, including all those insured under social security laws. Disagreement was to be found on the .question of a minimum standard versus a standard of social security based on past income. A coalition of Social Democrats, Social Liberals and Christian Democrats carried through the double principle of both a minimum standard for all citizens and a standard related to former income for the employed, based on salary-related contributions.

Political Consensus. Though various differences exist between the political parties, an overall consensus on Norwegian welfare policy has developed (Seip 1981; Kuhnle & Solheim 1985;

Kolberg & Pettersen 1981). This consensus is partly related to an ideology of conservative collectivism, which has made the non-socialist parties accept limited state regulation in order to reduce injustice, and partly to the social democratic ideology of a public responsibility for equality and redistribution of resources. A psychologically important influence was the unifying influence created by the Second World War. The War experiences and the post-War situation helped build support for public regulation and resulted in the emergence of a temporary common programme for both socialist and non-socialist parties (Kuhnle & Solheim 1985). A precondition for achieving a social policy consensus has been Norway's stable economy (Seip 1981).

Political and Socio-Economic Environments

The Political System. Norway is a stable parliamentary democracy based on a multi-party system. Politically the first part of the century was dominated by non-socialist parties, the latter by the Social Democrats. Since 1965 non-socialist coalitions and minority governments of Social Democrats have shared power.

Administration. There are three tiers of government: central, county and municipal levels, all with popularly elected political assemblies.

The Norwegian Population. This is quite stable numbering about four million people with a recent yearly mean population growth of 0.33 (1979-84). However, the total fertility rate was 1.66 in 1984 compared with 2.72 in 1968-9 (Statistical Yearbook 1986). The age structure of the population is characterised by an increasing proportion of elderly people. In 1985 about 14 per cent of the population was over 67 years, but in 2025 the proportion will have increased to about 17 per cent. Immigration, primarily from elsewhere in Europe and the United States of America, has contributed to the population growth in a small way. Except for a small minority group of Lapps the racial composition is homogeneous.

Employment and Unemployment. For 30 years after the Second World War there was no serious unemployment in Norway. In 1984, however,

Norway

unemployment increased to about three per cent of the workforce, which is high for Norway. It has especially affected the young. Public efforts through the labour exchange, together with an increasing demand for labour, have reduced unemployment. From the 1970s female employment has risen about six per cent, with this increase being primarily in the public sector (Statistical Yearbook 1986).

Economic Growth. Sustained economic growth has been a characteristic of the Norwegian economy ever since the Second World War. From the 1970s oil production became a dominant economic factor accounting for about 19 per cent of the Gross Domestic Product (GDP) in 1984. Norway was thus insulated from the international economic crises of the 1970s. Economic policy of the 1970s was characterised by large public sector spending, resulting in a growing inflation rate. The tendency of the 1980s has been towards a more limited public economy. In the 1980s mean annual inflation rate has been estimated at about nine per cent (CBS 1986c).

THE WELFARE SYSTEM: AN OVERVIEW

Social Welfare Administration

The dominant features of the social welfare administration are the National Insurance Scheme (NIS) and the Social Care System (SCS). As regards health and social welfare, services are decentralised to a municipal or county level. Labour exchange services are the responsibility of the state and are located at the county and the municipal level.

National Insurance Scheme (NIS). The National Insurance Act came into effect in 1967. The object of the NIS is to provide benefits in the case of sickness, physical defect, pregnancy, unemployment, old age, disablement, death, loss of supporter and one-parent families.
 The system is both compulsory and universal. It provides social security benefits as well as various health services. It is partly based on the insurance principle, favouring members who have paid insurance contributions during their working career, and partly on the redistributive

principle which guarantees all citizens a minimum pension, health services or various other minor benefits.

The NIS is centrally administered by the National Insurance Administration (<u>Rikstrygdeverket</u>) and locally by National Insurance Offices mainly located in each municipality.

Country Committees and their secretariats are responsible for decisions about long-term benefit grants, such as disability pensions and rehabilitation allowances. The National Insurance Administration is the highest administrative body of appeal for disputes.

Special pension schemes are available for seafarers, fishermen, forestry workers, reindeer-herding Lapps and war invalids. These pension schemes are mainly amended to the NIS, and administered by the National Insurance Administration.

Unemployment benefits are administered centrally by the Directorate of Labour. A County Labour Committee and Development Board decide and control claims for unemployment benefits in the county. In the labour exchange district, decisions are often delegated to managers of the local Labour Exchange Offices. Appeals of decisions may be brought before the County Labour Committee and Development Board.

<u>The Social Care System</u>. This is based on the Social Care Act of 1964, which includes various forms of social services as well as economic support. The responsibility of implementing the Act is delegated to the municipality in which there is a Social Welfare Board elected by the Municipal council. The Social Welfare Board coordinates the social welfare activities in the municipalities and prepares a joint annual budget for these activities.

The Social Welfare Board provides information, advice and guidance to those individuals who need it in order to be self-supporting, or to overcome or adjust to difficult personal situations. According to the law persons who are not in a position to support themselves and provide for their own needs are eligible for social assistance (such as loans, grants, admission to homes for the aged, nursing homes or other suitable institutions). The services and benefits offered are given on an individual basis and are usually means-tested. The economic support is not given according to a uniform set of national standards. The administration of the Social Welfare Board's activities is delegated to a Social Welfare Office. Its personnel are usually professional social workers. The official in charge of the Social Welfare Office has the authority to make decisions pursuant to the daily administration of care. An applicant for social benefits may appeal a decision to the County Governor.

County Social Services. The county is responsible for the planning and running of institutions for child and youth welfare, residential homes for young mothers, foster home arrangements and institutions for the treatment of alcohol abuse.

Social Welfare Finance

The National Insurance Scheme. The financing of the NIS is based on compulsory contributions from employees and employers, together with a state grant determined by the Parliament.

A contribution set as a percentage of income exceeding NOK 17,000 per year is paid by the employees and the self-employed, partly based on the net income assessed for state tax purposes and partly on gross income. In 1986 the contribution based on net income was 4.4 per cent for both employees and the self-employed, while the contribution based on gross income was respectively 7.4 and 12.3 per cent. The employer's contribution is calculated on the basis of wages. Since 1975 this contribution has been stipulated according to variations in regional employment. In 1983 the maximum level of contribution was 16.8 per cent.

Contributions from the government are determined by the Parliament each year. The state grant compensates for deficits in income compared with expenses. From 1967 onwards, the level of government grants financing the NIS has increased dramatically, as a consequence of various reforms which have both widened insurance coverage, and thus increasing the number of recipients, and increased the benefits given.

The Social Care System (SCS). This is financed from general tax revenue. A central government grant is determined for primary health and social services in each of the municipalities. The expenses of financing the SCS have increased in the 1980s, especially in relation to economic aid. Research has shown that this development is due to an increase in unemployment, especially among young people, and to an increase of the single-parent families not being able to support themselves on the NIS allowances (Terum 1987).

The economic grant allocated under the Social Care system is supposed to maintain a minimum standard of living. There has been a debate about standardising economic aid at the same level as the minimum pension of the NIS (Oeyen 1981). A government commission has also supported this idea (NM HSA 1985; CP 18).

County Social Services. These are generally financed by block grants from the central government.

THE AGED

Until the twentieth century the responsibility for the aged was the prerogative of the families. During this century, public responsibility for the aged as regards both insurance benefits and social services has been acknowledged. When it comes to who actually cares for the aged, however, the majority of the aged who need care are nursed by female relatives.

Social Security

Social security is provided by the National Insurance Scheme (NIS) primarily through old age pensions and through the Social Care Act, if the daily expenses are greater than the pension provided by the NIS.

Old Age Pension. Since 1973, the retirement age after which one receives a pension from the NIS is 67 years. Special rules apply to taking a reduced old age pension in conjunction with earned income between the ages of 67 and 70. A full retirement pension is given after the age of 70.

The old age pension consists of a basic pension and a supplementary pension, and possibly special supplements, compensation supplements and carer's allowances. The basic pension is the basic amount stipulated by the Parliament, to which most of the NIS benefits are related. This amount was NOK 28,000 in 1986. The basic pension and the special supplements are the main elements of a guaranteed minimum old age pension, which was NOK 40,128 per annum in 1986 (RTV 1986).

The supplementary pension payable is dependent on the length of the working career and the amount of the annual income for the 20 best-paid years. Pension points are calculated for each pension-earning year between the ages of 17 and 67. Pensionable income which is between 8.33 and 12 times the basic pension generates reduced pension points. Pensionable income in excess of 12 times the basic pension is, however, disregarded.

For citizens without any former income or a very low one, the special supplement is designed to secure a minimum standard of living which the basic pension alone cannot provide. The special supplement is usually about one half of the basic amount. Both the basic pension and the special supplements are intended to be related to the cost of living and to the general income level in the society.

For the aged who incur expenses as a result of permanent injury, disablement or illness the NIS provides compensation supplements. These cover expenses related to the cost of necessary transport, a more expensive diet, clothes, certain costs of medicine and various costs of technical aid, and so forth.

A carer's allowance is granted to a person who is in need of special care or help in the house. The conditions for receiving this allowance is that the aged person is dependent on paid help or that help from relatives is a hindrance for their own possibilities of paid employment.

Social Assistance. People who are not able to support themselves on their own income may claim extra financial support through the Social Care Act. Due to a high cost of living in Norway, some pensioners with minimum grants find themselves obliged to apply for this extra assistance. Some municipalities pay an extra carer's allowance as financial assistance to old people who need care and receive help from relatives. The care allowance is paid in addition to any basic or allowance from the NIS.

Occupational Insurance Schemes. Private insurance schemes, often related to employment, are regarded as supplements to the old age pension of the NIS.

Norway

In 1984 about 36 per cent of the old age pensioners had a supplementary income from such private occupational insurance schemes (CBS 1986b).

Personal Social Services

Policy initiatives in the personal social services have until recently been primarily aimed at building nursing and residential institutions for the aged. Studies have shown that the aged want to live at home as long as they can and that institutional care often makes the inhabitants passive and more dependent on professional care. Recent social policy initiatives for the aged have therefore been aimed at providing services to enable them to remain at home.

Domiciliary Services. These consist of home-help, meals-on-wheels, handyman service and cleaning patrols. At the end of 1984, all the municipalities provided home-help services. The other services, however, are rather new and, according to public statistics, only two municipalities had organised such services in 1975. By 1982, 392 of the 455 municipalities provided such services to some degree at least (CBS 1986b). The domiciliary services are normally financed in part by means-tested fees.

Home Nursing. In addition to the domiciliary services, the home nursing service constitutes the major municipal welfare service provided to the aged living at home. Home nursing service became a municipal responsibility in 1984.

Day Centres. These provide medical supervision and aid to the needy aged who are living at home. In 1986 the municipality was given total responsibility for these services. Day centres are located in almost all counties of Norway (Guntvedt 1985). A day patient usually pays for the medicine and a nominal amount to cover the cost of food.

Service Centres. Traditionally service centres have been initiated and maintained by voluntary organisations. Much of the financial responsibility has recently, however, been taken over by the municipalities. The services provided are excursions, chiropody, exercise classes, hairdressing, a cafeteria, meals-on-wheels and visiting services. Centres are staffed mostly by volunteers but they often have a professional social worker to provide counselling services. These services are also financed by payment of fees.

Telephone Allowance. The elderly and disabled with a total income not exceeding the basic pension from the National Insurance Scheme may receive telephone allowances to cover the registration fee, subscriber fee and any expenses in connection with moving a telephone. These telephone allowances are granted by the municipalities.

Transport Concessions. Most of the municipality-operated transport companies give transport concessions to citizens over the age of 67. The ticket concessions also apply on all state-owned or state-subsidised transport services.

Improvement of Dwellings. To improve the standards of old houses and flats inhabited by the aged (and disabled) people, the Norwegian State Housing Bank may grant loans for renovation, depending on the age of both the applicant and the dwelling. The interest rate is quite favourable and the arrangement covers all kinds of housing. A grant for the improvement of dwellings lived in by the aged with special needs may also be sought. This grant is means-tested and applies to all dwellings regardless of age.

Housing Subsidies. People aged over 65 years of age with a low income and high housing expenses are entitled to housing subsidies. The dwellings must either be built after 1974 or before that with loans from the State Housing Bank or Agricultural Bank. These subsidies are means-tested and financed by a central government allocation. Since 1977, the central government has allocated grants through the municipalities so as to reduce total housing expenses for pensioners. These grants are means-tested.

Apartments for the Elderly. This involves the provision of purpose-built apartments for the aged (and other pensioners). This programme is rather new. Since 1974 about 1,000 apartments have been built yearly, often combined with built-in-services from service centres for the aged. These purpose-built flats are the responsibility of the municipalities and are financed by the State Housing Bank.

Homes for the Aged. Residential homes for the aged are a municipal responsibility and covered by the Social Care Act. A residential home is primarily for the aged who have a need and a desire to live in circumstances where household work is taken care of and they are offered supervision and a certain amount of socio-medical care.

Somatic Nursing Homes. A nursing home is a medical institution which provides nursing and care such that hospital care is rendered unnecessary. The nursing home may be an independent unit or a combination of residential institution and nursing home.

Psychiatric Nursing Homes. Psychiatric nursing homes are covered by the Mental Health Act. These institutions are regarded as long-term institutions for the mentally ill.

Geriatric Wards. In a few of the county hospitals, there are special wards for the aged. In 1983 there were only 265 beds in these wards (Guntvedt 1985).

Evaluation

The Norwegian Welfare State provides a range of measures of financial support and social services for the aged, while family care is acknowledged as supplementary assistance. However, there are discrepancies between political initiatives and the needs of the aged dependent on social welfare. Waiting lists exist for people wanting to stay in nursing homes. Claims for domiciliary aid cannot be met. This indicates a maladjustment between the need for and supply of services. Despite considerable variations in the rate of income replacement after retirement, the pensioners receiving only the minimum guaranteed pension constitute a low income group. Some of them have considerable difficulties in managing their daily expenses. The aged have, however, been made a high welfare policy priority with broad political backing. The great challenge regarding welfare for the aged is to use resources

THE DISABLED AND HANDICAPPED

To obtain any help the disabled person has to be medically invalid, dependent on assistance or unable to work. The total situation of the individual is assessed, which includes medical, physical and occupational disability. The provision of services to the disabled has been in the past provided through institutionalising and segregating measures. The aim of current policy is to integrate the needs of the disabled into municipal and county social welfare and education services.

Social Security

Social security includes two major systems of support, the National Insurance Scheme (NIS) and the Social Care Act (SCA).

<u>Labour Insurance Benefits</u>. Labour insurance benefits refer to the NIS disability pension. To qualify insured persons must meet certain insurance period and residency requirements. The disability must be of a permanent nature, caused by medical illness, injury or defect and must prevent the person from earning an income as a consequence. However, those with a primary medical diagnosis of alcoholism or narcomania are not entitled to a disability pension. Nevertheless, a disability pension may be awarded on the basis of other serious illnesses caused by these primary diagnoses. In 1984 there were 184,176 disability pensioners. From 1980 until 1984 there was a net growth of pensioners of about 37 per cent (RTV 1986).

A basic pension and special supplements are payable. To be entitled to a supplementary pension the pensioner must have had a reduction in working capacity of 50 per cent and have an annual pensionable income of at least the basic pension each year after 1967. People suffering from congenital disablement or who were disabled before the age of 21 are granted a supplementary pension based on a future annual number of pensions points where a minimum level is set at 2.5 points.

Norway

Extra Financial Allowances. From the NIS a basic grant is given if the disease, injury or defect involves heavily increased expenses for the disabled or occupational injured. As of 1 May 1985 the minimum basic grant was around NOK 3,500.

An assistance grant may be awarded to those who are injured or disabled who need nursing, domestic help or special care. As of 1 May 1986 the minimum assistance grant was NOK 5,856 per annum.

Technical Appliances. The NIS includes a varied set of rules for financing and provision of technical appliances for the disabled. Regional centres for the coordination of testing, purchase, allocating, repair and recirculation of such appliances have been established in all counties.

Social Assistance. The SCA programme ensures the financial existence for those who do not qualify for NIS benefits, such as alcoholics, drug addicts and socially divergent people. In addition, it covers those who receive funds from the NIS, but where these funds are insufficient to make ends meet. The support is given as a means-tested supplement to the NIS benefits.

Personal Social Services

Domiciliary Services. Services such as home-help services, meals-on-wheels, caretaker-service, cleaning patrols and so forth are available for the disabled living at home. These services are financed by means-tested fees, but the rates vary from municipality to municipality.

Relief Assistance. The disabled living at home or in institutions may receive social visits by special social workers. The purpose is to stimulate social participation in ordinary cultural or social activities. Home services are supplied by the municipalities, whereas county government is responsible for institutional services.

For families who care for disabled family members, supplementary care is offered to make holidays or relaxing weekends possible. These services are administered by municipalities and are means-tested. Families whose children receive supplementary care in an institution for more than one month lose their benefits such as basic and supplementary allowances while their child receives care.

Day Centres. Day centres provide services for disabled adults living at home, including social and cultural activity, information and social contact. Additional services, such as hairdressing, physiotherapy and ergotherapy, may be provided as well. The municipal Social Welfare Office is the administrative office of the activity.

Information and Counselling. Social welfare consultants have been employed at some of the county medical offices to counsel parents of disabled children.

Transportation Service. The municipalities obtain extra central government grants to accommodate the transportation needs of the disabled or to establish special transport services when regular transport services are not provided.

Housing Subsidies and Loans. The disabled may obtain housing subsidies or loans to manage general housing expenditure or renovation of dwellings.

Institutions for the Disabled. Various institutions are available for the disabled, such as large central institutions, smaller homes, day centres, sheltered workshops, and so forth. The administration of these institutions is under the Hospital Act of 1969, which designates the county as responsible.
The initial purpose of the large central institutions was to increase efficiency in the provision of specialised medical care. Current policy, however, is to provide for the needs of the disabled through local social services. The objective now is to provide individual housing, integrated with social and medical services and available work opportunities. A government study in 1985 (NOU 1985, p.34) proposed that the social service system for the disabled be transferred from the county level to the municipality. It is proposed that the institutions are to be used only to provide services for the extremely disabled. Medical care in such an institution is free. However, after a month's stay, pensioners' supplementary pension is reduced.

Norway

Health Centres. To prevent disability and physical or mental illness or injury, free health centres for children have been established in all municipalities. Physicians examine the children regularly between birth to the age of four.

Kindergartens. Disabled children have priority access to kindergartens if attendance is deemed beneficial. Less than one per cent of the children in kindergartens were disabled in 1984 (CBS 1986b).

Vocational Training. Nine years compulsory school is available for all children. After nine years of school, the disabled are given priority access to secondary school. Special lessons for the disabled may be available in ordinary classes, segregated schools, or in medical or social institutions. There are also special technical colleges for the disabled.

Labour Exchange Services. The disabled over 16 years of age are entitled to services from special rehabilitation consultants at the Labour Exchange Offices regarding employment in private or public enterprises, sheltered work or various forms of employment-preparing activities. Regional professional teams are established at special institutes to develop individual and realistic plans for rehabilitation. This service is free. The rehabilitation service is administered by the Labour Exchange Offices in cooperation with the National Insurance Offices, Social Welfare Offices, rehabilitational institutions, social medical departments in hospitals and psychiatric institutions.

Rehabilitation Allowances and Benefits. If a medically disabled person is provided with paid work, the NIS may provide a wage subsidy for a preliminary period of three years. The NIS also allows the combination of pension benefits and reduced working hours. In institutions for sheltered work training the workers have disability pension in addition to a symbolic salary. In sheltered workshops the disabled are ordinarily employed and are paid wages on a negotiated basis.

A rehabilitation allowance is paid during the rehabilitation period from the NIS, according to the same criteria as the disability pension, as

Norway

long as the disabled person is under medical treatment, occupational rehabilitation or waiting for a suitable rehabilitation programme. The socially disabled, such as those who misuse alcohol or drugs, may receive a means-tested allowance from the NIS during planned occupational rehabilitation.

Evaluation

Special emphasis has been placed on providing an income to the handicapped suffering from congenital disablement or those disabled before the age of 21, as they will not be able to raise their pensions income level by gaining pensions points during a working career. The new government policy of extended social and cultural integration of the disabled and the handicapped at the local government level, offers a challenge to the municipalities as those primarily responsible for this integration process. As regards the provision of employment, various measures of financial support are provided from the NIS to train or educate the occupationally disabled to help them readjust and enter the labour market. The integration of the mentally disabled or the severely physically handicapped is likely to depend on economic growth and the general employment situation.

NEEDY FAMILIES

Needy families are defined as families experiencing extraordinary situations of life which reduce the possibility of maintaining a stable income, such as pregnancy and child-birth, single-parenting and the loss of a breadwinner.

Social Security

Maternity Allowances. The NIS provides a maternity allowance of 100 days if the mother has worked for six of the last ten months before child-bearing. Periods of sickness or unemployment allowances may be included. The amount paid is based upon the mother's former income. Working mothers who do not so qualify are unconditionally entitled to a maternity allowance for the first six weeks after child-birth.

Norway

In contrast to many countries, there is a recognition in Norway of the role of the father and his rights in taking care of the newly born. The parents may share the allowance period, but 30 of the 100 days allowance period are reserved for the mother. To be entitled to the maternity allowance, the father must satisfy the same requirements as the mother.

Lump-sum Birth Grant. Mothers who do not meet the requirements for NIS maternity allowances are paid a lump sum after giving birth. The amount payable was NOK 4,000 in 1986.

Family Allowances. Family allowances were introduced in 1946 and granted to all families supporting children under 16 years of age. The benefits vary from the first to the later born children. The annual amount for the first child was NOK 5,256 in 1986 and for the fifth and additional child NOK 8,232.

Extra Birth Grants for Single Mothers. A birth grant is paid to an unmarried mother after the delivery. The annual amount in 1986 was NOK 7,740. In special cases, this grant may be paid before the child is born. If the unmarried woman has been in paid work, she is granted the NIS maternity allowance. If she has not been in paid work, she is entitled to the general lump sum birth grant in addition to the maternity grant.

Transitional Allowance for Single-parent Families. A transitional allowance is paid to a one-parent family supporter who is temporarily unable to support themself because of the need to care for the child/children or because of their participation in necessary vocational training or education to become self-supporting. The right to benefits usually lapses when the child has completed the third year of school, but it may be prolonged. The full transitional allowance corresponds to the guaranteed minimum pension of the NIS.

Educational Allowances for Single-parent Families. Educational allowances are provided if single-parents need education or training in order to become self-supporting. The NIS covers the necessary expenses for courses, school fees and accessories and examination fees.

Extra Family Allowances for Single-parent Families. Single-parent families are entitled to a family allowance for one child more than they have under the age of 16.

Assistance for Child Care for Single-parent Families. Assistance for child care is granted if single parents must leave the care of the children to others while being educated or in paid work.

Social Assistance. The social assistance granted under the Social Care Act is available to single parents and other low-income families, depending on the needs of the family. In spite of being awarded insurance benefits, single-parent families constitute a low-income group in Norway, especially those with a female head living exclusively on social insurance benefits. Studies have shown that about 60 per cent of the fatherless families living on the transitional allowance claim additional social assistance (Terum 1987).

Social Security Benefits to Surviving Spouse. A spouse is entitled to a survivor's pension if the marriage has lasted for at least five years, or if he/she is taking care of the children of the deceased. The pension is calculated according to the insurance period and the pension points of the deceased. If the deceased was entitled to a supplementary pension, the spouse gets 55 per cent of the previous pension. The pension is reduced if the spouse is in paid employment with a salary exceeding half the basic amount which the NIS normally provides.

If death was caused by occupational injury or illness, the survivor's pension is paid regardless of the circumstances.

In the case of divorce when the former spouse is not remarried, unemployed and under the age of 67, a pension may be awarded depending upon the duration of the marriage, the number of children and if the divorced person was receiving support from the deceased.

Orphans' Pensions. An orphan's pension is usually provided to children under 18 years of age who have lost their father or mother or both. If the child has lost the mother and paternity has not been decided, the pension is granted as if both parents were deceased. The annual pension corresponds to 40 per cent of the basic amount if one of the parents is deceased. Where both parents are deceased, the children will receive a pension equal to a survivor's pension, but stipulated in rates according to the number of children in the family. The total pension amount shall be divided equally among the children.

Allowance for Surviving 'Family Nurse'. A surviving 'family nurse' is entitled to a special benefit when unmarried, under the age of 67 and if he or she has stayed in the home for at least five years to give necessary care and attention to parents or near relatives. The care must have reduced the family nurse's opportunities of getting employment and may be permanent if the opportunities of employment are scarce.

Personal Social Services

Housewife Stand-in. If, during pregnancy or after, a single-parent mother family is in special need of domiciliary aid or of assistance in taking care of the baby, the municipal Social Welfare Office may provide a housewife stand-in for a limited amount of time.

Counselling and Information. The Social Welfare Offices offer various forms of assistance including social information and the communication with other welfare offices such as the Labour Exchange Office. Most of the Social Welfare Offices have special social workers who advise families who have severe problems concerning bringing up their children or other family issues.

Crisis Centres for Mistreated Women and Children. Severe cases of wife and child abuse have been given more publicity lately. Due to voluntary action amongst women, crisis centres have been established to give shelter and social assistance to women trying to cope with a difficult life situation. The centres are usually subsidised by the municipalities.

Evaluation

Compared to Sweden the period of maternity allowance is remarkably short in Norway; 20 weeks as compared to one year. A mobilisation of women in political process in Norway during the 1970s and the 1980s focused on maternity care and the Socialist government, which has eight female Ministers, intends to extend the period to 30 weeks in the years to come, depending in part on general economic growth. Studies have shown that single-parent families are in the lower income group, especially those whose total income comes from transitional allowances (Kjeldstad 1986; Dahl 1987). Unintended effects of taxation and social insurance rules make it unprofitable to seek reduced working hours in employment, and single parents often find themselves in a poverty trap (Hatland 1985).

THE SICK AND INJURED

Social welfare support for the sick and injured is granted in cases of sickness, physical defect or pregnancy. Additional sickness benefits are granted as health care services and are financed by refunds from the NIS, public expenditures and fees paid by the patients.

Social Security

Sickness Allowances. The general requirement for entitlement to sick allowances is a fixed earned annual income and employment or self-employment for at least 14 days before the sickness or injury occurred. Employees are entitled to 100 per cent of their gross earned income from and including the first day of absence. The employer must pay the allowance for the first 14 days, after which the allowance is paid by the NIS. Self-employed persons are entitled to sickness allowance amounting to 65 per cent of assumed annual income from the fifteenth day of sickness. A voluntary supplementary NIS insurance may be taken out covering up to 100 per cent of the income basis from the first day of illness. Persons in temporary freelance employment may also receive a 100 per cent sickness allowance from the fifteenth day of illness. Military personnel, seamen, unemployed with daily unemployment allowance receive sickness allowances according to special rules. No allowance is payable which exceeds six times the NIS basic pension. Sickness allowances are subject to taxes and the insured person is credited with pension points on the sickness allowance in the same way as on earned income.

Norway

For patients undergoing long-term treatment in approved health institutions the sickness allowance or other NIS benefits to an insured person will be reduced unless they are supporting a family. A supplement is payable if patients are supporting a spouse or children, while the insured person receives a lesser amount for himself.

The sickness allowance is paid up to 260 days for one sickness period. In cases of prolonged sickness, the insured person is eligible for rehabilitation assistance if receiving approved medical or rehabilitation treatment.

Medical Benefits. Medical benefits are granted in the form of free service or repayment of costs partly or fully from the NIS irrespective of work history. The services provided are:

- care from physicians, psychologists and in some cases from dentists;
- physiotherapeutic treatment and treatment from chiropractors prescribed by a physician;
- assistance from midwives, family planning, regular examination during pregnancy and health centres for children;
- medicaments of major importance (including vaccines and various prostheses) or treatment to counteract the effect of functional disturbances;
- medical treatment and care in approved health institutions; and
- transportation and board in connection with travelling for examination and/or treatment for which benefits are granted.

Minor fees are paid by patients for medical treatment and medicine, limited to an annual amount of NOK 840 in 1986. Expenses exceeding that amount per annum are free. Some of the municipalities have special arrangements for free medical care for pensioners, especially the aged. Free medical service is granted in the case of occupational injury or illness or confinement. Seamen on Norwegian ships engaged in foreign trade and public officials abroad are entitled to completely free medical assistance from the NIS.

Occupational Injury Benefits. The NIS provides benefits for occupational injury, meaning bodily injury or illness caused by an occupational accident. Self-employed businessmen under 67 may take out voluntary insurance for occupational injury coverage. During treatment of the injury or illness the injured person is generally entitled to sickness benefits and the NIS covers all the expenditure of medical assistance, physiotherapeutic treatment, medical costs and various remedies for rehabilitation.

If the capacity for work has been reduced at the end of the treatment period, a pension may be payable according to the same rules as the disability pension, but subject to certain modifications. There are no requirements of a minimum insurance period, number of point years or period of stay in Norway. A pension is paid even if the earning ability has not been permanently reduced. If the degree of disability is finally determined to be less than 30 per cent, the pension is paid out as a lump-sum based on an estimated annual pension according to disability degree.

Personal Social Services

Those who are sick or injured with difficulties in managing to live at home may receive home nursing service or domiciliary services such as housewife stand-in or home-help service from the Social Welfare Office.

Evaluation

Social security allowances based on the NIS criteria are payable while sick or injured, or attending rehabilitation programmes and provide an economic basis for maintaining the previous living standard. Sickness or injury resulting in disability normally reduces income level as a result of less favourable insurance rules for disability pensions. A private insurance market of injury and disability pension schemes is therefore emerging to help provide for maintenance of an individual's living standard.

CHILDREN AND YOUTHS

The care and upbringing of children is traditionally viewed as the responsibility of the parents. A modest level of income security is provided through a family allowance programme enacted in 1946 and granted to all families with children under 16 years of age. In cases where economic, social or environmental circumstances may threaten the families' ability to secure their children's welfare, various forms of assistance may be provided by the welfare state.

Social Security

Social Assistance. Young people who have passed the age of 18, who are unemployed and not in school, may ask for social assistance from the Social Welfare Office according to the Social Care Act. Studies have shown that this group of youngsters has increased during the 1980s constituting a major group recipient for social assistance (Terum 1987).

Personal Social Services

In the municipalities Child Care Committees implement the Child Welfare Act of 1953, which requires them to examine the living conditions of children and adolescents and, in cooperation with other organisations, to promote measures for the improvement of child welfare. Measures may be applicable to children under 18 years of age if they:

- are facing serious physical or mental health risks;
- are severely maladjusted to society;
- have no one to provide for them or their parents are not able to; or
- are physically or mentally ill, or suffering from other defects or disabilities that require extra nursing or treatment.

The general child welfare policy is that children shall stay at home with their family. The Child Care Committee, therefore, first adopts preventive measures to secure living conditions in the children's homes by offering home assistance services as well as financial help when needed. If none of these measures are successful, the committee may consider taking custody of the child and having it brought up in a foster home, children's home or other suitable institution. To assist the child a supervisor is appointed to take care of contact between the foster home, or other institution, and the parents. The administration of the measures are usually dealt with by professional social workers at the Social Welfare Offices.

Institutional Child Care for Pre-school Children. Traditionally, the rearing of children has been the responsibility of housewives. Due to the sudden increase of female workers especially in the 1970s and 1980s stronger demands have been made to build more kindergartens and play centres. The number of children accommodated in kindergartens increased by nearly 300 per cent in the period 1975-84. However, in 1984 there were still only kindergarten facilities for 26 per cent of the children under seven years of age (CBS 1986b).

Kindergartens operate on a fee basis, but this often depends on the income of the parents. Therefore subsidies are given if the family has two or more children using the service and, in addition, families with low income may apply for free service. Disabled children or children of single parents are given a priority access to kindergartens. Political refugees are entitled to free service for a limited period. The construction and administration of kindergartens is the responsibility of the municipalities, however, there is a large number of voluntary programmes and facilities operated by various religious or humanitarian organisations.

Out-of-School Care. For children attending primary school some municipalities have established play centres to supervise the children and provide cultural activities while their parents are still at work. In 1984 only 3,500 children were provided with this service. The responsibility for building play centres is municipal, but this is not stated in any law (CBS 1986b).

Support for Children Affected by Marriage Breakdown. Children of single parents have priority in attending kindergartens. Moreover single parents are entitled to extra family allowance, child care assistance and various allowances from the NIS securing a minimum standard of living or the possibility of occupational education.

Support for Illegitimate Children. Welfare services for the unmarried woman and her child or children are the same as for separated or divorced families. Extra economic support is granted at the time of the child's birth if the mother is not living with the child's father. In addition, there are special homes available for unmarried mothers with infants needing care and treatment after child-birth. In law, an illegitimate child has the same rights of inheritance as legitimate children, if the father is known.

Foster Homes. Children for whom the Child Welfare Committee has assumed custody are preferably placed in foster homes. Foster homes must be approved of by the Child Welfare Committees and must be regular families. The foster parents are paid for their service and the placement is administered by the official Foster Home Centres which are the responsibility of the county. Of the children under custody care in 1984, 70 per cent were living in foster homes and only 14 per cent in children's homes (CBS 1986b).

Institutions for Children and Adolescents. Institutional care is provided if the parents are unable to take care of the children in accordance with the Child Welfare Act, and there has been no success in attempts to either support the family or provide a foster home.
Children's homes are small institutions catering for a maximum of 12 children under the age of 13. Homes for adolescents are institutions for young people between the age of 13 and 18. The demand for this type of institution is far greater than supply. The youngsters attend regular schools or have regular jobs. Teachers with special training play an important role in encouraging the youngsters to take part in various activities and in helping them to adjust to a more normal life.
Psychiatric institutions for children and adolescents are available if behavioural difficulties are such that consultation and treatment by psychiatrists is necessary. This service consists of polyclinics and treatment homes. On the national level a State Centre for Child and Adolescent Psychiatry has been established. For young drug addicts there are special therapy homes, but the services available are far from meeting the demand. Except for treatment and therapy, vocational training and leisure activities are provided in the

institutions. Public responsibility has increased in this area, but voluntary initiative is still quite strong.

<u>Young Boys with Criminal Records</u>. Other institutions are provided for young boys between 14 and 18 years of age with criminal records. Youngsters under the age of 14 who have commited crimes are not tried in a criminal court. They become the responsibility of the Child Welfare Committee which is responsible for finding suitable measures in each case in cooperation with various professionals.

<u>Adoption</u>. To qualify for an adoption a couple must be married, over 25 years of age and Norwegian citizens. The proposals for adoption are decided upon by the Child Welfare Committee, the Municipal Health Advisory Board and the County Governor. With foreign children, the Ministry of Health and Social Affairs and the Board for International Adoptions must accept the application. If both the adopting parents are in paid employment they are entitled to a maternity allowance for 12 weeks from the NIS. In some cases a lump sum benefit of NOK 4,000 (1986) is payable as supplementary assistance.

<u>Evaluation</u>

Care and upbringing of children is traditionally acknowledged as a parental responsibility. In cases when the parents are unable to raise their children, because of work, social problems or the death of one or both of the parents, the Welfare State provides measures to secure the welfare of the children through various social services or economic support. However, welfare services in this area fall far short of meeting the demand. There is a lack of kindergartens and especially of institutional treatment for maladjusted youths with criminal records, psychiatric problems or drug abuse. Moreover, the growth of unemployment in the early 1980s especially affected young people, making those young people into clients dependent on social welfare assistance. The number of new child welfare cases was stable for many years, but from 1975 to 1982 it doubled. Though these problems affect a minority of children and youngsters, they represent a clear challenge for the welfare system to secure the welfare of maladjusted children and youth.

THE UNEMPLOYED

As in the rest of the industrialised world, there has been an increase in unemployment in Norway, especially in the 1980s. The rate of unemployment reached its peak in 1984 at 3.2 per cent of the total workforce. By 1986 the unemployment rate had fallen to 1.8 per cent. (These figures include those available for immediate employment.) A significant proportion of the unemployed are youths without a professional education (Arbeidsdirektoratet 1987). At the same time there is a tendency to exclude older workers in private enterprises, resulting in an increase of hidden pre-pension retirement of older workers. Curtailment of operations or temporary dismissals of employees have affected the heterogenity of the unemployed. In addition, surveys have shown there is a concealed unemployment in workers who delay entry into the labour market, because of the lack of suitable jobs.

Social Security

Unemployment in Norway is viewed as a legitimate reason for receiving welfare benefits. The requirements for entitlement to NIS unemployment benefits are having been in paid employment before being unemployed, and having earned a fixed income. Means-tested social assistance is available if the benefits paid from the NIS do not cover daily expenditure.

Daily Cash Allowance. Unemployment benefits are payable as a daily cash allowance for a period of 80 weeks. The allowance is calculated on the basis of daily wages, however, it cannot exceed six times the basic amount. Minor supplements are payable if the unemployed person is supporting a family. To be eligible for the daily cash allowance, the unemployed person must be able to work, willing to accept any work which the Labour Exchange Office finds suitable, and be in regular contact with the Labour Exchange Office for as long as daily allowances are granted.

Norway

Social Assistance. Social welfare assistance may be payable to unemployed persons not eligible for the benefits granted by the NIS. If recipients of unemployment benefits from the NIS find themselves in financial hardship because of highly reduced income, means-tested social assistance may be granted. Investigations have shown that this group of social welfare recipients is small in number compared to the unemployed youngsters with no or little former experience of employment (Terum 1987).

Personal Social Services

There are no special personal social services for the unemployed. The Social Welfare Office, however, does provide a range of services.

Job Search Services. The Office of the Labour Exchange, generally located in every municipality, may offer a range of services for the unemployed. All who seek employment are given free advice by special occupational consultants concerning different occupations or educational alternatives. In the bigger cities, special divisions have been established to cope with unemployment among youth. Some of the Labour Exchange Offices have special consultants to deal with the unemployment of foreigners. At the county level, special programmes have been initiated for the purpose of increasing the employment of women.

Voluntary Training. Persons having difficulties in getting a new job because of lack of vocational or occupational training, may attend special work training courses in order to qualify for various handicraft or industrial occupations. To a certain extent, these courses are provided in collaboration with private enterprises. They are free and travelling expenses are also paid for.

Wage Subsidies. To enable an unemployed person to obtain employment the Labour Exchange Office may provide grants from the NIS or from a special state budget which subsidises wages in public or private enterprises for a limited period, when the intention is to provide regular employment. These subsidies are usually reserved for certain groups such as youth, the elderly, women, foreigners and the long-term unemployed.

Norway

Job Creation Programmes. At the peak of the unemployment period, special governmental employment programmes were implemented to temporarily employ people in public services. A decline in unemployment has led to the termination of these programmes.

Training and Counselling Centres. For people having severe difficulties obtaining gainful employment, regional Labour Market Institutes have been established to test working ability and increase employment opportunities. The service is free and is provided in collaboration with the local Labour Exchange Offices.

Recreational Facilities and Programmes. The greatest challenge in the sector of employment is to prepare the mentally, physically or socially disabled to earn a stable income. Special programmes have been developed for these groups either individually or collectively providing vocational and occupational education as well as job-training. While attending an acknowledged rehabilitation programme, benefits are available from the rehabilitation scheme of the NIS.

Evaluation

Although there has been a minor increase in unemployment in the 1980s, the growth of employment has been notably stronger in Norway than in any other Western-European country, growing by 20 per cent from 1973 to 1984. The most dramatic trend is the growth in the number of married women entering the labour market, amounting to four-fifths of the total growth of the work force for the period (NMFA 1982). Despite increasing unemployment, there have been a considerable number of vacancies in many sectors where educational skills are required, which indicates that the labour market is undergoing severe adjustment problems. Besides wage subsidies and various job-creation and skill-training programmes, the government policy is to stimulate business and industry to give guidance, practical experience and training for young people and to promote in-house training schemes to deal with readjustment of their own employees to prevent future unemployment. Due to an annual increase of 12,000 to 14,000 potential employment seekers between the age of 16 and 67 in the years to come, the future challenge in the economic policy is to create around 20,000 to 30,000 new jobs per year (NMFA 1982).

ASSESSMENT OF THE NORWEGIAN WELFARE SYSTEM

The two systems of welfare, the NIS and the SCS provide financial assistance in cases of temporary or permanent loss of income. Included are welfare benefits given to citizens for the purpose of covering training or education taken in order to obtain a new job. Social services are primarily considered to be a public reponsibility. In spite of a considerable expansion in social security benefits and the personal social services, demand exceeds supply. In the social services there are shortages in the services offered, especially in respect to the needs of the aged, children and youths. Both the NIS minimum pension and the social assistance have been shown to be insufficient to cover daily expenditure.

The Norwegian social welfare policy implemented after 1945 has concentrated on reducing economic and welfare inequalities through a policy of redistributing the benefits of economic growth. Sociologists have found that inequalities have been reduced, but they have not disappeared. In spite of general economic welfare, social problems have increased and various groups of poor people have not benefitted from the redistribution that has taken place (Hanoa 1977; Lingaas 1983). In addition, there has been a tendency for recipients to become dependent on the welfare support (Kolberg 1970; Leonardsen & Roenning 1982).

In the 1980s both politicians and social scientists have been occupied by the crises of the Welfare State resulting from a decline in economic growth (Kuhnle & Solheim 1985; Kolberg 1983; Ringen 1981; Stjernoe 1982). Despite a general reduction in the public sector's size, health and social welfare are still high priority areas. There is general agreement between both the political parties and within the community at large about the need to maintain the legitimacy and the strength of the welfare system (Kuhnle & Solheim 1985). To do this the question of a possible commercialisation of welfare benefits in the years to come has been raised (Kuhnle & Solheim 1985).

In the future, great challenges will occur in maintaining the Norwegian welfare system, especially in the NIS. As the NIS is financed by current contributions the increase in the proportion of retirees compared with contributors in the future may threaten the stability of this method of financing. There is, therefore, an inherent demographic problem facing the NIS. In addition, increases in future supplementary pensions will cause a considerable growth of expenditure. Proposals integrating housewives into the supplementary pension scheme and reducing retirement age, which are now under debate, will probably result in increased future NIS contributions. The economic future of the NIS may therefore encourage a debate about the universal principle of allocation versus a principle of providing benefits for the needy.

A second challenge relates to the impact of the entrance of women into the labour market. Studies show that women provide the major source of care for children, the aged and the disabled (Waerness 1982). This source of support will be more and more difficult to obtain as women enter the labour market. The present policy on first-line welfare services is to offer services to the aged or disabled in their home with some professional assistance from the Welfare State, and with some support of an extended family. There seems, therefore, to be a problem in the relationship between the limited services rendered by the public services and the possible future care provided by women.

A further consequence of women's increased work participation is a tendency for them to choose non-traditional careers, away from employment in health care and social services. Thus the combination of hard work and low incomes have reduced the recruitment of personnel in the welfare services. This situation threatens the delivery of services, when hospital departments and kindergartens are temporarily closed because of lack of personnel. The public authorities, therefore, have to take measures to improve working conditions for the health care and social service workers in order to provide stable public welfare services in the years to come.

Norway

REFERENCES

Arbeidsdirektoratet, <u>Arbeidsmarkedsstatistikk nr 2</u>, Oslo 1987.

Central Bureau of Statistics of Norway (CBS) (1986a), <u>Health Statistics 1984</u>, NOS B608, Oslo.

───── (1986b), <u>Social Statistics 1984</u>, NOS B615, Oslo.

───── (1986c), <u>Statistical Yearbook of Norway</u>, Oslo.

Dahl, Espen (1980), <u>Sosiale fordelingsvirkninger av ny egenandels-ordning</u>, Oslo: Sosialdepartementets utredningsserie, rapport nr 10.

───── (1987), <u>Enslige forsoergeres oekonomi. En analyse av foreliggende data.</u> Upublisert, Statistisk Sentralbyraa, Oslo.

Guntvedt, Odd H. (1985), <u>Services, Housing and Institutions for the Elderly in Norway</u>, Oslo: The Norwegian Institute of Gerontology, report nr 6.

Hanoa, Rolf (1977), <u>Sosialmedisinske behov og ufoerhet i et saneringsstroek i Oslo</u>, Oslo: Gyldendal.

Hatland, Aksel (1984), <u>Folketrygdens Framtid</u>, Oslo: Universitetsforlaget.

───── & Tore Johannesen (1985), <u>Trygd, skatt og arbeids-inntekter</u>, notat nr 5, Oslo: Institutt for anvendt sosialvitenskapelig forskning.

Kjeldstad, Randi (1986), <u>Forsoergermoenster i forandring. Folketrygdens og barnetrygdens rolle</u>, Olso: Stensil, Institutt for anvendt sosialvitenskapelig forskning.

Norway

Kolberg, Jon-E. (1970), 'Det klientskapende systemet', Kontrast nr 1.

───── (1974), Trygde-Norge, Oslo: Gyldendal.

───── (1983), Farvel til velferdsstaten?, Olso: Cappelen.

───── & Per Arnt Pettersen (1981), 'Om velferdsstatens politiske basis', Tidsskrift for samfunnsforskning bd 22 nr 2-3, Oslo.

Kuhnle, Stein (1978), 'The Beginnings of the Nordic Welfare States: Similarities and Differences', Acta Sociologica 21, Supplement.

───── (1983), Velferdsstatens utvikling. Norge i et komparativt perspektiv, Bergen: Universitetsforlaget.

───── & Solheim, Liv (1981), 'Party Programmes and the Welfare State: Consensus and Conflict in Norway 1945-1977', Skrifter nr 3, Institute of Sociology, University of Bergen.

───── & Solheim, Liv (1985), Velferdsstaten - vekst og omstilling, Oslo: Tango.

Leonardsen, Dag & Roenning, Rolf (1982), 'Det klientskapende samfunn', i Stjernoe, S. (red.), Velferd eller noed, Oslo: Pax.

Lingaas, Lars Gunnar (1983), (red.), Myten om velferdsstaten, Oslo: Pax.

Norwegian Ministry of Foreign Affairs (NMFA) (1982), The Disabled in Norway, UDA 734 10/82.

───── (1983), Norwegian Child Welfare, UDA 701 06/83.

───── (1985a), The Labour Market in Norway, UDA 170 06/85.

───── (1985b), Voluntary Action in Health and Welfare Services, UDA 10/85.

Norway

———— (1986), Social Administration in Norway, UDA 740 03/86.

Norwegian Ministry of Health and Social Affairs (NMHSA) (1983a), The Social Care Act of 5 June 1964, Oslo.

———— (1985b), Lov om sosiale tjenester m.v., NOU, 18.

———— (1985c), Levekaar for psykisk utviklingshemmede, NOU, 34.

———— (1986), Samordning i helse - og sosialtjenesten, NOU, 4.

———— (1987), Norwegian Report to Conference of European Ministers Responsible for Social Affairs, Warsaw, 6-11 April 1987, Oslo.

Oeyen, Else (1974), Sosialomsorgen og dens forvaltere, Bergen: Universitetsforlaget.

———— (1975), 'En beskrivelse og sammenligning av to sosialpolitiske system', Tidsskrift for samfunnsforskning, bd 16.

———— (1981), Garantert minsteinntekt i Norge, Oslo: Universitetsforlaget.

Ringen, Stein (1981), Hvor gaar velferdsstaten?, Oslo: Gyldendal.

Rikstrygdeverket (RTV) (1986), Statistisk aarbok, Oslo.

Seip, Anne-Lise (1981), Om velferdsstatens framvekst, Oslo: Universitets-forlaget.

Stjernoe, Steinar (1982), Velferd eller noed, Oslo: Pax.

Terum, Lars Inge (1987), 'Trygd og sosialhjelp. Boer forholdet mellom hjelpesystema vurderast?' Sosial trygd, nr 1.

The National Insurance Administration (1986), Social Insurance in Norway, Oslo.

Norway

Titmuss, R.H. (1974), <u>Social Policy</u> (eds Brian Abel-Smith and Kay Titmuss), London: Allen & Unwin.

Waerness, Kari (1982), <u>Kvinneperspektiv paa sosial-politikken</u>, Olso: Universitetsforlaget.

SWEDEN
Sven E. Olsson

THE WELFARE SYSTEM ENVIRONMENT

The focus of this analysis of the Swedish welfare system scrutinises the balance between the social service state and the social security state in Sweden in the mid-1980s after a decade of major concern about the future of the welfare state. This balance differs quite considerably between different Western welfare states - a few of them have large public consumption sectors, while the majority have more or less all-encompassing income maintenance schemes. The Swedish case represents an attempt to bring the two types together.

Historical and Ideological Environments

Even before the notion was widely accepted in the first post-war decades, in the 1960s in particular, Sweden was regarded as a democratic model Welfare State (Childs 1936). As early as 1938, the American Academy of Social and Political Sciences launched a broad presentation - mainly by Swedish contributors like the then little-known economist Gunnar Myrdal - of the social policy programmes that were underway in Sweden as part of the new, Labour-dominated, Left-Centre political regime (Ohlin 1938).
Situated on the Western corner of Siberia, this North-European Welfare State shares many basic characteristics with surrounding nations in the advanced capitalist world. In particular the social developments in the neighbouring states of Denmark, Norway and Finland have given birth to a broader concept, the Scandinavian or Nordic Welfare State model (Deadalus 1984).

Attempts have been made to conceptualise this 'model' not only along territorial lines, but in a more plainly scientific form. Among the first was Richard Titmuss (1974), who talked about an institutional model of social welfare as compared to a much more limited residual or marginal social policy approach. In recent years, a growing theoretical interest has produced dichotomies like 'strong' vs 'weak' Welfare States, and so forth, but still there is no common terminology in this field of social research (Amenta & Skocpol 1986).

In the 'residual' or 'weak' welfare state, responsibilities for social contingencies rest almost entirely with individuals, either through their own market capacity or through social relations of dependency inside the family as a social institution. Only when these 'natural' mechanisms do not function is social policy to enter the stage, and then only as a temporary substitute. The state intervenes as a patron of marginal groups that are unable to survive, while the majority of the non-working population are to be sustained and protected by the family, where the individual male wage-earner is the patron in charge.

In the 'institutional' or 'strong' social policy model, the state is no longer the 'lender of last resort'. It is firmly a state model, and social policy is an integrated part of society offering citizens services outside the market on criteria of need. Firstly, it is a universalistic model, bring all residents under the shelter of their state. Secondly, the relationship between work activity and job rewards is at the same time - dialectically - reinforced and abolished. Thirdly, in the event of illness, old age or whatever contingency may disturb the ability to earn a living through the market, economic support is provided to match the average standard of living (Korpi 1980).

State intervention in the economy and in the maintenance of the population have old roots in the Nordic countries. Solidaristic and egalitarian values too have long had a strong backing in this part of Europe. Serfdom was never imposed on the rural population, and feudal magnats never succeeded in pushing the peasantry out of the representative four Estate-system (nobility, clergy, merchant and peasant) which dates back to medieval times. Literacy has for centuries been widespread. The central state is contemporaneous with the sixteenth century Lutheran reformation, when the Church was deprived of its property and thoroughly subordinated to state power, which after a 'Great power' period in the seventeenth century, degenerated into weakness. After the Tzarist take-over of Finland in 1809, language became uniform. And for more than 170 years, Sweden has been spared the ravages of war (Koblik 1975).

A 'peasant democracy' emerged with the new bi-cameral Parliament in 1866, at a time when suffrage was still severely limited but the emergent industrial and financial tycoons were not yet strong enough to dominate the semi-feudal state. At the local level, the free peasant had considerable influence over public affairs, too. Before the process of industrialisation and urbanisation developed roughly a hundred years ago, Sweden was a poor but fairly egalitarian society. Responsibility for the maintenance of work discipline and work ability lay with the state, although central and local authorities quarrelled over the performance of the task. Strong popular movements - the teetotallers, the non-conformist churches, centre-left middle and working class political parties as well as socialist trade unions - soon became recognised 'social partners' which were able to form coalitions, struggling and negotiating with the upper social classes around the ruling royal order. This was the background to the social policy events that started around the turn of the century inspired by working class demands, middle class liberal humanitarianism, and paternalistic, Bismarckian social legislation in neighbouring Prussian Germany (<u>Acta Sociologica</u> 1978).

For example, poor relief and work houses were not regarded any more as proper means to care for the sick, aged, needy and able-bodied poor by the popular movements. They tried instead to secure the existence of their members through voluntary self-help by friendly societies (sickness funds and burial societies), and unemployment and strike funds, and demands sent to Parliament. In 1891, two years after a Factory Inspectorate had been established sickness funds received state subsidies. From that time until the Second World War, a rudimentary public network of social protection was developed: universal old-age and invalid pensions, motherhood insurance and child allowances to children without parents (or with widows or invalids as parents), state subsidies to recognised unemployment funds, and compulsory occupational injury insurance (see table 1).

Universal suffrage and representative democracy was instituted under the impact of the insurrections that shook the world at the end of the First World War. After a decade, the Social Democrats took a firm grip over the helm for almost half a century. In addition, the closely affiliated blue collar Trade Union Confederation achieved in the 1930s an agreement with the Employers' Confederation that strengthened their power position in society and paved the way for gradual and incremental developments on the labour market up to the 1970s (Korpi 1978; Therborn 1985). From this time on, concerted welfare programmes influenced by a labourite ideology and the rationality of social engineering were outlined, a few of them in effect from the late 1930s but generally set in motion in the late 1940s. These programmes more or less continuously expanded during the post-War decades up to 1980, with increasing support from the newly unionised white collar employees, in particular in the public sector (Marklund 1982). This was accompanied by stable economic growth up to the mid-1970s. Thus, in material terms, progress in Sweden has been extraordinary: one of the poorest countries in Europe in the mid nineteenth century, it became in the second half of the next century one of the most prosperous in the world (Jorberg 1984). A summary of the post-War expansion of welfare programmes is given in Table 2.

Currently the positive consequences of social policy measures for both the market and the individuals have a strong ideological bearing. In contrast to a small minority consisting of professional economists and neo-liberal ideologists, social policy is not seen by the great majority as a threat to the smooth functioning of the market mechanisms (Heckscher 1984). Unemployment is seen as a social cost, not as a price signal to the workers to adjust their demands to what the market for the moment can offer as in traditional laissez-faire economics. The Keynesian theme of full employment via state intervention has been developed into the full responsibility of all citizens to provide mutual support - solidarity - through public authorities. Thus, policies directed towards increasing labour-force participation and

Sweden

TABLE 1: SWEDISH WELFARE PROGRAMMES PRIOR TO THE SECOND WORLD WAR

1763	Poor Law
1842	Compulsory state education
1847	Poor law (more generous; recognition of right to appeal)
1862	Foundation of county councils to cover the country with a network of hospitals
1871	Poor Law (more severe; right to appeal withdraw)
1889	Factory Inspection Act (Industrial Safety Act 1912)
1891	Subsidies to voluntary sickness benefit societies
1901	Employers made liable for reimbursement in cases of industrial accidents, changed to compulsory occupational injury insurance in 1916
1906	State subsidies to municipal employment offices
1913	Universal and compulsory old-age and invalidity insurance; National Board of Social Welfare instituted as well as Pension Board instituted
1914	State Board for Relief work and unemployment cash support
1918	Poor Law (more generous, right to appeal re-installed)
1919	Act on eight-hours working day
1920	Separate Ministry for Health and Social Affairs
1924	Child Care Act
1931	Act on recognition of voluntary sickness benefit societies and improved state subsidies to them
1933	New employment policy; housing grants and rent rebates
1934	State subsidies to recognised unemployment funds
1937	Motherhood insurance, preventative maternity and child care Act (free delivery), child allowances to children without parents (or with widows or invalids as parents), maintenance advances.
1938	Public dental care.
1939	State grants to homes for the aged

SOURCE: Elmer 1986; Olsson 1986

decreasing unemployment are another important aspect of the institutional model, that is, a commodification of the great majority of the adult population as no individual ought to be dependent upon another through the market wage. In particular, women should not be dependent upon men and equality between the sexes is part of the official ideology.

Contrary to countries where living on welfare is synonymous with being poor and relying on public support, these stigmatising effects are more or less avoided where the Welfare State receives strong support in public opinion (Svallfors 1987). Thus, in a universalistic approach social policy assumes a major role, potentially of the same scope and significance as the market in effecting allocative and distributive processes in society. The institutional types of social policy will attempt to prevent needs from arising rather than being limited to alleviating needs which already have become manifest.

Socio-economic and Political Environments

Sweden is a non-aligned country, which belongs neither to North Atlantic Treaty Organisation (NATO) nor to the European Economic Community. Nevertheless, it is firmly situated inside the Western economic hemisphere of advanced capitalist countries and is extremely dependent upon developments in world markets. The transformation into an industrial society mainly producing technologically advanced manufactured goods for exports was aided by Sweden's abundant natural resources (iron ore, timber and water), the proximity to the European markets, and the reconstruction of a continent that had been plagued by two world wars that Sweden escaped. The long recession from the mid-1970s onwards adversely affected the Swedish economy.

State intervention in the economy is frequent, but in industry and trade the role of state enterprises is marginal. Agricultural employment is currently below five per cent, and most farmers belong to the Federation of Swedish Farmers - the central co-operative, which is closely affiliated with the Centre Party. In the retail industry, consumers' co-operatives are important. Otherwise, business is in the hands of a highly concentrated private ownership, mainly through

TABLE 2: MAJOR CHANGES IN THE SWEDISH WELFARE SYSTEM AFTER 1945

Area	Year	Change
Labour market and unemployment insurance	1948:	Nationalisation of local employment offices under a new National Labour Market Board, also supervising voluntary unemployment relief funds
	1974:	Cash benefits to non-insured
Industrial safety and injury insurance	1949:	New safety law and central agency
	1955:	Old compulsory insurance coordinated with sickness insurance
	1976:	Safety law replaced by Work Environment Act
Health insurance	1946:	Parliament approves principle of flat-rate insurance (never implemented)
	1955:	Compulsory earnings-related insurance
	1963:	County councils take over responsibility for state-provincial physicians
	1967:	County councils responsible for psychiatric care; i.e. the whole health system
	1974:	Cash benefit level raised to 90 per cent of gross earnings (became taxable). Dental insurance
Pension	1948:	Universal flat-rate pension
	1960:	Earnings-related compulsory supplementary pension for employees Pensions paid from 1963
Family policy	1948:	General child allowance
	1974:	Parental insurance replaces maternity benefits
Municipal poor relief	1957:	Social assistance law replaces poor law
	1982:	Social service law replaces social assistance law

SOURCE: Olsson 1986.

institutions like insurance and investment companies as well as private foundations. The dominant group, the Wallenberg dynasty employing half a million Swedes, has been called the financier of the Welfare State. Nowadays, Swedish multi-nationals like Volvo operate to an increasing degree overseas, and employment abroad had grown considerably in the last two decades (Hermansson 1981, 1986). At home, industrial employment grew up to the mid-1960s, but has since declined or stagnated, and has been surpassed by the tertiary sector in both employment and Gross Domestic Product (GDP) terms (see table 3). Overall, private enterprise accounts for almost two-thirds of employment (SCB 1985). The public sector, accounting for almost one-third of employees has grown rapidly in the last decades, and here, more than every second employee is a female, often working part-time. In the future labour force participation is projected to grow in the private service sector (SOU 1987:3).

In 1985 there were 4.4 million people in the labour force (of which 47 per cent were women). Unionisation is very high both in the private and the public sector. More than 90 per cent of the blue-collar workers belong to the Trade Union Confederation (LO) with some two million members. The non-partisan Central Organisation of Salaried Employees (TCO) and Confederation of Professional Associations (SACO/SR) have succeeded to unionise most white-collar employees. The labour market is thus characterised by strong and centralised organisations, which also holds true on the part of employers, where one confederation is representing both big business and smaller firms in industry and commerce (Kjellberg 1983). Between these organisations, or affiliated sectorial unions, national wage agreements are negotiated each or every second year. These organisations also frequently take part in public life and are often on the boards of various state administrative organs. All three levels of government have their own negotiating bodies, which make agreements with unions belonging to the abovementioned central organisations.

Politically, the Swedish system is based on representative democracy on three levels: national, county (24) and municipal (284) (see Graph 1), all with tax-raising powers. The unicameral Parliament is chosen in direct elections and is situated in Stockholm, where the

TABLE 3: SECTORAL CHANGE OF GROSS DOMESTIC PRODUCT AND EMPLOYMENT

Percentage Distribution[1]	1950	1960	1970	1980	1985
Gross Domestic Product					
Agriculture	11	10	5	4	3
Industry	48	47	44	35	34
Services	40	44	49	60	63
Employment					
Agriculture	20	13	8	5	3
Industry	39	45	40	36	33
Services	39	41	52	59	64

Note: 1 Percentage distributions do not add to 100 due to rounding

SOURCE: SCB 1985.

Head of State, the King, who only has ceremonial functions, also resides. Parliamentary seats are distributed proportionally above a four per cent threshold, and the cabinet is dependent upon the relative strength of parties in Parliament. A working class party, the Social Democrats, has for decades dominated political life (Himmelstrand 1982, Olofsson 1979). They were continuously in office between 1932 and 1976, partly in coalitions or in working agreements with mainly the non-socialist Centre party (earlier Farmer's League). There has, however, been considerable competition between the three bourgeois parties - Centre, Liberal and Moderate/Conservative - non of which has consistently dominated the other two. Between 1976 and 1982, four non-socialist cabinets were in power, but since 1982 the Social Democrats have been back in office (Korpi 1983, Esping-Andersen 1985).

Demographically, the population is fairly uniform in terms of language (Germanic), race, religion and similar characteristics. The Laplanders, a very small ethnic and linguistic minority in the far North, have lived there for thousands of years. Approximately 95 per cent of Swedes belong to the Lutheran State Church but a secularised culture is dominating everyday life

Sweden

(Deadalus 1984). Sweden has a low birth rate, but life expectancy is rather high: 80 years for women and 74 for men. Since the Second World War a net immigration of some 600,000 persons has accounted for more than half of the population growth. Still, the newcomers, mainly from neighbouring Finland, but also from Southern Europe and other continents, constitute a relatively small part of the population (Leinio 1984). As in most European countries, the population is ageing: a decline in the share of youth (just below 20 per cent) has been accompanied by an increase for those aged over 65 (17 per cent in the mid-1980s). In a comparative perspective, the economically active population is still large, and the dependency ratio - so important in all social policy discussions - is thus remarkably unaltered. Again, immigration has helped to maintain this balance.

THE WELFARE SYSTEM - AN OVERVIEW

The Structure and Administration

Graph 1 provides an overview of the Swedish political and administrative system (Vinde & Petri 1978). On the national level, political power rests with the Cabinet, which organisationally consists of twelve rather small Ministries. They prepare budgetary and policy matters for Parliament and issue instructions to the general administration. The main 'welfare ministries' are the Ministries of Health and Social Affairs, of Labour, of Housing, and of Education and Cultural Affairs. The Ministry of Finance is the co-ordinating public cashier, including social security, although formally the National Superannuation Pension Funds are not included in the yearly budget of the government.

Under the government's authority, 24 State County Administrations, and a number of often rather powerful and independent, central agencies implement the policies decided upon. The latter ones sometimes have independent regional sub-units, or affiliated semi-public organs like the regional Social Insurance Funds, but in most cases their regional administration is part of the general State County Administration. The most important 'welfare agencies' are: the National Social Insurance Board, the Housing board, the

GRAPH 1: THE POLITICAL AND ADMINISTRATIVE SYSTEM IN SWEDEN

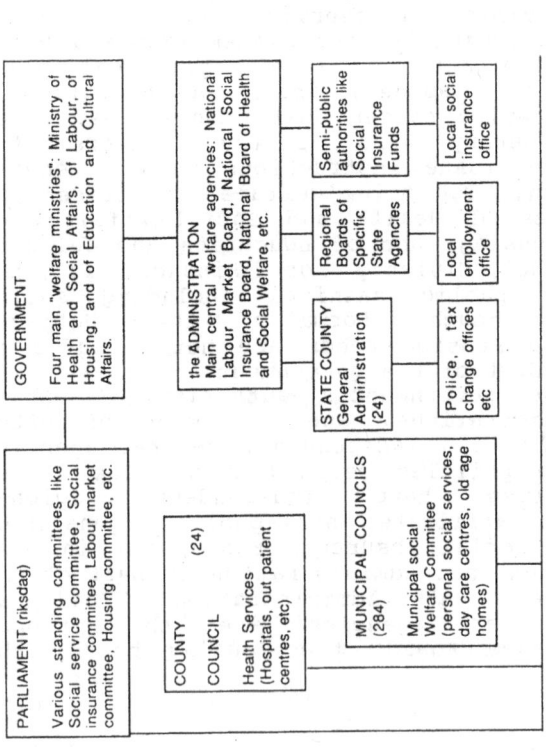

General elections to policy-making bodies are held at three levels: national, county council and municipal. Overriding responsibility at all three levels is vested in the State, acting through the Riksdag and Government. The 'staircase' above serves to illustrate the mutually independent status of county councils and municipalities.

SOURCE: Adapted from Lundquist, L., Förvaltningen i det politiska systemet, 2 uppl., 1977.

Board of Health and Social Welfare, the Board of Industrial Safety, the Board of Education, the Immigration Board, and the Labour Market Board. The latter one has, like the Social Insurance Funds', local employment offices (employment services are a state monopoly) in each municipality. Senior civil servants in the Ministries, as well as in the County Administration and the central agencies, are appointed by the Cabinet.

Labour market and manpower policy is the task of the central government (Rothstein 1986). The responsibility for and financing of education is shared between central and local authorities. Housing is shared between the administrative levels, while social security is tightly controlled by central authorities but carried out by formal private social insurance funds. The exception to centralised authority is unemployment insurance, which is administered by the trade unions under the inspection of the Labour Market Board (Edelbalk 1975).

In each county, there is a directly elected representative County Council. The population of these regional units ranges from 60,000 to 1.6 million. Their main field of responsibility is the administration and performance of health and medical care. Advisory guidelines are given in the new national Health and Medical Services Act, in force since 1983 (SFS 1982:763).

The task of providing personal social services has traditionally been the duty of the 284 municipalities, which have populations ranging from 3,000 to 700,000 (Stockholm). They also have a directly elected representative body, the Municipal council, and their own agencies for different branches of administration. These are under the control of committees elected by the municipal council, but they also have a number of salaried employees. The Social Welfare Committee is usually the one with the largest share of the municipal budget, and the most personnel. Central guidelines for municipal social work are given in the new Social Service Act, in force since 1982 (SFS 1980, p.620).

As indicated, a comprehensive social welfare system exists in Sweden. Nevertheless, in the housing sphere, fiscal welfare is important through deductions in taxable income, and similar public subventions not directly seen in the state budget (Olofsson 1986). In the pension sector,

Sweden

occupational welfare, through a network of negotiated nationwide pensions agreements, is of some importance for white collar employees (Stohlberg 1985). The private pension insurance market has been expanded in the first half of the 1980s, but is still only for a wealthy minority. Private welfare through the church and other charitable organisations plays an insignificant role in Swedish society. There are both national and local fund-raising campaigns, organised by various voluntary organisations, but these are of negligible importance and often aimed at international assistance.

Social Welfare Finance

A comprehensive welfare system is, of course, not free of charge and imposes certain limitations on the individuals' freedom of spending. However, in return for taxes and - to a much lesser extent - contributions, people are provided with a broad spectrum of public services and social benefits which include the following: guarantee a job or education/retraining, a decent standard of living, aid in emergencies, redistributed income more evenly over a person's life cycle, and narrows the financial gaps between various groups (Eriksson & Aberg 1987). The extent of these interventions can be measured in a number of ways. Total public sector expenditure - including public consumption, public investments, social and other transfers and subsidies, as well as the interest payments on the public debt - is higher as a percentage of Gross Domestic Product (GDP) than in any other industrialised country and amounted to no less than 65 per cent in 1985, especially in the area of non-military public consumption - mainly social services - which is the largest segment reaching almost 30 per cent of GDP (OECD 1985).

Graph 2 shows an overview of the main welfare outlays in 1985 at current prices and their financing. Income maintenance, (in particular basic and superannuation pension benefits, but also sickness benefits, allowances, parental insurance benefits, and a variety of smaller expenditure items) makes up the majority of social outlays. A growing item is child care, as a result of a concerted programme for the expansion of day nursery places. Education expenditure, roughly of the same order as public health, is not

Sweden

GRAPH 2: SOCIAL EXPENDITURE 1985 (Current prices).

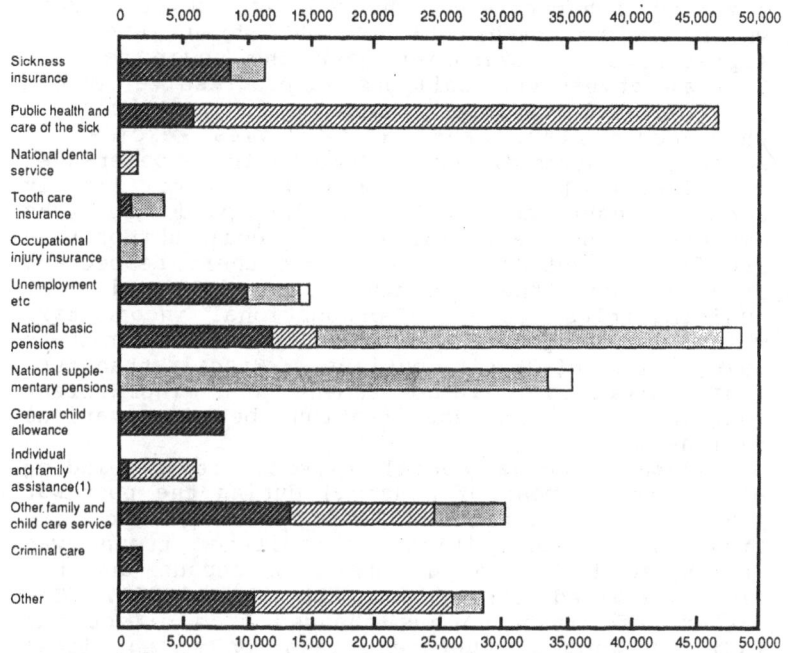

LEGEND

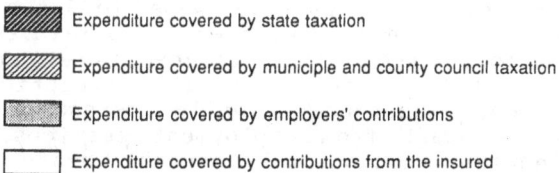

NOTE: (1) Including temperence welfare, public child welfare and social assistance

SOURCE: The cost and financing of social services in Sweden in 1985 (SCB, S42 SM 8601).

included in the graph. Most public expenditure on housing is not included, but is in toto comparable to sickness insurance expenditures.

Almost all personal social services and social security schemes are financed by public taxes, which are relatively high. All three levels of representative government have the power to tax. Central government collects a progressive income tax, several indirect taxes - in particular a value-added tax, and also levies excise on selected commodities (alcoholic beverages, gasoline, etc) - as well as a payroll tax (mainly social insurance contributions paid by the employers and self-employed). Local authorities are free to set the tax rates in their respective areas, and the County Councils and the municipalities collect a proportional income tax, which varies greatly throughout the country, to cover part of their outlays. Fiscal transfers from central to local government to a minor extent contribute to an equalisation between various regions.

Graph 3 shows social expenditure (excluding education and most of housing) during the post-war period at constant (1950) prices, and its financing. The rising expenditure trend was broken at the turn of the last decade and has since remained fairly constant (SCB 1986). The pattern of financing has changed from direct and indirect central government taxation to the local proportional income tax and charges imposed on the employers. As of 1987 these levies amount to about 35 per cent of the wage bill, and are treated as business expenses. Social security contributions from the insured are nowadays marginal with the partial exception of unemployment insurance. While personal social services - apart from employment services, which are financed through the central state - are mainly financed by local taxation, social security schemes are financed by contributions from the employers.

Sweden

GRAPH 3: SOCIAL EXPENDITURE 1950, 1960-85 AND ITS FINANCING (in 1950 PRICES)

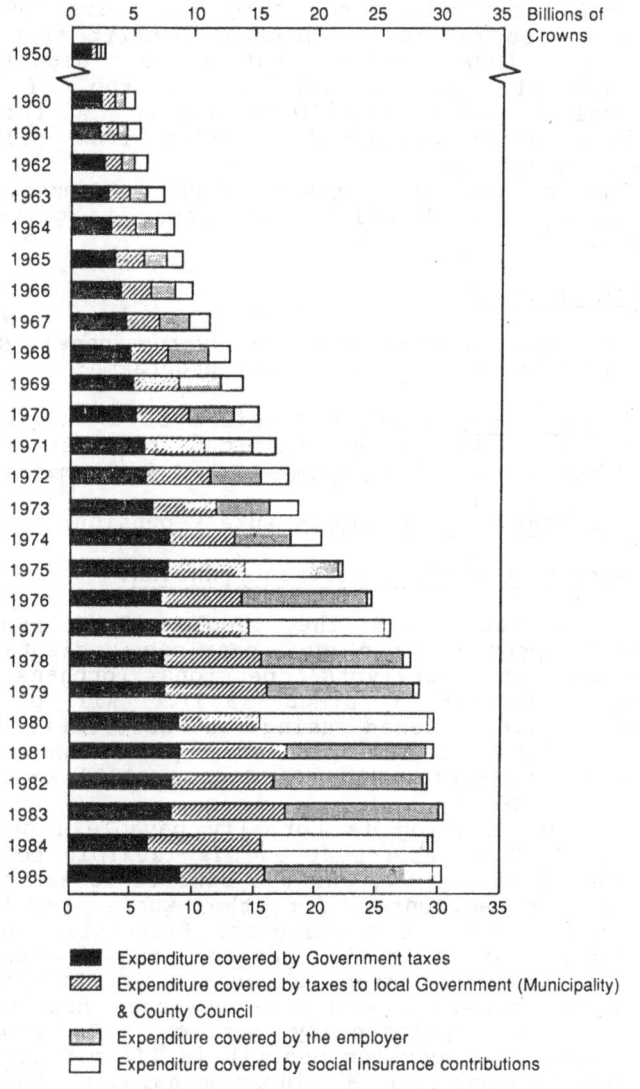

■ Expenditure covered by Government taxes
▨ Expenditure covered by taxes to local Government (Municipality) & County Council
▧ Expenditure covered by the employer
☐ Expenditure covered by social insurance contributions

SOURCE: The cost and financing of the social services in Sweden in 1985 Statistics Sweden (SCB S42 SM 8601).

Sweden

THE AGED, DISABLED AND HANDICAPPED

In the mid-1980s, well above two million Swedes were in receipt of pension benefits from the national programmes (see table 5). Some 750,000 of them also received a pension benefit from one of the four major nationwide negotiated occupational pension schemes on top of the national benefits (Stahlberg 1985). A further 200,000 persons received benefits from private pension insurances.

Public spending on the pension programmes, and on old age and disability services, is given in table 4.

Social Security

The national Swedish pension system consists of two major and one complementary programme:

- <u>basic pension</u>, which consists of a universal, minimum flat-rate pension together with various partially income-tested supplements;

- <u>earnings related supplementary pension</u>; and

- <u>part-time early retirement pension</u>.

Both the basic and the supplementary pension schemes provide old-age pensions, disability pensions, and survivors' pensions (orphans and widows) (Edebalk & Elmer 1983). All pension benefits are indexed using an artificial <u>base amount</u>, linked to the consumer price index and adjusted annually, which in January 1987 amounted to 24,100 SEK.

Old age pension is normally payable from the age of 65, but retirement age is flexible between the age of 60 and 70, and the benefit consequently reduced or augmented for the whole remaining life-span. This is a universal flat-rate benefit consisting of a basic pension and a special pension increment which is payable in addition to the basic pension, where a pensioner has no or only a low supplementary pension. In January 1987, the total pension benefit is 144 per cent of the base amount for a single pensioner (96+48), and 253 per cent for a couple (78.5+78.5+48+48). In 1987, the pension has reached the sum of 34,992 SEK for single and 61,479 SEK for couples and are the guaranteed minimum hand-outs.

Sweden

TABLE 4: PUBLIC OUTLAYS ON PENSION PROGRAMMES AND ON SOCIAL SERVICES FOR THE ELDERLY, DISABLED AND HANDICAPPED 1984 (MILLION SEK)

	Total Outlays	Central Government Contributions	Local Government Contributions
Social Security Expenditure			
Basic pension scheme:			
old age pension	30,920	30,920	-
disability pension	7,420	7,420	-
widows' pension	1,330	1,330	-
orphans' supplement	198	198	-
wife's supplement	707	707	-
handicap allowance	395	395	-
child handicap allowance	383	383	-
child's supplement	64	64	-
municipal housing allowance	4,040	719	3,321
Sub Total	45,457	42,136	3,321
Supplementary pension scheme:			
old age pension	24,620	24,620	-
disability pension	7,850	7,850	-
widows' pension	3,345	3,345	-
orphans' pension	357	357	-
Sub Total	36,172	36,172	-
Part-time early retirement scheme	1,135	1,135	-
TOTAL	82,764	79,443	3,321
Personal Social Services			
Care of the disabled (Technical aids and so forth)	3,746	3,744	-
Domiciliary service	6,112	1,925	4,190
Homes for the aged	4,149	-	4,149
Care of mentally retarded	3,995	504	3,491
TOTAL	18,002	6,173	11,830
Total Public Outlays	100,766	85,616	15,151

SOURCE: National Social Insurance Board, and Statistical Yearbook.

Sweden

TABLE 5: NUMBER OF PENSIONERS IN 1984 BY TYPE OF PENSION AND PENSION SCHEME ('000)

Pension Scheme	old age	Number of Pensioners disability[1]	widows	orphans	Total Number
Basic pensions[2]	1,435	321	78	37	1,871
Supplementary pension	912	252	281	41	1,486
Part-time pension	47				47
Other supplementary[3]	53	22			76
Estimated number of pensioners	1,535	343	281	41	2,200

SOURCE: SCB 1986, pp.303-5.

Notes:
1. Includes disability pensions and temporary disability pensions for both the basic and the supplementary pension schemes. Under 'other', handicap allowance is reported.
2. In 1984, 847,323 persons were in receipt of the special pension supplement and 648,965 in receipt of municipal housing allowances.
3. Other supplements in the basic pension scheme: in 1984, 53,349 persons were in receipt of wives' supplement, 9,448 in receipt of handicap allowances and 12,948 in receipt of disability allowances for children. The way these supplements are incorporated under pensioner categories does not correspond to official Swedish classification.

In principle, all pension benefits (except the housing allowance) constitute taxable income. However, pensioners whose only source of income is the minimum pension do not pay tax because of a special tax exception rule. With any additional income, this tax deduction is reduced proportionally.

Sweden

Disability pension is paid to persons over 16 years of age whose working capacity is reduced by at least 50 per cent due to illness, physical disability or mental handicap. If people are expected to recover wholly or partially, they may receive a temporary disability allowance. An unemployed person who has used all their rights to unemployment benefits can retire at the age of 60 if their working capacity is not reduced, under the disability programme. A full disability pension equals the old age pension, but with the difference that a double pension increment is paid, if the disabled has either no or only a low supplementary pension. At the age of 65 the disability pension is replaced by the old age pension and the pension increment is reduced correspondingly.

In addition, these benefits can be combined with the following supplements: income-tested wife's supplement; child's supplement; child care disability allowance; handicap allowance; and income-tested municipal housing supplement. The amount of the latter is determined by the municipal councils and may vary from one municipality to another. This is the most important supplement, and together with the basic pension and the pension increment if forms the foundation of the non-taxed pension benefit, which amounts to roughly two base amounts for a single person and three base amounts for a couple.

The general supplementary pension scheme is compulsory and covers all (employed and self-employed) persons over 16 years of age. The supplementary pension is earnings-related, and is payable to persons who have yearly earned more than the 'base amount' for at least three years (old age pension rule).

The benefit from this scheme depends on the 'average pensionable income' earned in previous years and on the number of years of gainful activity. For each year, a ratio is calculated by dividing the individual income by the general base amount for the respective year ('pension points'). However, only the income up to a ceiling of 6.5 times the base amount is taken into account. The average number of pension points for all years of gainful activity (for a period of more than 15 years, the average is calculated for the 15 best years but 30 years' of accumulated pension points for full benefit) is then multiplied by the base amount for the year in which a person retires. For each missing year the pension is reduced by 1/30. This gives the 'average pensionable income'. A smaller number of years (but at least 20) is required for persons born between 1896 and 1923 to qualify for a full pension. For the supplementary old age pension the normal age of retirement is 65, with the same possibilities of early or deferred retirement as in the case of the basic pension scheme.

To qualify for a supplementary disability pension, a person must have accumulated pension points for at least one year of gainful activity. The rules are in principle the same as for the supplementary old age pension, with the difference being that pension points (above one year) are calculated on the basis of present or former (particularly in case of total disablement) income in relation to the reduction of the working capacity, and for future assumed income to 65 years of age ('normal career'). Finally, a supplementary family or survivors' pensions are payable to children under the age of 19 on the death of one or both parents, and to widows (but not widowers) under certain conditions.

Personal Social Services

The guiding principle in both Swedish old-age and disability policy - which have a common universalistic approach - is that the aged, disabled and handicapped should be part of the community and not be treated as special or separable groups of people (Sundstrom 1983). Each individual is given the opportunity to live and function in as near normal a setting and under conditions as near normal as possible. This also applies to the handicapped, as a handicap is not regarded as an individual characteristic but considered as a relationship between the society and the individual.

Following this policy, the state offers a number of services, but individuals are responsible for most of their own care, with the assistance of relatives, friends and neighbours. The great majority of the disabled and those aged over 65 live in their own homes or in rented apartments (over 80 per cent of the latter group). Pensioners living at home are entitled to a means-tested non-repayable grant for housing improvements, and in the 1980s over 90 per cent of the aged have modern facilities (Jonsson & Lundberg 1984). However, anyone needing help to sustain themself in everyday life has the right to claim other types of assistance if their need cannot be met in other ways. In particular the municipalities, but also the country councils, provide a number of personal social services.

The most important of these is domiciliary service, which includes services such as cleaning, cooking, laundry, shopping on a basis ranging from daily to bi-weekly visits depending on the needs of the recipients. This enables many aged and disabled people to stay out of nursing homes and in their own apartments much longer than otherwise possible. This service is subsidised variably according to the recipient's income. Generally the fees are very low. In 1985, some 330,000 pensioners received help from some 65,000 home-helpers.

As a complement, the County Councils provide a similar - but free of charge - home health service, which provides regular medical care in the homes of the aged and disabled, both day-care and night-care if necessary (SPRI 1984). Some 43,000 persons were in 1984 in receipt of home nursing. A home health allowance can be paid to relatives assisting in this job, and 7,000 relatives received this allowance in 1983.

Both levels of local authority provide several housing alternatives for the aged and handicapped, which vary in degrees of independence. The present policy is to build 'service houses', which are not nursing homes but individual apartments, for persons who are capable of living on their own with a little extra help. In 1985, there were 30,000 such apartments, and another 30,000 'pensioner's dwellings', an earlier alternative to institutional living. There are also Old-Age-Residential Homes, which are run by the municipalities, and cater to the aged needing care and supervision. In these residential homes residents have their own rooms which are usually furnished with their old familiar things. Income-related fees are charged by the residential homes, but the residents can retain a guaranteed minimum, which in 1986 amounted to 30 per cent of a single old age pension. In 1985, some 50,000 people lived in homes for the aged, of which over 70 per cent were aged over 80.

Sweden

The County Councils provide two types of lodging as part of regular medical long-term treatment. Integrated with district out-patient health care centres (see below) local nursing homes combine in- and out-patient care. In 1985, almost 20,000 beds were available. Patients with more difficult rehabilitation problems are cared for in hospitals with some 30,000 beds for chronic invalids.

The County Councils are also responsible for the care and development of disabled children, and the rehabilitation of adults belonging to various disability groups. Technical aids for the disabled, with the exception of spectacles, are in principle supplied free of charge without a means test, and with no upper limit to the cost of the aid. However, the scope of this service varies greatly between different parts of the country. In general, for the partially disabled, the ambition of Swedish disability policy is to facilitate their placement whenever possible in the open labour market and only to create more or less sheltered employment for those who cannot be gainfully employed (Wadensjo 1985).

In cases of multiple disabilities, the care can only be provided on a nationwide basis and this may have to be in institutions often far away from the person's home region. For example, the education of the visually and auditorally impaired and mentally retarded persons is provided for in special state schools.

In recent years there has been a clear trend towards transferring people from institutions to various forms of independent, integrated housing, which is particularly noticeable concerning the mentally retarded. More than half of this group (over 20,000) live either with their parents or in their own homes. A further 15,000 live either in boarding homes or in the old-fashioned mental hospitals, which are gradually closing down. However, it is too early to measure the outcome of these integrative attempts.

There is a problem in co-ordinating services since it is unclear where municipal services end and health services begin, but in collaboration the municipalities and the County Councils try to develop a round-the-clock service, designed to provide help at any hour in case of acute illness or other difficulties. This is absolutely necessary if the aged and disabled are to feel a sense of security. Assessment of the functioning

Sweden

of services for the aged and disabled is not easy but it seems that in general they are fairly well developed (Bengtsson 1985). There are queues for the institutions taking care of the very aged, and the burden will increase as the population ages. In particular, the group over 80 and over 90 is markedly increasing.

Evaluation

It is generally agreed that the basic pension - including the increment and the rent allowance - make possible a life with dignity and self respect for the aged and disabled. Whilst income differences remain due to previous occupation, sex and age differences, they are considerably reduced through the progressive income tax. A wide range of personal social services augment the support rendered by the social security system in Sweden.

CHILDREN, YOUTHS AND FAMILIES

In Sweden, all families with children receive a number of universal benefits in cash and kind. In addition to the actual payment of money - of which the most important family benefits are visible in graph 4 - there are a great many programmes which relate to almost all phases of life and seek to give extra attention to the welfare of children. Social assistance - the last resort in the Swedish income support system - is not included in the graph, as it is negligible as a share of total social expenditure (below one per cent).
 The number of social assistance recipients is an indication of family welfare in Sweden. The hardship found is primarily among three different categories: ordinary families and single women living with their children; youngsters not yet established on the labour and housing market; and finally middle-aged singles, mainly men, with one or more traditional social and personal problems (divorced, alcoholism and so forth).

Personal Social Services

For children, youths and families, services can be summarised under five sub-headings: child and maternity health services; pre-school activities; general education; labour market introductions; and various kinds of protective measures.

Sweden

GRAPH 4: GOVERNMENT SUPPORT FOR FAMILIES 1982-3 to 1986-7[1] (BILLION SEK IN CURRENT PRICES)

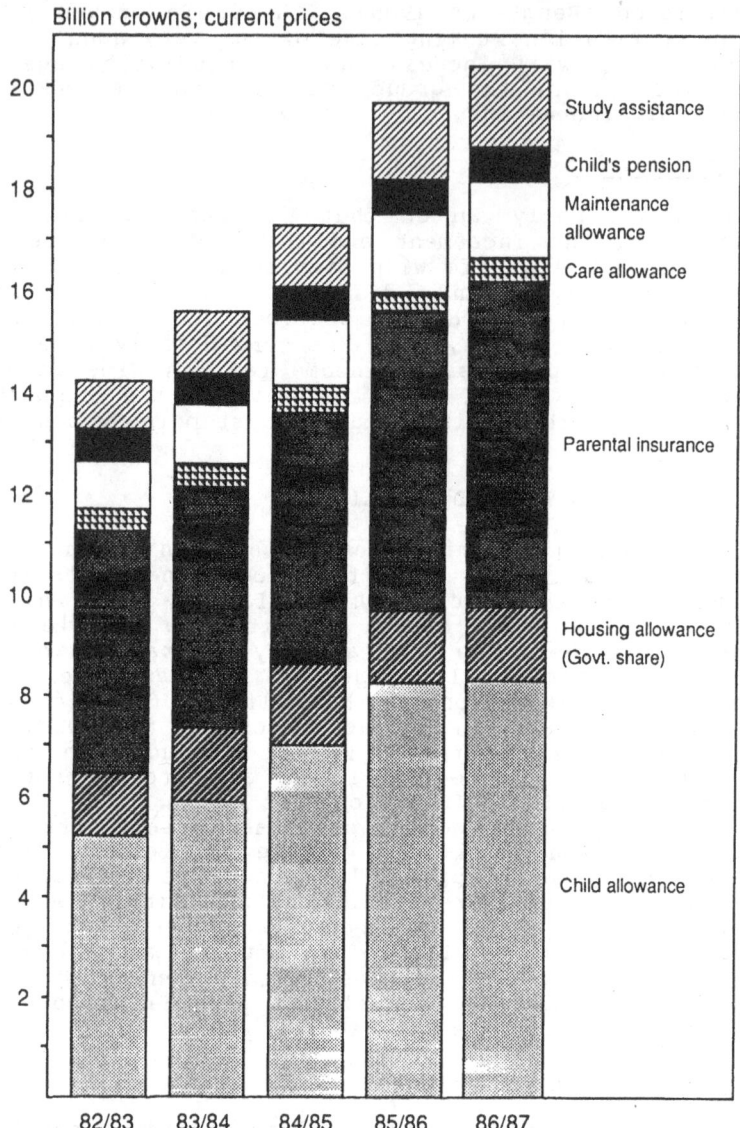

Note: 1 In addition a grant-in-aid is provided for child minding facilities.

SOURCE: The Swedish Budget

Sweden

A system of preventive maternity care (pregnancy controls, prophylactic medicines, and parental education), deliveries at special clinics at most hospitals (home delivery is extremely rare but midwife service is free), and child guidance centres are part of the in- and out-patient health service organised by the County Councils. All services are provided free of charge. During a two year period, the development from a specie-in-being to a one-and-a-half year old baby is closely followed by health personnel, in particular midwives. They give advice about life with a child, and very early visit the home of the newborn.

From the ages of one and a half to six most children are expected to be embraced by the public child-minding programme, as both parents are supposed to work (though women often part-time). Child care facilities are organised in several ways: day care centres/day nurseries; family day care (the municipality hires child-minders who take children to their own apartments); and child care parents' co-operatives provide, if necessary, full-time rearing, while kindergartens and open pre-schools offer activities for children on a part-time basis (the latter case often require the participation of one of the guardians). Some of these activities can be combined. In most cases, the parents have to pay according to their income, but at a rather subsidised rate (Sideback & Sundbom 1985). From the age of six, the municipalities are obliged to offer a full-time place in the pre-school system, without charge, or on a half-time basis from the age of five. In 1985 there were roughly 420,000 places in the public day care centres and another 100,000 places in family day care. The number of parents' co-ops are rather small, 125 with some 2,000 places. Although the expansion of day care facilities has been rather ambitious, as yet demand by no means meets supply.

Compulsory schooling starts at the age of seven, for a nine-year period (Rehn 1980). For the youngest school-children, after-school activities are provided in recreation centres affiliated with the day nurseries or the school, but here, too, demand is by no means met by supply (SCB 1984). Through the school, free dental and health service is offered by the county councils. Otherwise, schooling is organised by the municipalities with financial support (the teachers salaries) from the central government. Schooling is semi-compulsory between the age of 16 and 18, and most youngsters generally complete one-to-three year courses (Jonsson 1987). If not in school, the schools are responsible for the labour market performance of those leaving school.

At the age of 18, labour market authorities are responsible for the support of those not having regular employment. Unemployed youth are offered a half-time place in a youth team up to the age of 20, and no unemployment assistance is paid out if the youth-team place is refused. However, as youth unemployment is a problem in the age-group 20-24, labour market authorities offer special programmes for this group (Bjorklund & Persson-Tanimura 1983).

Public welfare authorities intervene to protect children under the age of 18 from physical and mental maltreatment or neglect, and to prevent delinquent behaviour among children and youth under the age of 20. Children under the age of 15 cannot be brought to court, and those under 18 only in exceptional circumstances (NCCP 1985). Alcoholism and drug dependency is a major concern - not only for youngsters - for the municipal welfare authorities. The sale and production of alcoholic beverages is a state monopoly, while the selling of drugs for non-medical use is forbidden by law. Drug abuse and related problems (e.g. AIDS) receive a lot of attention in the media, but the care of drug addicts, whilst both time-consuming and expensive as measured per case, does not represent a sizeable proportion of social welfare outlays.

Alcoholism is widespread, and through pressure from the temperance movement, policies on alcohol have a strong impact on public life. Treatment of alcoholics and drug addicts may be either voluntary or compulsory. If the municipal welfare authorities consider the individual's problem too great and the person refuses to co-operate, a social court may decide compulsory care is necessary. A variety of treatments exist for alcoholics, both public and voluntary (the latter generally heavily state-subsidised).

There are a number of other cases when social welfare authorities intervene and offer various forms of assistance, such as conflicts inside families and between neighbours, maltreatment and personal neglect (Nasenius & Veit-Wilson 1985). The County Councils, for example, run special

Sweden

family guidance centres to cope with the problems of living together, family planning, psychiatric problems and so forth. Immigrants having problems adjusting to entirely new surroundings are the concern of public authorities, as well as publicly supported voluntary organisations (such as information centres at public libraries, entitlement to language courses, interpreter service and so forth). However, as in many areas and sectors of society the gap between demand and supply is considerable.

Social Security

A general child allowance is payable to all persons resident in Sweden with at least one child under the age of 16 (Bridgeland et al. 1985). It is a flat-rate and tax-free benefit payable monthly. It is not indexed, but regularly adjusted by parliamentary decision. In 1987, the annual benefit amounted to 5,820 SEK. Families with three or more children receive a supplement (50 per cent allowance for the third child and an extra full allowance for each child above).

One-parent families are entitled to either a maintenance allowance from the deserting parent, or an advance maintenance payment, where that parent does not, or cannot pay. This advance payment is a way of guaranteeing a minimum subsistence for the child (in addition to the general child allowance). A full maintenance allowance amounts to 41 per cent of the base amount or 9,881 SEK in 1987.

A parental allowance is claimable by every family for 270 days in connection with child-birth at a replacement level of 90 per cent of taxable income (same rate as sickness cash benefit). Economically non-active persons (such as housewives) are entitled to a minimum daily allowance which amounted to 60 SEK in 1987. Parents choose who will stay at home with the child, but both are entitled to cash benefits for 10 days in connection with delivery. Parents are also entitled to draw an allowance up to 60 days prior to the delivery. In addition, a flat-rate minimum daily allowance (60 SEK) is payable for another 90 days, if one of the parents abstains from work to take care of the child. The parental benefit may be drawn at any time during the first four years of a child's life. Parents' benefit for temporary child care for a period of up to 60 days per child a year is payable if a parent has to stay away from work in order to look after a sick child under the age of 12. The replacement rate is the same as sickness cash benefit. Parents' insurance also covers adoptive parents. They are entitled to parental allowances for a maximum of 270 days when they adopt a child under the age of 10, and they are also entitled to draw parents' benefits for temporary child-care.

Families with children living in rented or owner-occupied dwellings are entitled to income-tested housing allowances. In 1986 less than 400,000 families with children received this benefit.

Between the ages of 16 and 19, pupils in lower and upper secondary schools are entitled to educational allowances. The study allowance consists of a general allowance payable to all pupils, equal to the general child allowance, and a special income-tested educational allowance which equals the housing allowance. There are also travel and lodging allowances for pupils studying away from home, in addition to special means-tested study grants and repayable loans. At the age of 20, pupils become entitled to study loans, which is a kind of social security although the benefit is a loan and repayment compulsory.

Benefits for widows and orphans can be drawn from the basic as well as the supplementary pension schemes. A widows' pension is payable to a widow from the time of her husband's death until the age of 65, if she has the care of a child under 16 (living permanently in her household), or if she is at least 36 years old and has been married or has been living together for a minimum of five years. The widows' pension ceases on remarriage. In the first half of the 1980s, there have been some attempts to replace widows' pension with some kind of temporary (transitional) benefit, but so far no legislative change has occurred.

Childrens' or orphans' pensions are payable to children under 18, whether either one or both parents are dead. They receive at least 25 per cent, and up to 40 per cent of the base amount, if they have either no or only small benefits from the supplementary pension scheme.

Social assistance is the final resort for securing the livelihood of children as well as adults. According to the Social Service Act

Sweden

municipalities have the responsibility for providing maintenance for those who, due to illness, childhood or old age or other social contingencies are unable to maintain themselves. This assistance corresponds to need and is thus means-tested. In 1983 social assistance was given to 474,657 relief recipients (namely all persons in a family in receipt of social assistance irrespective of whether the whole family or only one of its members has been assisted), 160,041 of whom (33.7 per cent) were children under the age of 16. In that year social assistance costs amounted to 2,276 million SEK, equivalent to 4,794 SEK per relief recipient.

Evaluation

An extensive net of protective and supportive services is available to Swedish families. Generally, under the present Social Service Act, people unable to provide for their subsistence or unable to satisfy other basic needs is entitled to assistance. This is not limited to well-defined categories, but rather it is supplied by public authorities in the manner most appropriate in each individual case. The hidden demand is thought to be greater than the fullest possible supply. Still, the stigmatising effects of poor relief characterise the utility of this last resort of the comprehensive welfare system.

THE UNEMPLOYED

In Sweden, unemployment is not regarded as an individual characteristic, but something for which society is responsible. There is a stress on employment programmes in contrast to reliance on unemployment cash benefits (see Graph 5). Thus, labour market issues have been closely bound up with welfare policies, and full employment, the major target of the government (Rehn 1985). Here, the extremely close socio-political links between the Social Democratic party and the trade unions are perhaps most visible. The National Labour Market Board is the central agency in charge of most of these activities. Through its local offices, information about the available jobs and educational opportunities are provided, and matching is done (job placement).

Sweden

Personal Social Services

Job creation is at the heart of Sweden's manpower policy. If the job supply and demand can be maintained and overall employment security be provided, it is more meaningful to try to rehabilitate groups earlier outside the labour market in order to strengthen their position in society.

Labour market training, carried out since 1986 by the newly created National Board of Labour Market Training, is one of the most important means of influencing and changing the available labour supply, serving to facilitate both occupational and, to some extent, regional mobility. It is aimed at those who are unemployed, in danger of unemployment or hard-to-place job seekers who lack occupational skills. Courses are given at labour market training centres or in the upper secondary schools. The vast majority of these courses are vocationally oriented, but there are also preparatory courses for advanced schooling and Swedish language courses for immigrants. These are free of charge and participants over the age of 20 receive a training grant, equal to an unemployment insurance cash benefit. The total number of participants in 1984-5 was approximately 100,000. Occupationally handicapped persons and immigrants each represent about 20 per cent of the trainees. Young persons aged 20-24 are also well-represented at the training courses. Follow-up studies show that over 70 per cent of those completing their vocational training were gainfully employed six months later.

Measures to influence demand for labour can either be aimed at companies or at individuals. On-the-job training is an example of the former. Other employment promotion measures for persons already in employment are orders to industry, temporary employment subsidies (for elderly workers in the textile industry) and recruitment subsidies aimed at speeding up recruitment plans in anticipation of an economic upswing. In addition, regional employment subsidies are given to firms in the northernmost counties, where unemployment is above the average.

Relief-work projects are arranged in order to create temporary jobs for the unemployed persons who cannot find jobs on the regular market for various reasons. These projects are used as a

Sweden

GRAPH 5: LABOUR MARKET EXPENDITURE 1983-84 AND 1984-85

Acitivity	1983/84 MSEK	1984/85 MSEK	1984/85 PERCENTAGES
The Employment Service	**1,107**	**1,285**	**5.9**
Placement, counselling	752	786	
Labour market information	138	157	
Relocation assistance	217	342	
Labour market training	**3,909**	**3,888**	**17.7**
Training grants	2,053	2,110	
Training costs	1,856	1,778	
Special measures for the occupationally handicapped	**2,846**	**3,143**	**14.3**
Wage subsidies	2,145	2,416	
Working aids	89	118	
Employability Assessment Institutes (Ami) including training grants	612	609	
Job creation measures	**5,984**	**6,530**	**29.8**
Relief work	4,854	3,612	
Recruitment subsidies etc.	600	1,267	
Youth teams	147	1,541	
Other measures	383	110	
Unemployment benefits	**6,078**	**6,596**	**30.1**
Reimbursement of unemployment insurance funds	5,359	6,102	
Severance pay subsidies		13	
Cash labour market assistance	719	481	
Administration	**447**	**465**	**2.2**
County Employment Boards	237	257	
AMS	124	117	
Other administration	86	91	
Total	**20,371**	**21,907**	**100.0**

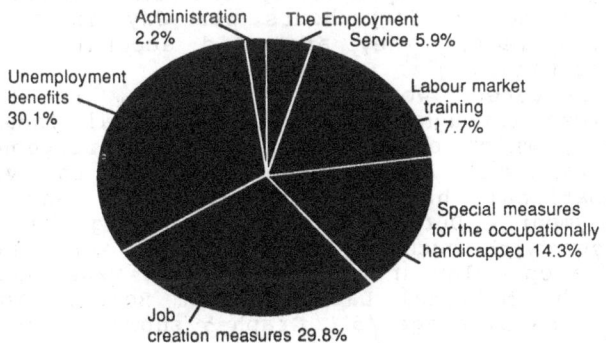

Sweden

Notes:

1   Placement costs include salary costs, the cost of facilities, travel expenses, etc.

2   Labour market information costs include Platsjournalen, computerised placement activities, etc.

3   Administrative costs include the cost of salaries and facilities and the procurement of equipment etc, for AMS, the County Employment Boards and the regional offices.

SOURCE: AMS, Verksamhetsberattelse, p.14.

supplement for other measures to counteract unemployment from the structural transformation of business, or to counteract seasonal or cyclical unemployment.

Since 1983, jobless members of unemployment insurance societies with less than 50 days left before the expiration of their unemployment cash benefit are automatically entitled to relief work. So far, this social right has not been used very often and there are still a number of unemployed who lose their right to economic support without having a job (Johansson 1984).

Youngsters aged 18-19 are guaranteed a place in a youth team if not under an education programme or having a regular job. These places are provided inside the public sector, and most youngsters are employed by the municipalities on an average of four hours per day in a normal working week. They are paid according to the market wage.

Sheltered workshop employment is usually provided through the Swedish Communal Industries groups, which employs some 25,000 throughout the country who are unable - due to various occupational handicaps - to find any other employment. During 1984-5, an average of 64,000 persons with occupational handicaps were employed on the open labour market but with wage subsidies from the National Labour Market Board. Most of them were over age 45. Graph 5 shows the manpower policy budget.

Sweden

Social Security

Most full-time employees and two-thirds of the total labour force belong to an approved voluntary unemployment insurance fund operating in close connection with their trade union and under the supervision of the National Labour Market Board (Bjorklund & Holmlund 1986). To be eligible for unemployment benefits, a person must: be a member of a fund for at least 52 weeks, including 20 weeks during the 12 months preceeding unemployment; be registered at the local employment office; and be capable of work. Unemployment must be involuntary and the unemployed must not decline any offer of a 'suitable job' (work tests are rather harsh).

The cash benefit is an earnings-related daily allowance, payable for not more than five days a week. Payments start after a waiting period of five days for a maximum duration of 300 days, but up to 450 days for members between 55 and 65 years of age. Every insured person is placed by the unemployment insurance society into one of 10 daily allowance groups, but most full-time employees are in the 'top group' in which the daily allowance in 1987 amounted to 400 SEK (or about 70 per cent of a manufacturing worker's daily wage).

Unemployment cash assistance is granted to persons who are not covered by unemployment insurance, who do not have 12 months prior membership of an insurance fund, or who have fallen out of unemployment insurance after the maximum payment period has lapsed. In principle an applicant must have worked for five of the last 12 months and have applied unsuccessfully for a job via the Employment Service before a benefit is payable. Unemployed school-leavers can also obtain unemployment assistance, provided they have applied for a job through the Employment Service, but they must wait three months after having finished their courses. Unemployment assistance is a flat-rate daily allowance amounting to 140 SEK in 1987. The duration of the benefit varies with age: 150 days up to the age of 55, 300 days from the age of 55 to 60, and without limitation from 60.

As part of the unemployment programmes a number of cash benefits are provided (such as mobility allowance, training allowance).

Sweden

Evaluation

Unemployment cash benefits are rather low in Sweden as compared with other types of social security benefits. This can be seen as part of a set of policies to promote employment, and not maintain unemployment.

THE SICK AND INJURED

In Sweden, health care delivery is definitely regarded as a public task (Heidenheimer & Elvander 1980). Out- and in-patient medical treatment, care of the mentally retarded, as well as some dental care are organised by the County Councils and subsidised by the general health insurance. Within the in-patient sector, there are only a limited number of private alternatives, chiefly nursing homes for long-term care (roughly 15 per cent of the available beds), and two regular hospitals in Stockholm and Gothenburg respectively. Some five per cent of the physicians are private practitioners, while more than 50 per cent of the dentists are in the private sector (Olsson 1987). All pharmacies are owned by a public monopoly, and prescribed drugs are heavily subsidised by health insurance.

Structurally, the health care system can be divided into three, functional levels. At the district level out-patient health centres are responsible for the district's population. Health insurance covers most of the costs according to a standard rate as well as reimbursing patients for their travel expenses. When medical resources are insufficient at this level, responsibility is transferred to the county level.

At the county level responsibility for patients with life-threatening injuries, diseases or other illnesses requiring access to technical and medical skills is necessarily concentrated at a few hospitals within each County Council area. In general, hospital treatment is free of charge, but there can be a small reduction of the patient's sickness cash benefit (55 SEK in 1986). Pensioners have to pay an income-related fee.

At the regional level the medical care system is organised jointly by several County Councils. It is responsible for those few patients with medical problems requiring special treatments and special equipment (such as burns units). Sweden is divided into six regions, each with a

Sweden

population above one million, having one or more hospitals with a high degree of specialisation.

In close co-operation with the schools, the County Councils provide dental care for all children and youngsters below the age of 20 free of charge. At these clinics, some services are offered to the adult population, at fees set by the health insurance, but most adults go to private dentists, most of whom work on contract with the health insurance system. Dental insurance covers everybody above the age of 20. Through this system the patient never pays more than 60 per cent of the cost for a visit if the charge for full treatment is less than 2,500 SEK.

Occupational safety and health is the responsibility of the firms, under the supervision of bipartisan workplace safety committees (with full-time working trade union safety stewards at major plants). Regional public Labour Inspectorates have the right to intervene and forbid certain activities unless safety measures are undertaken. The National Board of Occupational Safety and Health monitors legislation on working hours and work environment matters.

Social Security

The health insurance programme is divided into two parts: subsidies for in-kind medical benefits, and sickness cash benefits (RFV 1984). Whilst health care is available for the entire population, cash benefits can be drawn only by the economically active population. All residents above the age of 16 are entitled to cash benefits if their annual income from gainful activity is estimated to be at least 6,000 SEK. Benefits amount to 90 per cent of gross income up to an income ceiling of 7.5 base amounts. To qualify for a benefit, a person must have been reported sick to the local Social Insurance Office. A doctor's certificate is necessary after one week of illness. The benefit is payable for an unlimited duration after a one-day waiting period.

In addition, housewives and men under 65 who permanently cohabitate as well as unmarried persons who have children under 16 years of age who still live at home, are guaranteed a flat-rate cash benefit, even if the annual income is less than 6,000 SEK. These persons received a non-taxable daily allowance of eight SEK in 1986. Voluntarily, this allowance can be increased up to a maximum of 20 SEK. This possibility is also available for university students. Voluntarily insured as well as self-employed persons can choose a waiting period for sickness cash benefit of three, 33 or 93 days.

Health services are quite well developed, but concerning certain diseases, in particular those affecting the aged, there are rather long waiting periods, up to two years (Kjellstrom & Lundberg 1987). The standard of medical care is generally good, but in some areas there is a shortage of trained personnel, and in other areas a high turnover amongst the unskilled employees.

Health and social insurance programmes provide an extensive range of benefits to support the sick and injured.

The health insurance programme is administered by 26 semi-public regional social insurance funds. They handle claims for cash benefits, collect charges payable by patients, and pay hospitals, doctors, dentists, and others, the sums due to them (see Graph 6). The National Social Insurance Board supervises the funds and their local offices.

The social insurance funds also administer the oldest component in the social security system, the work injury insurance, which is compulsory and universal in coverage for all gainfully employed. It provides benefits in cash and kind for accidents occurring in connection with employment, occupational diseases, and accidents on the way to or from work. It is co-ordinated with health insurance during the first 90 days of illness, after which time work injury insurance takes over sole responsibility, thereby raising the cash benefit to the same level as the former income. Other benefits provided by this insurance are medical care benefits, life annuities (for those with lasting impairments and to dependants in case of death), and a funeral allowance. In particular the procedure leading to the establishment of a life annuity has been severely criticised by the trade union movement in recent years. Too many workers, the unions argue, have had to wait too long for the authority's classification as to the degree of their injuries (Eriksson & Hetzler 1984).

AN ASSESSMENT OF THE SWEDISH WELFARE SYSTEM

Sweden has long had an institutional type of Welfare State. This was developed from the 1940s

Sweden

GRAPH 6: INCOME, EXPENDITURE AND SURPLUS OF SICKNESS INSURANCE IN 1984.

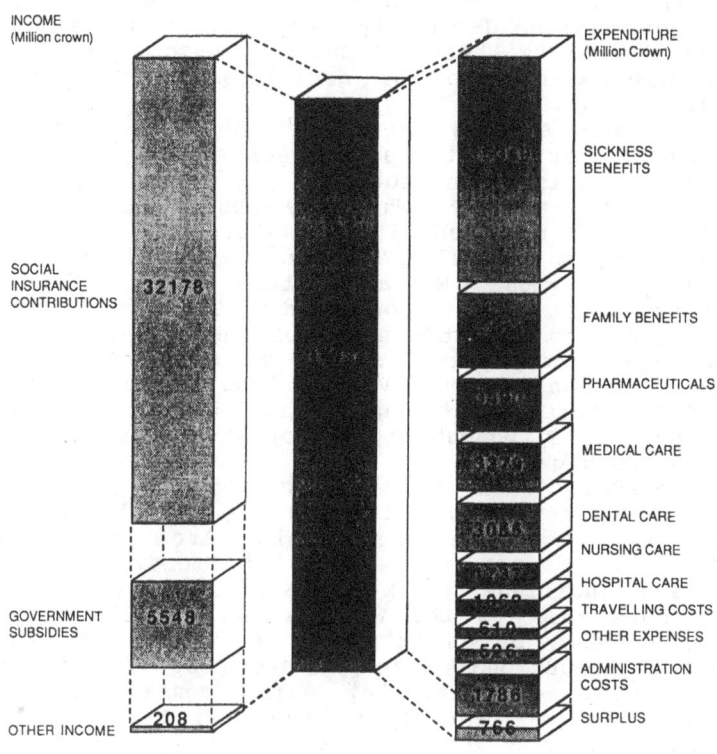

Note: Expenditure on public health by the county councils is not included in this graph (44 billion SEK in 1984).

SOURCE: National Insurance (Allman Forsakring) 1984. National Social Insurance Board, Stockholm 1986.

onwards. The social security coverage had reached its current high levels by the late 1950s (parental insurance, however, was thoroughly reformed in 1974), and the personal social services expanded rapidly over the next decade. Since the 1970s there has been no major change in the balance between the social service and the social security system.

To what extent, then, has the Welfare State managed to attain its main objectives, eliminating poverty and improving social security and equality among its citizens? When the public Low Income Commission presented its results in the late 1960s, great inequalities were discerned in some areas, and the Welfare State was accused, particularly by the young, new Left, of being inadequate to meet the needs of the working class and other subordinated social stratas. A decade later, the new, conservative Right attacked the Welfare State for being costly, inefficient and too much of a roundabout, all of which was keeping taxes too high.

However, when the replication of the Low Income Study presented its results from 1981, and compared them with the results from the late 1960s, there were clear signs of improvements in social conditions (Eriksson & Aberg 1987). To attribute this to the Welfare State alone would most probably be an exaggeration, but the impact of redistributional attempts are most likely not negligible. For example, while pension income grew by 79 per cent during the period 1967-1980, annual full-time earnings rose only 19 per cent. According to another recent investigation of official statistics, average household income for the severely disabled was only slightly lower than for households aged 20-64 without any handicapped member (Wadensjo 1985).

The general conclusion from the new Low Income Study covering the period 1967-81, is that the average standard of living rose in some respects (housing conditions in particular, but also income and other economic resources), and in others did not change at all (health and working conditions). In no field was an average deterioration detected. Similarly, the differences between various socio-economic groups in the population have either diminished or remained unaltered: none have increased. Swedes are not necessarily more satisfied with their situation, but the average well-being measured as actual conditions and resources, seems to have improved during the 1970s.

Another important welfare component is unemployment. On the European continent, and in near by Denmark, there has been a tremendous deterioration during the same decade. Whilst the employment situation has been strained in Sweden, the unemployment rate has never exceeded four per cent even during the worst recessionary years in the early 1980s. Of course, social outlays on the active manpower policy have helped to avoid open unemployment of continental proportions. Also the labour force has continued to grow (in particular women have received permanent positions in the public sector).

One policy area, which is regarded as rather unsuccessful, is education. Although a comprehensive school reform was carried out in the last decades, great inequalities still persist in the school system (Arnman & Jonsson 1986). Further, the real value of education has decreased considerably with the explosive increase in the number of students in higher education. Concerning pre-school children, demand for day care facilities in the 1980s far exceeds supply, although a concerted programme is underway and will most likely be implemented in the 1990s.

Finally, in health care, where a tremendous amount of money, energy and resources have been spent in recent times, the results vary from one sub-area to another.

Despite the reported shortcomings in actual welfare, the Welfare State must be regarded as not only being fairly successful, but also, as a new century looms, an irreversible feature of Sweden for the foreseeable future. However, a new pattern of socio-political forces, under different economic conditions, can, of course, considerably change this prediction.

ENDNOTE

This article is based on my contribution to the research project The West European Welfare State Since the Second World War. (See Olsson, 1986). The Swedish part of this project was generously supported by a grant from the Commission for Social Research, Ministry of Health and Social

Affairs, Stockholm, Sweden (DSF 84/51:1). A major general source for the main target populations is Elmer 1986.

REFERENCES

Acta Sociologica (1978) Vol.21 Supplement (Special Congress Issue: The Nordic Welfare States).

Allardt, E. et al. (eds) (1981), Nordic Democracy, Copenhagen: Det Danske Selskab.

Amenta, E. & Skocpol, T. (1986), 'States and Social Policy' in Annual Yearbook of Sociology, Palo Alto: Annual Reviews.

Arnman, G. & Jonsson, I. (1986), Olika for olika, Lund: Arkiv.

Bengston, G (1985), Vad vet vi om aldres liv och omsorgsarbeters villkor, Stockholm: Stockholms socialforvaltning, Forsknings- och utvecklingsbyran, Report No. 5.

Bjorklund, A. & Persson-Tanimura, I. (1983), 'Youth Employment in Sweden' in Ruebens, B. (ed.), Youth at Work - An International Survey, Toronto, NJ: Allenheld, Osmun & Co.

_____ & Holmlund, B (1986), The Economics of Unemployment Insurance: The Case of Sweden, Stockholm: The Industrial Institute for Economic and Social Research, Report No. 167.

Bridgeland, W., Smith, P. & Duane, E. (1985), 'Child-care Policy Arenas: A Comparison between Sweden and the United States', International Journal of Comparative Sociology, Vol 26, pp.35-44.

Childs, M. (1936), Sweden: The Middle Way, New Haven: Yale University Press.

Deadalus (1984), Vol.113, Nos.1&2 (Winter and Spring 1984).

Edebalk, P.G. (1975), Arbetsloshetsforsakringsdebatten, Lund: Ekonomiskhistoriska instutionen.

Sweden

_____ & Elmer, A. (1983), 'Social Insurance in Sweden' in Soderstrom, L. (ed.), *Arne Ryde Symposium on Social Insurance*, Amsterdam: Elsevier - North Holland.

Elmer, A. (1986), *Svensk socialpolitik*, Lund: Liber.

Erikson, K. & Hetzler, A. (1984), *Arbetsskadeforsakringens tillampning*, Lund: EKNA.

Eriksson, R. & Aberg, R. (eds) (1987), *Welfare in Transition*, Oxford: Clarendon Press.

Esping-Andersen, G. (1985), *Politics against Markets*, Princeton: Princeton University Press.

Flora, P. (ed.) (1986), *Growth to Limits?* Berlin & New York: De Gruyter, Vol. 1, 2 & 4.

Heckscher, G. (1984), *The Welfare State and Beyond*, Minneapolis: University of Minnesota Press.

Heidenheimer, A. & Elvander, N. (1980), *The Shapening of the Swedish Health System*, London: Croom Helm.

Hermansson, C.H. (1981 & 1986), *Kapitalister 1 & 11* Stockholm: Arbetarkultur.

Himmelstrand, U., Ahrne, G. & Lundberg, L. (1982), *Beyond Welfare Capitalism*, London: Heinemann.

Johansson, L. (1984), *Vilka blir utforsakrade?* Utforsakringsprojektet: Socialhogskolan, Stockholms universiter, Report No. 1.

Jonsson, I. (1987), 'Educational resources' in Eriksson, R. & Aberg, R. (eds), *Welfare in Transition*, Oxford: Clarendon Press.

_____ & Lundberg, O. (1984), 'De aldre i valfarden' Stockholm: Swedish Institute for Social Research.

Jorberg, L. (1984), 'Svensk industri under 100 ar' in Sodersten, B. (ed.) *Svensk ekonomi*, Stockholm: Raben & Sjogren.

Kjellberg, A. (1983), *Facklig organisering i tolv lander*, Lund: Arkiv.

Kjellstrom, S-A. & Lundberg, O. (1987), 'Health and Health Care Utilization' in Erikson, R. & Aberg, R. (eds), *Welfare in Transition*, Oxford: Clarendon Press.

Koblik, S. (ed.) (1975), *Sweden's Development from Poverty to Affluence, 1750-1970*, Minneapolis: University of Minnesota Press.

Korpi, W. (1978), *The Working Class in Welfare Capitalism*, London: Routledge & Kegan Paul.

───── (1980), 'Social Policy and Distributional Conflict in the Capitalist Democracies', *West European Politics*, 3(3).

───── (1983), *The Democratic Class Struggle*, London: Routledge & Kegan Paul.

Leinio, T. (1984), *Inte lika men jamlika*, Stockholm: Swedish Institute for Social Research.

Marklund, S. (1982), *Klass, stat och socialpolitik*, Lund: Arkiv.

Nasenius, J. & Veit-Wilson, J. (1985), 'Social policy in a cold climate: Sweden in the eighties', *The Yearbook of Social Policy 1984-85*, London: Routledge & Kegan Paul.

National Council for Crime Prevention (NCCP) (1985), *Predicting Social Maladjustment*, Stockholm: The National Council for Crime Prevention, Report No. 17.

Ohlin, B. (ed.) (1938), 'Social Problems and Policies in Sweden', in *The Annals of the American Academy of Political and Social Science*, special issue.

Olofsson, G. (1979), *Mellan klass och stat*, Kristianstad: Arkiv.

───── (1986), 'Stat, bostad och subvention'. Paper presented at the Annual Meeting of the Swedish Sociological Association, Umea.

Olsson, S.E. (1986), 'Sweden' in Flora, P. (ed.) (1986), *Growth to Limits*, Berlin & New York: De Gruyler.

Sweden

Organisation for Economic and Cultural Development (OECD) (1985), Social Expenditure 1960-1990, Paris: OECD.

Rehn, G. (1980), Education and Youth Employment in Sweden and Denmark, Carnegie Council of Policy Studies in Higher Education.

_____ (1985), 'Swedish Active Labour Market Policy: Retrospects and Prospects', Industrial Relations, 1(1).

Riksforsakringsverket (RFV) (1983), Allman forsakring 1982, Stockholm: Riksforsakringsverket (National Social Insurance Board).

Rothstein, B. (1986), Den socialdemokratiska staten, Lund: Arkiv.

Sideback, G. & Sundbom, L. (1985), 'Agents of change. On the driving forces behind child care revolution in Sweden'. A paper presented at the ECPR Joint Session of Workshops, Barcelona, March 25-30.

Sjukvardens och socialvardens planerings- och rationalise-ringsinstitut (SPRI) (1984), Aldreomsorg och ekonomi, Stockholm.

Statens offentliga utredningar (1987), No.3 (State Commission on the Prospects of the Economy into the 1990s, Stockholm: Ministry of Finance.

Statistiskacentralbyran (SCB) (1984), Levnadsforhallanden, Stockholm: Report No. 40, Statistics Sweden.

_____ (1985), Statistical Yearbook of Sweden, Sweden: Statistics Sweden.

_____ (1986), Statistical Yearbook of Sweden, Sweden: Statistics Sweden.

_____ (1987), Statistiska Meddelanden - Socialutgifterna och dessas finansiering 1985, S 42 SM 8701, Stockholm: Statistics Sweden.

_____ (SFS) (1982), No.763 (Government Bill).

Stohlberg, A-c (1985), *Public and Negotiated Pension Wealth in Sweden and their Distributions*, Stockholm: Swedish Institute for Social Research. Meddelanden 16/1985.

Sundstrom, G. (1983), *Caring for the Aged in Welfare Society*, Stockholm Studies in Social Work No.1, Stockholm: Stockholm School of Social Work.

Svallfors, S. (1987), 'Vem alskar valfardsstaten', *Zenit*, 94.

Svensk forfattningssamling (SFS) (1980), No.620 (Government Bill).

The Swedish Budget 1987/88, Stockholm: Ministry of Finance.

Therborn, G. (1983), 'The working class and the welfare state'. Paper presented at the fifth Nordic congress of research in the history of the labour movement.

——— (1985), 'The Coming of Swedish Social Democracy' in *"Annali" della Fondazione Criamgiacomo Feltrinelli 1983-84*, Milan.

Titmuss, R. (1974), *Social Policy*, London: Allen & Unwin.

Vinde, P. & Petri, G. (1978), *Swedish Government Administration*, Stockholm: Prisma.

Wadensjo, E. (1985), 'Disability Policy in Sweden' in Haveman, R., Halberstadt, V. & Burkhauser, R. (eds), *Public Policy Toward Disabled Workers: Cross-National Analyses of Economic Impacts*, Ithaka: Cornell University Press.

UNITED KINGDOM
Jane Keithley

THE WELFARE SYSTEM ENVIRONMENT

Ideological Environment

The United Kingdom (UK) is a capitalist society with a growing commitment, over most of this century, to collectivist state welfare. Beveridge, in his report (1942), laid down the principles on which he argued the post-war welfare state should be based: universality, comprehensiveness and adequacy. 'Cradle-to-grave' provisions would tackle want (through income maintenance), disease (health services), squalor (housing programmes), ignorance (education) and idleness (full employment policies). Schemes would cover all contingencies and groups on the basis of citizenship, without occupational or income differentiation. Cash benefits would be flat-rate and adequate for subsistence, but above that level individuals should be encouraged to make private provision. The government would actively pursue full employment policies, based on Keynesian demand management of the economy. This was not a socialist transformation (indeed capitalist state welfare has been viewed as an antidote to socialism), although the 1945 Labour government was elected on the basis of support for a fairer and more equal society.

Beveridge's principles were never fully enacted, but there does seem to have been a degree of consensus from the late 1940s to the early 1970s that the state had a responsibility to provide welfare and maintain employment and that social expenditure should increase as part of a thriving capitalist economy. Most criticisms of state welfare focused on gaps in coverage and inadequate benefits.

By the mid-1970s, views were becoming more polarised. The origins of this shift can be located in the economic downturn, following the 1973 oil price increases and the ascendancy of a 'public burden' model of state welfare. The ideological shift gained momentum with the election of the 1979 Conservative government, committed to 'rolling back the frontiers of the State.' It believed that high taxation and public spending were inflationary, reduced productive investment and damaged incentives to work. In addition, state services were criticised as monopolistic, inefficient and limiting consumer choice.

It is arguable how far the public supports a 'welfare backlash'. The Conservative government was re-elected in 1983 and 1987. A much quoted 1976 Eurobarometer survey found the British more likely than any other European Economic Community (EEC) nationals to blame the poor for their poverty (EEC 1977). A survey published in 1979 claimed there was considerable support for reducing state intervention and 'reprivatising' welfare services (Harris & Seldon 1979). However, others have produced evidence of people's willingness to pay higher taxes for better state services (Taylor-Gooby 1985).

Despite political rhetoric, social expenditure has continued to increase, although recently slightly less than national wealth. However, these ideological shifts have had their impact. There has been a shift towards greater selectivity (that is, means-testing) in cash benefits and more occupational provision. In health care, the government has encouraged the private sector and attempted to expose the National Health Service (NHS) to greater competitive pressure. In the personal social services, the emphasis has been on a 'mixed economy of welfare', with the family as the 'front line' providers of care.

Historical Origins

State intervention in welfare provision dates back to the Poor Laws, originating in the fourteenth century, which, although primarily punitive measures designed to repress vagrancy, were also concerned with the relief of destitution. During the middle and late nineteenth century, the increased pace of industrialisation was accompanied by increased state regulation and provision for working conditions, public health, education and housing. Much of the legislation was limited and difficult to enforce, but it did mean that by the late nineteenth century the principle of state intervention, although at a minimal level, was accepted in a variety of social welfare areas. Outside the state sphere, some employers and trade unions began to provide services and benefits to their employees and members. This period also witnessed an enormous expansion in voluntary philanthropy. In the 1850s, London charities had an annual income in excess of that spent by the capital's Poor Law authorities (Fraser 1973, p.116).

Private charities and voluntary organisations still play a significant part in some areas of welfare provision (for example, residential care). However, it is state and occupational welfare which have expanded most during the twentieth century. In 1897 the first social security provision outside the Poor Law was introduced, in the form of a Workmen's Compensation Act. The Liberal government of the next decade introduced means-tested old age pensions, and limited social insurance schemes for unemployment and sickness benefits.

The contributory principle was extended to retirement, invalidity and widows' pensions in 1925 and coverage of social insurance was extended during the inter-war period. In response to high levels of unemployment, a national scheme of unemployment assistance was introduced in 1934.

The best-selling Beveridge Report, published during the Second World War, influenced and symbolised much of the subsequent State welfare. By 1948, the claim was made that legislation had secured 'cradle-to-grave' provision of cash benefits for the whole population, with flat-rate social insurance and family allowances backed up by a 'safety net' of means-tested benefits and accompanied by a 'free' National Health Service and local authority-run personal social services for children, the aged and the disabled. Other measures, outside the scope of this chapter, in education, housing and the environment, also formed an important part of the post-War settlement.

These measures still constitute the framework of state welfare in the contemporary United

United Kingdom

Kingdom. However there have been important developments. In income maintenance, there has been a continuing and expanding dependence on means-tested benefits, the introduction of some earnings-related supplements and increasing reliance on occupational benefits. Local authority personal social services have been unified and, during the early and mid-1970s, expanded rapidly. The NHS has undergone several reorganisations and some charges have been introduced. More generally, following over two decades of continuous, if uneven growth, the period since the mid-1970s has seen governments attempting, with varying degrees of success, to halt and even reverse the expansion of state welfare and to place more reliance on alternative welfare mechanisms, such as the market, employers, and formal and informal voluntary provision. Table 1 shows selected significant events in the evolution of social welfare policy.

TABLE 1: THE EVOLUTION OF THE WELFARE SYSTEM IN THE UNITED KINGDOM SINCE 1897 - SELECTED DATES AND EVENTS

1897	Workmen's compensation scheme introduced
1908	Means-tested old age pensions introduced
1911	National Insurance for some sick and unemployed workers established
1925	National Insurance for widows, orphans and the retired created
1934	National scheme of unemployment assistance established
1942	Beveridge Report published
1945	Family allowances scheme introduced National Insurance for those injured at work introduced
1946	National Insurance for the sick, unemployed, widows, orphans and retired, and for maternity, reformed and extended National Health Service created
1948	National Assistance scheme created Local Authorities given responsibilities for personal social services - especially residential and child care
1959	Graduated pension scheme introduced
1966	Earnings-related supplements to sickness and unemployment benefit introduced
1970	Local Authority social services Departments set up (Social Work Departments in Scotland, 1968)

United Kingdom

1972	Family income supplement scheme established
1974	National Health Service reorganised
1978	Earnings-related pensions scheme created
1982	National Health Service reorganised
1982	Earnings-related supplements to short term benefits abolished
1983	Statutory sick pay introduced
1985	Major changes to income maintenance system proposed in <u>Reform of Social Security</u>

POLITICAL ENVIRONMENT

Both central and local government provide welfare services. The United Kingdom is a parliamentary democracy, with general elections held at least every five years, with secret ballots and universal adult suffrage. Most parliaments are dominated by one party, from which a Prime Minister is selected who appoints her or his Ministers. Ministers are generally responsible for particular government departments and the most senior constitute the Cabinet, which is the government executive. For much of recent history, two parties - Labour and Conservative - have, in turn, formed governments. However, there are also significant nationalist parties in Wales, Scotland and Northern Ireland and an alliance of Social Democrats and Liberals is currently attracting support, although with little parliamentary representation.

Local Authorities (LAs) are regularly elected and are frequently not of the same political complexion as the central government. They have had considerable responsibilities devolved upon them and a significant degree of autonomy within a framework of national legislation. However, they are heavily dependent on the central government for finances and are currently experiencing an erosion of their powers.

SOCIO-ECONOMIC ENVIRONMENT

The United Kingdom (comprising England, Wales, Scotland and Northern Ireland) had a population of 55.9 million in 1984, and currently there is almost zero population growth. Population density is relatively high, especially in England, and the society is highly urbanised. The number and proportion of aged people (mostly women) have increased substantially during this century, from under five per cent of the population aged over 65 to 15 per cent in 1981 (Family Policy Studies Centre 1986a). Another important change has been the increase in divorce, accompanied by a growth in one-parent families. In 1983, the divorce rate was about 12 per 1,000 married couples: two and a half times the figure for 1970. About 13 per cent of all families with dependent children are headed by a lone parent (Family Policy Studies Centre 1985). Birth rates have fluctuated considerably, but there has been a steady decline in completed family size, so that relatively few women now have more than three children and most have one or two.

Immigration of Asians and West Indians from the 'New Commonwealth' into the United Kingdom was encouraged during the labour shortages of the post-war period. This has changed the racial composition of some of the larger conurbations and racism has become a serious political issue. Religious dichotomies are important in Northern Ireland, where Roman Catholicism is associated with support for a united Ireland.

The United Kingdom experienced sustained economic growth during the post-War period, although at lower rates than many other Western countries (about 2.7 per cent per annum on average) until the mid-1970s (Walker 1982, p.28). Growth was accompanied by low inflation and unemployment rates and substantial increases in living standards for almost everyone. Between 1951 and 1976, real disposable income per capita (1980 prices) rose from 1,375 pounds to 2,536 pounds. The average real weekly earnings of adult male manual workers rose from 60 pounds in 1951 to 111 pounds in 1983 (Halsey 1987). Relative inequalities have, however, remained substantial. In 1982, the bottom 20 per cent of households received 8 per cent of disposable income and the top 20 per cent, nearly 40 per cent (O'Higgins 1985). Recently, very high inflation rates - an annual average of about 14 per cent during the 1970s compared with 4.6 per cent between 1961 and 1971 (Central Statistical Office 1987) - and government attempts to control this (quite successfully currently) are associated with rapid rises in unemployment. From an average of about 250,000 in the mid-1960s, recorded unemployment rose to nearly 3.3 million in 1985-6 (Central)

United Kingdom

Statistical Office 1987). This is a conservative estimate of the total number unemployed. The pattern of employment has also changed, with a decline in heavy industry and manufacturing jobs and an expansion in the service sector. Part-time employment has shown considerable growth, largely taken by married women, whose participation in the labour force has increased greatly. In 1951, 21.7 per cent of married women were economically active. By 1982, the figure was 50 per cent, with over 40 per cent of these in part-time employment (Beechey 1986).

THE WELFARE SYSTEM: AN OVERVIEW

The Structure and the Administration of the Welfare System

Central government responsibility for welfare services rests principally with the Department of Health and Social Security (DHSS). Income maintenance is centrally administered, with national benefit rates and entitlement conditions, through regional and local DHSS offices. A range of benefits is provided through the National Insurance Scheme, to which all those earning 39 pounds a week or more must contribute (except some married women). Means-tested benefits provide a 'safety-net' for many with few or no resources. There are also non-contributory child and disability benefits.

The National Health Service (NHS), provides comprehensive and virtually free health care for all residents. It is also centrally administered. However, responsibility for hospital and community services is devolved to Regional and District Health Authorities (Health and Social Services Boards in Northern Ireland): appointed bodies with policy-making and executive responsibilities, who have some autonomy in utilising their allocated resources to meet local needs. Local Family Practitioner Committees contract on a nationally determined basis with self-employed doctors, dentists and opticians to provide primary care. Appointed Community Health Councils are intended to give consumers a voice.

Personal social services, on the other hand (except in Northern Ireland), are a LA responsibility although central government places duties on LAs, provides policy guidelines and much of the finances. Each LA has a social services department, but its structure, resources and the mix and level of provision vary considerably.

The tax system includes various reliefs and allowances which influence the distribution of resources between different population groups. This fiscal welfare can be an alternative to direct state cash and service provisions.

Voluntary welfare organisations are of most importance in the personal social services. Many depend partly, some almost entirely on central or local government grants. Some have service provision as their primary function; others concentrate on campaigning on behalf of a particular group. Although there is substantial local variation, the large organisations (Age Concern, Marriage Guidance Councils, Citizens' Advice Bureaux, and so forth) are found in most areas.

Private sector welfare services can supplement or replace state welfare and are often linked to government through regulation and subsidies. Of particular importance is occupational welfare; many employers provide more than the statutory minima in sickness, maternity and redundancy cash benefits. They can also provide occupational pensions which replace part of the state pension. Much of the recent growth in private health insurance has resulted from employers taking out group plans for selected employees. These, and other occupational benefits, tend to benefit the best paid and those working for large firms most. They are encouraged by considerable fiscal subsidies.

In addition, many individuals purchase services akin to state welfare in the market. Life insurance and assurance provide for income in retirement or for surviving dependents. 'Over the counter' purchases of drugs cost more than the NHS drugs bill. Many personal social services have their market equivalent: for example, domestic help, residential homes, child care and financial advice. The present government favours encouraging these private, as well as voluntary services and thus a 'mixed economy' of welfare.

Financing Social Welfare

National insurance benefits are financed from contributions and an Exchequer subsidy. Employees pay nine per cent on earnings between 100 pounds and 295 pounds a week (less if contracted-out of

United Kingdom

the state earnings-related pension) with lower rates on earnings between 39 pounds and 100 pounds a week. Employers' contributions are similar, except that the rates are higher on earnings above 150 pounds a week (10.45 per cent) and there is no upper earnings limit. The self-employed pay a flat-rate contribution of 3.85 pounds a week plus 6.3 per cent on annual profits between 4,590 pounds and 15,340 pounds. In recent years, the Exchequer subsidy has averaged 13 per cent (Department of Health and Social Security 1986b, table 44.04).

Social assistance benefits and demogrants are financed entirely from general tax revenues.

General taxation provides around 85 per cent of the total finance of the NHS, national insurance contributions about 10 per cent and charges (for example, on prescriptions, dental treatment, private patients in NHS hospitals) the remaining five per cent. A very minor role (although it can be important at a local level) is played by fund-raising and charitable contributions.

Statutory personal social services are financed by local government, whose income comes principally from central government grants (about one half), from local property taxes (about one third) and from council house rents (less than one tenth). Charges also contribute to the revenue of the personal social services. Table 2 illustrates some aspects of expenditure on statutory services.

Voluntary, non-profit-making organisations are, as mentioned above, most important in the personal social services. Financed by local and central government grants, national and local fund-raising and donations, many also charge for services. Some charges, especially for residential accommodation, are met by public authorities.

Private health services are financed partly by direct patient charges. However, insurance meets much of the cost, particularly of hospital care. Three non-profit-making companies dominate the field. Employee group plans are the most common.

Occupational pensions are usually financed by both employee and employer. However, some schemes do not involve direct employee contributions. Non-statutory occupational maternity, sickness and redundancy benefits are employer-financed.

While describing the major patterns of expenditure, Table 2 does not show where the cost ultimately falls. Finance by public authorities derives from taxation. The United Kingdom has mildly progressive income taxes combined with regressive indirect taxes. Employer and employee contributions to statutory and non-statutory services may come from profits and wages, or be passed on to consumers in higher prices. In addition, the complex system of tax allowances and reliefs alters the incidence of the financial burden. For example, tax reliefs on occupational pension contributions, house mortgage interest and the operations of charitable organisations lower the real cost of benefits to the recipients and spread that cost amongst the whole tax-paying population. As tax-efficient occupational benefits and substantial house mortgages are more widespread for the better-off, the effects can be regressive.

TABLE 2: PUBLIC EXPENDITURE ON INCOME MAINTENANCE, HEALTH AND PERSONAL SOCIAL SERVICES IN REAL TERMS (MILLION POUNDS, BASE YEAR 1984-85)

	Health & Personal Social Services	Income Maintenance	Total Public Expenditure
1980-81	18,194	31,086	119,196
Percentage of Public Expenditure	15.3	26.1	100.0
1981-82	18,500	34,394	121,471
Percentage of Public Expenditure	15.2	28.3	100.0
1982-83	18,810	36,513	123,757
Percentage of Public Expenditure	15.2	29.5	100.0
1983-84	19,136	37,908	125,735
Percentage of Public Expenditure	15.2	30.1	100.0
1984-85	19,601	39,320	129,638
Percentage of Public Expenditure	15.1	30.3	100.0
1985-86	19,747	40,482	127,812
Percentage of Public Expenditure	15.5	31.7	100.0

SOURCE: Central Statistical Office 1987, table 6.21.

United Kingdom

THE AGED

Most people in the United Kingdom survive into old age and many well into their 70s and 80s. As a result of the institutionalisation of retirement, the first welfare problem which confronts most of them is loss of income. High unemployment in recent years has encouraged earlier retirement and thus increased the number of years for which a replacement for earned income is necessary. Women, a majority in the aged population, are especially vulnerable to poverty.

Ageing can also mean a decline in health and a loss, sudden or gradual, in functional capacities. The availability and cost of health services are thus of particular concern to the aged. Some may also need help with daily living, ranging from assistance with household tasks to residential care. The aged may suffer from loneliness and social isolation, especially if they have no family near by. Over one-quarter of the people aged 65 to 74 and nearly half of those aged 75 or more live alone (Central Statistical Office 1986, table 2.7), although many of these will have frequent contact with neighbours and kin.

Social Security

Entitlement to the full, flat-rate, national insurance pension depends on contributions for nine-tenths of a full working life. However, those receiving state benefits, those caring for children or disabled people and the wives of insured workers are credited with contributions. Thus, in practice, the pension is virtually universal. It can be claimed at age 60 for women and 65 for men, but for the first five years it is reduced if earnings exceed 75 pounds a week. The pension is 39.50 pounds a week for a single person and 63.25 pounds for a married couple: about 29 per cent and 43 per cent, respectively, of average net male earnings for manual work (Department of Health and Social Security 1986b, table 46.15), and is taxable. There are also additions of 8.05 pounds a week for each dependent child. Those with no or little other income can also claim means-tested supplementary benefits and/or housing benefits which meet all or part of the cost of rent and rates. Although the basic supplementary benefit rates are slightly lower than the pension, claimants are entitled to lump-sum payments and weekly benefit additions for exceptional needs, such as the purchase of furniture and bedding, special diets, extra heating, or help with housework.

The aged also receive an extra personal tax allowance, lifting those solely dependent on state benefits above the income tax threshold.

Earnings-related pensions are increasingly important and, since 1978, almost all those in employment have to contribute either to the state earnings-related pension (SERPS) or, preferably, an occupational pension. Currently, nearly two-thirds of aged couples, but only one-third of aged single women receive some occupational pension (Central Statistical Office 1986, table A.8).

Health services are available to the aged in the same manner as other residents and they are exempt from NHS charges. Many hospitals contain specialist geriatric wards, but many beds in other wards are also occupied by those over age 65.

General practitioners receive an extra capitation fee for patients over age 65 and much of the work of community nurses and health visitors is in domiciliary care and health education for this group. The NHS on average spends nearly four times as much on those between the ages of 65 and 74 and over nine times on those over age 75, as compared with younger adults (Department of Health and Social Security 1983).

Personal Social Services

Many clients of the personal social services are the 'frail aged'. Local Authorities (LA) provide residential accommodation, usually in purpose-built homes with between 30 and 70 residents, for about two per cent of the aged population. Accommodation is also provided by private, often profit-making, residential nursing homes. These have increased greatly from 1980, since 'reasonable charges' can be met through the supplementary benefit scheme.

A range of domiciliary services are also provided by local authorities, including social work support, help with household tasks, 'meals-on-wheels' and a variety of aids and adaptations. Less widely available are lunch clubs, day centres, transport and telephones. There are some charges but these are usually modest and related to means. Voluntary

United Kingdom

organisations such as Age Concern provide similar services, often grant-aided by local authorities, and their volunteers are frequently the 'young aged'.

By far the most important source of care for the aged is their families. There is no evidence that modern families have transferred their responsibilities to the state (Department of Health and Social Security 1981). State and voluntary organisations see their role primarily as helping families to care for aged members and only taking the major role where there are no available relatives (or neighbours). 'Community care', involving domiciliary services and family care, has become a popular catch-phrase for governments: partly reacting to criticism of the effects of large, impersonal institutions on their inmates and partly in the hope that care in (or, rather, care by) the community would strengthen mutually rewarding kin and neighbourhood networks and save money. This latter motivation has been strengthened by increases in the very aged population at a time when governments are attempting to reduce state expenditure.

Evaluation

The aged in the United Kingdom are guaranteed a minimum state income, 'free' and comprehensive health services and access to a variety of personal social services. The government also encourages and subsidises voluntary and occupational provision. Pensioners' incomes have increased considerably since 1945 and have improved relative to average incomes (Central Statistical Office 1986, table A.1).

However, the average disposable income of the aged is still only 70 per cent of those of working age (Central Statistical Office 1986, table A.1). More than one-fifth depend on means-tested supplementary benefits (Central Statistical Office 1986, table A.5). Higher, earnings-related pension schemes take decades to mature. In addition, particularly if current proposals to reduce the SERPS pension are accepted (Department of Health and Social Security 1985), the considerable inequalities amongst the aged will increase. Some will, on top of the basic state pension, receive a generous occupational pension and income from accumulated private assets. Others will continue to depend on the basic state pension, with perhaps (if they have not suffered long spells of unemployment) small additions from SERPS, which may need 'topping up' by means-tested benefits.

The aged are heavy users of health and personal social services. Although both (especially the NHS) have continued to consume more resources since the mid-1970s, this growth has been insufficient to compensate for the growth in needs - particularly deriving from increases in the very aged population - and thus the real level of provision has fallen. In addition there are variations in the extent and quality of services in different parts of the country, and the poorest provision tends to be in the areas of greatest need.

Finally, there are problems associated with 'community care'. 'Community' in practice overwhelmingly means close female kin (Finch & Groves 1983). Some services do exist to help people caring for relatives, such as laundry services, 'respite care' and limited financial assistance. However, the chief material and emotional burden of what can be a very demanding and exhausting task falls on daughters, wives and sisters, many of whom are not young themselves.

THE DISABLED AND HANDICAPPED

There is no certain estimate of the number of disabled people in the United Kingdom. A 1971 survey concluded that about three million people (around 5.5 per cent of the population) had some measurable physical, mental or sensory disability (Harris 1971). The majority were over retirement age. However this group is very heterogeneous in age, extent and type of disability and in how far a given disability results in a handicap for the individual.

Social Security

Lack of income is a problem for many disabled people. They may find difficulty in obtaining employment, especially when unemployment is high, and their disability may necessitate extra expenditure.

Disability benefits have developed on a piecemeal basis, and individuals with similar disabilities can have very different

United Kingdom

entitlements. Historically, those injured at work and war pensioners have been treated most generously, followed by others who become disabled while in employment and, with the poorest provision, those with no or no recent history of employment.

Cash benefits for short-term sickness are described later. Those with the necessary contribution record can claim invalidity benefit if inability to work continues past 28 weeks. This consists of invalidity pension (39.50 pounds a week) with additions for adult and child dependents, plus a small earnings-related addition for those first claiming after April 1979. Invalidity allowance of up to 8.30 pounds a week is also paid if the onset of invalidity was five or more years before retirement age. These benefits are reduced during a hospital stay of more than eight weeks. In addition, most occupational pension schemes (covering just over half the working population) include provision for an earnings-related invalidity pension. Those disabled through industrial injury or disease may, however, qualify for more generous benefits. For example, industrial disablement benefit can be paid on top of earnings and entitlement to other benefits. A lump sum is paid for permanent disablement of 14 per cent to 19 per cent; a weekly pension of up to 64.50 pounds for more severe disablement. The maximum disablement benefit is paid during hospital stays arising from the disability. Inability to return to as well-paid a job qualifies the individual for a reduced earnings allowance of up to 25.80 pounds a week. Moreover, where the employer is at fault, injured employees or their dependents can claim compensation through the courts.

If disability originated during childhood or develops when the individual is out of paid employment, benefit entitlement is more limited. Until recently, only means-tested benefits could be claimed. These are still of major importance for the severely disabled, even those with some insurance entitlement. They qualify for the higher, long-term rate of supplementary benefit (38.50 pounds a week for a single person, 61.85 pounds for a married couple) and maybe also for additions which recognise that extra costs can be associated with disability, such as laundry, heating, extra wear and tear on clothing, special diets and domestic assistance. The blind receive

United Kingdom

a small addition to their weekly benefit. Low income, disabled people can also claim housing benefit.

However, reliance on means-tested benefits has been reduced for some disabled people with no insurance entitlement. A severe disablement allowance is now payable to those unable to work, but not qualifying for invalidity benefit. However, the benefit is only 60 per cent of the invalidity pension and, where incapacity for work began after age 20, the individual must be at least 80 per cent disabled.

There is a range of benefits applicable to all disabilities. The attendance allowance is for those aged over two who need substantial care because of physical or mental disabilities. It is payable at two rates (21.10 pounds and 31.60 pounds a week) dependent on the amount of care needed. The mobility allowance can be claimed by those aged five to 65 likely to incur extra transport costs because of inability to walk (22.10 pounds a week). The invalid care allowance is for those who give up work to care for someone receiving attendance allowance. The amount is only 60 per cent of the invalidity pension.

Disabled people are entitled to NHS care in the same way as are other residents of the United Kingdom. Long-term care for the most severely physically and mentally disabled is provided either in specialist hospitals or in units of general hospitals. Rehabilitation services such as occupational therapy and physiotherapy can help to minimise the effects of disabilities.

'Community care' programmes, similar to those for the aged, have become a priority. However, unlike the aged, large numbers, especially of severely mentally disordered people, used to be in hospitals, mostly large, isolated institutions, criticised for their effects on patients and, in some cases, low standards of care. There have been substantial reductions in hospital beds and a consequent increase in disabled people receiving 'community care'. Community nursing services, including a developing community psychiatric nursing service, can enable people to return to or remain in their homes. Some hospitals provide day care and workshops, hostels or discharge units which are 'halfway houses' for the mentally disordered. However, community care policies mean a larger role for the family and the personal social services.

United Kingdom

Personal Social Services

Successive recent government documents have urged LAs to expand provision for the disabled. In 1970, a duty was placed on LAs to assess the numbers and needs of disabled people in their areas. However, services have developed slowly and unevenly.

All LAs employ social workers to support and give practical advice to the disabled and their families, and to provide aids and adaptations, home helps and meals-on-wheels. Many LAs have day centres, residential homes, sheltered accommodation, holiday and transport schemes, laundry services and services for the blind and deaf.

Joint consultative committees, involving health authorities and LAs, plan services for the disabled (and the aged), and joint funding is available from the central government for a limited number of years for schemes promoting community care, acknowledging that this policy involves a transfer of costs and responsibilities to LAs.

Voluntary organisations contribute much to the care of the disabled. Some LAs use them as an alternative to direct state provision, for example, meals-on-wheels and residential accommodation. They vary enormously in size and activities: some promote medical research, others are primarily campaigning bodies, some concentrate on developing self-help groups, others provide more traditional services.

Evaluation

The cash benefits and service provision available for the disabled in recent years have undoubtedly improved. This has given some help to groups (especially married women) who previously received none. However there is still much variation depending in the income maintenance system on the origins of the disability and in the more locally administered health and personal social services on geographical locations. Many severely disabled people still live at the minimal supplementary benefit level and rely on family and friends for care. Current proposals to reform the supplementary benefit system (Department of Health and Social Security 1985) will substantially worsen the financial situation of some disabled people by abolishing many of the additions they can claim.

Despite the priority given by successive governments, health and personal social service provisions for the disabled have been affected by recent public expenditure constraints, inhibiting the development of adequate 'community care' facilities. There is also the problem that, especially in the case of the mentally disordered, 'the community' often appears unwilling to accept the integration of disabled people, particularly if it involves a hostel or day centre next door. In addition to material disadvantage, the disabled often face social stigma, prejudice and rejection from 'normal' people. Once again, major responsibilities are placed on families, especially the spouses and the ageing parents of severely disabled adults.

For those without family support, extensive use has been made in some areas of 'bed and breakfast' accommodation for the ex-patients of psychiatric hospitals. Despite the criticisms of long-term hospital care, it is doubtful how far the quality of life of these people could be said to have been improved.

CHILDREN AND YOUTHS

Currently, about 21 per cent of the population is aged under age 18. The size of this group has fluctuated considerably since 1945, due to fluctuations in the birth rate. At any time, only about one-third of households contain children. Education is compulsory between the age of five and 16. In 1984-5 45 per cent of young people stayed in full-time education after 16 and about 15 per cent after 18 (Central Statistical Office 1987, table 3.10). Most 16 year old school leavers are unable to find employment and enroll in a government-sponsored two-year training programme. The United Kingdom has no coherent 'family policy', but in various ways policies operate to redistribute resources towards families with children and encourage what is considered to be a 'good' family life.

Social Security

Maternity benefits have recently undergone considerable reform. Women working in the same

United Kingdom

employment for at least six months and earning at least 30 pounds a week are entitled to statutory maternity pay of 32.85 pounds a week for 18 weeks, subject to tax and national insurance contributions. However, those who have been in the same employment for at least two years (five years if part-time) receive 90 per cent of wages for the first six weeks, then 32.85 pounds a week for 12 weeks. These benefits are administered by employers, who are then reimbursed by the government. Women who have recently changed jobs, or have been self-employed, and have an adequate contribution record, can claim state maternity allowance (30.05 pounds a week). Some employers, in addition, provide extra benefits for women who are returning to work. A statutory right to return exists for up to six months after the baby is born for those in the same job for at least two years.

Families with children receive child benefit of 7.25 pounds a week for each child under 16 (19 if in full-time education). The benefit is normally paid to the mother, is tax-free and not subject to income or contribution conditions. The take-up rate is virtually 100 per cent. Child benefit recognises that children place a strain on most family budgets. It also represents a partial socialisation of the costs of children, acknowledging that resources invested in the younger generation can benefit the whole society.

Long-term national insurance benefits have additions for dependent children (8.05 pounds a week for each child). Supplementary benefits are also increased for each child and this will be discussed, along with other benefits for needy families, in the next section.

Some older children are entitled to state benefits in their own right. Unemployed school-leavers can claim supplementary benefits regardless of their parents' income, although the rate is lower for the under-18s (18.75 pounds a week). Those on the government's Youth Training Scheme receive an allowance of 27.30 pounds a week (35 pounds in the second year). Most education grants go to those over 18, but LAs can pay discretionary grants to students aged 16-18 on full-time education courses.

Babies and young children are heavy users of health services. Besides general practitioner services, there are maternal and child welfare services ranging from ante- and post-natal

United Kingdom

check-ups and care during confinement, to regular visits from a health visitor with a statutory responsibility to monitor the development of children under five, to a programme of immunisation and vaccination. A school medical service carries out regular checks on the health of school-children. All children under 16 are exempt from NHS charges.

For more serious illness, most hospitals have special wards for children and there are a few hospitals treating only children. There has recently been an increase in the number of special care baby units, associated with advances in the ability to save the life of very premature babies. However, the availability of beds in some areas does not meet the demand.

Personal Social Services

Much of the work of Social Services Departments involves children and this area of their responsibilities is often contentious. LAs have a statutory duty to promote the welfare of children, provide for children in trouble, and receive children deprived of a normal family life into substitute care. However, while all children use health services, only a small proportion ever have direct contact with personal social services. The clientele for these services are disproportionately drawn from the poorer sections of society, although the services are available to all.

LAs provide social work services, residential care, fostering and adoption services, day nurseries, home helps and services for young offenders (those aged under 17). They also register private nurseries and childminders. Charges operate for some of these services, usually according to income. Statutory youth services, including clubs and outdoor pursuit centres, are provided by the Education Department.

Twin beliefs which are widely held though not unchallenged are that, other than in exceptional circumstances, the best place for children is with their natural family, and that a welfare rather than a punishment approach is the most appropriate for all children 'in trouble', whether they have committed an offence or are suffering parental abuse. Thus the emphasis of social work with families is on preventing break-down, by counselling, practical advice, day-care and, in an emergency, limited financial assistance. If parents are unable to cope, they can ask for their children to be taken into care. Where children are at serious risk from parental abuse, or have committed offences and are considered to be beyond parental control, the LA can, with a court order, compulsorily take children into care. This may involve placing children in a residential home, or temporarily or permanently with foster parents, or even adoption. Courts can also send young offenders aged 14 or more to special institutions run by the Prison Department, under sentences ranging from 21 days to life. Alternatively (providing the court has not specified a residential care order) children may remain with parents under social work supervision, perhaps with day-care or, for older children, compulsory participation in an intermediate treatment project run by LAs or voluntary organisations. Intermediate treatment is for young offenders, or those at risk of offending, designed to develop their interests, sense of responsibility and involvement in the community.

Voluntary organisations, often working with LAs, are also widely involved in providing practical and counselling support for families with difficulties, residential care, adoption and fostering services, and in the prevention and detection of child abuse.

Evaluation

Social policy in the United Kingdom does involve some redistribution of resources towards children. Free state education is a major example, although it also places a burden on parents in compulsorily removing their children from the labour market. In social security the NHS covers the whole population, but includes some well-developed and popular services for babies and children and the income maintenance system has higher benefit levels for families with children. However child benefits (and their predecessors, family allowances) have not increased or even maintained their value as have other social security benefits. Neither do they cover anything like the full cost of children, especially older children. In addition, the abolition of child tax allowances in the late 1970s has been accompanied by a shift in the tax burden towards families with children.

United Kingdom

Personal social services only directly affect the lives of a minority of children, although it could be argued that the ideals of family life which they attempt to uphold influence the experience of many more. The twin beliefs in a welfare approach to young offenders and in the superiority of the natural family as an environment for children have both come under attack recently. A number of well-publicised, tragic cases of children being killed by relatives while in LA care, has led many social workers to adopt a more cautious (perhaps defensive) approach and be less willing to take risks. Criticisms of a 'soft' approach to juvenile offenders and concern over the rising rates of delinquency have led to an increase in the power of the courts as opposed to that of the LA, exemplified by their recently acquired ability to specify that children convicted of an imprisonable offence while in care must spend up to six months in a residential institution.

NEEDY FAMILIES

The number of poor families with children has increased substantially, due mainly to rising unemployment. The other major cause of family poverty is the dependence of a number of individuals on one modest wage. Those most likely to be poor thus include families headed by female single parents and the unskilled, minority ethnic groups and those in areas of high unemployment, including the inner-cities. In 1983, just under 10 per cent of couples with children and 52 per cent of one-parent families were living at or below the supplementary benefit level (Department of Health and Social Security 1986a).

Social Security

Although some family benefits are available regardless of income, recent trends have been towards selectivity, in two ways: the expansion of means-tested benefits and the introduction of benefits for one-parent families.

Family Income Supplement (FIS) was introduced to tackle family poverty and increase work incentives by improving the in-work income of those on low wages with children. It is means-tested and paid to those in full-time work,

United Kingdom

making up half the difference between income and a needs level which varies with the number of children. The maximum payment for a family with two children under 11 is 28.45 pounds a week.

Poor families without a full-time breadwinner can claim Supplementary Benefit (SB), a general social assistance scheme which takes the number and ages of children into account when entitlement is assessed. This is also a feature of housing benefits. Families with children are more likely to receive the single payments for 'exceptional needs' already described than other SB claimants. Those on SB and FIS or living on a very low income are entitled to a maternity payment of 80 pounds on the birth of a child, free milk and vitamins for pregnant and nursing mothers, and children up to five, free school meals and, depending on the LA, an educational maintenance allowance if over 16 and still in full-time education.

The national insurance widows' pension is the only longstanding benefit specifically (though not exclusively) for single parents. All widows receive 55.35 pounds a week, plus 8.05 pounds for each child, for the first six months. After this, a taxable pension of 39.50 pounds plus 8.05 pounds for each child is given to widows, regardless of other income, if they have dependent children or are over age 50 (or between 40 and 50, at a reduced rate). The pensions last until remarriage or retirement age.

However, single parents can now claim an extra child benefit (4.70 pounds a week for the first child). Their tax allowances, FIS and housing benefit entitlements are calculated as if two adults were present. They can qualify for FIS by working 24 hours a week (instead of 30). They are not required to look for work if claiming SB and can also earn more before losing entitlement. Single parents believed to be cohabiting are treated as married for social security purposes.

Poor families are exempt from NHS charges. Their poverty is sometimes associated with illness or disability of a breadwinner; in addition recent research has shown a continuing link between poverty, poor health and the relative under-utilisation of health services.

United Kingdom

Personal Social Services

As noted earlier personal social services are available to everyone, but most used by the less well-off. It is not necessarily that the poor are particularly prone to personal difficulties. Managing on low incomes and finding a way through the benefits maze, however, demands knowledge, personal competency and coping skills. In addition, better-off families can secure services such as domestic help and child care privately.

The services for families with children have already been described. Poor families can receive social work advice on their benefit entitlements. Some LAs have advice services which aim to improve communication with clients from ethnic minority groups, especially those whose first language is not English. In the voluntary sector, besides the Citizens' Advice Bureaux, many large conurbations have welfare rights or legal advice centres, offering free services and funded mainly by local or central government grants. In day care, many LAs give priority to single parents, but demand is well in excess of supply.

Evaluation

SB and FIS provide a 'safety-net' below which, in theory, no families with children fall. There is considerable debate over the adequacy of this safety-net. Many two-parent families only receive the lower rate of SB which, for a family with two children is 70.15 pounds a week, plus housing costs. Average male weekly earnings in April 1986 were 203.40 pounds (Department of Employment 1987, table 5.6). It is now proposed to replace SB with an income support scheme which, by including a premium for families with children (doubled for each disabled child) and a lone-parent premium, is likely to increase their basic entitlement. However, the proposed replacement of the present system of extra special needs payments by a system of recoverable loans, will particularly affect this group.

FIS increases the income of low-paid families, especially single parents. In 1985 one-parent families were 13 per cent of all families but 42 per cent of families receiving FIS (Family Policy Studies Centre 1986b). However, the take-up rate is low (about 50 per cent of those eligible) and

United Kingdom

FIS is criticised as enabling employers to pay low wages. It has also contributed to the 'poverty trap'. The combined effects of low tax thresholds and entitlement to means-tested benefits results in increases in the income of poor families being more than offset by loss of benefits and increased taxes. Current proposals to replace FIS with Family Credit, administered through the wage packet by employers, may increase the take-up rate, but will give the benefit to the man instead of (as at present) the woman in most two-parent families and will make it even more evidently a low-wage subsidy. Combined with reforms in housing benefit, marginal tax rates of over 100 per cent will be eliminated, but rates of 90 per cent or more will still be common.

Attitudes towards public support for one-parent families are ambivalent. Concern about the effects of material and social deprivation on the children mingles with fear that generous treatment may encourage marital breakdown and illegitimacy. Widows attract more sympathy and entitlement to benefits as a right. For the never-married, the divorced and the separated, there is the issue of the degree of support from the other parent and from public funds. There is also continuing ambivalence over whether single mothers should support themselves through employment or remain at home with their children. Mothers at home suffer a low standard of living on SB and constant vigilance from social security officials to ensure they are not cohabiting. Those at work may well receive low wages, thus still depend partly on means-tested benefits, and have difficulty in finding good, low-cost child care.

Another contentious issue is the degree to which lack of income is associated with a need for other social services. In the context of a universal non-stigmatised NHS, concern is about relative under-utilisation of services by the poor, although there is a debate over whether their greater ill-health derives from genetic and behavioural characteristics or from environmental and structural features of the society. The issue in regard to the personal social services, which has a high proportion of poor clients, is how far problems associated with low income warrant the intervention of social workers into other aspects of a client's personal life.

United Kingdom

THE UNEMPLOYED

The substantial increase in unemployment has been an outstanding feature of recent history in the United Kingdom. Although all groups and areas are affected, unemployment continues to be unequally distributed. Those at most risk include the least educated, ethnic minorities and those living outside the southern and south-eastern parts of the United Kingdom. Official unemployment ranged from 8.2 per cent in the South-East to 15.9 per cent in the North of England and 18.8 per cent in Northern Ireland in December 1986. As unemployment has risen, so has long-term unemployment. In January 1987, 40.5 per cent of the unemployed had been out of work for more than 52 weeks (Department of Employment 1987, table 2.8). These figures only include those claiming benefits and not others seeking work, the early retired or those on one of the many government-sponsored training and employment schemes.

Social Security

Income maintenance for the unemployed is still based on the system introduced in the late 1940s which assumed that unemployment would be an infrequent, short-term contingency. Unemployment Benefits (UBs) are part of the national insurance scheme. Former employees (not the self-employed) with sufficient contributions receive a flat-rate benefit of 31.45 pounds a week, plus 19.40 pounds for an adult dependant. The benefit is taxable and payable after three waiting days for a maximum of 52 weeks. Claimants are only allowed to earn two pounds a day before losing entitlement and must demonstrate they are available and capable of work. They can be disqualified from UB for leaving their last job voluntarily for no good reason, dismissal for industrial misconduct, refusal to accept a suitable job or training, making a fraudalent claim, or involvement in an industrial dispute. The stringency with which these are interpreted varies but disqualification is for 13 weeks and, in the case of industrial disputes, for the whole duration.

Those not entitled to UB or whose entitlement has run out, rely on means-tested supplementary benefit (SB). This has become the major source of support for the unemployed. In 1985, 18 per cent of the male unemployed received only UB, eight per cent received both UB and SB, and 62 per cent relied entirely on SB (Central Statistical Office, 1987, table 5.8). Because of concern that benefit levels should not approach wages, the unemployed are restricted to short-term SB rates. The long-term rates received by the elderly, long-term sick and one-parent families are over 25 per cent higher. Householders receive a higher rate than non-householders. Individuals disqualified from UB can claim SB, but at reduced rates. Claimants can only earn four pounds net a week and their spouses four pounds before SB is reduced pound for pound.

Loss of a job through redundancy qualifies for a lump-sum payment, if the individual has worked for the employer for at least two years, the amount of which depends upon pay, age, and length of service. Some employers have redundancy schemes which provide more than the statutory minimum. Redundancy payments are made even if the individual finds another job immediately. If they amount to more than 3,000 pounds, they can affect the individual's claim to SB.

The expansion of government-sponsored training and work experience programmes has blurred the boundaries of income maintenance for the unemployed. The incomes received by those participating varies between schemes, but sometimes, as in the two year Youth Training Scheme, and the new Job Training Scheme for the adult unemployed, they are very close to benefit levels. There is mounting evidence that unemployment, particularly if it is prolonged, is associated with a deterioration in health, especially mental health (Whitehead 1987). Thus the unemployed may make heavier demands on the NHS. Those on low incomes will be exempt from NHS charges.

Personal Social Services

Social Services Departments make little special provision for the unemployed, although they are likely to figure disproportionately among clients, from participants in intermediate treatment (as unemployment increases the risk of juvenile crime), to family casework clients. In some areas, 'drop-in' centres for the unemployed have developed with social activities and information centres, run by LAs or voluntary organisations. Their welfare rights services are also important

United Kingdom

for the unemployed. Many LAs offer concessionary rates to the unemployed for leisure and transport facilities.

Vocational counselling and job placement are provided through the Careers Service (administered by local education authorities) for the under-19s and through the Manpower Services Commission, part of the Department of Employment, for adults.

Evaluation

One major priority for the unemployed - increased job opportunities - lies largely outside the remit of the social services and, some would argue, of government, although the public sector itself provides many jobs. However, the social services seem primarily concerned with the alleviation of the effects of unemployment and the maintenance of work incentives. These two concerns are difficult to reconcile and the balance between them arouses much debate. Concern about 'scroungers' and fear that people may 'settle down' on benefits has produced a variety of controls (financial and otherwise), which make the unemployed, in many ways, the least generously treated of social security recipients.

For those entirely dependent on benefits, entitlement to UB would often be no higher than SB and many UB recipients are also claiming means-tested benefits. However, dependence on a means-tested rather than an insurance benefit may have a psychological impact, adding to the stigma experienced by many unemployed. Means-testing also excludes some individuals from receiving any benefits at all, for example, unemployed individuals (especially women) with working spouses. In addition, the system acts as a disincentive to work for many wives of unemployed men, as their earnings will reduce the family's entitlement to SB, but are unlikely to be sufficient to raise their standard of living to a level appreciably higher. Another disincentive to work could operate through the very low allowable income in both UB and SB.

There is a widespread assumption that to maintain work incentives benefits must be substantially lower than wages. Because of the flat-rate nature of the benefits, this means that most unemployed suffer a considerable fall in income, especially if they have children, and find it difficult to make ends meet (Bradshaw et al.

United Kingdom

1983). The proposed income support scheme may increase basic benefit entitlements for this group, but will reduce the amounts they receive in special needs payments.

THE SICK AND INJURED

When the NHS was set up, many envisaged that after initial high demand for the treatment of a backlog of illness, the availability of free, comprehensive care would improve the nation's health and thus, demand would eventually decline. Subsequently, by many measures, people have become healthier. Mortality rates at all ages have continued to decline, although the contribution of medicine to this progress is debatable. However, expenditure on the NHS has risen substantially. In 1949-50, 3.75 per cent of Gross National Produce (GNP) was devoted to the NHS. By 1980 this had increased to 6.1 per cent (Allsop 1984, pp.75-6). These increases stem from higher expectations and lower tolerance thresholds, advancing medical technology, widening definitions of ill-health and the availability of largely free, good quality health services.
   It is difficult to estimate accurately the extent and patterns of sickness (as opposed to mortality) among the population. The annual General Household Survey of about 16,000 households, includes information on self-reported health. In 1985 about 30 per cent of the respondents reported some long-standing illness and 12 per cent had suffered a very recent acute illness (Office of Population Censuses and Surveys 1986). Information on recorded use of health services will only show a very partial picture as only a small proportion of episodes of sickness ever reach the NHS (Office of Health Economics 1975).
   Patterns of mortality and morbidity have changed over this century. The incidence and virulence of the major infectious diseases has declined and that of diseases of the circulation, cancer and respiratory diseases has increased (Allsop 1984, p.149). The former affected primarily younger age-groups, whereas the latter are diseases mostly of middle and old age. These changes have important implications for the type of health serivces required and for the type of patients who predominate.

United Kingdom

Social Security

Employees earning enough to pay national insurance contributions (39 pounds a week) are entitled to statutory sick pay (SSP) if unable to work because of sickness. This is paid at two rates (47.20 pounds or 32.85 pounds a week) depending on earnings, taxable and administered and 'policed' by employers who reclaim the money from the government. Those not qualifying for SSP (including the self-employed and unemployed) can claim sickness benefit instead (30.05 pounds a week). This is the national insurance benefit partly replaced by SSP in 1983. It is taxable and, unless the illness is work-related, entitlement depends on having paid sufficient contributions. Self-certification is required for sickness benefit and in most SSP schemes for the first seven days, after which medical certificates must be produced. Many people relying entirely on SSP or sickness benefit will also be entitled to means-tested supplementary and housing benefits. These short-term benefits for the sick are paid after three waiting days, for up to 28 weeks. After that, there are long-term benefits, described in a previous section.

Many employees are also covered by occupational sick pay schemes, varying considerably in amount and duration. Some (especially for white collar workers) fully replace earnings during short-term sickness.

Comprehensive, virtually free health services are obviously important to the sick and are available regardless of age, employment or financial status. Exemption from NHS charges and help with hospital travelling costs depends on low income, but anyone who needs a number of prescriptions can buy a 'season ticket' for a fixed charge. Almost all of the population is registered with a general practitioner (GP), who is (except in emergencies) the first point of contact with the NHS. Access to specialists must be through GP referral. Hospital treatment is completely free, although a long stay may lead to reduced social security benefits.

The NHS is still primarily a 'national sickness service'. However, mounting evidence of the lack of a relationship between increased expenditure and better health has led to more emphasis on prevention (Department of Health and Social Security 1976). This has mainly consisted of exhorting individuals to change their lifestyles and, in terms of resources, has not posed a threat to curative medicine.

Occupational health provision is only well developed in the larger companies and more hazardous industries. However, private health insurance is an expanding 'fringe benefit', especially for white-collar employees. In 1981, just over seven per cent of the population was covered, although almost all of these use the NHS as well. Expenditure by the three major associations that dominate the private market was less than two per cent of NHS expenditure in 1981 (Maynard and Williams 1984). The present Conservative government is encouraging the expansion of private health insurance to lower income groups through tax concessions to employers. The major advantages of the private sector are shorter waiting times for 'cold' surgery (hernias, varicose veins, and so forth) and more comfortable accommodation. Half of all abortions are also carried out privately (Allsop 1984, p.34).

Personal Social Services

Some local authority social workers are based in hospitals and specialise in the social and financial problems associated with sickness. Others are 'attached' to general medical practices and work with the doctors and for their patients. Home-helps can provide domestic assistance to those incapacitated through sickness. One of the most frequent reasons for the short-term admission of children into care is that the responsible parent is admitted to a hospital. However, most of the sick will not be in contact with personal social services.

Evaluation

Most of those unable to work because of sickness (the major exceptions being housewives and those on low, part-time earnings, mostly married women) are entitled to social security benefits and many will also receive sick pay from their employer. Their recovery need not be impeded by the fear of huge medical costs. Health services are virtually free, accessible and more evenly distributed than in many other Western societies, although patients can wait many months for surgery for conditions which, while not life-threatening, can cause considerable pain and limitation of function. Extra resources have recently been allocated for the reduction of hospital waiting lists.

The private health sector is small, but does symbolise (but not cause) a continuing division which has attracted considerable recent attention: class differences in health and the use of health services. A variety of measures of mortality and morbidity and of NHS utilisation show that at all ages, health status appears poorer and use of health services (especially preventive services) less in relation to need in the lower socio-occupational classes and in poorer areas (Le Grand 1982). More contentiously, some have argued that these differences have remained stable or even increased over time (Townsend & Davidson 1982; Whitehead 1987). Reforms within the NHS such as improved health education and more resources to poorly served areas may contribute towards lessening this division, but improvements in income, housing and environmental conditions may well be more valuable in tackling the social bases of much ill-health.

AN ASSESSMENT OF THE UNITED KINGDOM'S WELFARE SYSTEM

State welfare services and fiscal policies influence the lives of everyone living in the United Kingdom. Social expenditure (including education, as well as income maintenance, health and personal social services, but not fiscal welfare) comprised 24.9 per cent of GNP in 1981, compared with 13.9 per cent in 1960 (Jones 1985). This increase has not produced an overall trend towards equality of income, but there is evidence it has significantly modified pressures towards increased inequality (O'Higgins 1985).

Beveridge's vision of comprehensive, universal and adequate provision has partially been fulfilled, with a National Health Service covering all residents and a comprehensive system of cash benefits which has improved coverage for the disabled, one-parent and low-wage families and married women. Personal social services are also available to all, but in practice are used mainly by particular groups (poor families, the aged and disabled).

United Kingdom

In some respects there have been important shifts away from the Beveridge principles in income maintenance. He envisaged flat-rate social insurance as the main form of state provision, and did not anticipate the growth of social assistance nor of statutory earnings-related and occupational benefits. He was particularly opposed (as are many contemporary critics) to the widespread use of means-testing, because of problems of stigma, low take-up rates and complex, high-cost administration. In 1986, 14 per cent of the population were dependent on supplementary benefit (Department of Health and Social Security 1986b, table 34.31). One reason for the continuing importance of social assistance is that, contrary to Beveridge's recommendations, social insurance and child benefits have never been considered to be, by themselves, at an adequate level. That this is so, despite considerable increases in their real value and as a proportion of average earnings (except for child benefits), indicates a rising level of expectations and the relative nature of deprivation.

The National Health Service is popular and is one of the services to which the present government declares itself most committed. There are debates over whether expenditure increases are keeping pace with need, especially given demographic changes, about whether the United Kingdom's relatively low expenditure rate compared to other Western societies reflects greater efficiency or chronic underfunding, and about the efficacy of curative medicine in promoting better health. There is also some concern over the persistence, despite 'free' access to the NHS, of continuing class and geographical inequalities both in health and the use of health services.

Personal social services, after rapid expansion in the early 1970s and the accumulation of a wide range of statutory responsibilities, have come under increasing financial pressure in recent years. This has had serious implications for the development of community care for the aged, the physically handicapped and the mentally disabled. 'Care in the community', involving comprehensive statutory and voluntary support services, has been transformed into 'care by the community', with responsibilities falling mainly on female kin.

United Kingdom

The economic recession of the mid-1970s, with inflation and unemployment as its most striking symptoms, imposed considerable strains on state welfare, both in terms of increasing demand and of encouraging a more critical view of its relationship to the economy. In 1979, 1983 and 1987 Conservative governments were elected, committed to a very different economic strategy from that which had dominated much of the period since 1945. Whether this strategy will involve only a trimming at the edges of the Welfare State, or a more wholesale 'rolling back of the frontiers of the State', with more emphasis on self-help, private and occupational welfare, is as yet unclear.

REFERENCES

Allsop, J. (1984), Health Policy and the National Health Service, London: Longman.

Beechey, V. (1986), 'Women's Employment in Contemporary Britain', in Beechey, V. and Whitelegg, E. (eds) Women in Britain Today, Milton Keynes: Open University Press.

Beveridge, W. (Chairman) (1942), Report of the Committee on Social Insurance and Allied Services, Cmnd 6404, London: HMSO.

Bradshaw, J., Cooke, K. & Godfrey, C. (1983), 'The Impact of Unemployment on the Living Standards of Families', Journal of Social Policy 12 (4), 433-52.

Central Statistical Office (1986), Social Trends 1986, London: HMSO.

_____ (1987), Social Trends 1987, London: HMSO.

Department of Employment (1987), Employment Gazette, April, London: HMSO.

Department of Health and Social Security (1976), Prevention and Health: Everybody's Business, London: HMSO.

_____ (1981), Growing Older, Cmnd 8173, London: HMSO.

United Kingdom

_____ (1983), Health Care and Its Costs, London: HMSO.

_____ (1985), The Reform of Social Security, Cmnd 9691, London: HMSO.

_____ (1986a), Low Income Families - 1983, London: HMSO.

_____ (1986b), Social Security Statistics 1986, London: HMSO.

European Economic Communities (1977), The Perception of Poverty in Europe, Brussels: Commission of the European Communities.

Family Policy Studies Centre (1985), The Family Today, London: Family Policy Studies Centre.

_____ (1986a), An Ageing Population, London: Family Policy Studies Centre.

_____ (1986b), One-Parent Families, London: Family Policy Studies Centre.

Finch, J. & Groves, D. (1983), A Labour of Love, London: Routledge & Kegan Paul.

Fraser, D. (1973), The Evolution of the British Welfare State, London: Macmillan.

Halsey, A. (1987), 'Social Trends Since World War II', in Central Statistical Office, Social Trends 1987, London: HMSO.

Harris, A. (1971), Handicapped and Impaired in Great Britain, Part 1, London: HMSO.

Harris, R. & Seldon, A. (1979), Over-Ruled on Welfare, London: Institute of Economic Affairs.

Jones, C. (1985), Patterns of Social Policy: an Introduction to Comparative Analysis, London: Tavistock Publications.

Le Grand, J. (1982), The Strategy of Equality, London: George Allen & Unwin.

United Kingdom

Maynard, A. & Williams, A. (1984), 'Privatisation and the National Health Service' in Le Grand, J. and Robinson, R. (eds), *Privatisation and the Welfare State*, London: George Allen & Unwin.

Office of Health Economics (1975), *The Health Care Dilemma*, London: Office of Health Economics.

Office of Population Censuses and Surveys (1986), *OPCS Monitor - General Household Survey*, GHS 86/1, London: HMSO.

O'Higgins, M. (1985), 'Inequality, Redistribution and Recession: The British Experience 1976-1982', *Journal of Social Policy*, 14 (3), 279-307.

Taylor-Gooby, P. (1985), *Public Opinion, Ideology and State Welfare*, London: Routledge and Kegan Paul.

Townsend, P. & Davidson, N. (eds) (1982), *Inequalities in Health*, Harmondsworth: Penguin.

Walker, A. (ed.) (1982), *Public Expenditure and Social Policy*, London: Heinemann.

Whitehead, M. (1987), *The Health Divide*, London: Health Education Council.

UNITED STATES OF AMERICA
Robert S. Magill

THE WELFARE SYSTEM ENVIRONMENT

Ideological Environment

Values are especially important in American social welfare since many Americans have strong opinions about social welfare problems. In addition, the absence of definitive research results in policy choices which rely heavily on broadly held values and on the preferences of powerful interest groups.

The central values which have contributed to American social welfare policy include capitalism, classical liberalism, positivism, pragmatism (Dobelstein 1980), humanitarianism (Magill 1984) and social and economic mobility (Tropman 1981).

Capitalism. Capitalism emphasises the work ethic and the importance of the private sector. Under capitalism, the individual has the moral authority to pursue wealth in the market-place. Strong negative sanctions are applied to those who seem able to work but do not. The goal of social welfare is to help people become socially and economically independent. However, capitalism supports help for the non-able bodied who are seen as deserving charity.

Liberalism. Classical liberalism is based on the values of individualism and personal freedom. Government should have a minimal function in the economy and in the social welfare system. Issues of social justice are best resolved by the free operation of the market-place without outside intervention (Friedman 1972). If government is needed in social welfare, local and State government should be employed before the federal government. Overall, classical liberals feel that too much help for those in need is harmful because it creates dependency. Classical liberals believe that 'self help is the best help'.

Social Darwinism. Social Darwinism or Positivism states that the laws of biological evolution can be applied to social organisation. If left alone, the natural progress of society will allow the fittest to survive. Those in need are blamed for their condition. Positivism can be used to justify inequalities in society and minimal help for those in need (Hofstadler 1955). Because of positivism, there is often a stigma attached to those who receive financial, emotional or social help through the social welfare system.

Pragmatism. Pragmatism emphasises policies which seem to work in the short run. Pragmatism focuses on means rather than goals. Its importance helps to explain the resistance to centralised long-range planning in social policy (Dobelstein 1980).

Humanitarianism. Humanitarianism stresses concern for those in need. While not a dominant American value, it has contributed to the development of the social welfare system. Humanitarianism is based in the Judeo-Christian ethic of the groups' concern for those in need. Humanitarianism was especially important during the major expansions of the social welfare system in the 1930s and the 1960s (Magill 1984).

Social and Economic Mobility. Social and economic mobility may be the dominant American value. In American society, social and economic mobility is the yardstick used to measure personal worth. High social mobility is valued while the absence of social mobility is scorned. The valuing of social mobility explains the hostility towards welfare recipients and the unemployed, who are failing in this central American value (Tropman 1981).

In general, dominant American values emphasise individual freedom and responsibility (Magill 1984). The result is a social welfare system that is neither as extensive nor as generous as in many other developed countries.

United States

Historical Origins

The history of American social policy is the history of the change from charity to social welfare (Leiby 1987) and the change from State and local support to federal participation in providing for those in need (Magill 1979). Early social welfare measures were based on the English Poor Law and emphasised community responsibility. Outdoor relief was provided for the deserving poor who could live in their homes, whole others were placed at community expense in private homes, and later in public institutions called almshouses. During colonial times, 'most communities attacked the problem of poverty with a high degree of civic responsibility' (Trattner 1974).

The revolutionary war caused social and economic dislocations which disrupted many community-administered social policies. In addition, there was an increase in the percentage of the population which was poor. European population economists were disputing the supportive approach to charity. The building of community almshouses, which housed all those who could not take care of themselves, was the beginning of the change towards a more institutional, less neighbourly approach to taking care of those in need. It soon became clear that more specialised care was appropriate for different clients who had been housed together in the almshouses. States were pressured by crusaders like Dorothea Dix to establish specialised institutions for clients such as the emotionally ill and the hard of hearing (Magill 1984). The system of outdoor relief and institutionalisation at the community and State level was supplemented by private charity supported by wealthy individuals. Both were '... based on a much honored religious commandment to love others as one loves God' (Leiby 1987, p.760).

Early efforts to involve the federal government in providing for those in need were largely unsuccessful. President Pierce wrote, in vetoing a measure inspired by Dorothea Dix to provide federal lands to the States to support emotionally ill persons, '... I cannot find any authority in the Constitution for making the Federal Government the greater almoner (provider) of public charity throughout the United States' (Congressional Globe 1854).

United States

As society became industrialised and urbanised, Social Darwinism became a powerful ideology. Ideas such as the 'survival of the fittest', 'the least government is the best government' and 'blaming the victim' dominated public policy.

With social needs growing, and the government reluctant to take responsibility, private charity became more developed. This was in part to help the waves of Eastern European immigrants who were entering the country to power the transition from an agricultural to an industrial society. The first Charity Organisation Society was established in Buffalo, New York in 1877. These groups became known for 'scientific charity' since they attempted to apply the new approach of the scientific method to changing human behaviour. Mary Richmond was an early leader of the movement and her book, <u>Social Diagnosis</u>, published in 1917, is recognised as the first social casework book. The Charity Organisation Societies sent volunteers to work with the urban needy in order to help them to adjust to society. The Charity Organization Societies were the predecessors of American family counselling agencies.

In contrast to the individual approach of the Charity Organization Societies, the settlement houses worked to change social institutions. The first American settlement was established in New York City in 1886. Outsiders, such as James Adams of Chicago's Hull House, 'settled in' working class communities, developed needed services, and participated in the growing community, state and federal efforts at reform (Davis 1974).

With the proliferation of private agencies, efforts at community planning and federated fund-raising eventually resulted in the creation of the United Way.

The Great Depression was a turning point for American social welfare. In response to an economic crisis, the federal government promoted a series of broad social welfare programmes, implemented in large part through the States, to provide employment and social assistance. The Social Security Act, passed in 1935, established, for the first time, the legitimacy of the federal government in providing for the general social welfare.

During the 1930s, under the leadership of President Franklin Roosevelt and the New Deal, social welfare became institutionalised in society. While the private efforts continued, government assumed the basic responsibility for a 'safety net' of programmes for those in need.

The second major advance in social welfare policy occurred during the 1960s. Society was again in crisis, this time due to racial inequality. In part in response to the civil rights movement, a broad series of social welfare policies in the areas of health, education and welfare were developed. A backlog of social legislation created during the 1950s was implemented by President Lyndon Johnson as part of his Great Society programme.

Since this period, efforts have been made to consolidate, reduce, and decentralise the major policies of the 1930s and the 1960s. There has been a disturbing return to some aspects of Social Darwinism. During the 1980s, economic and defence policy has predominated over social policy in the contest for public attention and support.

The following table shows some significant dates in the development of social welfare programmes in the United States (US).

TABLE 1: SIGNIFICANT DATES IN THE HISTORY OF SOCIAL WELFARE

1647	First colonial poor law enacted by Rhode Island
1773	First public mental health hospital established in Virginia
1790	First public orphanage founded in South Carolina
1793	US Public Health Service established
1817	Gallaudet School, first free school for deaf founded in Connecticut
1822	First State institution for deaf established in Kentucky
1824	First State institution for juvenile delinquents in New York
1837	First State institution for the blind in Ohio
1853	First independent child placement agency founded by Charles Loring Brace in New York
1854	President Pierce vetos federal aid to mentally ill
1855	YMCA organised in Massachusetts
1863	First State Board of Charities, Boston, Massachusetts

United States

1865	Freedmans' Bureau to help freed men; first federal welfare effort
1866	YWCA established in Boston, Massachusetts
1877	First Charity Organization Society founded in Buffalo, New York
1886	First Settlement House in New York City
1899	First juvenile court in Chicago, Illinois
1908	First Community Welfare Council in Pittsburgh, Pennsylvania
1911	Urban League organised Predecessor of Family Service Association of America organised
1912	Children's Bureau in federal government established Girl Scouts of US founded
1913	Modern Community Chest movement began in Cleveland, Ohio
1917	First textbook on social casework written by Mary Richmond First State department of public welfare in Illinois
1918	Vocational Rehabilitation Act passed
1920	Boy Scouts of America founded
1921	Maternity and Infancy Hygiene Act passed
1930	American Public Welfare Association founded
1933	Civilian Conservation Corps provided work and education programmes for the unemployed Federal Emergency Relief Act provided relief for unemployed
1934	National Housing Act was first law promoting housing construction
1935	Social Security Act passed
1942	First federal support for day care for working mothers
1946	National Mental Health Act passed; recognised mental illness as a national public health problem Hill-Burton Hospital Construction Act passed
1950	Social Security Act Amendments, established aid to disabled, extended coverage to elderly and children
1953	US Department of Health, Education and Welfare created
1957	Civil Rights Act of 1957 established Commission on Civil Rights
1962	Social Security Act Amendments increase services for families with dependent children

United States

1964	Civil Rights Act promoted policies to reduce discrimination based on race Food Stamp Act passed Economic Opportunity Act creates the poverty programme
1965	Older Americans Act creates the Administration on Ageing Medicare and Medicaid Act created health care for poor and aged Elementary and Secondary School Act provides federal funds for schools in poor neighbourhoods
1966	Narcotic Addict Rehabilitation Act created providing for treatment of addicts
1973	Health Maintenance Organization Act provides federal aid to support group medical practice
1974	Child Abuse and Prevention Treatment Act passed
1975	Social Security Act Amendments provide services through block grants to States
1981	Omnibus Budget Reconciliation Act and Social Service Block Grant Act resulted in reductions to the federal government's social welfare role and financial support provided and increased State responsibility.

SOURCE: Based on Alexander 1987

THE POLITICAL AND SOCIAL-ECONOMIC ENVIRONMENT

The United States is a democratic society with a system of free elections and rule by law. In addition to the federal government, there are 51 state, as well as county, city, village and special district governments. The relationship between the central government and the States and municipalities has been characterised by federalism, or the sharing of responsibilities. The relative power and specific responsibilities of each level of government has changed within this framework over time. At present, in domestic policy, and especially in social welfare, the major trend is the decentralisation of programmatic and financial responsibilities from the federal government to the States and counties (Magill 1979).

In 1985, there were 238,631,000 Americans living in the United States. Between 1980 and

1984, the US population grew by 4.2 per cent. Ninety-one per cent of this growth occurred in the South and the West (NASW 1987, p.3).

Eighty per cent of Americans are white. Of the non-white population, 12 per cent are black, six per cent are Hispanic and two per cent are American Indian, Asian Americans and other non-whites (Hopps 1987, p.163). There are also significant numbers of newer immigrants from South-East Asia, South America and the Caribbean who are settling in urban areas and are not included in the most recent census (Magill 1985). The non-white population grew faster than did the white population between 1980 and 1984. Among non-whites, the Spanish-speaking population is the fastest growing minority group.

The US is predominantly a Christian country: 57 per cent of the population is Protestant, 28 per cent is Catholic, and two per cent is Jewish (Census 1987, p.33). Recently, there has been an increase in fundamentalist Christian religious groups.

The US is primarily an urban and suburban country. In 1985, over three quarters of the population (76 per cent) lived in metropolitan areas.

The major demographic trend is the ageing of the population, which will continue. At the other end of the age spectrum, most children live in two-parent families. However, in 1984, one in four families with children was a single parent family. Other demographic trends include: the increase in the percentage of the population which is poor, particularly evident among children; the relative decrease in the percentage of the population of teenagers and young adults; and the increase in the percentage of women in the labour force.

The American economy, like that of many other industrial nations, is changing from a manufacturing to a service dominated economy. During the 1980s the economy has been characterised by relatively slow and steady growth and low inflation, rising trade deficits, the international dispersion of economic activity, and increased inequalities of income and wealth (NASW 1987, p.12). The high amount of debt owed by Third World countries to American banks and the high national government deficit, are also areas of concern.

United States

Employment has been characterised by:

> ... the stagnation of earnings and decline of job-quality measured by income, stability, and opportunity-accompanied by the long-term increase in unemployment and underemployment among all groups (NASW 1987, p.23).

These trends are expected to continue in the near term (Thurow 1980). Economists project that by the turn of the century there will be a labour shortage in many high skill jobs.

The 1980s in America has been characterised as the 'retreat from social welfare' (Ginsberg 1987). A conservative trend which emphasised individual responsibility has resulted in significant cutbacks in federal social welfare responsibility and financing. Efforts to repair the damage created by these cuts have been limited by the high federal deficit and expenditures which are locked into the defence budget for the next decade. It is probable that in the future, major new federal social programmes can only be financed by increases in taxes.

THE WELFARE SYSTEM: AN OVERVIEW

The Structure and Administration of the Welfare System

The American social welfare system is decentralised and characterised by a strong private sector which supplements governmental provisions. Using a broad definition of social welfare, the national government funds and directly operates programmes for war veterans, federal personnel, native Americans, and violators of federal law. The federal government also administers most parts of the social security programme, including old age, survivors and disability benefits, hospital insurance and supplementary security income for the aged and disabled. The federal government also undertakes and sponsors research efforts in the areas of health, education and welfare.

The States administer unemployment insurance (apart from special federal programmes for veterans, railroad workers, and government employees) and workmen's compensation (apart from special federal programmes). The States and/or the counties also administer income maintenance programmes (general (social) assistance and aid to families with dependent children), medical care for the poor, education, child care, direct delivery of goods and services, housing programmes, personal social services, correctional programmes and food stamp programmes. In some States, some of these policies are delegated for implementation to the county level of government. In a few cases, these programmes are implemented by municipal government.

At the county and municipal level of government, there may be social welfare programmes in the areas of health, personal social services, housing, community development, education and financial assistance. Usually these programmes receive all or a part of their funding from federal and state sources through transfers in the form of block grants.

At the federal level, the Departments of Health and Human Services, Education, Labour and Housing and Urban Development administer most social policies. Virtually every federal department operates some social welfare programmes. To an extent, there is coordination on the federal level between departments through the President's Domestic Council and the Office of Management and Budget. In Congress, there are committees concerned with social security, income maintenance, health, education, the work force, and related policies (Kammerman & Kahn 1976).

Most States have departments of health and social services, with related committees composed of State legislators. Since, in many States, counties now play a role in the delivery of health, mental health, and income maintenance programmes, there are county administrators and county legislators as well who become involved in social welfare policy.

Almost one-third of social services in the US are delivered by non-governmental organisations. These services tend to be personal social services for middle and upper income clients, although substantial programmes may exist for lower and working class individuals and families. In all major communities, established voluntary agencies are affiliated with the United Way, a predominantly North American institution characterised by federated fund-raising and some community planning (Kramer 1984). In addition, some services are provided by religious

United States

organisations and interest groups. Private and proprietary services are increasingly important as alternatives to established voluntary agencies, especially now that many workers can receive third party payments from the government and from insurance companies (Barker 1987).

There has been a reaction against the significant increases in social welfare policy by the federal government during the 1960s. Since then, important efforts have been made to decentralise the responsibility for many social welfare programmes to the states and to the counties. In addition, governments at all levels have decreased their support of social welfare. As a result, the private and voluntary sector have been asked to assume new responsibilities.

Financing Social Welfare

In 1984, all federal governmental expenditures constituted 18.6 per cent of the Gross National Product (GNP). When State and local expenditures are added, government spending at all levels constituted 28.8 per cent of the GNP (US Office of Management and Budget 1985). Table 2 shows the percentage distribution of the federal budget outlays excluding Social Security and Medicare for 1984.

The rate of increase in public social welfare spending began to slow during the late 1970s, after a decade and a half of rapid increases (Doolittle 1986). There has been growth in spending since then, but it has been uneven. Between 1975 and 1983, spending for social insurance programmes which are supported by their own tax rose 168.8 per cent. During this period funding for all other social welfare programmes rose only half as fast, at a rate of 86.3 per cent. Further, except for Social Security insurance for the elderly, the imbalances between the level of need and spending has increased. Social security payments to disabled workers was cut substantially between 1981 and 1983, although Congressional action eventually slowed the cuts. As unemployment rates reached post-war highs, unemployment insurance covered a decreasing share of the unemployed (NASW 1987, p.49).

Table 3 shows public social welfare spending for 1975, 1980 and 1983.

Table 4 outlines the social security contributions paid by employees, employers and government.

United States

TABLE 2: PERCENTAGE DISTRIBUTION OF FEDERAL BUDGET OUTLAYS (EXCLUDING SOCIAL SECURITY AND MEDICARE), 1984

Category	1984
National Defence	36.9
Income Security	18.3
Net Interest	18.0
Health	4.9
Education, training & employment	4.5
Veterans	4.2
Transportation	3.8
International Affairs	2.5
Agriculture	2.2
Natural resources	2.0
All others	2.7
Total (per cent)	100.0
Total Outlays (in $US billions)	616.0

SOURCE: Budget of the United States 1986, pp.3.2(4)-3.2(5)

Programmes for the poor comprise about one-tenth of the federal budget. However, programmes for the poor bore almost one-third of the federal budget cuts made between 1981 and 1983 (Center on Budget and Policy Priorities 1985). In other terms, non-defence spending in 1985 was reduced by $56 billion, or about 10 per cent of the levels needed to continue existing programmes at the same real service levels (Mills 1984).

'The United States is unique among industrialised countries in its dual system of social welfare - a public system for some and a private system for those who qualify through their employment' (NASW 1987, p.51). These private benefits were estimated at $US435 billion in 1980. They provided pension, medical care, psychiatric and other benefits to those who are enrolled.

In addition to the above expenditures, private philanthropy contributes extensively to social welfare as shown in Table 5 (NASW 1987, p.63).

United States

TABLE 3: PUBLIC SOCIAL WELFARE EXPENDITURES, 1975, 1980 and 1983 (in $US billions)

Category	1975	1980	1983
Total	290.0	493.2	641.9
Social Insurance	123.0	229.8	330.6
Old Age, Survivors, Death and Health Insurance	78.4	152.1	224.7
Public employee retirement	20.1	39.5	54.8
Unemployment insurance - employment service	13.8	18.3	25.3
Workers' compensation	6.5	13.5	17.4
Medicare	14.8	34.9	56.9
Other	10.6	-	-
Public Aid	41.4	71.8	85.8
Public Assistance[1]	27.4	44.9	56.6
Supplementary Security Income	6.1	8.2	10.8
Food Stamps	4.7	9.1	11.7
Other	3.2	9.6	6.7
Health & medical programmes[2]	17.8	28.3	36.9
Veterans' programmes	17.0	21.5	25.8
Education	80.8	121.0	141.5
Housing	3.2	7.2	9.1

Notes:

1. Cash and medical payments under the Social Security Act and state and local general assistance
2. Excludes Medicaid

SOURCE: NASW 1987, p.52

United States

TABLE 4: SOCIAL SECURITY CONTRIBUTIONS PAYABLE

Employees	Percentage of Earnings
Old age, invalidity and death benefits[1]	5.7 [2]
Hospitalisation of Insured Workers[3]	1.35 [4]
Sickness Benefits[3]	1.2 [5]
Work injury benfits	[6]
Unemployment benfits[7]	[8]

Employers	Percentage of Payroll
Old age, invalidity and death benefits[1]	5.7
Hospitalisation of Insured Workers[3]	1.35
Sickness benefits[3]	[9]
Work injury	Whole cost[10]
Unemployment	[11]

Government	
Old age, invalidity and death benefits	Whole cost of means-tested allowances
Hospitalisation of Insured Workers	[12]
Unemployed	[13]

Notes:
1. Maximum earnings for contribution and benefit purposes $US39,600 a year, automatically indexed to wage levels.
2. Self-employed 11.4 per cent less transitional tax credit of 2.3 per cent in 1985.
3. Provided in only five States. Maximum earnings for contribution purposes $US39,600 a year (hospitalisation) and $US6,240-$US22,150 a year (cash benefit).
4. Self-employed 2.7 per cent
5. Maximum rate, varies according to State.
6. Nominal contributions in a few States.
7. Maximum earnings for contributions and benefit purposes $US7,000 (under federal and 19 state programmes. Higher in remaining states).
8. None except in Alabama, Alaska and New Jersey.
9. Varies according to State.

United States

10. Whole cost in most states, and most of cost in others, through compulsory insurance premiums (public or private cover), war injury with risk or self-insurance.
11. Federal tax, 0.8 per cent of taxable payroll. In most states 5.4 per cent, but varying from 0-0.5 per cent according to individual employer's experience averaging 3.1 per cent in 1985.
12. Cost of hospitalisation for certain non-insured aged persons. Balance of cost of voluntary insurance for all medical services.
13. Federal government pays for administration of state programmes.

SOURCE: US Social Security Administration 1986.

TABLE 5: PRIVATE PHILANTHROPY: ESTIMATED ALLOCATION FOR 1975, 1980, 1984 (in $US millions)

Category	1975	1980	1984
Total	29,680	47,740	74,250
Religion	12,910	22,150	35,560
Education	3,950	6,680	10,080
Social Welfare	3,140	4,730	8,010
Health & Hospitals	4,420	6,490	10,440
Arts & the Humanities	1,720	2,960	4,640
Civic & public	890	1,360	2,080
Other	2,650	3,370	3,440

SOURCE: NASW 1987, p.63.

Table 5 shows that the total amount given more than doubled between 1975 and 1984, with more than half of the contributions going to religion

THE AGED

The ageing of the population has become a dominant demographic characteristic of the twentieth century, a condition that will continue into the twenty-first century as well (Maldonado 1987, p.95).

United States

In the US the proportion of aged in the population is expected to increase. By 1983 there were 26.8 million aged in the US comprising 11 per cent of the population. By the year 2030, it is expected that there will be 64.3 million elderly persons comprising 21 per cent of the population (US Bureau of the Census 1982).

The elderly population can be divided into the young old (55-64 age group), the old (65-74 age group), the older old (75-84 age group) and the very old (85 and older age group) (US Senate 1984). Some experts suggest that it would be more accurate and useful to base these categories on social and functional abilities rather than on age (Neugarten 1982).

Health issues are of the most immediate concern to the aged, especially to the Black, Hispanic and poor elderly. Elderly people also worry about their economic status. In general, the economic status of the aged in the United States is somewhat lower than that of other population groups, although it has improved markedly over the past decade.

Cognitive impairment is the primary health problem of the elderly. Alzheimer's disease contributes to this condition and affects more elderly persons than any other disease involving cognitive impairment (Maldonado 1987, pp.95-106).

Social Security

Retirement Insurance. An earnings-related benefit (or social security grant) is provided to insured workers aged 65 and over and who are able to satisfy a contribution test (35 quarters of coverage before age 62, up to a maximum of 40 quarters of coverage), an income test if aged between 65 and 69 (grant reduced by 50 per cent of earnings above $US7,320 a year); almost all workers are covered by social security. A maximum grant is specified $US717 a month for workers retiring at age 65 in 1985. No minimum grant is specified for insured workers who have retired since 1981. The grant is based on covered earnings averaged over a period since 1950 or age 21 if later, up to age 67. Grant is also available at age 62, but is reduced for each month of receipt prior to age 65. A deferral increment is provided if retirement is deferred between the ages of 65 and 69. Dependents' allowances are also provided. The maximum grant available to retired workers aged 65 and over in 1985 was $US1,255 per month. Automatic cost of living adjustments are also paid.

<u>Social Assistance</u>. Social security grants are not sufficient to cover all retirement living expenses. For the poor aged, now about 13 per cent of the older population, supplemental security income (SSI) programme provides additional means-tested allowances. SSI created a national minimum income for all aged persons, which can be supplemented by the States. Both programmes are administered by the federal government and funded by employee and employer contributions. The universal coverage aspect of the Social Security programme has been under attack and small changes have been made which have the effect of taxing some Social Security programme benefits of upper income persons.

<u>Employment Retirement Income Security</u>. This programme was established in 1974 primarily to protect the pension rights of workers and their beneficiaries. It provides full pension rights after 10 years of employment with a company, guarantees benefits from government-approved pension plans, and establishes approaches to save and invest money for retirement which defer taxes until retirement for some individuals (Brody & Brody 1987).

<u>Medicare</u>. Medicare was enacted in 1965 and amended in 1973. It is a universal programme which reimburses private health service providers. Medicare provides in Part A for hospital services, post-hospital skilled nursing services, and home health services. Physicians' services, home health services, out-patient hospital services and therapy and other services are provided under Part B under a voluntary programme. The aged person who wishes to participate in this programme pays a monthly fee for this insurance (Marcus 1987, p.701). Payment for services was originally on a fee for services basis. In order to try to control costs, current practice is to pay established amounts for each medical procedure and to use prepaid group plans, or Health Maintenance Organisations, as major service providers (Marcus 1987).

<u>Personal Social Services</u>

<u>Long-term care</u>. Long-term care refers to services delivered over a sustained amount of time to

people who are functionally impaired. It may include institutionalisation although prolonged home health care and other services can also be identified as long-term care. About five per cent of the aged population are in long-term care institutions, such as nursing homes, at any one time, although 20 per cent of the aged will spend some time during the year in an institution (Blackburn 1987). Due to the cost, increasing attention is being paid to community care alternatives where home health care is provided (Kane 1987).

Mental Health. It has been estimated that between 18 per cent and 25 per cent of the aged have symptoms of significant mental health problems (Cohen 1980). These needs are addressed in nursing homes, psychiatric hospitals and community mental health centres. There is general agreement that inadequate provisions are available for aged individuals with mental health needs.

Other Personal Social Services. With increasing community care, in home services such as help with money management, case planning and advocacy, in home medical care, out-patient counselling are being developed.

Informal System. Family, including spouses and children, provide up to 80 per cent of the health and social services received by the elderly. This includes help with health, transportation, financial care and planning, housing, and emotional support (Brody & Brody 1987).

Evaluation

During the past two decades, there has been a dramatic increase in the provisions for the aged in the area of health and social services. This can be expected to increase somewhat, as their already significant political power grows. More adequate medical coverage, including catastrophic health insurance, and more attention to the mental health problems of the aged are priorities for service.

At present, most service is oriented towards the co-operative aged who live in the community and those who are institutionalised. There is a large population of the aged who are ambulatory but non-cooperative. They may have significant mental health problems, such as depression, no support system, and may have problems with alcohol or drug abuse. This is the group which is the most difficult to work with and is receiving the least amount of service.

The projected growth of the aged as a percentage of the population in the years ahead, their increasing political power, and the significant costs of important services such as medical care, raise some fundamental social policy issues. How does a society take care of its ageing population while at the same time provide resources for less politically powerful groups, such as children? Can universal policies continue such as Social Security and Medicare, given current and projected cost constraints? Alternatively, what would be the negative consequences for the aged of moving more towards means-tested programmes? There is already evidence of tension between groups representing the aged and those representing other needy individuals. This conflict will probably increase and may constitute one of the major issues facing social policy in the United States in the next decade.

THE DISABLED AND HANDICAPPED

The scope of the problem of disability is based on the definition used. For example, there were eight million mentally retarded individuals in 1974 and it is expected that there will be 12 million by the year 2000 (The President's Commission on Mental Retardation 1976). In contrast, there were approximately four million individuals in 1980 with serious developmental disabilities. This newer estimate was based on a more restrictive definition of disability, which only included severe and chronic developmental disabilities (US Department of Health and Human Services 1981). According to this definition, disabilities must be related to mental or physical impairment and result in substantial limitations in functioning. This more restricted definition tends to exclude a large number of people with mild developmental disabilities, many of whom are poor.

The most frequent categories used to describe those with developmental disabilities include mental retardation, cerebral palsy, autism,

United States

orthopaedic problems, hearing problems, epilepsy, specific learning disabilities and co-occurrence of disabilities (McDonald-Wikler 1987).

There is also controversy in defining physical disability. Definitions include those who are unable to work in the same way as an able bodied person could work and the inability to perform certain functions which able bodied persons can perform. More recently, physical disability is understood as a problem located in the interaction of the individual with various parts of the society. With this definition, the emphasis on adjustment is on society as much as it is on the physically disabled person (Roth 1987).

It has been estimated that the number of disabled constitute from 8.5 to 17 per cent of the population, depending on the definition of physical disability (Haber 1985). Physical disability is more common among the aged, the poor, Blacks, and blue collar workers.

Social Security

Disability Insurance. An earnings related benefit calculated on the same basis as the retirement benefit is available to covered workers who are unable to engage in substantial gainful activity due to impairment expected to last at least one year, provided they have contributed one quarter for each year since 1950 (or age 21 if later) up to the year the disability began (maximum contribution period permitted 40 quarters), and 20 quarters of contributions in the 10 years prior to the disability occurring. More liberal requirements apply to young workers and the blind. The maximum grant for a disabled worker in 1985 was $US1,363.

Social Assistance. Means-tested allowances are payable to needy invalid and blind under the Supplementary Security Income (SSI) programme.

Programmes generally available for low income persons, such as Assistance to Families with Dependent Children, Food Stamps, and Medicaid are also used by members of this population category who are poor.

Personal Social Services

Education and Training. The education of disabled children is provided for by the Education for All

United States

Handicapped Children's Act of 1975. Where possible, disabled children are to be integrated with non-disabled children. Individual education plans are developed for each child (Roth 1987). In addition there is federal support for the education of children with developmental disabilities. Vocational rehabilitation services are provided for adults with developmental disabilities. States have departments of vocational rehabilitation which are responsible for the education, retraining and job placement services for the disabled adult. These State programmes provide financial assistance, medical care and counselling services. One of the major objectives of the vocational rehabilitation programmes is independent living for the disabled. In addition to public sponsored programmes, there are a large number of private and proprietary agencies which provide services for the disabled.

Health Care. Many disabled individuals are treated in hospitals for at least part of the time. For those who live at home, some home health care services are available.

Institutional Care. Forty per cent of federal costs for the developmentally disabled are used for institutionalisation, although these services are used by only six per cent of the developmentally disabled population. Recent trends are to promote community care for all except the most seriously retarded and emotionally ill individuals.

Community Care. A wide range of community care provisions are available for handicapped and developmentally disabled persons. Often individuals live at home with their family. These programmes include counselling, foster care, day activities, case management, money management, respite care, advocacy, transportation, sheltered workshops and other services (McDonald-Wikler 1987).

Evaluation

The major trend in services for the disabled is to provide the least restrictive care to those with developmental disabilities. Over the past decade, individuals with a history of institutionalisation

United States

have been sent to live in their home communities. This new direction has been based on studies showing client improvements in non-institutional settings. In addition, community care is less costly to states than is institutionalisation.

While institutions have been emptied, community care programmes have not generally been increased sufficiently. In many communities, there are inadequate services available to those who previously were institutionalised. Many individuals have been unable to cope and have swelled the ranks of the homeless. Some have been taken advantage of by unscrupulous landlords and business people. In the absence of adequate alternatives, some individuals become a part of the criminal justice system, even though they have mental health problems (Adler 1986; Hochstedler 1986).

The pressure for the least restrictive treatment has meant that some individuals have been denied institutional care even when it was in their own best interest. How to protect the rights of the individual, along with those of society in decisions relating to institutionalisation is one of the most difficult and pressing problems in this area.

CHILDREN AND YOUTHS

A little over one-third (37.1 per cent) of American households in 1982 had children. During this year, there were 63.7 million children in the US. Since 1979, there has been a significant increase in the number of children who are growing up in poor families. In 1984, 21.3 per cent of all children were in families who were below the poverty line (US Department of Commerce 1985). Although 63 per cent of all children grow up in two-parent families, children increasingly are being brought up in families headed by women (20 per cent of all children in 1982). In addition, there has been a dramatic increase in the percentage of women who have entered the labour force. At present, a majority of children grow up in families in which both parents are working (House of Representatives 1983, pp.2, 5, 8-13).

As a result of these trends, children are increasingly spending some part of their day in the care of someone other than their parents, such as relatives. It has been estimated that this can

United States

include 3.5 million children under the age of 13. An additional seven million children under the age of 13 may spend some part of their day without any adult supervision (Children's Defense Fund 1984).

Major changes in the family unit are having profound effects on children. As Giovannoni (1987, p.247) notes:

> Unless these changes are abated (and there is no indication that they shall be) traditional ideas about the family unit - the most fundamental element of children's lives - will soon be in need of revision if not largely obsolete.

Social Security

Family Allowances. Payments are made under the Aid to Families with Dependent Children (AFDC) programme for children in poor families. Tax-payers are allowed to take deductions for their minor children for federal income taxes.

Maternity Leave. Pregnant women are permitted by law to stay home from work during the last part of their pregnancy and for several months after the baby is born. While there is no governmental subsidy, employers are required to hire mothers after the pregnancy leave.

Personal Social Services

Day Care Services. Some day care services are provided by the government, social agencies and private business for the children of working parents. Telephone contact and emergency services are also available for some school-age children who go home after school to a home without adult supervision.

Youth Service Programmes. Recreation and character building programmes for children and youth are provided by public and private organisations. Public schools, public recreation departments, settlement houses, and youth serving organisations, such as the Boy and Girl Scouts, the Boys and Girls Clubs and the Young Mens and Womens Christian Associations offer winter after-school activities and summer camping experiences for some children and youth.

United States

Foster Care and Adoption. Temporary placement in homes for children who must be removed from their families is available through community-based public welfare departments. Permanent placement of infants and children is provided by public and private agencies through adoption.

Counselling, Advocacy, and Information Referral. These services are available through schools, family counselling agencies, and residential institutions.

Child Protective Services. Supported primarily by government, child protective workers investigate and act on cases of child neglect and abuse. While attempting to keep the family intact, they will initiate proceedings to remove children from dangerous and abusive situations.

Children's Court. The Children's Court or Juvenile Court was established in the United States in 1899. Its purpose was to give individual attention to delinquent children and youth. Judges, with the assistance of lawyers and social workers, make dispositions for delinquent children. These may include returning the child to the custody of parents, placement in a community-based youth programme, or placement in an institution for delinquent children (Gumz 1987).

Institutional Services. Each state operates penal institutions for delinquent youth. There are also public and private institutions, such as residential treatment centres for children with serious emotional problems.

Health Care. Governmentally subsidised health care is available for poor families who are eligible for AFDC. Nutritional counselling, food supplements and some health services are available to some poor mothers before and immediately after delivery under the Special Supplemental Nutrition Programme for Women, Infants and Children (WIC) programme.

Evaluation

There is a serious lack of services of all types for children and youth. All aspects of the child welfare system from economic assistance to day care to correctional services needs improvement and expansion. Recent cuts in social welfare programmes by the Reagan administration have been particularly difficult and have contributed to an extremely high rate of poverty among children and youth.

NEEDY FAMILIES

The problems of needy families have grown more serious during the past 10 years. At present, 14.4 per cent of the population, or 33.7 million individuals, are below the poverty line (a standard developed by the federal Labor Department). At present, the poverty line is $11,000 (1986 standard) a year for an urban family of four.

Two related trends characterise the problems of poor families. There has been a dramatic increase in single-parent families and in the percentage of children who are poor. In 1984, almost half of the poor families, 48.1 per cent, were composed of female-headed households. Persons living in families headed by single women are more than three times as likely to be poor as other families. During the same year, there were 13.3 million children below the poverty line. In other terms, one in every five American children (21.3 per cent) was growing up in a poor family.

In the United States in 1984 68.1 per cent of the poor were white and 31.9 per cent non-white; 56.9 per cent were female and 43.1 per cent male; 32.1 per cent worked part of the year and 17.1 per cent worked year-round full-time. Twelve and a half per cent of the poor were ill or disabled and 9.9 per cent were over 65 years of age in 1984.

While most poor people are white, non-Whites are more vulnerable to poverty. Blacks are three times as likely as Whites to live in poverty whereas Hispanics are twice as likely as non-Hispanic whites to be poor. Finally, the poor are getting poorer. In recent years, the percentage of the poor whose income is less than half of the poverty line has increased. In addition, the 'poverty gap', the total amount of dollars by which the incomes of all poor families and individuals fall below the poverty line has increased (Center on Budget and Policy Priorities 1985). Since most new jobs are being created in urban metropolitan areas, rural poverty is becoming more serious and extensive. In 1985, the poverty rate for rural counties was 18.3 per cent

United States

as compared with 12.7 per cent for metropolitan areas (Robbins 1987).

Social Security

Aid to Families with Dependent Children (AFDC).

AFDC is the major income maintenance programme for poor families. It was developed during the Depression as a federal-State grant-in-aid programme. In 1983, the programme served 3,720,000 families at a cost of about $US15.4 billion, slightly more than half of which was paid by the federal government. Thirty-six states administer the programme directly while 18 delegate administrative responsibility to counties (and in a few instances, cities) (Carerra 1987). AFDC provides a monthly grant to eligible families. Each State or jurisdiction determines the minimal level needed for a family to exist. States or jurisdictions then pay recipients a percentage of this amount with only rare increases for inflation. Depending on the State or jurisdiction, grants range from a low of $US112 a month to a high of $US673 for a family of two. AFDC is a means-tested programme primarily for mothers and their children. Some States or jurisdictions also cover unemployed fathers. As a condition of their grant, able-bodied women with children aged over six are required to participate in the Work Incentive Programme (WIN) which provides employment counselling, minimal training and placement services. AFDC provides only minimal support. Since in most States recipients cannot earn money and retain their AFDC benefits, the programme does not usually include the working poor; those whose incomes are below the poverty line but above a given State's level for AFDC. While some AFDC recipients make use of benefits over a long period of time, most are on the programme only temporarily (less than a year and a half) until some crisis in their life is resolved.

Survivor's Insurance.

Survivors (including surviving divorced spouses if marriage lasted 10 years) of deceased pensioners or insured workers able to satisfy the retirement and disability insurance contributions test receive the full grant for which the deceased worker qualified at age 65, but reduced if the deceased worker was an invalid aged 50 to 59 or aged 60 to 64. These are reduced contribution requirements yearly for orphans and non-aged widows with eligible orphans (or six quarters coverage in the 13 quarters preceeding death).

The survivor's pension is equal to 75 per cent of the deceased pension entitlement at any age if recipient is a widow; widower or surviving divorced spouse caring for child under 16 or an invalid. An orphan's allowance (75 per cent of deceased's pension or pension entitlement for each child under age 18, aged 18-19 but still at school, or invalided before age 22) and a dependent parent's allowance (82.5 per cent of deceased's pension or pension entitlement at age 62 or 150 per cent for two eligible parents) are also provided.

The maximum total family pension assuming workers died at age 65 in 1985 was $US1,255.

Worker's Compensation. Survivors of workers who die through work injury receive an earnings-related benefit (35-70 per cent of deceased's last earnings to widow, or 60-80 per cent if widow has dependent children). The maximum weekly pension varied (by State) from $US107 to $1,114 in 1985. This benefit is for up to 231-600 weeks in work, in 50 per cent of States.

Other eligible survivors in some States include dependent parents and siblings.

A funeral grant is paid in all States, varying from $US300 to $US3,200 in 1985.

Medicaid. Medicaid provides medical care to AFDC families and is also a federal-State programme. While there are growing restrictions imposed by States regarding the services provided and the choice of providers, the programme is valued by AFDC recipients. At present, Medicaid is not made available to the working poor by most States.

Food Stamps. Food stamps are in-kind benefits available to AFDC recipients and to some working poor families and individuals. Food stamps are restricted to the purchase of food at participating food stores. Food stamps are means-tested benefits and administered by states and counties with federal support.

General (Social) Assistance. General assistance is a non-federally supported (usually county) income maintenance programme for clients not covered by AFDC. It covers needy individuals and some families. General assistance is not available in all communities and the grants are usually low.

Earned Income Credit. Working poor individuals and families may file a federal income tax form and receive a refund, in excess of their taxes, if their income for the year was below the poverty level. This is a small form of a negative income tax, and is dependent upon the applicants' initiative.

Energy Grant. Low-income individuals and families may apply to local community agencies for a small grant to help them with their winter utility bills. In most States, this grant is federally funded and is means-tested.

Public Housing. Some housing is available for low-income and working class families. Most of the housing programmes are federally supported, although States and cities are beginning to assume housing functions. At present, the demand for this housing far outstrips the need.

Personal Social Services

Shelters. Shelters have expanded during the past eight years in response to the dramatic increase in homelessness. They are funded through a variety of governmental and private sources. Originally for single individuals, shelters are increasingly used on a temporary basis by poor families.

Food Pantries. As with shelters, food pantries have grown much more extensive during the past eight years, as the condition of the poor has worsened. Food pantries distribute food and are supported through the private sector. They vary in terms of their eligibility criteria and provisions.

Poverty Programme. Started in the 1960s with a community action emphasis, poverty programmes provide a variety of personal social services for low-income people. The Economic & Opportunity Act of 1964 was a multi-faceted approach to alleviate the problem of poverty. The War on Poverty included education programmes, retraining programmes, job placement, job creation, business

United States

loans, pre-school programmes, personal social service programmes, minority programmes, and so forth. Many of the programmes established under the Economic & Opportunity Act of 1964 have either been dismantled or severely curtailed in funding.

These programmes are funded with some Federal support and a variety of other public and private means. The programmes are usually delivered on the community level, are more common in urban than in rural areas, and vary widely according to local conditions.

Title XX Social Services. Amendments to the Social Security Bill, Title XX provides Federal money to States to fund a variety of social services at the local level including services for child abuse, day care, addiction, housing weatherisation and so forth. In many States, these monies are administered on the county level through grants to public and private organisations.

Counselling and Family Planning. In some communities, family counselling, budget counselling and help with other individual and family problems is available to poor families. Counselling and family planning services are primarily provided by private individuals and social agencies, sometimes with governmental funds.

Information, Referral and Advocacy. These services are becoming increasingly important and are provided primarily by private agencies and individuals, sometimes with grants from public agencies.

Evaluation

The income maintenance system developed as a categorical system primarily for women and their children. Its benefits are inadequate and inequitable, as it treats similar clients differently. Benefits vary from State to State and other jurisdictions and do not cover all needy families and individuals. The situation has become more serious after the significant cutbacks in programmes affecting low-income people enacted by the federal government during the Reagan administration. In addition, dislocations created by the crisis in agriculture and the shift from a manufacturing to a service economy have exacerbated the problem. Current proposals

United States

receiving substantial attention are to change the income maintenance programmes into workfare-type programmes. Workfare means that a needy family is expected to provide a number of hours in meaningful work in order to obtain assistance. It is doubtful that sufficient resources will be available to make significant impact on the welfare population through the workfare programmes.

THE UNEMPLOYED

Some level of unemployment seems to be acceptable to modern United States society. The percentage of the unemployed has been rising over the past decade. From 1950 to 1970, the official national unemployment rate averaged about five per cent of the population. In 1975 the rate increased to 8.5 per cent and has averaged somewhat over eight per cent of the population since then (US Department of Labor 1986, p.288) although it has decreased in 1987. Unemployment is particularly high for Blacks and Hispanics, teenagers, especially inner city minority teenagers, women, and individuals with inadequate education. In July 1985, unemployment rates were 41.3 per cent for Black teenagers, 16.3 per cent for white teenagers, 15.0 per cent for all Black persons, 11.7 for young men aged 20-24, 11.2 per cent for persons of Hispanic origin, 10.6 per cent for women aged 20-24, and 10.2 per cent for women heads of households (Monthly Labor Review January 1986, pp.89, 90). The shift in the economy from manufacturing to service employment and the decline in farming has increased the problem of underemployment, in addition to unemployment.

Social Security

Unemployment compensation programme. Unemployment compensation covers almost nine million insured workers who have lost their jobs. About 75 per cent of all states require a minimum-earnings loss to be satisfied before insured workers are eligible for unemployment benefits. Thirteen States specify a minimum employment period. All specify a work test and disqualify insured workers for varying lengths of time if unemployment is caused by voluntary leaving, misconduct, labour dispute, or the refusal to accept a suitable

United States

employment offer. Unemployment compensation is generally payable after a one week waiting period, for up to 26 weeks; longer in States with higher unemployment rates.

Unemployment compensation is about 50 per cent of earnings, according to diverse state formulas (minimum $US5 per month, maximum $US224 per month). Dependents' supplements are available in some States.

The Unemployment Compensation programme is a joint federal and state programme, with broad federal guidelines and a wide variety of benefits among the states. Financing comes from a payroll tax on employers (Wolf Jones 1987). Since unemployment compensation is a time-limited programme, persons whose benefits expire may participate in other income support programmes appropriate for needy families.

Personal Social Services

Employment Agencies. States have established employment services where unemployed persons can be matched with employers who are looking for workers. In addition, private companies perform this service for specialised needs, such as temporary workers, office workers, or nursing care.

Job Training and Placement. The federal Job Training and Partnership Act provides limited federal funds for job training and placement. Job placement and some job training is available to some recipients of public assistance although there is wide variation among the States. Private organisations, sometimes with some public funds, such as the Opportunities Industrialization Centers (a private manpower programme for the inner cities) provide job training and placement.

Economic Development. States, and to some extent municipalities and counties, have increased their economic development efforts in order to attract industry and reduce employment.

Evaluation

In the past, unemployment-related programmes, such as unemployment compensation and job training and placement, have expanded when unemployment has increased. However, during the most recent recession, these programmes were cut back (Piven &

Cloward 1982). The result was a dramatic increase in unemployment, poverty and a reduction in wages. This was associated with increases in individual and family stress, violence within the family, and crime. For the first time since the 1930s, the assumption that the federal government has a responsibility in reducing unemployment and poverty, and in affecting the overall distribution of resources was questioned. Those who support an activist government role in this area feel that the unemployment compensation programme is under-financed, covers only a small portion of the unemployed and often provides inadequate benefits. Many experts feel that the economy will change rapidly in the future, and demand a higher level of job training of workers. The importance of training and retraining programmes for workers should increase in significance in the years ahead.

THE SICK AND INJURED

There have been important improvements in the health care for the poor and the aged over the past two decades. However, for the working poor, minorities, and the increasing number of individuals not covered by health insurance on their job, adequate and affordable medical care has become a more serious problem. During a typical year, 18.5 million people lacked coverage throughout the year while an additional 16 million people lacked coverage for five months or more. This constituted 12 per cent of the population. Young people, Blacks and Hispanics with low incomes, and rural residents are most vulnerable to inadequate health insurance coverage (NASW 1987, p.75).

The cost of American health care has increased dramatically. In 1950, health care expenditures constituted 4.4 per cent of the GNP. In 1984, they constituted 10.6 per cent. Between 1960 and 1984, individual payments for health care decreased from 54.9 per cent of all payments for health care to 27.9 per cent, whereas government payments increased from 21.8 per cent to 39.6 per cent (NASW 1987, p.78).

Increasing government participation in paying for health care has led to cost containment through the payment of fixed fees for specific procedures and the development of Health Maintenance Organizations, which are a pre-paid

United States

health facility that provides multi-services for a pre-determined cost. The 1980s have also seen the development of private, investor-owned, for-profit clinics and hospitals.

Social Security

Medicare and Medicaid. These are the major government supported health care programmes. Medicare is for older people. Medicaid is for some low income people.

Workers Compensation. Temporary disability benefits are provided in most states in the event of work injury. This benefit is generally two-thirds of earnings, with dependents' supplements provided in about 20 per cent of states. The maximum benefits provided varied from $US126 to $US1,114 per month according to state. It is payable after a two to seven day waiting period and may be paid retrospectively if injury lasts a special (variable) period (three days to six weeks according to state).
    Permanent disability pensions are also generally provided in most States in the event of total disability due to a work injury. This benefit is generally two-thirds of prior earnings. In most states this is payable for life or throughout the period of disability. Constant attendance and dependents' supplements are provided in some states.
    Partial disabilities due to work injury attract, in most states, a pro rata benefit or full benefits for fewer weeks for certain scheduled injuries.
    Medical care is also provided for as long as required in all states.

Sickness Insurance. Five states provide earnings-related sickness insurance benefits to covered employed (limited scope).

Personal Social Services

Hospitals. Medical hospitals are supported by municipalities, counties, states, universities, charities and religious groups, and private entrepreneurs. The federal government operates hospitals for veterans and for native Americans. The majority of hospitals are for short-term care with an average bed capacity of 450 patients.

United States

There are, in addition, speciality hospitals for long-term care of emotional illness, tuberculosis, chronic disease and other ailments (Lum 1987).

Health Maintenance Organizations. HMOs provide comprehensive health services to enrolled members for a prepaid fixed fee, rather than on the basis of a fee for service. HMOs provide group practice under fixed cost contracts with insurance companies. They emphasise prevention and limit, somewhat, patient choice in the selection of health providers. While not replacing independent medical care, HMOs are growing in an effort to control medical costs.

Evaluation

While the United States citizens spend more per capita on health care than do citizens in other industrialised countries, there are serious inequities in the availability and adequacy of health care services. There is a trend towards more expensive and higher quality care for upper income persons. The ageing of the population and associated increase in the need for health care, the increase in the availability of expensive technology, and the potentially severe demands of AIDS patients on the health care system are going to precipitate serious ethical, practical and financial policy questions. Issues such as: Should society maintain terminally ill elderly patients and severely handicapped infants? How can we sustain a basic health care system in the face of an epidemic of AIDS patients? How can we provide affordable health care coverage for the increasing number of United States citizens who have little or inadequate health care coverage? These will be central to health policy in the years ahead.

ASSESSMENT OF THE AMERICAN WELFARE SYSTEM

Social welfare in the US has been characterised by a relatively strong private sector and an often reluctant public commitment. Alexis De Tocqueville (1956) noted that whereas in Europe the government would be asked to undertake projects that benefit the community, in the US the preferred approach was for private citizens to band together in a voluntary effort. This distrust of government, especially the federal government in domestic policy, is still powerful.

In addition, US citizens have generally felt that individuals should be responsible for their own behaviour. In a land of opportunity, all could succeed if they applied themselves. Because of the strong emphasis on individualism, group support for individual problems has generally not been a strong priority. In true Poor Law tradition, with support from Social Darwinism, individuals have felt that too generous a social welfare system would create dependency and reduce the work ethic.

Further, the sheer size and diversity of the United States, in comparison to other Western industrialised countries, has fostered a decentralised approach to domestic policy. It has been argued that State and regional authorities were more able to make decisions about local problems than were distant Washington bureaucrats (Magill 1979).

The Reagan administration has been the most actively anti social welfare of any government in modern United States history. Many feel that the strategy of increasing defence commitments and creating a large federal budget deficit were conscious policies aimed at controlling domestic spending. Regardless of the motivation, defence commitments and the budget deficit are going to limit increases in social welfare spending for the next decade. In addition, the much heralded switch from a farming and manufacturing economy to a service economy may limit the ability of the federal government to raise significantly larger revenues through increases in taxes.

The result of these factors is an inadequate social welfare system which is under-financed, disorganised, and lacks strong public support. Increasingly, it is a two tier system, with upper and upper middle class individuals relying on private agencies and lower middle and low income persons relying primarily on charity and a fragmented public system for the basic needs of food, shelter, income and health care.

In addition to being somewhat class-biased, the welfare system benefits different client groups differentially. As is characteristic in countries with a growing number of aged citizens, services for the ageing receive the most attention and support (Magill 1984). In contrast, services for most other groups, and especially for children, minorities and the poor, have deteriorated markedly during the past eight years. While the country has significantly reduced the percentage of the aged who are poor, one-in-five children in the United States now grow up in a home whose income is below the poverty line. The mental and physical health care system, policies for the unemployed, programmes for the disabled and handicapped, and services for children and youth, among others, are all in a state of serious disrepair (Center on Budget and Policy Priorities 1985). There seems to be no consensus about the most basic social welfare questions of who should be covered against what risk, and by whom (Rimlinger 1971).

In the past the social welfare system in the United States has reacted to major threats to the country. During the Great Depression, and again, during the civil disruptions of the 1960s, significant expansion of the social welfare system contributed to solving basic social and economic problems and to returning stability to the country. At other times, the growth of the social welfare system has tended to mirror the economy, with moderate increases during periods of growth (Magill 1979). Specific areas of growth are dependent on economic, demographic and political factors (Zald 1977).

There are serious unmet social needs that directly bear on the future of the US. Given the seriousness of the economic and political issues facing the country, it seems unlikely that a needed major recommitment to providing for basic human needs will occur in the near future.

REFERENCES

Adler, M.F. (1986), 'Jail as a Repository for Former Mental Patients', *International Journal of Offender Therapy and Comparative Criminology*, 30, 225-232.

Alexander, C. (1987), 'History of Social Work and Social Welfare: Significant Dates', *Encyclopedia of Social Work (Eighteenth Edition)* Silver Spring, Maryland: National Association of Social Workers (NASW).

United States

Barker, R.L. (1987), 'Private and Proprietary Services', in National Association of Social Workers, <u>Encyclopedia of Social Work, (Eighteenth Edition)</u>, Silver Spring, Maryland: NASW.

Blackburn, J. (1987), Personal Communication, Milwaukee, Wisconsin.

Brody, Elaine M. & Brody, Stanley J. (1987), 'Aged: Services' in National Association of Social Workers, <u>Encyclopedia of Social Work, (Eighteenth Edition)</u>, Silver Spring, Maryland: NASW.

Carerra, Joan (1987), 'Aid to Families with Dependent Children', in National Association of Social Workers, <u>Encyclopedia of Social Work, (Eighteenth Edition)</u>, Silver Spring, Maryland: NASW.

Center on Budget and Policy Priorities (1985), 'Smaller Slices of the Pie: The Growing Economic Vulnerability of Poor and Moderate Income Americans', Washington, DC, November, 22.

Children's Defense Fund (1985), <u>A Children's Defense Budget: An Analysis of the President's FY 1985 Budget and Children</u>. Washington, DC: Children's Defense Fund.

Cohen, G.D. (1980), 'Prospects for Mental Health and Ageing', in J.E. Birren & R.B. Sloane (eds), <u>Handbook of Mental Health and Ageing</u>. Englewood Cliffs, NJ: Prentice-Hall.

<u>Congressional Globe</u>, Thirty-Third Congress, 1st Session, May 3 1854, 1061.

Davis, A.F. (1974), <u>Spearheads for Reform: The Social Settlements and the Progressive Movement 1890-1914</u>. New York: Oxford University Press.

de Tocqueville, A. (1956), <u>Democracy in America</u>. New York: Mentor Books.

United States

Dixon, John & Scheurell, Robert (1987), 'Social Security in Australia and the United States: A Comparison of Value Premises and Practices', *Journal of International and Comparative Social Welfare* 4(1&2), 1-18.

Dobelstein, Andrew (1980), *Politics, Economics and Public Welfare*. Englewood Cliffs, NJ: Prentice-Hall.

Doolittle, Fred C. (1986), 'Social Welfare Financing', in National Association of Social Workers, *Encyclopedia of Social Work (Eighteenth Edition)*. Silver Spring, Maryland: NASW.

Friedman, Milton (1972), *Capitalism and Freedom*. Chicago; University of Chicago Press.

Ginsberg, Leon (1987), 'Economic, Political and Social Context', in National Association of Social Workers, *Encyclopedia of Social Work (Eighteenth Edition)*. Silver Spring, Maryland: NASW.

Giovannoni, Jeanne (1987), 'Children', in National Association of Social Workers, *Encyclopedia of Social Work (Eighteenth Edition)*. Silver Spring, Maryland: NASW.

Gumz, Edward (1987), *Professionals and Their Worth in the Family Divorce Court*, Springfield, Ill: Charles C. Thomas.

Haber, L.D. (1985), 'Trends and Demographic Studies on Programs for Disabled Persons', in L.G. Perlmand & G. Austin (eds), *A Report of the Ninth Annual Mary E. Switzer Memorial Seminar*, Alexandria, VA: National Rehabilitation Association.

Hochstedler, E. (1986), 'Criminal Prosecution of the Mentally Disordered', *Law and Society Review*, 20, 279-92.

Hofstadler, Richard (1955), *Social Darwinism in American Thought*. Boston: Beacon Press.

United States

Hopps, J.G. (1987), 'Minorities of Color', in National Association of Social Workers, *Encyclopedia of Social Work (Eighteenth Edition)*. Silver Spring, Maryland: NASW.

House of Representatives (1983), *US Children and Their Families: Current Conditions and Recent Trends*. New York: Foundation for Child Development.

Kammerman, Sheila B. & Kahn, Alfred J. (1976), *Social Services in the United States: Policies and Programs*. Philadelphia: Temple University Press.

Kane, Rosalie (1987), 'Long-Term Care', in National Association of Social Workers, *Encyclopedia of Social Work (Eighteenth Edition)*. Silver Spring, Maryland: NASW.

Kramer, Ralph (1984), *Voluntary Agencies in the Welfare State*. Berkley and Los Angeles: The University of California Press.

Leiby, James (1987), 'History of Social Welfare', in *Encyclopedia of Social Work (Eighteenth Edition)*. Silver Spring, Maryland: NASW.

Lum, D. (1987), 'Health Service System', in *Encyclopedia of Social Work (Eighteenth Edition)*. Silver Spring, Maryland: NASW.

Magill, Robert (1979), *Community Decision Making for Social Welfare: Federalism, City Government and the Poor*. New York: Human Sciences Press.

_____ (1984), *Social Policy in American Society*. New York: Human Sciences Press.

_____ (1985), 'Ethnicity and Social Welfare in American Cities: A Historical Overview', in L. Maldonado and J. Moore (eds), *Urban Ethnicity in the United States: New Immigrants and Old Minorities*. Beverly Hills: Sage Publications.

Maldonado, David Jr. (1987), 'Aged', in *Encyclopedia of Social Work (Eighteenth Edition)*. Silver Spring, Maryland: NASW.

United States

Marcus, Leonard (1987), 'Health Care Financing', in *Encyclopedia of Social Work (Eighteenth Edition)*. Silver Spring, Maryland: NASW.

McDonald-Wikler, Lynn (1987), 'Disabilities-Development, in *Encyclopedia of Social Work (Eighteenth Edition)*. Silver Spring, Maryland: NASW.

Mills, G. (1984), 'The Budget: A Failure of Discipline', in J. Palmer & I. Sawhill (eds), *The Reagan Record: An Assessment of America's Cahnging Domestic Priorities*. Cambridge: Ballinger Publishing.

Monthly Labor Review (1986), January.

National Association of Social Workers (NASW), (1987), 'Face of the Nation 1987', *Statistical Supplement to the 18th Edition of the Encyclopedia of Social Work*. Silver Spring, Maryland: NASW.

Neugarten, Bernice (1982), *Age or Need? Public Policies for Older People*. Beverly Hills, California: Sage Publications.

Piven, F.F. & Cloward, R. (1982), *The New Class War: Reagan's Attack on the Welfare State and It's Consequences*. New York: Pantheon.

President's Committee on Mental Retardation (1976), *Report to the President*. Washington, DC: US Government Printing Office.

Rimlinger, G. (1971), *Welfare Policy and Industrialisation in Europe, America and Russia*. New York: John Wiley & Sons.

Robbins, William (1987), 'Cities Luring People and Jobs, Widening Rural-Urban Gap', *The New York Times*, March 3, p.8.

Roth, William (1987), 'Disabilities-Physical', in *Encyclopedia of Social Work (Eighteenth Edition)*. Silver Spring, Maryland: NASW.

United States

Scheurell, Robert (1987), <u>Introduction to Human Service Networks: History, Organization and Professions</u>. Lanham, Maryland: University Press of America Inc.

Thurow, Lester (1980), <u>The Zero Sum Society: Distribution and the Possibilities for Economic Change</u>. New York: Basic Books.

Trattner, Walter (1974), <u>From Poor Law to Welfare State: A History of Social Welfare in America</u>. New York: The Free Press.

Tropman, John E. (1981), 'Societal Values and Social Policy: Implications for Social Work.', in George Martin & Mayer Zald (eds), <u>Social Welfare in Society</u>. New York: Columbia University Press.

United States of America, (US) Bureau of the Census (1982), <u>Decencial Censuses of Population, 1900-1980 and Projections of the Population of the United States: 1982 to 2050</u>, (Current Population Reports, Series p.25, No.922). Washington, DC: US Government Printing Office.

_____, _____ (1986), <u>Statistical Abstract of the United States: 1987</u> (107th Edition), Washington, DC: US Government Printing Office.

_____ Department of Commerce, Bureau of the Census (1985), <u>Money, Income and Poverty Status of Families and Persons of the United States: 1984</u>, Washington, DC: US Government Printing Office.

_____ Department of Health and Human Services (1981), <u>Special Report on the Impact of the Change of Developmental Disabilities</u>. Washington, DC: US Government Printing Office.

_____ Department of Labor (1986), <u>Economic Report of the President, 1986</u>. Washington, DC: US Government Printing Office.

_____ Office of Management and Budget (1985), <u>Budget of the United States, Fiscal Year 1986</u>. Washington, DC: US Government Printing Office.

United States

    _____ Senate. Special Committee on Ageing (1984), <u>Ageing America: Trends and Projection</u>. Washington DC: American Association of Retired Persons.

    _____ Social Security Administration (1986), <u>Social Security Programs Throughout the World</u>, Washington, DC: Department of Health and Human Services.

Wolf Jones, L. (1987), 'Unemployment Compensation and Worker's Compensation Programs', in <u>Encyclopedia of Social Work (Eighteenth Edition)</u>. Silver Spring, Maryland: NASW.

Zald, M. (1977), 'Demographics, Politics and the Future of the Welfare State', <u>Social Service Review</u>, March.

APPENDICES

SOCIAL SECURITY PROVISIONS

COUNTRY	SERVICE PROVIDERS	THE AGED	THE DISABLED AND HANDICAPPED	CHILDREN AND YOUTH	NEEDY FAMILIES	THE SICK AND INJURED	THE UNEMPLOYED	METHODS OF FINANCING	RESPONSIBLE GOVERNMENT ADMINISTRATIVE AGENCIES
AUSTRALIA	Central government administrative agencies	• Flat-rate means-tested age pensions for men 65+ and women 60+ • Parallel pensions for war veterans with theatre of war experience men 60+ and women 55+	• Flat-rate pension for 85 per cent incapacity • Allowances • Wives pensions	• Family allowance (means-tested) • Austudy assistance for education and training	• Supporting parent benefits (means-tested) • Family income supplement for needy families not receiving pensions or benefits	• Sickness benefits (means-tested)	• Unemployment benefits (work-tested)	• General revenue (non-contributory)	• Departments of Social Security Veterans Affairs (except Dept of Employment Education and Training for Austudy)
	Regional government administrative agencies				• Family allowance supplement • Emergency assistance			• Commonwealth grants and state taxes	• Parallel State Departments
	Voluntary agencies				• Emergency assistance			• Private donation and government grants	
	Private enterprise	• Occupational superannuation				• Workers' compensation and paid sick leave	• Redundancy payments	• Employer and employee contributions	

PROVISION OF PERSONAL SOCIAL SERVICES

COUNTRY	SERVICE PROVIDERS	THE AGED	THE DISABLED AND HANDICAPPED	CHILDREN AND YOUTH	NEEDY FAMILIES	THE SICK AND INJURED	THE UNEMPLOYED	METHODS OF FINANCING	RESPONSIBLE GOVERNMENT ADMINISTRATIVE AGENCIES
AUSTRALIA	Central government administrative agencies	• Residential/ institutional care • Home and community care	• Disability services programme • Home and community care	• Child care and welfare family support • School to work transition programme • Youth support schemes		• Universal health insurance	• Labour market programmes • Employment services	• General revenue excepting Medicare financed by levy on income	• Departments of: Community Services, Health, Veterans' Affairs, Aboriginal Affairs, Immigration & Ethnic Affairs
	Regional government administrative agencies	• Hospitals • Residential/ institutional care • Home and community care	• Home and community care • Medical services	• Children's services • Educational services • Hospitals	• Family casework	• Medical services	• Job creation programmes	• Commonwealth grants and state taxes	• Parallel State Departments
	Voluntary agencies	• Home and community care	• Home and community care • Sheltered workshops	• Childcare and family support	• Women's shelters • Family planning			• Private donation and government grants	
	Private enterprise	• Leisure services • Retirement housing	• Sheltered workshops	• Childcare • Maternity leave		• Health services and programmes at work	• Employment counselling	• Employer financing	

SOCIAL SECURITY PROVISIONS

COUNTRY	SERVICE PROVIDERS	THE AGED	THE DISABLED AND HANDICAPPED	CHILDREN AND YOUTH	NEEDY FAMILIES	THE SICK AND INJURED	THE UNEMPLOYED	METHODS OF FINANCING	RESPONSIBLE GOVERNMENT ADMINISTRATIVE AGENCIES
CANADA	Central government administrative agencies	• Stacked demogrant, contributory and income-tested benefits • Spouse's allowance at age 60 • Special tax deduction at age 65 • Registered private plans tax deductible • Social assistance	• Disabled veterans and dependants • CPP disability benefit	• Family allowance (except Quebec tax credit) • Child income tax deduction	• CPP-survivor and lump sum death benefit	• Unemployment insurance Maternity (17 weeks); Illness benefit for claimants (15 weeks max.) • Wage-related benefits	• Unemployment insurance up to age 50 • Wage-related training allowance	• Employer/employee contributions: CPP and UIC • General tax revenues (corporate, personal and others)	• Unemployment Insurance Commission • Department of Manpower and Immigration • Health • Welfare Canada • Finance Canada • Revenue Canada
	Regional government administrative agencies	• Property tax credit • Sales tax rebates • Quebec - QPP contributory	• Social assistance • In-training allowances • QPP disability benefit • Worker compensation	• Quebec family allowance	• Social assistance for needy long term • QPP survivor and lump sum death benefit	• Social assistance for needy long term	• Social assistance for needy (supplement low insurance or alternative for uninsured)	• Employer/employee contributions • General revenues • Federal grants-in-aid	• Provincial social welfare ministries • Treasury • Workers compensation boards
	Local government administrative agencies				• Social assistance for needy short term 'employable'	• Social assistance for needy short-term 'employable'		• Local property tax • Federal and provincial cost sharing	• Municipal departments of social services
	Private enterprise	• Occupational pensions contributory & non-contributory (RRPPs) • Personal plans (RRSPs)				• Commercial insurance personal non-contributory, occupational contributory or non-contributory			

PROVISION OF PERSONAL SOCIAL SERVICES

COUNTRY	SERVICE PROVIDERS	THE AGED	THE DISABLED AND HANDICAPPED	CHILDREN AND YOUTH	NEEDY FAMILIES	THE SICK AND INJURED	THE UNEMPLOYED	METHODS OF FINANCING	RESPONSIBLE GOVERNMENT ADMINISTRATIVE AGENCIES
CANADA	Central government administrative agencies	• Housing subsidies (shared cost) • Grant to provinces under Canada assistance plan for social services • Grant to provinces for universal health services	• Housing subsidies (shared cost) • Grant to provinces under Canada assistance plan for social services • Grant to provinces for universal health services	• Grants to provinces under Canada assistance plan	• Housing subsidies • Grants to provinces under Canada assistance plan	• Universal health care grants to provincial programmes	• Jobs strategy • Job entry (youth) • Job re-entry • Job development • Skill investment • Skill shortages • Community futures (special aid) • Innovations	• General tax revenue	• Ministry of Man Power and Immigration • Health and Welfare Canada • Mortgage and Housing Corporation
	Regional government administrative agencies	• Grant to local government and voluntary agencies under Canada assistance plan (some provinces administer services directly) • Subsidised housing	• Vocational rehabilitation • Grant to local government and voluntary agencies under Canada assistance plan (some provinces administer services directly) • Hospitals for mentally ill and retarded	• Licensing & supervision • Grants to local governments and voluntary agencies • Contracts with voluntary and proprietary services for children with special needs	• Grants to local governments and voluntary agencies • Housing subsidies	• Payments to service providers • Ancillary services (air transport; service in remote areas)	• Placement of social assistance recipients	• Federal grants and subsidies • Health care federal grants, provincial taxes, insurance contributions in some provinces • User charges	• Provincial housing ministries • Provincial ministries of social welfare • Provincial health agencies
	Local government administrative agencies Voluntary agencies	• Residential / institutional care • Homemakers and other support in home • Recreational services • Counselling • Subsidised housing	• Residential / institutional care • Subsidised housing • Sheltered workshops • Vocational assessment and rehabilitation (under contract with provinces) • Prostheses • Subsidised housing	• Residential / institutional care • Recreation • Day-care • Protection, foster care, adoption (some provinces provide)	• Counselling • Foodbanks • Hostels • Subsidised housing	• Visiting nurse and homemakers		• Federal and provincial grants • Local taxes (property) • User charges	• Municipal departments of social service • Provincial ministries of social services (licensing and inspection)
	Private enterprise	• Residential / institutional care • Home help services	• Residential care • Prostheses	• Day-care Residential care for special needs		• Home help		• Government contracts • User charges	• Provincial ministries of social service (licensing and inspection)

SOCIAL SECURITY PROVISIONS

COUNTRY	SERVICE PROVIDERS	THE AGED	THE DISABLED AND HANDICAPPED	CHILDREN AND YOUTH	NEEDY FAMILIES	THE SICK AND INJURED	THE UNEMPLOYED	METHODS OF FINANCING	RESPONSIBLE GOVERNMENT ADMINISTRATIVE AGENCIES
GERMANY, WEST	Central government administrative agencies	• Contributory earnings-related benefits for blue collar workers and employees and their dependants	• Contributory earnings-related benefit • Social assistance	• Maternity benefits • Child benefits • Tax exemptions • Educational fee for parent staying at home with a newborn child for one year		• Contributory earnings-related sickness benefits • Contributory earnings-related work injury benefit	• Contributory earnings-related unemployment benefits • Unemployment relief	• Contributions of employees and employers • A fixed or flexible grant by federal government and / or the States	• Statutory Social Health Insurances Agencies • Statutory Federal Social Security Agencies • Federal Institute of Labour
	Regional government administrative agencies				• Social assistance at fixed regional standards after a careful examination of each individual case • Housing allowance				
	Voluntary agencies								
	Private enterprise	• Additional retirement programmes by some companies	• Private insurances			• Private health insurances			• Statutory Social Health Insurances Agencies

PROVISION OF PERSONAL SOCIAL SERVICES

COUNTRY	SERVICE PROVIDERS	THE AGED	THE DISABLED AND HANDICAPPED	CHILDREN AND YOUTH	NEEDY FAMILIES	THE SICK AND INJURED	THE UNEMPLOYED	METHODS OF FINANCING	RESPONSIBLE GOVERNMENT ADMINISTRATIVE AGENCIES
GERMANY, WEST	Central government administrative agencies	• Research • Employment promotion services	• Research • Employment promotion • Vocational training	• Research	• Research	• Research	• Research • Employment promotion • Vocational training • Vocational and career counselling	• Federal taxes	• Ministry of Labour and Social Affairs • Federal Institute of Labour
	Regional government administrative agencies	• Supervision of standards of other institutions and programmes	• Supervision of standards of other institutions and programmes • Residential/institutional care • Sheltered workshops	• Supervision of standards of other institutions and programmes	• Fixing public assistance standards	• Supervision of public health service institutions and programmes		• Local taxes	• State authorities
	Local government administrative agencies	• Recreational programmes • Day-care centres • Residential care • Home help • Interpersonal help and counselling • Visiting services • Meals-on-wheels	• Home help • General casework and groupwork services • Self-help groups • Residential care • Rehabilitation services	• Day nurseries • Recreational activities • Institutional care for children at risk • Foster home care • Adoption • Youth services • Probation • Youth groups • Youth services	• Allocation of resources and individual counselling	• Public health service counselling • Individual counselling		• Federal government grants to voluntary agencies and self-help groups	• District Youth Welfare Offices • District Social Welfare Offices • District Health Service Offices
	Voluntary agencies	• Home help • Residential institutional care	• Residential care • Medical rehabilitation	• Day nurseries • Institutional care	• Allocation of resources and individual counselling	• Individual counselling • Self-help groups	• Initiatives of the unemployed • Self-help groups	• Regional government grants to voluntary agencies and self-help groups • Public foundations • Private foundations • User charges	• District and Commune authorities
	Private enterprise								• District and Commune authorities

SOCIAL SECURITY PROVISIONS

COUNTRY	SERVICE PROVIDERS	THE AGED	THE DISABLED & HANDICAPPED	CHILDREN & YOUTH	NEEDY FAMILIES	SICK & INJURED	THE UNEMPLOYED	METHODS OF FINANCING	RESPONSIBLE GOVERNMENT ADMINISTRATIVE AGENCIES
ITALY	Central government administrative agencies	• Contributory earnings-related minimum pensions (employees) • Contribution-related and minimum pensions (self-employed) • Social assistance (needy elderly)	• Contributory invalidity pensions (national minimum) • Means-tested allowances to the deaf and blind	• Earnings-related maternity benefits • Family allowances	• Family allowances	• Earnings-related sickness cash benefits • Earnings-related pensions to the injured	• Full unemployment indemnity (flat rate) • Earnings-related benefits for temporary or partial unemployment	• Social security contributions and general revenue	• Ministries of Health, Labour and Social Insurance • National Institute for Social Insurance • National Institute for Occupational Injuries Insurance
	Regional government administrative agencies	• Discretionary cash support	• Discretionary cash support to the disabled	• Discretionary allowances to single parents	• Discretionary cash support	• General health care		• Transfers from central government	• Regional Councils • Local Authority Departments
	Voluntary agencies								
	Private enterprise					• Sick leave			

394

PROVISION OF PERSONAL SOCIAL SERVICES

COUNTRY	SERVICE PROVIDERS	THE AGED	THE DISABLED & HANDICAPPED	CHILDREN & YOUTH	NEEDY FAMILIES	SICK & INJURED	THE UNEMPLOYED	METHODS OF FINANCING	RESPONSIBLE GOVERNMENT ADMINISTRATIVE AGENCIES
ITALY	Central government administrative agencies								
	Regional government administrative agencies	• Institutional care • Community care • Domiciliary help • Recreation	• General health care • Rehabilitation • Institutional care • Training programmes	• General paediatric care and counselling • Day nursing • Recreation • Institutional and foster care • School assistance	• Family counselling • In-kind assistance	• General health care • Rehabilitation services	• Vocational training • Labour re-training schemes	• Transfers from central government	• Local Health Units of the National Health service • Local Authority Departments
	Voluntary agencies	• Same as above	• Training programmes	• Recreation • Nurseries				• Donations, subsidies, charges	
	Private enterprise			• Nurseries				• User charges	

SOCIAL SECURITY PROVISIONS

COUNTRY	SERVICE PROVIDERS	THE AGED	THE DISABLED AND HANDICAPPED	CHILDREN AND YOUTH	NEEDY FAMILIES	THE SICK AND INJURED	THE UNEMPLOYED	METHODS OF FINANCING	RESPONSIBLE GOVERNMENT ADMINISTRATIVE AGENCIES
NETHERLANDS	Central government administrative agencies		• Invalidity pension • Special income-tested supplementation	• General orphans pensions • Family allowances • Educational allowance	• General widows pension • Maternity allowance • Rent subsidies	• Sickness pension	• Earnings-related unemployment benefits	• General revenue • Employer & employee contributions	• Ministry of Social Affairs and Employment • Insurance Council • Supervision of Industrial Insurance Boards • Social Security Bank
	Local government administrative agencies		• Social assistance		• Social assistance		• Social assistance	• Central government allocation • Municipal government allocation	• Local Social Offices
	Voluntary agencies								
	Private enterprise		• Supplementation • Occupational pensions		• Health insurance • Occupational insurance			• Employer and employee contributions • State subsidies	• Social Insurance Council supervision of Pension and Sickness Funds

396

PROVISION OF PERSONAL SOCIAL SERVICES

COUNTRY	SERVICE PROVIDERS	THE AGED	THE DISABLED AND HANDICAPPED	CHILDREN AND YOUTH	NEEDY FAMILIES	THE SICK AND INJURED	THE UNEMPLOYED	METHODS OF FINANCING	RESPONSIBLE GOVERNMENT ADMINISTRATIVE AGENCIES
NETHERLANDS	Central government administrative agencies						• Employment creation programmes • Training programmes • Employment centres	• Allocation from central government	• Regional Employment Offices
	Local government administrative agencies								
	Voluntary agencies	• Homes for the elderly • Nursing homes • Domiciliary services • Provision of meals • Family care	• Sheltered workshops • Rehabilitation • Domiciliary services • Nursing • Family help • Nursing homes • Housing programmes • Information centres • Specialised housing • Day care for disabled children	• Day-care centres • Foster help • Centres for drug help • Advising centres	• Social counselling • Meals-on-wheels • Family care	• Domiciliary services • District home nursing services • Family help • Information services	• Self-help programmes	• Allocation from Social Security Institutions • User charges • Central government allocations	• Local authorities
	Private enterprise			• Nursing schools • Day-care centres				• User charges • Central government allocations	• Local authorities

SOCIAL SECURITY PROVISIONS

COUNTRY	SERVICE PROVIDERS	THE AGED	THE DISABLED & HANDICAPPED	CHILDREN & YOUTH	NEEDY FAMILIES	SICK & INJURED	THE UNEMPLOYED	METHODS OF FINANCING	RESPONSIBLE GOVERNMENT ADMINISTRATIVE AGENCIES
NEW ZEALAND	Central government administrative agencies	• Universal non-contributory flat-rate pension payable to all aged 60 and over.	• Flat-rate invalids benefit • Flat-rate disability allowance offset expenses incurred due to disability • Flat-rate handicapped childs allowance where constant care required	• Family benefit universal allowance for each child • Family support income-tested allowance for each child	• Domestic purposes benefit solo-parents, women alone aged 50 and over those caring for sick or infirm • Flat-rate widows benefit • Flat-rate orphans benefit • Flat-rate special benefit paid on discretionary basis related to hardship	• Flat-rate sickness benefit • Accident compensation payments earnings-related and lump sum payments	• Flat-rate unemployment benefits	• Government tax income • Levies on employers, self-employed and car owners	• Department of Social Welfare • Accident Compensation Corporation • Inland Revenue Department
	Regional government administrative agencies								
	Voluntary agencies								
	Private enterprise								

PROVISION OF PERSONAL SOCIAL SERVICES

COUNTRY	SERVICE PROVIDERS	THE AGED	THE DISABLED & HANDICAPPED	CHILDREN & YOUTH	NEEDY FAMILIES	SICK & INJURED	THE UNEMPLOYED	RESPONSIBLE GOVERNMENT ADMINISTRATIVE AGENCIES
NEW ZEALAND	Central government administrative agencies		● Rehabilitation league fully funded agency serving physically handicapped	● Residential / institutional care ● Social work services ● Foster care ● Te Kalanga Peo Maori pre-school centres ● School-based counselling services	● Social work services	● Rehabilitation and prevention		● Department of Social welfare ● Department of Health ● Department of Education ● Department of Labour ● Department of Maori Affairs ● Department of Internal Affairs ● Accident Compensation Corporation
	Regional government administrative agencies	● Hospital boards ● Residential / institutional care ● Home-based services (meals-on-wheels, home help, laundry)	● Hospital boards ● Residential / institutional care ● Assessment services					● Regional authorities
	Local administrative agencies	● Pensioner housing ● Day care services		● Child-care centres /family day care ● Community work/detached youth work				● Local authorities
	Voluntary agencies	● Residential / institutional care ● Day care ● Counselling services	● Residential / institutional care ● Rehabilitation services ● Sheltered workshops	● Residential / institutional care ● Child-care centres ● Family day care ● Foster care ● Telephone counselling	● Counselling services, including budgeting advice ● Family support ● Womens refuges	● Counselling ● Rehabilitation services	● Work schemes ● Counselling services	● Department of Social Welfare
	Private enterprise	● Residential care ● Retirement villages						

SOCIAL SECURITY PROVISIONS

COUNTRY	SERVICE PROVIDERS	THE AGED	THE DISABLED AND HANDICAPPED	CHILDREN AND YOUTH	NEEDY FAMILIES	THE SICK AND INJURED	THE UNEMPLOYED	METHODS OF FINANCING	RESPONSIBLE GOVERNMENT ADMINISTRATIVE AGENCIES
NORWAY	Central government administrative agencies								• Ministry of Local Government & Labour • Directorate of Labour • Ministry of Health & Social Affairs • Directorate of Public Health • National Insurance Administration
	Regional government administrative agencies		• Disability pension • Rehabilitation allowances • Technical appliances			• Sickness benefit	• Daily cash allowances	• National insurance scheme (contributions from employers, employees, self employed and state grants)	• County Committees of National Insurance Secretaries • County Labour Committees • Development Boards
	Local government administrative agencies	• Old age pension • Extra financial allowances • Social assistance	• Labour insurance benefits • Extra financial allowances • Technical appliances • Rehabilitation • Social assistance	• Childrens pensions Social assistance	• Maternity allowances • Family allowances • Extra child-birth allowances to single mothers • Transitional allowances to single-parent families • Extra financial allowances for single-parent families • Social security benefits to surviving spouse • Childrens pensions • Allowances for surviving family nurse • Social assistance	• Sickness allowances • Occupational injury benefits • Sickness benefits • Social assistance	• Daily cash allowances • Social assistance	• National insurance scheme (contributions from employers, employees, self-employed and state grants) • State block grants	• Local National Insurance Offices • Social Welfare Offices • Local Labour Exchange Offices
	Private enterprise	• Private insurance schemes	• Private insurance schemes			• Private insurance schemes			
	Employers	• Occupational insurance schemes				• Sickness allowance (for 14 days)		• Employer allocations	

400

PROVISION OF PERSONAL SOCIAL SERVICES

COUNTRY	SERVICE PROVIDERS	THE AGED	THE DISABLED AND HANDICAPPED	CHILDREN AND YOUTH	NEEDY FAMILIES	THE SICK AND INJURED	THE UNEMPLOYED	METHODS OF FINANCING	RESPONSIBLE GOVERNMENT ADMINISTRATIVE AGENCIES
NORWAY	Central government administrative agencies	• Transport concessions • Improvement of dwellings • Housing subsidies	• Improvement of dwellings	• Psychiatric assistance • Foreign adoption				• Government subsidies and grants	• Ministry of Local Government and Labour • Directorate of Labour • Ministry of Health & Social Affairs • Directorate of Public Health
	Regional government administrative agencies	• Somatic nursing homes until 1988) • Geriatric wards • Psychiatric nursing homes	• Counselling & information • Institutional care • Vocational training in secondary school	• Foster home centres • Psychiatric institutional ward • Children's homes • Homes for adolescents	• Residential homes for young mothers		• Training and counselling services • Job creation programmes	• Government grants	• County Government • County Labour Exchange
	Local government administrative agencies	• Domiciliary services • Home nursing service • Day centres • Service centres • Somatic nursing homes (from 1988) • Residential homes • Old age housing • Telephone allowance • Transport concessions • Housing subsidies	• Domiciliary services • Relief assistance • Day centres • Transportation service • Housing subsidies • Health centres • Kindergartens • Smaller homes • Primary vocational training • Labour exchange service • Sheltered workshops • Job training programmes	• Child welfare assistance • Kindergartens • Play centres • Adoption	• Housewife stand-in • Counselling & information • Crisis centres for mistreated women & children	• Housewife stand-in • Home help services • Home nursing service	• Labour exchange service • Recreational facilities and programmes • Job creation programme • Vocational & occupational training • Occupational counselling service	• Government grants • User charges	• Municipal Government • Local Labour Exchange Office
	Voluntary agencies	• Service centres • Residential homes • Transport services	• Centres for rehabilitation • Technical colleges for the disabled • Transport services	• Kindergartens • Play centres	• Crisis centres for mistreated women & children			• Government grants • User charges	
	Private enterprise	• Residential homes		• Kindergartens • Play centres				• User charges	

SOCIAL SECURITY PROVISIONS

COUNTRY	SERVICE PROVIDERS	THE AGED	THE DISABLED AND HANDICAPPED	CHILDREN AND YOUTH	NEEDY FAMILIES	THE SICK AND INJURED	THE UNEMPLOYED	METHODS OF FINANCING	RESPONSIBLE GOVERNMENT ADMINISTRATIVE AGENCIES
SWEDEN	Central government administrative agencies	• Universal minimum flat-rate age pension • Partially income-tested supplementary pensions • Earnings-related supplementary pensions • Part-time early retirement pensions • Wife's supplement	• Universal minimum flat-rate disability pensions • Handicapped allowance • Child minding allowance • Medical care • Wife's supplement	• Child's supplement • Orphan's pensions • Universal child allowance • Universal education allowance • Income-based education allowance	• Basic widows pensions • Supplementary widows pensions • Single parent allowances (income-tested)		• Earnings-related unemployment insurance benefit • Training allowances • Mobility allowance	• Central government taxes • Employer/ employee contributions	• Ministries of: Finance • National superannuation pension fund • National social insurance board • National labour board
	Regional government administrative agencies		• Work-injury insurance benefits • Medical benefits			• Health insurance Sickness benefits • Medical benefits			• Social insurance funds with local social insurance offices
	Local government administrative agencies	• Social assistance	• Social assistance	• Social assistance	• Municipal housing allowance • Social assistance		• Social assistance	• Central government allocations • Local taxes	• Municipal authorities
	Voluntary agencies								
	Private enterprise	• Occupational pensions	• Occupational pensions					• Employer and employee contributions	

PROVISION OF PERSONAL SOCIAL SERVICES

COUNTRY	SERVICE PROVIDERS	THE AGED	THE DISABLED & HANDICAPPED	CHILDREN AND YOUTH	NEEDY FAMILIES	THE SICK AND INJURED	THE UNEMPLOYED	METHODS OF FINANCING	RESPONSIBLE GOVERNMENT ADMINISTRATIVE AGENCIES
SWEDEN	Central government administrative agencies	• Home improvement grants	• Home improvement grants				• Labour market training	• Government allocation	• Ministries of: Health and Social Affairs, Labour, Housing, Education and cultural affairs • National labour market board • National board of health and social welfare
	Regional government administrative agencies	• Nursing Homes • Home health service • Special apartments • Domiciliary service	• Half-way houses • Rehabilitation centre • Nursing Homes • Home health service • Special apartments • Domiciliary service		• Child and maternity health services • Family guidance centres			• Government allocation	• County authorities
	Local government administrative agencies	• Special apartments • Homes for the aged • Domiciliary service	• Sheltered workshops • Special apartments • Homes for the aged • Domiciliary services	• Pre-schools • Family day-care • Day-care centre • Protective services	• Counselling		• Job Creation programmes	• Government allocation • User charges	• Local employment offices • Municipal social welfare committees
	Voluntary agencies			• Child care (parents cooperatives)				• Government allocation • User charges	• Municipal authorities
	Private enterprise		• Occupational safety & health			• Occupational Safety and health		• Government allocation • User charges	• Municipal authorities • Regional office labour inspectorates

SOCIAL SECURITY PROVISIONS

COUNTRY	SERVICE PROVIDERS	THE AGED	THE DISABLED & HANDICAPPED	CHILDREN & YOUTH	NEEDY FAMILIES	SICK & INJURED	THE UNEMPLOYED	METHODS OF FINANCING	RESPONSIBLE GOVERNMENT ADMINISTRATIVE AGENCIES
UNITED KINGDOM	Central government administrative agencies	• Flat-rate & earnings-related contributory pensions • Free health care • Means-tested supplementary benefits • Means-tested housing benefits • Additional personal tax allowance	• Flat-rate & earnings-related contributory pensions, or non-contributory severe disablement allowance • Industrial disablement & reduced earnings benefits for those injured at work • Attendance allowance • Mobility allowance • Invalid care allowance (for carers) • Means-tested supplementary benefits • Means-tested housing benefits • Free health care (minor charges if not on low income)	• Statutory maternity pay • Earnings-related & flat-rate contributory maternity allowance • Child benefit • Training allowances • Means-tested supplementary benefits for school leavers • Free health care (minor charges if 16 and not on low income) • Maternal & child health services.	• Family income supplement • Supplementary benefits • Housing benefits • Maternity grants • Free milk & vitamins for expectant mothers & children under 5 • Flat-rate contributory widows' pensions • Extra child benefit & tax allowance for single parents • Free health care	• Earnings-related statutory sick pay or flat-rate contributory benefits • Means-tested supplementary benefits • Means-tested housing benefits • Free health care (minor charges if not on low income)	• Flat-rate, contributory benefits • Means-tested supplementary benefits • Means-tested housing benefits • Redundancy payments • Training & special employment programme allowances • Free health care (minor charges if not on low income)	• Employee/employee earnings-related contributions • General Taxation	• Department of Health & Social Security
	Local government administrative agencies			• School medical services	• Discretionary means-tested educational allowances for 16-18 year olds			• Grants from central government • Local property taxes	• Local Authority Education Department • Health Department
	Private enterprise	• Occupational pensions • Private pensions	• Occupational pensions • Compensation for those injured at work where employer at fault • Private pensions	• Administration of statutory maternity pay • Additional occupational maternity pay		• Administration of statutory sick pay • Additional occupational sick pay • Occupational health services • Private health insurance • Private cash benefits • Private health insurance & health services	• Additional redundancy payments	• Employer/employee contributions • Employer subsidies • Tax subsidies • Individual contributions • Tax subsidies	

PROVISION OF PERSONAL SOCIAL SERVICES

COUNTRY	SERVICE PROVIDERS	THE AGED	THE DISABLED AND HANDICAPPED	CHILDREN AND YOUTH	NEEDY FAMILIES	THE SICK AND INJURED	THE UNEMPLOYED	METHODS OF FINANCING	RESPONSIBLE GOVERNMENT ADMINISTRATIVE AGENCIES
UNITED KINGDOM	Central government administrative agencies						• Vocational counselling • Job placement services	• General taxation	• Manpower Services Commission
	Regional government administrative agencies								
	Local government administrative agencies	• Residential homes • Social work support • Home help • Meals-on-wheels • Aids and adaptions • Lunch clubs • Day centres • Transport • Telephones	• As for the aged plus: • Services for the blind and deaf • Laundry services	• Social work support • Residential care • Fostering and adoption services • Day nurseries • Home help • Services for young offenders • Registration of private nurseries & child minders • Youth services	• As for children and youth, plus • Welfare rights services	• Medical social work services • Home help	• Drop in centres • Welfare rights service • Concessionary rates for transport & leisure facilities • Vocational counselling • Job placement services for young people	• Central government grants • Local property taxes • User charges	• Local Authority • Social Services Department • Education Department
	Voluntary agencies	• Residential homes • Day centres • Lunch clubs • Meals-on-wheels • Decorating • Transport	• As for the aged plus: • Services for the blind and deaf • Subsidised holidays	• Social work support • Residential care • Fostering and adoption services • Child abuse services	• As for children and youth, plus: • Welfare and legal rights services		• Drop in centres • Welfare and legal rights services	• Grants from central and local government • Voluntary donations • User charges • Tax subsidies	
	Private enterprise	• Residential homes • Domestic help	• Residential homes • Domestic help	• Day nurseries • Child-minders • Domestic help				• User charges	

SOCIAL SECURITY PROVISIONS

COUNTRY	SERVICE PROVIDERS	THE AGED	THE DISABLED AND HANDICAPPED	CHILDREN AND YOUTH	NEEDY FAMILIES	THE SICK AND INJURED	THE UNEMPLOYED	METHODS OF FINANCING	RESPONSIBLE GOVERNMENT ADMINISTRATIVE AGENCIES
UNITED STATES	Central government administrative agencies	• Contributory earnings-related pensions • Social assistance allowance to indigent • Subsidised health care	• Contributory earnings-related disability pensions • Social assistance • Disability social assistance	• Family assistance	• Income maintenance programme • Survivors insurance • Workmans compensation • Medical care • Food stamps • Income tax relief • Energy grant • Public housing	• Partial insurance for elderly • Partial insurance for poor	• Contributory earnings-related unemployment benefits	• Governmental subsidies • Employer/employee contributions	• Federal Departments of Health and Human Services, Agriculture, Labour, Housing and Urban Development and Commerce
	Regional and local government administrative agencies				• Income maintenance • Workmans compensation • Medical care • Food stamps • Income tax relief • General assistance • Energy grant	• Earnings-related Partial insurance for poor • Earnings-related temporary disability benefits • Earnings-related sickness benefits (contributory)	• Contributory earnings-related unemployment benefits	• Federal, state and local government subsidies	• State Department of Health and Human Services • County Departments of Human Services
	Voluntary agencies			• Discretionary assistance • Maternity benefits				• Employer-financed	• Health Insurance Agencies
	Private enterprise			• Discretionary assistance • Maternity benefits				• Employer financed	• Health Insurance Agencies

PROVISION OF PERSONAL SOCIAL SERVICES

COUNTRY	SERVICE PROVIDERS	THE AGED	THE DISABLED AND HANDICAPPED	CHILDREN AND YOUTH	NEEDY FAMILIES	THE SICK AND INJURED	THE UNEMPLOYED	METHODS OF FINANCING	RESPONSIBLE GOVERNMENT ADMINISTRATIVE AGENCIES
UNITED STATES	Central government administrative agencies	• Residential / institutional care • Housing • Home care	• Education and training • Institutional care	• Day care • Foster care and adoption • Institutional services • Health care	• Shelters • Personal services • Education and training	• Hospitals for veterans and native Americans • Partial support for some hospitals		• National government in form of conditional grants-in-aid and block grants	• Federal Departments of: Health and Human Services, Labour, Housing and Urban Development
	Regional government administrative agencies	• Residential / institutional care • Housing • Home care • Mental health services	• Education and training • Health care • Institutional care	• Health care • Institutional services • Day care • Recreation • Foster care and adoption • Childrens court • Health care • Institutional services	• Shelters • Personal social services	• Hospitals	• Employment and training • Economic development	• State, county and city governments subsidies	• State Department of Health and Human Services
	Voluntary agencies	• Residential / institutional care • Housing • Home care • Mental health services	• Health care • Institutional care • Community care • Institutional care	• Day care • Recreation • Foster care and adoption • Counselling advice • Information and referrals	• Shelters • Food pantries • Counselling services • Education and training	• Hospitals	• Employment and training	• Donations • Government subsidies • Client fees	• County Departments of Health and Human Services
	Private enterprise	• Residential institutional care • Housing • Home care • Mental health service	• Institutional care	• Day care	• Food pantries	• Hospitals	• Employment and training • Economic development	• Government grants • Fees	• Federal and State Labour Departments

INDEX

accidental injury benefit
    New Zealand 217; see also occupational injury and sickness benefits, sickness benefit
adoption
    Australia 76; Canada 78; Germany, West 106, 107; Italy 136; Norway 254-5; Sweden 292; United Kingdom 328, 329; United States 368
adoption leave
    Canada 78
advocacy services
    Canada 76; United States 362, 365, 368, 373
age pensions
    Australia 18; Canada 68-71; Germany, West 100; Italy 131; Netherlands 164; New Zealand 201-2; Norway 235-6; Sweden 280, 282, 283-4; United Kingdom 319; United States 360
aged, personal social services for the
    Australia 19-20; Canada 71-2; Germany, West 102; Italy 132; Netherlands 167-8; New Zealand 203-5; Norway 237-9; Sweden 284-7; United Kingdom 320-1; United States 361-2
aged, social security
    Australia 18-19; Canada 68-71; Germany, West 100-2; Italy 131; Netherlands 164-7; New Zealand 201-3; Norway 235-7; Sweden 280-4; United Kingdom 319-20; United States 360-1
aged, the
    Australia 16-17; Canada 67-8; Germany, West 100; Italy 130-1; Netherlands 164; New Zealand 200-1; Norway 235; Sweden 280; United Kingdom 319; United States 364
apartments for aged
    Canada 72; Norway 239; Sweden 285
attendance allowances
    United Kingdom 324; United States 377

attendant care
    Canada 76

Beveridge, influence of
    Canada 49; Italy 124; Netherlands 147, 148, 185-6; Norway 229; United Kingdom 305, 311
birth grants
    Norway 245; United Kingdom 331 see also maternity benefits, maternity care, maternity leave
Bismarck, influence of
    Netherlands 147, 148, 185; Norway 228-9; Sweden 266
blind, welfare of the
    Australia 18, 21; Italy 134; Netherlands 174; Sweden 286; United Kingdom 323, 325; United States 364

capitalism
    United States 345
carer's allowances
    Australia 23; New Zealand 220; Norway 236-7; Sweden 285; United Kingdom 322, 324
child abuse
    Canada 79; New Zealand 211; Norway 248; Sweden 290; United Kingdom 329; United States 368, 373
child benefits
    see family allowances
child care
    see family day care, out-of-school care, day-care centres
children and youths
    Australia 24; Canada 77; Germany, West 105; Italy 135; Netherlands 175; New Zealand 206; Norway 251; Sweden 287; United Kingdom 326; United States 366-7
children and youths, personal social services
    Australia 26-7; Canada 78-80; Germany, West 106-8; Italy 135-6; Netherlands 176-7; New Zealand 210-12; Sweden 287-91; United Kingdom 328-9
children and youths, social security
    Australia 24-5; Canada 77-8; Germany, West 105-6; Italy 135; Netherlands 175-6; New Zealand 206-9; Norway 251; United Kingdom 326-8; United States 367
Christianity
    Germany, West 89, 90, 91, 92; Italy 122, 123; Netherlands 147-8; Norway 228

community (neighbourhood) centres
    Australia 26; Canada 72; New Zealand 205;
    Norway 237-8, 242; United Kingdom 320, 325
congenitally handicapped, welfare of
    Australia 21; Canada 76
conservatism
    Australia 8; Canada 47, 48, 50; Netherlands
    148; Norway 230; United Kingdom 310
counselling services
    Canada 61; Germany, West 104, 106, 111; Italy
    136-7; Netherlands 180; New Zealand 204;
    Norway 242, 247; Sweden 290; United Kingdom
    325, 328, 329, 332; United States 362, 365,
    368, 369, 370, 371
crisis centres
    Norway 248
cross-organisations (Netherlands)
    see voluntary agencies

day-care centres
    Australia 26; Canada 59-60, 76; Germany, West
    107; Netherlands 177; New Zealand 210; Norway
    252; Sweden 289; United Kingdom 328 see also
    child care
deaf, welfare of the
    Italy 134; Netherlands 174; Sweden 286; United
    Kingdom 325
death grants
    Germany, West 109 see also funeral grants
democratic socialism
    see socialism
demogrants
    see universal pension and allowances
disability allowances
    New Zealand 219; Sweden 284 see also invalid
    pensions
disability pensions
    Canada 74; Germany, West 103-4; Italy 133-4;
    Netherlands 172; New Zealand 217; Norway
    240-1; Sweden 283-4; United Kingdom 322-3;
    United States 364 see also invalid pensions
disabled and handicapped, personal social services
    Australia 23; Canada 74-6; Germany, West 104;
    Netherlands 174-5; New Zealand 219-20; Norway
    242-4; Sweden 284-5; United Kingdom 324-5;
    United States 364-5
disabled and handicapped, social security
    Australia 21-3; Canada 73-4; Germany, West
    103-4; Italy 133-4; Netherlands 171-2; New
    Zealand 218-19; Norway 240-1; Sweden 280-4;
    United Kingdom 322-5; United States 364

disabled and handicapped, the
    Australia 20-1; Canada 73; Germany, West 103;
    Italy 133; Netherlands 169; New Zealand 218;
    Norway 240; Sweden 280; United Kingdom 333;
    United States 363-4
domestic violence
    Canada 60; Norway 248; United States 376
domiciliary services
    Australia 18; Canada 67, 72; Germany, West
    102; Italy 132; Netherlands 167-8, 180; New
    Zealand 204; Norway 237, 241-2, 247, 250;
    Sweden 285; United Kingdom 320, 325; United
    States 362

early retirement benefits
    Canada 69; Germany, West 101; Italy 131;
    Netherlands 165; Sweden 280, 283; United
    States 360 see also age pensions
economic environment of welfare systems
    see socio-economic environment of welfare
    systems
economic growth
    Australia 9; Canada 55; Germany, West 96;
    Italy 127-8; Netherlands 156; New Zealand 191;
    Norway 232; United Kingdom 314; United States
    352
educational allowances
    Australia 26; Germany, West 106; Italy 136;
    Netherlands 175-6, 176-7; Norway 246; Sweden
    292; United Kingdom 331
egalitarian principles
    New Zealand 198; Sweden 265-6 see also equity
    principles
emotionally disturbed, welfare of
    Germany, West 104
equity principles
    Australia 1-3, 16, 24-5; New Zealand 198;
    Norway 231; United Kingdom 309, United States
    2, 9

family allowances
    Australia 25, 28, 29; Canada 77; Germany, West
    105-6; Italy 137; Netherlands 175-6, 177; New
    Zealand 206-7, 208-9; Norway 245, 246; Sweden
    291; United Kingdom 327; United States 367
family and welfare
    Australia 4, 23; Canada 49-50, 68, 77; Norway
    235; Sweden 265; United Kingdom 321, 342;
    United States 362
family assistance benefits
    United States 370

family day-care
    Australia 26; New Zealand 210; Sweden 289 <u>see also</u> child care
family support services
    Australia 26; Germany, West 111; Italy 134; Netherlands 181; New Zealand 204; United Kingdom 328
fascism
    Germany, West 93-4, 101, 108, 119; Italy 123, 124
fatherless families
    <u>see</u> sole parents, welfare of
federalism and social welfare policy and practice
    Australia 8, 9-10, 12, 15, 16, 19, 42; Canada 49, 50, 51, 52, 53, 59, 64-6, 71, 72, 73, 74, 77, 79-80, 81; Germany, West 95, 108, 112, 114; United States 347-9, 351, 353-4
female workforce participation
    Australia 33; Canada 58, 77; New Zealand 206, 213; United Kingdom 315; United States 352, 366
fiscal welfare
    Australia 13, 16, 18, 25, 29, 35, 38, 40; Canada 53, 56, 57, 70-1, 77-8, 80; Germany, West 105, 108; Italy 137; New Zealand 197, 203, 208, 212; Sweden 275, 282-3; United Kingdom 316, 318, 319, 329, 331, 339; United States 275
food supplements
    Canada 60-1; United States 368, 371, 372
foreign workers, welfare of
    Germany, West 106
foster care
    Australia 26; Canada 78; Germany, West 106; Italy 136; New Zealand 212; Norway 252, 253; United Kingdom 328, 329; United States 368
funeral grants
    Sweden 300; United States 371 <u>see also</u> death grants

handicapped child's allowance
    New Zealand 219
health insurance
    Australia 5, 24, 26, 38; Canada 48, 65-6, 72; Germany, West 115-15, 117-18; Italy 128, 130; Netherlands 159, 172-3; Sweden 298-9, 300; United Kingdom 316, 324, 325, 327-8, 339; United States 331, 362, 376

health services
    Australia 38, 40; Canada 64-6, 67; Germany,
    West 116, 117; Italy 140-2; Netherlands
    159-60, 172; New Zealand 217; Norway 243,
    249-50; Sweden 298-9; United Kingdom 320, 329,
    337-8, 338-9, 339-40, 341; United States 361,
    365, 368, 371, 376-7, 378
historical origins of welfare systems
    Australia 4-6, 7; Canada 49-51; Germany, West
    92-4; Italy 124-6; Netherlands 149-53; New
    Zealand 192-4; Norway 228-31; Sweden 264-9,
    270; United Kingdom 310-11; United States 350-1
homes for single parents
    Netherlands 177; Norway 253
home-improvement subsidies
    Canada 76-6; Netherlands 167; New Zealand 219;
    Norway 238, 242; Sweden 284-5; United States
    373
homeless youths, welfare of
    Australia 26
home-maker services
    Canada 67, 72; New Zealand 104; Norway 237,
    247; United Kingdom 339
home nursing
    Australia 19; Canada 67; Netherlands 167, 173;
    New Zealand 204, 220; Norway 237, 250; Sweden
    285; United Kingdom 324; United States 361, 362
hostel accommodation
    Australia 19; Germany, West 102; United
    Kingdom 326
humanitarian principles
    Norway 220; Sweden 266; United States 346

ideological environment of welfare systems
    Australia 1-4; Canada 47-9; Germany, West
    89-92; Italy 122-4; Netherlands 147-9; New
    Zealand 194-6; Norway 228-31; Sweden 264-9;
    United Kingdom 309-10; United States 345-6
illegitimate children, welfare of
    Germany, West 107; Norway 253
immigrants, welfare of
    Australia 1, 12; Canada 74, 77; New Zealand
    214, 215; Norway 233; Sweden 291, 294
income distribution
    Australia 2; Canada 52, 80; Italy 127, 142;
    Netherlands 168, 187-8; Norway 259; United
    Kingdom 314; United States 352
income tests
    see means tests

indexation of pensions and benefits
    Australia 18; Canada 69, 77; Germany, West
    101, 104, 109; Italy 131; Netherlands 166; New
    Zealand 207, 208; Sweden 280; United Kingdom
    360
indigenous peoples, welfare of
    Australia 1, 12-13; Canada 53, 61, 78; New
    Zealand 210, 212, 213, 215, 221-2; United
    States 353, 377
inflation
    Australia 9; Netherlands 156; Norway 232;
    United Kingdom 314; United States 352
injured, the
    see sick and injured, the
intellectually handicapped, welfare of
    Australia 21; Canada 74; Germany, West 103;
    Italy 134; New Zealand 220; Sweden 286; United
    Kingdom 324, 326; United States 363
invalid pensions
    Australia 21-3; Germany, West 103-4; Italy
    133; Netherlands 171-2; United Kingdom 323 see
    also disability pensions, disability allowances

job creation programmes
    Canada 64; Germany, West 114; Italy 139;
    Netherlands 184, 185; New Zealand 215; Sweden
    294, 296; United States 372
job search services
    Australia 35; Germany, West 113; Italy 139;
    Netherlands 184; Norway 243, 256-7; United
    Kingdom 336; United States 365, 370, 372, 375
juvenile delinquency
    Canada 79; Germany, West 108; New Zealand 211,
    215; Sweden 290; United Kingdom 284, 285;
    United States 368

kindergartens
    Canada 78; Germany, West 107; Netherlands 177;
    New Zealand 210; Norway 243, 252 see also
    child care

labour market innovation subsidies
    Canada 64; Netherlands 184; New Zealand 215
liberalism
    Australia 4; Canada 47-8; Germany, West 89,
    91; Italy 122, 124; Norway 228; Sweden 266;
    United States 345

local government welfare services
    Australia 6, 7; Canada 49, 53, 54, 64;
    Germany, West 91, 92-3, 96-7, 106, 109; Italy
    126, 129, 132, 135, 136, 137, 139, 141;
    Netherlands 147-8, 159; New Zealand 196;
    Norway 232-4, 235, 238-9, 241-4, 247-8, 251-3,
    254-5, 256-7; Sweden 273, 278, 285, 286, 289,
    293; United Kingdom 311, 312, 313, 315, 320,
    325, 328-9, 330, 332; United States 345-6,
    351, 353-4, 370, 371, 372, 373, 375, 377, 379

marital breakdown
    Australia 9, 28; New Zealand 208; United
    Kingdom 314,
maternity benefit
    Canada 59; Germany, West 109; Italy 134;
    Netherlands 176; Norway 245; Sweden 291;
    United Kingdom 326-7 see also birth grants
maternity care
    Germany West 106, 115; Italy 134; Netherlands
    177; Sweden 289; United Kingdom 327-8 see also
    birth grants
maternity leave
    Canada 78; Germany, West 110; Italy 135;
    United States 367 see also birth grants
means tests
    Australia 2, 3, 5, 9, 18, 21, 25, 26, 33;
    Canada 50, 53, 62; Germany, West 101; Italy
    137; Netherlands 164, 170, 172, 183, 185; New
    Zealand 201, 206, 208, 210, 216; Norway 229;
    Sweden 280, 284, 292; United Kingdom 310-12,
    313, 330, 335, 336; United States 360, 363,
    370, 371, 372
mobility allowances
    Sweden 297; United Kingdom 324
motherless families
    see sole parents, welfare of
mothers' allowances
    Canada 50

national superannuation
    New Zealand 202-3
needs-testing
    Canada 53, 58-9; Germany, West 109, 112;
    Netherlands 178, 183
needy families
    Australia 28-9; Canada 58; Germany, West 109;
    Italy 137; Netherlands 177; New Zealand 206;
    Norway 244; Sweden 287; United Kingdom 330;
    United States 369-70

needy families, personal social services
    Canada 59-61; Germany, West 111; Italy 137;
    Netherlands 180; New Zealand 210-12; Norway
    247-8; Sweden 287-91; United Kingdom 332;
    United States 372
needy families, social security
    Australia 29-30; Canada 58-59; Germany, West
    109-11; Italy 137; Netherlands 177-80; New
    Zealand 206-9; Norway 245-8; United Kingdom
    330-1; United States 270-2
negative income tax
    United States 372
neglected children, welfare of
    Canada 49; Germany, West 105, 106; New Zealand
    211; Norway 252; Sweden 290; United Kingdom
    328; United States 368
nursing homes
    Australia 19-20; Canada 72-3, 79; Italy 132;
    Netherlands 167, 174; New Zealand 205; Sweden
    286, 298; United Kingdom 320; United States 362
nursery schools
    see kindergartens, child care

occupational injuries and sickness benefits
    Australia 39-40; Canada 66-7; Germany, West
    116-17; Norway 250; Sweden 300; United Kingdom
    323; United States 377 see also accidental
    injury benefits
occupational retirement benefits
    Australia 18-19; Canada 56-7, 71; Germany,
    West 101; Italy 130-1; Netherlands 164, 166,
    167; New Zealand 203; Norway 237; Sweden 286;
    United States 361
occupational welfare
    Australia 16, 18-19, 43; Canada 56-7, 71, 78;
    Italy 129; Netherlands 158, 169, 170, 171,
    184; Sweden 275-6; United Kingdom 311, 316,
    318, 320, 321, 338, 342; United States 358 see
    also occupational superannuation
orphan's benefits
    Australia 39; Canada 66; Germany, West 110;
    Italy 131; Netherlands 165, 176; Norway 247;
    Sweden 280, 283-4, 292; United States 371
out-of-school care
    Australia 26; Norway 253; Sweden 289 see also
    child care

paternity allowances
    Norway 245

personal social services, administration of
    Australia 11-12; Canada 53; Germany, West 96;
    Italy 129; Netherlands 160; New Zealand 196;
    Norway 233-4; Sweden 273, 275; United Kingdom
    315-16; United States 353-5
personal social services, financing of
    Australia 13-16; Canada 57-58; Germany, West
    98-100; Italy 129; Netherlands 162-3; New
    Zealand 199-200; Norway 235; Sweden 276-80;
    United Kingdom 317-18; United States 355-9
physically handicapped, welfare of
    Australia 21, 23; Canada 74, 76; Germany, West
    103; United States 363-4
political environment of welfare systems
    Australia 6, 8-9; Canada 51; Germany, West
    94-5; Italy 127; Netherlands 153-4; New
    Zealand 191-2; Norway 231; Sweden 271-2;
    United Kingdom 313; United States 351
Poor Laws
    Canada 49; Netherlands 148; Norway 229; United
    Kingdom 310-11; United States 347, 379
poverty
    Australia 30, 32, 36; Canada 52, 58, 80; Italy
    137-8, 140; Netherlands 187, 188; United
    Kingdom 319, 330; United States 347, 352, 367,
    369-70
private 'for profit' welfare services
    Australia 20; Canada 54-5, 72, 73, 78, 79, 81;
    New Zealand 195, 197, 205; United Kingdom 316,
    320; United States 354-5, 365, 375
probation services
    Canada 79; Germany, West 106, 108
prosthetic appliances and services
    Australia 23; New Zealand 219; Norway 241;
    Sweden 280; United Kingdom 325
public assistance
    <u>see</u> social assistance

redundancy payments
    United Kingdom 335
rehabilitation allowances
    Australia 23; Norway 244
rehabilitation services
    Australia 23; Canada 74, 75, 76; Germany, West
    104; Italy 134, 141; Netherlands 174; New
    Zealand 221; United Kingdom 324
rent allowances and subsidies
    Australia 20; Canada 71; Germany, West 110-11;
    Netherlands 167, 180; New Zealand 207; Norway
    238; Sweden 285, 288; United Kingdom 319, 324

residency tests
    Australia 18, 21, 30, 35, 38; Canada 68; New Zealand 201, 214, 216, 218; Norway 236; Sweden 291
residential care for adults
    Australia 19-20, 23; Germany, West 102; Italy 132; Netherlands 167, 168, 174; New Zealand 205; Norway 239, 242; Sweden 285; United Kingdom 320, 328; United States 365, 368
residential care for children and youths
    Australia 26; Canada 78, 89; Germany, West 106; Italy 136; New Zealand 211-12; Norway 253, 254; United Kingdom 329
respite care
    Australia 19; Canada 72; Germany, West 102; Italy 132; New Zealand 204, 219; Norway 242; United Kingdom 322; United States 242

self-help principle
    Australia 2-3, 8-9; Canada 47; Germany, West 91-2, 94; United States 346
sheltered employment
    Australia 23; Canada 75; Italy 134; Netherlands 183-4; New Zealand 218; Norway 242, 243, 244; Sweden 286, 296; United States 365
sheltered employment allowances
    Australia 23
sick and injured, personal social services
    Australia 40; Canada 67; Germany, West 117; Italy 142; Netherlands 173-4; New Zealand 217-18; Norway 250, United Kingdom 339
sick and injured, social security
    Australia 38-9; Canada 65-7; Germany, West 115-17; Italy 140-1; Netherlands 169-71; New Zealand 216; Norway 248-50; Sweden 299-300; United Kingdom 338-9
sick and injured, the
    Australia 37; Canada 64-5; Germany, West 115; Italy 140; Netherlands 169; New Zealand 216; Norway 248; Sweden 298-9; United Kingdom 337-8; United States 376
sick child leave
    Germany, West 106; Italy 135; Sweden 291-2
sick leave
    Germany, West 116, 117
sickness benefits
    Australia 38; Canada 67; Germany, West 115, 117; Italy 141; Netherlands 169-71; Sweden 299; United Kingdom 338-9; United States 377

single parents
    see sole parents, welfare of
Social assistance
    Australia 2, 3, 4-5, 9, 18-19, 21, 29-30, 33, 35, 38; Canada 50, 53, 54, 57, 58, 69-70, 74, 75-6, 80; Germany, West 91, 92, 94, 100, 101, 109, 112, 113; Italy 128, 129, 131, 132, 133, 135, 138; Netherlands 150, 158, 177-9, 180, 181; New Zealand 195, 198, 201; Norway 229, 237, 246, 248, 251, 256; Sweden 292-3; United Kingdom 331, 341; United States 348, 353, 361, 364, 370, 371
social Darwinism
    United States 346, 348, 349, 379
social environment of welfare systems
    see socio-economic environment of welfare systems
social harmony principles
    Italy 122
social insurance
    Australia 13; Canada 50, 51, 53, 56, 62, 68-9, 74, 80; Germany, West 90-1, 93, 100, 111; Italy 124; Netherlands 148, 157-8, 160-1; New Zealand 195, 198; Norway 228, 229; United Kingdom 311, 341
social insurance contribution rates
    Canada 56; Germany, West 99-100, 116; Italy 130; Netherlands 160-1; Norway 234-5; Sweden 278; United Kingdom 316-17; United States 355, 358
socialism
    Australia 4, 8; Canada 49; Germany, West 90, 91, 93; Italy 123; Netherlands 148; New Zealand 194; Norway 230; United Kingdom 309
social justice
    Australia 1, 16; New Zealand 198; Norway 231; United States 345
socially handicapped, welfare of
    Canada 74, 76; Norway 241, 244
social security, administration of
    Australia 11; Canada 53, 62, 66; Germany, West 96, 113, 115; Italy 128-9; Netherlands 157-60; New Zealand 196; Norway 232-3; Sweden 273, 275; United Kingdom 315; United States 353-4
social security, financing of
    Australia 13-15; Canada 55-7; Germany, West 98-100, 101, 116; Italy 129-30; Netherlands 160-2; New Zealand 198-9; Norway 234-5; Sweden 276-80; United Kingdom 316-17, 318; United States 355-9

social work education
    Germany, West 98, 118-19
socio-economic environment of welfare systems
    Australia 9; Canada 51-2; Germany, West 95-6;
    Italy 126-7; Netherlands 154-7; New Zealand
    190-1; Norway 231-2; Sweden 269, 271-2, 272-3;
    United Kingdom 313-15; United States 351-3
sole parents, welfare of
    Australia 28-9, 30; Canada 58-9, 60, 77, 80;
    Germany, West 111-12; Italy 135; Netherlands
    177, 178-9, 186-7; New Zealand 207, 208;
    Norway 245, 245-6, 252; Sweden 299; United
    Kingdom 330, 331, 332, 333; United States 366,
    369
solo parents
    see supporting parents, welfare of
supplementary dependents' benefits
    Australia 29; Germany, West 104, 117;
    Netherlands 180; New Zealand 207-8; Sweden
    283; United Kingdom 319, 323, 327, 331; United
    States 360, 375, 377
supporting parents benefits
    Australia 29, 30; New Zealand 207-8, 219;
    Norway 245, 246-7; Sweden 291; United Kingdom
    331
surviving family nurse's allowances
    Norway 247
survivors' pensions
    Australia 30, 39; Canada 66-7, 69, 73;
    Germany, West 109-10; Italy 131; Netherlands
    164-5, 166-7; Norway 246, 247; Sweden 281,
    283-4, 292; United Kingdom 331; United States
    370-1

take-up rates
    Australia 18; Canada 80; United Kingdom 332,
    333
tax credits
    Canada 53, 57, 59, 70-1, 77-8, 80 see also
    fiscal welfare
tax expenditures
    see fiscal welfare
thrift ethic
    Australia 2, 3, 4, 8-9
trade unions and welfare
    Australia 15, 43; Canada 60-1; Germany, West
    89-90, 93; Italy 138; Netherlands 148, 174;
    New Zealand 195, 203; Sweden 297; United
    Kingdom 311

training allowances
    Canada 63, 74; Germany, West 104; Sweden 294, 297; United Kingdom 327, 335
training subsidies
    Canada 64; Germany, West 113

unemployed, personal social services
    Australia 35-6; Canada 63-4; Germany, West 114; Italy 139; Netherlands 184; New Zealand 214-16; Norway 256-7; Sweden 294-5; United Kingdom 335-6; United States 375-6
unemployed, social security
    Australia 33-5; Canada 61-2; Germany, West 113-4; Italy 138-9; Netherlands 181-4; New Zealand 214; Norway 256; Sweden 297-8; United Kingdom 334-5; United States 374-5, 376
unemployed, the
    Australia 33; Canada 61; Germany, West 113; Italy 138; Netherlands 180-1; New Zealand 212-13; Norway 255-6; Sweden 293; United Kingdom 334; United States 374
unemployment
    Australia 3, 9, 26-8, 33, 36; Canada 52, 61, 64; Germany, West 95-6, 113, 114; Italy 126, 138; Netherlands 155-6; New Zealand 191, 212; Sweden 293, 303; United Kingdom 314-15, 319, 322, 330, 334; United States 374
unemployment benefits
    Australia 33, 35; Canada 62; Germany, West 113; Italy 138; Netherlands 178-9; New Zealand 214; Norway 251, 256; Sweden 297-8; United Kingdom 327, 334-5; United States 374-5, 376
universal benefits
    Australia 5, 25; Canada 48, 50, 53, 77, 80; Netherlands 175; New Zealand 198, 201-2, 207, 217; Norway 229, 230; Sweden 280; United Kingdom 317, 319; United States 363

vocational rehabilitation
    Australia 23; Canada 66-7, 74-5; Germany, West 104; Italy 134; Norway 243; United States 365
vocational training
    Australia 27, 35, 36; Germany, West 106, 114; Italy 139; Netherlands 184, 185; New Zealand 214-5; Norway 246, 257; Sweden 294; United Kingdom 326; United States 372, 375, 376

voluntary agencies
    Australia 9, 12, 15, 20, 23; Canada 49, 54, 58, 60-1, 63, 71, 73, 76; Germany, West 89, 93, 94, 96, 97, 102, 104, 109, 119; Italy 129; Netherlands 152, 160, 167, 173, 177, 180; New Zealand 195, 196-7, 199-200, 204-5, 215-16, 220, 221; Norway 238, 248, 253; Sweden 276, 369; United Kingdom 311, 316, 320, 321, 325, 329, 332; United States 348, 349, 353, 354-5, 365, 372, 375, 377

wage subsidies
    Australia 27; Canada 63; New Zealand 215; Norway 244, 257; Sweden 294, 296; United Kingdom 330-1, 331-2

war veterans, welfare of
    Australia 4-5, 11-12, 18, 21, 23; Canada 53, 74, 76; United Kingdom 323; United States 353, 377

widows, welfare of
    <u>see</u> survivors' pensions

workers' compensation
    Australia 16, 38, 39-40; Canada 50, 54, 47, 66-7, 73-4; United Kingdom 311; United States 353, 371, 377

work ethic
    Australia 2, 3, 4; Germany, West 112; United Kingdom 345, 379

workfare programmes
    United States 329

work injury benefits
    <u>see</u> occupational injury and sickness benefits

work tests
    Australia 33-35; Canada 59; New Zealand 214; Norway 256; Sweden 297; United Kingdom 319, 336; United States 374-5

youth labour market programmes
    Australia 27

youth unemployment
    Australia 26-7; Germany, West 111-12; New Zealand 213; Norway 251, 255; Sweden 290; United Kingdom 326, 327; United States 374

youths
    <u>see</u> children and youths